From James Beard Award–winning chef and author John Ash, *The Hog Island Book of Fish & Seafood* takes a comprehensive dive into the world of cooking shellfish, crustaceans, finned fish, and many more.

Featuring favorites from the kitchens of Hog Island Oyster Bars and other talented chefs who have embraced the company's sustainability ethos, this authoritative compendium showcases over 250 dishes from cuisines around the world, including regional favorites like San Francisco cioppino, Southern crayfish étouffée, and New England clam chowder. Presenting a wide variety of cooking methods—such as steaming, roasting, grilling, pan-frying, curing—along with illustrated techniques like shucking oysters, opening clams, and filleting fish, this authoritative cookbook will guide you through the basics of seafood preparation. And the extensive list of sauces, butters, and seasonings will help you turn your choice of seafood into a stellar dish. *The Hog Island Book of Fish & Seafood* is a master class from an award-winning chef who shows home and professional cooks how to bring culinary gifts from the water to the table at their peak of perfection.

"This wonderful book is a testimonial to two legendary stewards of great food in America: Chef Ash has been a sage leader with an innate ability to create food tied beautifully to the California cornucopia; Hog Island Oyster Co. has been a superhero for sustainable aquaculture since 1983 and is not stopping anytime soon. Together they show you a guide to all seafood, something that has been lacking on my cookbook shelf."

—CHEF HUGH ACHESON

# THE HOG ISLAND BOOK OF
# FISH & SEAFOOD

## Culinary Treasures from Our Waters

## JOHN ASH

Foreword by Stuart Brioza
Photographs by Ashley Lima

CAMERON + COMPANY
Petaluma, California

# CONTENTS

Foreword • 8

Introduction • 11

About Hog Island • 12

Sustainable Seafood • 17

How to Buy and Store Seafood • 20

MOLLUSKS • 26

CEPHALOPODS • 92

CRUSTACEANS • 112

THE SALMON FAMILY • 161

OTHER FINNED FISH • 187

HALIBUT AND OTHER FLATFISH • 222

BIG, MEATY FISH • 247

LITTLE FISH • 270

CANNED, TINNED, AND JARRED FISH • 284

OTHER GIFTS FROM THE SEA • 300

Basic Recipes and Techniques • 552

Index • 546

Acknowledgments • 552

# FOREWORD

Growing up in the Bay Area of California, I saw the ocean as a playground of vast beaches, surfable cold-water waves, and intense sunshine. A place of recreation, its creatures starred daily at the local aquarium. At home, seafood was a weekly meal—usually broiled white sole fillets or my mother's affectionately held Coquilles Saint-Jacques. It wasn't until my late teens, when I started working in professional kitchens, that my idea of the ocean shifted. It became an "unlimited" food resource—and a delicious one at that. I fell in love with everything ocean derived and feasted without question.

My first experience with Hog Island oysters occurred at the farm in Tomales Bay, which, at the time, felt like a private roadside party for some secret society of oyster connoisseurs. The shuck-your-own Sweetwater oysters harvested that morning changed everything I thought I knew about seafood. At first slurp, the intensely briny ocean sweetness grounded me, amplifying my senses: the offshore breeze, the sun peeking through the clouds, seabirds working and lurking around the native eelgrass, and the tide forcefully rising and falling. This indelible moment—eating this oyster in the very environment from which it came—was the impetus for my questing relationship with the oceans as inspiration, sustenance, and a sustainable resource. Notions of "taste of place" and the concordance between food production and environment became instantly obvious and imperative.

In the ensuing twenty years (about half of the farm's life), I've continued to admire Hog Island for its instrumental role in defining the California coast's merroir, a term I first heard from the farmers and marine-biologist owners of Hog Island: John Finger, Terry Sawyer, and Michael Watchorn. Over these many years working together, the truly profound lesson they've taught is that when the collaboration between farming, science, and the world is respectful and conscientious, you can produce not only the world's most perfect oysters, but also a synergistic, eco-positive oceanic habitat in which these farmed bivalves play an integral role of the health of our coastline.

Food just tastes better when you know the first name of the person growing it—a simple concept, really, and not too difficult to practice. When the relationship between producer and consumer is established, the food itself becomes a vessel of knowledge and trust. The more we talk about the food we eat, the closer we are to it and to each other. These are life lessons learned directly from John and Terry, who have built Hog Island Oyster Company from a nursery into a farming business that empowers an entire community of diners and chefs to make better choices. In this book, Hog Island Oyster Company and longtime collaborator chef John Ash explore oysters and much more of our ocean's abundance, citing current scientific material while proposing an easily followed approach to sourcing ingredients. The recipes and techniques are thorough and elegant, and they demonstrate how a passion for seafood can be simultaneously nourishing, sustainable, and impactful upon California and the greater world. In other words, we can have our oyster and eat it too.

**—STUART BRIOZA**
*Chef and co-owner of State Bird Provisions; The Progress; and The Anchovy Bar; San Francisco, California*

# INTRODUCTION

We are blessed. Look at all of the treasures from the waters that we are so lucky to be able to share! Despite the well-publicized concerns about the threats to our oceans, the waters of the world provide an immense amount of delicious, wholesome food for many cuisines.

There are a number of great books and spokespeople for seafood, and this book aims to expand that discussion and offer recipes that I've had a chance to discover during my long culinary career. Included are those from the talented chefs at Hog Island as well as from other chefs and friends from around the country who have embraced the Hog Island sustainability ethic. *The Hog Island Book of Fish & Seafood* explores the large world of shellfish, crustaceans, finned fish, and other gifts from the sea, including seaweeds and roes.

The recipes in this book feature a wide variety of cooking methods, including grilling, curing, and smoking, and showcase dishes from cuisines around the world, including regional favorites like San Francisco cioppino, Southern crayfish étouffée, and New England clam chowder. You will also find an extensive list of sauces, marinades, stocks, butters, and seasonings that can turn your choice of seafood into a stellar dish.

Some home cooks are wary of cooking seafood because it's often expensive (increasingly so), and perhaps because they are not as familiar with this cuisine. But seafood is one of the easiest of all foods to cook, and one of the quickest. The mantra here is, "Just don't overcook it!" The techniques in this book will help you learn basic seafood preparation, such as shucking oysters and filleting fish, and show you how to bring seafood dishes to your table at their peak of perfection.

This cookbook highlights seafood that is likely to be available to most readers. Some chapters are longer than others, reflecting the popularity and availability of such foods as shrimp and salmon. In recent years, the growth of online sources for fresh seafood has made it much easier to get top-quality fish and shellfish. Included here you will find tips on how and where to buy seafood, along with a discussion of sustainability aimed at preserving these gifts for future generations.

# ABOUT HOG ISLAND

The Hog Island Oyster Company was founded in 1983 by two young marine biologists with a big vision, a little cash, and a five-acre (two-hectare) aquaculture lease in Tomales Bay, California—a pristine coastal backwater less than fifty miles (80.5 km) north of San Francisco. John Finger and Michael Watchorn soon recruited Terry Sawyer (who had been an aquarist in the Husbandry Department at the nascent Monterey Bay Aquarium), and for many years, these three pioneered the emerging half-shell oyster trade in California. Of course, oysters had been a part of the California food scene for millennia. But until the 1980s, those oysters were either wild harvested from natural reefs or grown in gnarled clusters that had to be broken apart before they could shucked. They could be eaten raw, and certainly were, but they really didn't lend themselves to the half-shell experience we enjoy today. John, Mike, and Terry launched Hog Island at the dawn of a major technological revolution in the shellfish industry: the use of hatcheries. Shellfish hatcheries brought an unprecedented level of precision, reliability, and biosecurity to the production of small, single-set "seed" oysters. These hatchery-reared baby oysters could be efficiently delivered by the tens of thousands to oyster farms, tended in baskets in the intertidal zone, and harvested as beautiful, single oysters instead of the rugged old clusters.

In those early years, the founders embraced the hatchery single-set model, honed its farming techniques, and began producing a consistently beautiful and delicious half-shell oyster. The Hog Island Sweetwater was born! The emerging Bay Area farm-to-table dining movement was quick to take notice, and iconic restaurants like Chez Panisse and Zuni Café became customers and supporters. The team shucked and shared Sweetwaters via traveling oyster bars and sold oysters direct to the public at the farm site in Marshall. Yet even with the loyal patronage, the company still grew very slowly over those first twenty years. Shellfish farming is hard work, and even with modern advances there is a notorious amount of environmental uncertainty from year to year. Nevertheless, with time, the Hog Island brand earned more recognition, and a major turning point came in 2003 when the company was invited to open their first oyster bar in San Francisco's historic Ferry Building.

Today, Hog Island Oyster Company is a much bigger organization being led by John and Terry, along with a skilled leadership team. As of this writing, there are five Bay Area restaurants, thriving wholesale and catering divisions, two shellfish farms (on Tomales Bay and Humboldt Bay), a dedicated hatchery and nursery operation, a saltworks, and several seaweed initiatives. A family of more than three hundred employees keeps the boat moving forward as the team serves delicious, sustainably-sourced seafood experiences to more than half a million guests each year. Despite this quantum growth, Hog Island still maintains much of the original scientific and entrepreneurial spirit that has informed and guided the company since the beginning. Success is heady, but also deeply humbling. Ultimately, the viability of a seafood business is about stewardship of the marine ecosystems that make success possible. As those ecosystems have come under threat from climate change and other anthropogenic impacts, Hog Island has become deeply dedicated to research collaborations with the scientific community and policy makers. The company also provides educational programming for thousands of students and guests each year. Hopefully, these efforts will help cultivate the resilience, adaptive capacities, and ocean protections needed to thrive for the next forty years!

# SUSTAINABLE SEAFOOD

Sustainable seafood is a vast, controversial, and complicated topic. We have all heard how our oceans are in trouble (they are), how farmed fish and shellfish are problematic and shouldn't be consumed (not true for the most part), and how water quality and habitat are being irretrievably degraded (absolutely true). The truth is that 85 percent of the world's wild fisheries are either fully fished or overfished. That's why farmed seafood is becoming more important. It's estimated that at least 50 percent of the seafood that we consume today comes from farmed sources.

The well-publicized health benefits of seafood have made this gift from fresh and salty waters even more desirable today. Consumer demand, of course, adds to the depletion of the ocean's resources. While fish markets today offer many sustainable choices, they can be expensive, especially the wild species. But learning how and what to buy increases the odds that your favorite fish will be available in the future.

According to the Monterey Bay Aquarium in California, sustainable seafood "comes from sources, either wild or farmed, that can exist into the long term without jeopardizing the health of the fish population or the integrity of the surrounding ecosystem." The key factors that determine sustainability include population size, the percentage and types of bycatch, and the impact on the environment caused by fishing gear. Harvesting quantities of fish that leave too few to reproduce renders populations unsustainable.

Examples of fishery collapse include Atlantic cod and wild Atlantic salmon. Both are considered commercially extinct—only farmed Atlantic salmon appears in markets. Overfishing is especially troublesome for slow-growing fish such as Pacific rockfish and Patagonian toothfish (sold commercially as Chilean sea bass), which don't reach spawning age until about ten years of age or more. Some species of orange roughy need twenty years to mature. Bluefin tuna, the favorite fish at sushi bars, has been so overfished that some estimates say it will be commercially extinct in a decade or two.

Another issue is bycatch, which occurs when nontargeted ocean dwellers, such as sea turtles, dolphins, and "feeder fish," are caught along with the targeted harvest. Bottom trawling (basically scraping the seafloor for a target species like flatfish) brings up a tremendous amount of bycatch, estimated at ten times the weight of the target species. Thankfully, in the United States, turtle-release nets and fish-excluder devices are being used by some trawlers, and the availability of devices like baited mesh traps for shrimp help keep this number from escalating even higher.

Seafood Watch at the Monterey Bay Aquarium, among others, has noted that the future of seafood is farming. We'll all be better for it instead of depending on the "Wild West" attitude that currently exists in much of the commercial fishing world. Despite the bad press farmed salmon has had in the last few years, several producers have devised ways to reduce the impact fish farms have on the environment. Fish such as catfish, trout, and striped bass, and shellfish such as oysters, clams, and mussels have little bycatch and create little pollution thanks to current aquaculture methods such as zero-input farms, which are free from outside amendments, have low or no chemical usage, and an ability to manage waste.

Habitat destruction happens when manufacturing and agricultural waste pollutes streams, rivers, and oceans. Protective habitats, from coral reefs to mangroves, which provide important breeding grounds for the next generations of fish and shellfish, are being destroyed at an alarming rate. Dams, which prevent spawning fish such as salmon from returning to their natal waters, are especially problematic. In addition, harmful harvesting methods such as drag lines have the potential to make vast sections of the ocean barren of life.

Pollution, not only by fish waste and chemicals but plastic waste, has created gigantic islands of waste in the oceans, which, as they break down, are eaten and absorbed by fish and shellfish up and down the feeding chain. Unregulated pollution (especially by oil and gas drillers as well as by agriculture) is wreaking havoc with our ocean and freshwater sources. Ocean pollution is overwhelmingly from land sources, and the vast majority is food-related packaging, including take-out containers, napkins, and straws.

Climate change is a huge factor in the future of seafood. It is clear that the incidence of ocean acidification and warming will have an important impact on what the oceans and fresh waters can provide. Fish populations are already shifting their habitats as they move to find cooler waters. Seafood, coastal communities, and ocean ecosystems are all at risk as the oceans and planet warm.

What can we, as consumers of seafood, do? We can make a difference by choosing to buy, cook, and eat only seafood that is verified as sustainable. That means supporting the purveyors of seafood that is managed and fished using practices that ensure there will always be more to catch in the future. Jeremy Sewall, chef and owner of Row 34 restaurants in Massachusetts, who contributed to this book, says it well: "Seafood is to be celebrated. There are few harder ways to make a living than harvesting or growing seafood. Responsible aquaculture and well-managed fisheries are going to be crucial to the health of the oceans and the planet. Eat lots of seafood, eat lots of different seafood, and never be afraid to try something new."

The sustainability of seafood is constantly monitored by specific resources, and there are many to choose from. The gold standard is the Monterey Bay Aquarium's Seafood Watch initiative, which we've been involved with since its inception. Their consumer pocket guides pioneered simple-to-follow green/yellow/red recommendations. And their website, *seafoodwatch.org*, is an invaluable resource for both professionals and home cooks.

Some other resources that we support and follow include:

- **Seafood from Alaska:** The state of Alaska is truly dedicated to sustainability. It's a commitment that dates all the way back to Alaska becoming a state in 1959, when sustainability was written into their constitution. It calls for all its fisheries in the state to be sustainably managed and protected forever. See *alaskaseafood.org*.

- **Fish Watch:** From NOAA (National Oceanic and Atmospheric Administration, part of the U.S. Department of Commerce), this organization provides up-to-date information on marine fish harvested in U.S. federal waters as well as U.S. farmed fish. Sustainability is a top priority, and they provide strong monitoring, management, and enforcement to keep fish populations thriving. See *fisheries.noaa.gov*.

- **Oceana:** This international organization was established by a group of leading nonprofit foundations. They are dedicated to monitoring measurable change in the world's oceans by utilizing science-based studies and campaigns. See *oceana.org*.

- **Smart Catch:** A James Beard Foundation program that provides training and support for chefs in becoming environmentally responsible. By earning the Smart Catch seal, chefs give consumers a simple way to identify restaurants devoted to using sustainable foods. See *jamesbeard.org/smart-catch*.

- **Marine Stewardship Council:** Provides valuable consumer guides; their blue fish ecolabel identifies sustainable fish in the marketplace. Check out their website for a list of where to buy sustainable seafood: *msc.org*.

- **Fish Choice:** Provides a comprehensive guide for a broad range of species and includes data from many other sustainable guides: *fishchoice.com*.

- **Ocean Wise Seafood Program:** From the Vancouver Aquarium in British Columbia, this organization includes consumer recommendations and discussions of seafood-related issues. See *seafood.ocean.org*.

- **North American Native Fishes Association (NANFA):** Provides important information on seafood and promotes the conservation of native fishes and the protection of their habitats. It is useful for sport fishers. See *nanfa.org*.

The bottom line: Don't buy or consume seafood that doesn't have one or more recommendations/certifications from transparent and unbiased sources. Ask your fish markets and restaurants for proof of sustainability and support only those places that can provide it.

# THE HOG ISLAND APPROACH
# TO SOURCING SUSTAINABLE SEAFOOD

At Hog Island Oyster Company, we serve seafood to hundreds of thousands of guests each year, and we certainly want each of those dining experiences to be delicious and memorable. However, those meals must also reflect our commitment to protecting the ocean ecosystems on which we rely. In the case of our shellfish, we have direct stewardship over the entire supply chain—from hatchery to farm to table. But we also prepare and sell a wide range of other seafoods, and we have had to develop our own standards for how we source them. Rather than absolutes, we believe there are important questions we should always be asking, and conversations we should always be having about the seafoods we buy and support. What follows are some guiding values that are important to us. We hope they will help guide you as well, so you can source seafoods for the recipes in this book that are both delicious *and* sustainable.

1. **Start with good science**. We all need help with decision-making about something as complex as the sustainability of foods from the sea. As a company founded by marine biologists, we have always placed a high value on scientific research to inform our farming and business decisions. Along with Chef Ash, Hog Island has been involved with Seafood Watch since its inception, and we respect the program's goals, scientific methodology, and collaborative but independent approach to making recommendations. If you have questions, Seafood Watch is a great place to start. We do almost every day.

2. **Relationships matter.** Building and maintaining authentic relationships is a core value at Hog Island. Our customers trust us to provide the best shellfish possible, and we in turn seek vendors that we can trust to maintain the same high standards we have for our oysters. Ideally, we buy directly from farmers and fishers we know personally, and with whom we have established shared values—sometimes across generations! It's a type of quality assurance that can only be realized face-to-face. As a home cook, you too should seek out seafood sources that you can trust and that share your sustainability values. If you can buy directly from local fishers and growers you meet, that's great. If not, find a purveyor you trust or explore the many online options.

3. **Mileage matters**. We try to source as locally as possible. Close to home usually means fresh and in season, and the carbon footprint of transportation is lower. The majority of our wild seafood comes from the abundance of the West Coast, with much of it caught within one hundred miles of the Bay Area. We also keep space on our menus for some wonderful products from further afield: fish from Alaska and oysters from great shellfish farms on the East Coast, for example. But we don't really source further afield. Not that there aren't great products in other regions of the world—we just prefer to celebrate the diversity and abundance of seafoods available here in North America.

4. **Small is beautiful.** Hog Island's success is built on the ecological, nutritional, and culinary value of some very small ocean animals. And it turns out that the science around sustainable ocean food systems points in the same direction. Animals that eat low on the food chain (like shellfish and anchovies, sardines, and mackerel), along with seaweeds, represent the very best seafood choices. These are all highly nutritious, can be enjoyed often, and have the potential to feed billions of people sustainably. Of course, we still maintain a passion for those bigger, meaty fish too. But we are learning that those bigger species, like wild salmon and tuna, need to be treated as though they were something special and not as a bulk commodity. Indeed, large wild fish *are* something special, perched near the top the oceanic food chain, and often heavily overfished. We are striving to use those wild fish more thoughtfully and sparingly—through smaller portioning and with greater attention to using more of the fish than just a couple of thick fillets.

# HOW TO BUY AND STORE SEAFOOD

The first rule is to always buy seafood from a reputable fishmonger who is busy—that is, whose inventory turns over quickly. The simplest freshness test for any fish or shellfish you're thinking of buying is to use your nose. Seafood should *smell* fresh and not fishy. Unfortunately, much of what we buy in the market today has been prepackaged in plastic, so the smell test doesn't work in that case. Because of that, I generally avoid prepackaged raw seafood and suggest you do too. For seafood that isn't prepackaged, it's perfectly okay to ask the seller to let you sniff the seafood before buying. If they refuse, then go someplace else.

A good fishmonger will:

- clearly note if products have been previously frozen.

- keep display cases at or below 32°F (0°C). A thermometer should be visible to confirm.

- keep raw seafood separate from previously frozen.

- keep cut fish in trays or liners above the ice and do not arrange cut fish directly on ice.

If you can't find a good fishmonger near you, there are several reputable online sources that will get you properly frozen seafood overnight.

Buy raw, fresh seafood in season, when it is at its peak of flavor. When not in season, buy it cleaned and frozen.

## How to Buy Fresh Fish

- The eyes should be bright, clear, and big, not sunken.

- The gills of a whole fish should be bright and red, not dark and dried out looking.

- The flesh should be firm, moist, and elastic. It should not leave an indentation when you press it.

- The skin on a fish should be moist and viscous. The natural "slimy" coating on the skin of a fin fish is actually a good thing and a sign of a very fresh fish; it helps to keep the fish from drying out and extends its shelf life a bit. Wash it off before cooking.

## How to Buy Frozen Fish

- Previously frozen fish should be frozen rock hard.

- It should have no signs of freezer burn or snowy ice crystals.

- It should have tight vacuum-sealed packaging.

- If IQF (individually quick frozen), portions should not be clumped, which could be a sign of thawing somewhere along the line.

## How to Buy Shellfish

- Live crustaceans like lobster and crab should still be moving.

- Mollusks like mussels, clams, and oysters should have closed shells. Since they are "gappers" in the wild, their shells will sometimes be slightly open. If you give them a pinch and they don't close, discard them.

- Be careful not to seal live shellfish like mussels, oysters, and clams in a plastic bag. They need to breathe.

- Cooked shellfish looks moist and not dried out.

# FRESH FISH VS. FROZEN FISH

You may have heard that fresh fish is always better than frozen, but this isn't always true. The fish you see in the refrigerator case may have been there for a while and may not be in top shape. The truth is that most "fresh" fish we see in the market came in as frozen and then was defrosted for sale.

Since they are highly perishable, most fish are flash-frozen shortly after being caught, sometimes even on the boat it was caught on, which insures its "freshness." Frozen fish has better shelf stability. If it's properly vacuum-sealed, it should last for months in the freezer. When purchasing frozen fish, make sure that there are no ice particles in the plastic package. If there are, it probably has thawed and was then refrozen. Don't buy it! Also, make sure the package is fully intact with no tears. Finally, make sure your fishmonger posts the sources for their fish.

## Cooking Frozen Fish

Although it might seem counterintuitive, you can cook fish straight from frozen. Cooking fish from its frozen state is easier to manage than a fresh version, in part because it's harder to overcook it that way. (I helped create a training video with Alaska Seafood Marketing Institute a few years back for this technique. It's pretty straightforward and you can view a video on ASMI's website: *alaskaseafood.org*).

- Typically, frozen fish fillets are ice glazed before they are packaged. This helps preserve texture and moisture. Wash this glaze off under cold water and pat dry before proceeding to cook the fish.

- Oil the frozen fish well on both sides (not the pan) before placing in a single layer in a large skillet that has a lid. Heat the pan over medium-high heat before adding the fish, skin side up. Use an oil that can handle high heat, such as grapeseed or canola.

- Give the pan a little shake when you first put in the fish to keep it from sticking. Cook, partially covered, until the flesh is lightly browned, 3 to 4 minutes.

- Turn the fish over and season well with salt and pepper. Adding a little stock or wine helps keep frozen fish from drying out.

- Cover the skillet tightly, reduce the heat to medium, and continue to cook until done to your liking, 6 to 8 minutes, depending on the thickness of the fish.

- For very thick portions, finish in a preheated oven at 400°F (205°C), using an ovenproof pan.

- About three-quarters of the way through cooking, test the fish with a knife to see if the thickest part of the fish has turned opaque.

- Remember that fish retains heat after you take it out of the pan. This is called carryover cooking. Be sure to account for this and remove the fish from the pan just a tad before it's done so it won't overcook.

## Storing Fish and Seafood

If there is one overriding rule it is to keep all seafood cold. When you shop, bring along a sturdy cooler with ice to transport it home. Once you thaw fish or shellfish, do not refreeze it, and use it as soon as possible. Fresh or thawed frozen fish or shellfish is best the day it is purchased or thawed, or try to use it within a day or two.

Store all raw fish and seafood on the bottom shelf of your refrigerator (the coldest part).

The best way to store shellfish is in the refrigerator in a deep bowl covered with a wet towel, never in water or a bowl of ice.

# SEAFOOD SAFETY

Seafood in general is a very healthy source of nutrition. There is concern, however, that certain fin and shellfish should be avoided because of pollution and microbial contamination. The FDA is responsible for ensuring that the nation's seafood supply, both domestic and imported, is safe, sanitary, wholesome, and honestly labeled. Their seafood website, *fda.gov/seafood*, includes the most up-to-date consumer information and advice, guidance documents, regulation, and science and research content. This is the best resource I can think of to answer any questions you might have about seafood safety.

## Is Raw Fish Safe to Eat?

Raw fish-based dishes, like crudo, sushi, and ceviche, have become very popular, but are they safe to eat?

There is always a risk from microbes or parasites in raw fish, whether you are consuming sashimi or ceviche. Ceviche is marinated in citrus juice, which does "cook" the outside of the fish, but depending on how long you let the fish marinate, that marinade might not penetrate all the way through.

To minimize risk, you should invest in the best fish from a reliable fishmonger who understands that the fish is to be consumed raw. Get to know and talk to them so you can make an informed decision.

Simple refrigeration is not a good method of controlling parasites. Those parasites come from an aquatic environment and may thrive at refrigerator temperature. Thus, if fish is to be consumed raw, it must have been previously frozen, which kills parasites and most microbes.

According to the FDA, raw fish must first be frozen at specified temperatures and times to kill any parasites. They recommend that the fish must be:

Frozen and stored at a temperature of -4°F (-20°C) or below for a minimum of 168 hours (7 days) in a freezer; or

Frozen at -31°F (-35°C) or below until solid and stored at -31°F (-35°C) or below for a minimum of 15 hours; or

Frozen at -31°F (-35°C) or below until solid and stored at -4°F (-20°C) or below for a minimum of 24 hours.

NOTE  Not everyone observes this freezing protocol, most notably many Japanese and sport fishers.

# ABOUT THE RECIPES IN THIS BOOK

- The organization of the chapters doesn't follow a strict, scientific taxonomy. Instead, they are organized more according to a cook's view, with fish and shellfish grouped according to similarities in how they cook and taste.

- Times for recipe steps are often included but not always. I try to emphasize visual cues (color, texture, etc.). As I teach in my classes, visual cues are more reliable, given the vagaries of equipment and tools, and none of us stands there with a stopwatch while we are cooking.

- When salt is called for, it is always kosher salt unless otherwise specified; specifically, Diamond Crystal brand. Flavored salts add an interesting taste dimension and several ideas are included in the Basic Recipes and Techniques section on page 336.

- Use freshly ground black pepper unless otherwise specified. Avoid pepper that has been preground.

- When onions are called for, either yellow or white onions can be used unless otherwise specified.

- Try to buy whole spices. Once they are ground, they immediately begin to lose flavor and aroma. Spice grinders are inexpensive. I use an inexpensive electric coffee grinder. If you can, before grinding, toast the whole spices in a dry skillet over moderate heat, stirring regularly for about 3 minutes until they are fragrant.

- Do make notations in the cookbook about anything that you feel is important. Make your notes in the margins. It's best not to use a pencil because it can rub off. Your family will thank you.

- Remember that for the most part, recipes are just guides. Each of us has our own likes and dislikes. It's important to taste regularly as you cook so that you can adjust flavors to your own taste. Per the above, be sure to make a note if you have changed a recipe.

# MOLLUSKS

## oysters, clams, geoduck, mussels, scallops, abalone

Mollusks are an ancient and vast branch of life on Earth, encompassing marine animals as diverse as the gastropods (snails, like abalone), the bivalve shellfish (oysters, clams, mussels, and scallops) and the cephalopods (octopus and squid). This group represents about a quarter of all known ocean life. Of course, bivalves are particularly important to Hog Island, because they are the foundation of our business. But mollusks are important more broadly as one of the most sustainable categories of seafood available. They reproduce abundantly, feed very low on the ocean food chain (mostly algae), and in the case of oysters and mussels, provide critical ecosystem services like water filtration and structural habitat for a plethora of smaller sea creatures. As a result, the bivalves are almost universally considered a "Best Choice" by monitoring programs. Other mollusks, like squid and scallops, are well managed and highly abundant, making them a "Best Choice" as well.

# OYSTERS

Only five species of oysters are harvested in the United States. Oysters are, of course, the great passion at Hog Island. More than any other food from the sea, oysters reveal the qualities of the ecosystem in which they were grown. Tides, salinity, temperature, plankton abundance, and ocean chemistry all combine to create what shellfish growers like to call the "merroir" of an oyster, the taste of place. These differences can be dramatic—even across relatively small areas.

## THE TASTE OF AN OYSTER: SPECIES, LOCATION, AND SEASONALITY

When it comes to flavor, all three are important. Hog Island Oyster Co. grows five of the world's main oyster species side by side on the Tomales Bay farm—so they are all subject to the same local "merroir" factors. But each have a totally unique taste because they are totally different species. The species of an oyster always has the most important influence on flavor. However, the exact same Pacific oyster species at the Hog Island farms in Humboldt Bay and Tomales Bay will also taste very different because of the difference in geography of the two locations. Seasonality is an additional flavor factor that is often overlooked. An oyster preparing to spawn will taste wildly different than the same oyster in winter, fattened with stored glycogen and ready for dormancy.

### Pacific Oysters (*Magallana gigas* or *Crassostrea gigas*)

The vast majority of oysters eaten with any regularity are Pacific oysters, which account for about 90 percent of global oyster aquaculture. This global dominance and distribution is due to the Pacific oyster being tasty, fast-growing, and tolerant of a wide range of ocean conditions. In the past, the term *Pacific* was used to describe all small oysters, including Kumamotos. These were subsequently found to be their own species. Pacific oysters are usually named after the place where they are grown, such as Totten Inlet and Fanny Bay, but trade names are also used. The Hog Island Sweetwater, the flagship Tomales Bay oyster for nearly forty years, is a Pacific oyster.

### Kumamoto Oysters (*Magallana sikamea* or *Crassostrea sikamea*)

A close cousin to the Pacific oyster, Kumamoto oysters are originally from Japan but are now grown almost exclusively in Washington State and California's Humboldt Bay. The "Kumi" or "Kumo" are highly valued for their distinctive melon and cucumber flavors and small size. But they are slow growing (two to three years for market-size) and fussy about ocean conditions, which results in a higher price.

### Atlantic Oysters (*Crassostrea virginica*)

It may be hard to believe that Malpeques of Prince Edward Island, Blue Points of New York, and Apalachicolas of Florida are all the same species, but they are. The Atlantic oyster is native to the entire East Coasts of Canada and the United States, including every Gulf State. They have been a vital part of Eastern coastal foodways for millennia, evidenced by the huge shell mounds deposited by Native American communities throughout the region. Curiously, Atlantic oysters also found a foothold on the American West Coast. Originally transported in barrels on the transcontinental railroad in the late 1800s, "Atlantics" were viewed as a potential replacement for the smaller, struggling native Olympia oyster.

While the vast majority of West Coast oyster farmers eventually settled on fast-growing Pacific oysters from Japan, a few Atlantics are still nurtured in Pacific waters today. Hog Island has a special relationship with the Atlantic oyster going back to founder John Finger's time growing up on Long Island, and the very first Hog Island Atlantic oysters can be traced to the historic Flower and Sons Oyster Company in Oyster Bay, New York.

## European Flats (*Ostrea edulis*)

The European flat oyster is native and wild along the west coast of Europe, traditionally ranging from Norway to Morocco. Identified by their flat, as opposed to cupped, shape, these were once the most common oyster in Europe, but Pacific oysters have made big inroads there. Interestingly, European flat oysters are also available in New England and California. Small populations have established off the coast of Maine, and they are farmed in small numbers by Hog Island in Tomales Bay. European flats have a meaty texture and a delicious taste of seaweed and minerals.

## Olympia Oysters (*Ostrea lurida*)

Like the flat oyster in Europe, the Olympia is the only native oyster of the West Coast, ranging from British Columbia to Baja California. They are tiny compared to most other oysters—the meat being about the size of a quarter. Named for the Olympic Peninsula, where it was once abundant, it was the star of the gold rush era and made famous in Hangtown Fry (page 46), but was also decimated due to overharvesting. Wild populations still exist and are highly protected. "Olys" are a challenging business proposition because they grow so slowly. Several growers on the West Coast continue to produce this native oyster, including Hog Island, which grows Olympias in Tomales Bay. Hog Island is hosting research with conservation partners to better understand how farming these native oysters might benefit their recovery in the wild. They have a delicious celery salt and copper flavor that is surprisingly big, despite their small size.

# HOW TO SHUCK AN OYSTER

It can be intimidating to shuck an oyster, as it needs to be done carefully to protect your hands. Look for gloves made specifically for shucking, or use a heavy kitchen towel or an oven mitt to hold the oyster. Choose an oyster knife that is slender and long, with a pointed tip rather than a broad, stubby version. **1.** If using a kitchen towel, fold the towel into a square just large enough to hold the oyster, cupped side down and with the pointed end toward you. With a firm grasp of the knife, insert the tip into the hinge of the shell at the pointed end, using a side-to-side motion. **2.** Once the tip has slipped in, turn the knife handle to pry the shells apart. **3.** Run the blade against the top shell of the oyster to separate the muscle from the shell. **4.** Discard the top shell and slide the knife blade under the oyster to free the muscle and fully separate the oyster from its shell.

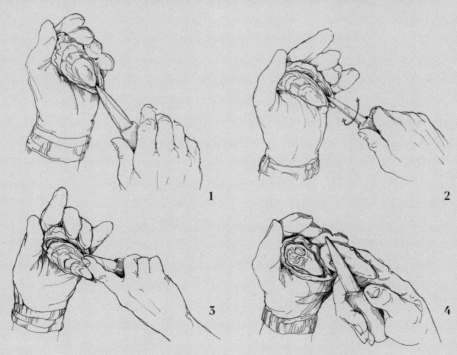

# CLAMS

Like oysters, clams are filter feeders and typically live in similar intertidal habitats. They also clean water, create habitat, reproduce quickly and abundantly, and convert microscopic plankton into a more nutrient-dense food resource for larger predators. As such, farmed clams are a "Best Choice" for the table—sustainable as seafood and providing regenerative ecosystem services in the ocean. There are hundreds of edible, wild clam varieties, but only a handful of them are commonly available commercially. All can be roughly categorized as "hard-shell" or "soft-shell" clams, which has more to do with burrowing depth and the length of their siphon (none have truly soft shells).

## Northern Quahogs (*Mercenaria mercenaria*)

Hard-shell clams, commonly known as quahogs (from the Narragansett word *poquauhock*), come in two main varieties: Northern quahogs and Southern quahogs. The Northern quahogs are also known as Atlantic hard-shell clams. These gray-white clams are found on the Atlantic coast from the Gulf of St. Lawrence in the north to the Gulf of Mexico. They have different names depending on their size:

- **Littlenecks** are the smallest of this group, and about 2 inches (5 cm) wide. Named after Little Neck Bay on Long Island, they are small and tender which makes them ideal for eating raw on the half shell or quickly steamed.

- **Cherrystones** are next in size, about 2½ inches (6 cm) wide. These are great grilled, raw, or stuffed.

- **Chowder clams** are the largest northern quahog. At least 3 inches (7.5 cm) across, they're pretty tough so are not eaten raw; instead, they're cooked and chopped for chowders.

## Southern Quahogs (*Mercenaria campechiensis*)

These hard-shell clams can be up to 6 inches (15 cm) long and live in intertidal zones from the Chesapeake Bay to the West Indies. Like northern quahogs, they are cooked and chopped for chowders.

## Mahogany Clams (*Arctica islandica*)

Also known as ocean quahogs, these hard-shell clams live in the North Atlantic, especially around Maine. They are distinct from northern and southern quahogs in that they have dark brown or black round shells and live deeper in the ocean. They have a slower life cycle than other clams, taking about six years to reach maturity, and they can live to be hundreds of years old. Mahogany clams have a stronger flavor than quahogs and are particularly suited to pasta dishes.

## Manila Clams (*Venerupis philippinarum* or *Ruditapes philippinarum*)

Manila clams, aka steamer clams, are small, sweet hard-shell clams found on the West Coast of the United States. They're best eaten raw, steamed, or in pasta. They are less briny than other types of clams. Hog Island Oyster Co. grows these and uses them in their famous clam chowder (page 52), as well as other dishes.

## Razor Clams

These are clams with long brittle shells resembling a straight razor. They have short siphons but a powerful digging foot that allows them to escape predators by rapid burrowing. The two most common razor clams on the market are both in the Pharidae family: the Pacific razor clam (*Siliqua patula*) and the Atlantic jackknife clam (*Ensis leei*). Both are tender and sweet and can be eaten raw or cooked.

## Soft-Shell Clams (*Mya arenaria*)

Also known as longneck clams, soft-shell clams are a staple in New England but are found on the Pacific coast as well. They are also known as Ipswich clams because Ipswich, Massachusetts, is a major processing center for soft-shell clams. They can grow up to 6 inches (15 cm) long and have relatively long siphons. They are gapers, which means they gap when they are above the sand and not buried, and this can make them sandy. Be sure to clean them before cooking (page 32). Serve smaller soft-shell clams either deep-fried or steamed and accompanied with their steaming liquid and butter. Use larger clams for chowder. '

## Geoducks

With its very long neck and equally long body, the geoduck (pronounced "gooey duck") looks nothing like other clams. In this country, geoducks are found wild and farmed in the Pacific Northwest, especially around the Puget Sound. Considered a delicacy in many countries, they're an important part of the commercial fishing industry in Washington, British Columbia, and Alaska. Their meat is chewy and crunchy, with a briny flavor.

The geoduck has a very small shell (6 to 8 inches/15 to 20 cm for its body, which can stretch to over 3 feet/0.9 m long). Their average weight is about 7 pounds (3.2 kg), although some have been reported to be up to 14 pounds (6.3 kg)! For cooking, look for the smaller ones, around 3 pounds (1.4 kg).

Like razor clams, geoducks dig into the ocean floor or mud beds and remain in the same place for the rest of their lives. When a predator approaches, they simply retract their siphon. There are two common species of geoduck:

- **Pacific geoducks** (*Panopea generosa*) live all along the Pacific Coast. Their 6-to-9-inch- (15-to-23-cm-) long shells are dwarfed by their siphons, which can be up to 4 feet (1.2 m) long. Weighing up to 8 pounds (3.6 kg), they are the largest burrowing clam. The siphon is often peeled and served raw in sushi and ceviche. The belly, which has a stronger flavor, is used in soups or stir fries.

- **Atlantic geoducks** (*P. bitruncata*) are found on the Atlantic coast from North Carolina to the Gulf of Mexico and are indistinguishable from their Pacific relatives.

## Surf Clams (*Spisula solida*)

Surf clams are large (up to 6 inches/15 cm long) and perfect for clam chowder. Mainly found in deep water off the coast of New Jersey, they account for almost one-third of the clam harvest in the United States.

## Washington Clams (*Saxidomus*)

A Pacific Coast clam, Washington clams are also known as butter clams for their smooth texture and are commonly steamed or grilled. There are two types:

- **Northern Washington clams** (*S. gigantea*) can be found from Alaska to San Francisco and are up to 4 inches (10 cm) in diameter.

- **Southern Washington clams** (*S. nuttalli*) are larger (up to 7 inches/17 cm) and have purple markings inside their shells. Despite their name, these clams are not found in Washington at all: They are harvested from Humboldt Bay in Northern California to Baja California in Mexico.

## Whole Belly Clams

You'll see this reference in New England; it refers to an entire clam that has been breaded and fried. The other designation is "clam strips," which are simply a clam with the belly removed.

# HOW TO CLEAN CLAMS

Clams that we buy from our fishmonger have usually been purged of sand and debris in salt water. Fresh water will kill clams. Pick through and discard any clams with broken or open shells or that do not close when pinched. Place them in a colander and run cold water over them. Scrub each shell under the water with a clean brush to remove any external dirt or sand.

# HOW TO OPEN CLAMS

Littlenecks and manila clams are excellent served raw. To open clams to serve raw, choose an oyster knife or other small-bladed knife known as a clam knife. **1.** Holding the clam on a small, folded kitchen towel, slide the sharp edge of the knife between the shells on the opposite side of the hinge. **2.** Run the tip of the knife all the way around the edge of the shell so that you don't damage the clam inside. You will eventually feel the resistance give way and be able to open the clam. Run the blade around the top inside shell to release the clam from the shell. Discard the top shell. **3.** Run the knife around the bottom shell to release the meat. Arrange the clams on their half shells on a plate of crushed ice and spoon sauce over.

# HOW TO PREPARE GEODUCK

You can buy geoduck online and often they come ready to prepare. If, however, you get a live one, the following simple steps will help you prep it for cooking: **1.** Insert a sharp knife between the shell and the clam and, keeping the knife pressed against the shell, cut the meat away from one shell, then repeat with the other shell. **2.** Cut away the entire soft belly section and discard. Be careful not to puncture the belly, or it will expel its contents. **3.** Cut the siphon away from the body meat with a single cut. **4.** Peel off as much of the tough skin as possible, using your fingers. The tough skin on the siphon is easier to remove if you blanch it in boiling water for 10 seconds and then shock it in an ice bath. Cut off any remaining skin with a knife. The tougher siphon meat is generally finely chopped or ground for chowder. The more tender body meat is typically sliced into clam "steaks," breaded, and fried, but it can also be chopped and used in chowders or fritters.

# MUSSELS

Mussels may be the most sustainable of all seafoods. Like oysters and clams, they improve the surrounding ocean environment by filtering water and providing habitat for other critters. What makes mussels unique is their sheer abundance. Farmed or wild, mussels reproduce and grow quickly, and at very high densities. This means that mussels can truly contribute to a global seafood solution for the growing human population. Mussels are widely available, either fresh, frozen, or tinned. A beloved traditional food in France and Belgium, mussels became popular in the United States when they began to be farm-raised in the European manner. Most frozen mussels are the green-lipped variety from New Zealand, and most tinned mussels are from Spain or Portugal.

The most common types of mussels found in the market:

- **Blue mussels** (*Mytilus edulis*) are the most popular mussels grown today. Indigenous to North America, they are farmed on the North Atlantic seaboard up to the Maritimes of Canada. The most famous are those from Prince Edward Island.

- **Bay mussels** (*M. trossulus*) are considered native to the Pacific Northwest but grow widely in the North Atlantic as well. Bay mussels from Penn Cove Shellfish in Puget Sound, Washington, are particularly prized by chefs. They have blue-black shells.

- **Mediterranean mussels** (*M. galloprovincialis*), are native to the Mediterranean region and are best known from France, Spain, and Portugal. They are also blue-black and are grown by a number of producers on the West Coast of the United States.

- **Green-lipped mussels** (*Perna canaliculus*) were first grown in Asia as a food source for Muscovy ducks. Now they are aquacultured in New Zealand and air-shipped to the United States. Much larger than the blues, above, their meat is a bit more chewy. The shell has a brilliant green edge, and the inside of the shell has a pearlescent finish.

## HOW TO CLEAN AND DEBEARD MUSSELS

Rinse the mussels thoroughly in cold running water. Most commercial mussels have already been debearded, but if your mussels are wild or still have their "beards" (the elastic threads that hold the mollusks to rocks), pull them off and discard them.

Note that a mussel's shell should close if it is tapped on a counter, or when squeezed shut. Any mussels that do not close are dead or possibly filled with mud and should be discarded.

# SCALLOPS

There are two main types of scallops in the North American market: sea scallops and bay scallops, which are both farmed and wild harvested. From a sustainability perspective scallops can be a bit more complicated than oysters and mussels. Farmed scallops, which may have a restorative impact on nearby wild scallop populations, are considered a "Best Choice" by Seafood Watch. Wild scallop fisheries that are well managed, as in the United States and Canada, can also be a good choice. The concern is with dredging and its impact on seafloor ecosystems.

Unlike oysters, clams, and mussels, scallops are highly mobile creatures. By clapping their shells shut rapidly, they propel themselves backward. Because they're not subject to tidal variation like other bivalves, scallops never evolved to keep their shells shut while out of water. Therefore, they dry out quickly and must be shucked on the boat promptly after harvest. The part of the scallop that we eat is the larger of its two adductor muscles, which is not affected by red tides or pollution.

Scallops have slight variations in color, which do not affect their flavor. Most are white to off-white; others are pinkish, beige, or grayish, or have a slight orange cast (these are known as "pumpkins").

When buying sea scallops, look for "dry-pack" scallops, which are always preferable to the "wet" scallops that come brined in a solution of trisodium phosphate to extend shelf life and boost weight (bathed in this solution, the scallops absorb liquid, which dilutes their flavor). This means you're paying more for water. During cooking, this water escapes, and the scallop shrinks to a fraction of its earlier size. Always look for the words *dry-packed bay scallops* and/or *chemical-free* on the label. When buying from your fishmonger, be sure to ask.

In Europe, scallops are often sold with their orange roe, which is considered a delicacy. American scallops are thought to have a gamier-tasting roe, and for that reason it is usually removed before the scallops reach the market.

**Day-boat scallops** are caught by smaller vessels that harvest closer to shore. **Diver scallops** are hand-harvested by scuba divers. Both of these are the larger sea scallops. Although they are generally available, it would be a good idea to order either of these ahead from your seafood supplier.

Other scallops that you might see on the market include:

- **Atlantic calico scallops** *(Argopecten gibbus)* are sometimes labeled as bay scallops, but they are found in the warm waters of the Atlantic and Gulf Coasts of Florida and Central and South America. They're even smaller than bay scallops (100 to 200 calico scallops to a pound/455 g) and are recognized by the patchwork of red and pink coloring on the shell. They are less expensive than other scallops.
- **Patagonian scallops** *(Zygochlamys patagonica)* are small, sweet, and tender, much like bay scallops. Rare in the market, they are harvested from the icy Antarctic waters just off the coast of Argentina.
- **Singing pink scallops** *(Chlamys rubida)*, aka steamer scallops, butterfly scallops, angel scallops, or scooter scallops, are a bay scallop variety from the Pacific Northwest. Noted for their pale pink shells, they are said to have more flavor than sea scallops. About 3 inches (7.5 cm) wide, they often come with a sac of pinkish roe and are called "singing" scallops because they make a small sound when propelling themselves through the water by clapping their shells.

## PREPPING SCALLOPS

When preparing scallops, trim or pull off and discard the tough bit of white tendon that attaches the adductor muscle to the shell.

# ABALONE

Abalone (*Haliotis*) is a large sea snail is found widely in the southern Pacific and off the coasts of Japan, as well as the west coast of North America. They have a single, powerful foot that allows them to hold firmly to rocks as they graze for bits of kelp. Like many mollusks, abalone can be found quite close to shore, making them easy prey for land predators and humans.

Until very recently, abalone was strictly a wild-harvested food, taken at low tides or by divers. But abalone (unlike the bivalves) are slower growing and subject to a boom-bust cycle in the coastal environment. Over the past one hundred years and around the world, many abalone species have been overharvested to the point of extinction. Today most abalone on the market are farm-raised to allow them to recover in the wild. Its slow growth and scarcity have made it one of the most expensive seafoods on the market. Abalone is sold live in the shell, frozen, canned, or dried. Fresh abalone is usually cut into steaks, tenderized by pounding (gently), and pan-fried, though it can be eaten raw as the Japanese do.

# HOW TO PREPARE ABALONE

Abalone is attached to its shell via a solid round muscle. **1. & 2.** To release the meat and not damage it, a wide wooden spatula or spoon comes in handy. **3.** Once out, cut off and discard the dark sac of guts, the rubbery dark lip around the edge of the abalone, and the tough outer skin. Scrub the abalone clean and cut off any remaining black stuff around the edges. **4.** The cleaned meat now needs to be tenderized, usually by pounding it whole or as thick-cut steaks. Like calamari, it can be made tender with long, slow braising. Usually, the tenderized steaks are cooked gently and quickly in a buttered skillet. It can also be eaten raw.

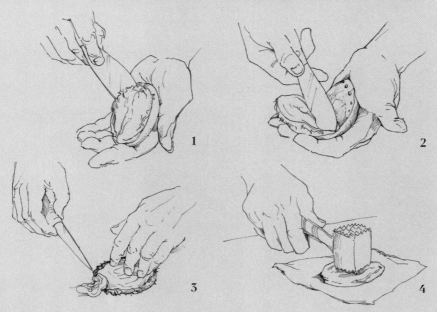

## Keeping Red Abalone on the Menu

Gary B. Fleener, director of science, sustainability, and farm education at Hog Island, writes: "At Hog Island Oyster Company, we work with our friends at the Cultured Abalone in Santa Barbara to procure farm-raised red abalone *(Haliotis rufescens)*. Farmed abalone are fed the same diet of wild kelp and other seaweeds as are wild but are grown in large tanks to protect them from predators and the uncertainties of the open coast. It takes three to four years to produce a red abalone about 4 inches (10 cm) long! Working with farmed abalone allows us to keep this ancient seafood on our menus without impact to recovering wild populations. In fact, some of the animals at the Cultured Abalone may eventually support restoration efforts in the wild."

## Where to Obtain Abalone

Farming abalone has become common in areas where this special animal lives. It ensures sustainably raised abalone if you buy it from a reputable supplier. Because they grow so slowly, farmed abalone is much smaller than those gathered in the wild. Remember that finding a deal on this or any other seafood can mean that it is inferior in quality or illegally harvested. Fresh abalone can often be shipped overnight.

As with all seafood, when buying it fresh make sure it has no off smells. Abalone should be cleaned and cooked the same day for best results. Canned, cleaned, and cooked abalone, as well as dried abalone, can be found in well-stocked markets. Though convenient, it is expensive.

Oysters on the half shell are one of my favorite things. Typically, extra-small oysters are best for this presentation. Place the oysters on a bed of rock salt or crushed ice to keep them from tipping and losing their delicious liquor. The simplest way to serve them is with a squeeze of lemon and/or a drop or two of hot sauce, but there are plenty of other toppings, such as Hog Island's Hogwash and classic French mignonette. Recipes for these and more follow this recipe.

# OYSTERS ON THE HALF SHELL

12 very fresh raw extra-small oysters in
the shell

Rock salt or crushed ice

Lemon wedges, hot sauce, or your favorite
sauce or salsa (see below or page 39)

Shuck the oysters (see page 29), leaving the meat on the half shell. Place on a bed of salt or ice to prevent the oysters from tipping. Serve with the lemon wedges and/or hot sauce, sauce, or salsa. **MAKES 12 OYSTERS; SERVES 4**

## FRENCH MIGNONETTE

A classic way to serve raw oysters on the half shell is with mignonette, a simple French sauce made with vinegar, minced shallots, and black pepper.

**Makes 1 cup (240 ml); enough for at least 24 oysters**

⅔ cup (165 ml) good-quality champagne vinegar
   or white wine vinegar
2 tablespoons finely diced shallots
2 teaspoons freshly cracked pepper

In a small nonreactive bowl, combine the vinegar, shallots, and pepper. Cover and refrigerate for at least 1 hour or up to 3 days before serving.

## MANGO-JALAPEÑO SALSA

Here's a fragrant Mexican-inspired salsa for raw oysters and other fish. Jalapeños can vary in their heat, so I suggest putting in half of what is called for in this recipe, then tasting after it has rested for at least half an hour. Add more if you like it hotter.

**Makes about 1 cup (165 g); enough for 24 oysters**

2 tablespoons extra-virgin olive oil
2 tablespoons fresh lime juice
2 teaspoons agave syrup or honey
½ cup (85 g) diced peeled mango
⅓ cup (40 g) finely diced sweet red onion
1 tablespoon seeded and finely diced jalapeño chile
2 teaspoons finely chopped fresh cilantro
¼ teaspoon ground cumin
Pinch of salt

In a small nonreactive bowl, whisk the olive oil, lime juice, and agave syrup together. Stir in the mango, onion, jalapeño, cilantro, cumin, and salt. Taste and adjust the seasoning. Let sit at room temperature for 1 hour to develop the flavors. Serve at once, or cover and store in the refrigerator for up to 3 days.

## HOGWASH

This sauce recipe was developed by Hog Island Oyster Co. founding partner Michael Watchorn many years ago. It remains a favorite.

**Makes about 1 cup (240 ml), enough for at least 24 oysters**

¼ cup (60 ml) seasoned rice vinegar
¼ cup (60 ml) unseasoned rice vinegar
1 large shallot, peeled and minced
1 large jalapeño chile, seeded and minced
½ bunch fresh cilantro, finely chopped
Juice of 1 lime

In a small nonreactive bowl, combine the vinegars, shallot, jalapeño, cilantro, and lime juice and stir until combined. Serve at once. If making ahead, mix dry ingredients and refrigerate for up to 3 days. Stir in the vinegars and lime juice just before serving.

## CANDIED CITRUS MIGNONETTE

This recipe from Tony's Seafood Restaurant chef John Lyell is adaptable to any citrus you may find at the farmers' market or growing in your backyard, including Cara Cara oranges, Meyer lemons, and grapefruit. Lyell notes that "it's a great way to play around with things we normally throw in the compost bin."

**Makes about 1 cup (240 ml); enough for at least 24 oysters**

½ cup (50 g) citrus zest strips, removed from fruit with a vegetable peeler
Pinch of kosher salt
½ cup (100 g) sugar
1 small shallot, finely diced
½ cup (120 ml) champagne vinegar
Pinch of cracked pepper

In a small saucepan, cover the zest with water. Add the salt and bring to a boil over high heat. Pour through a sieve to strain off the liquid. Repeat this process a total of three times. Cut the blanched zest into thin strips (julienne).

In the same pan, combine the sugar, water, and julienned zest and bring to a simmer; cook until the zest is translucent, about 12 minutes. Remove from the heat and let cool to the touch. Finely dice the zest.

In a small nonreactive bowl, combine the shallots, vinegar, diced zest, and pepper. Serve at once, or cover and refrigerate for up to 5 days.

## FRESNO CHILE MIGNONETTE

This recipe was created by Jamie Burgess, head chef and shuck master at the Boat Oyster Bar in Marshall, California.

**Makes 1 cup (240 ml); enough for 24 oysters**

2 Fresno chiles, seeded and minced (about ⅓ cup/50 g)
1 shallot, diced
1 teaspoon crushed pink peppercorns
⅔ cup (165 ml) champagne vinegar, or more to taste
½ teaspoon sugar

In a small, nonreactive bowl, combine the chiles, shallot, peppercorns, vinegar, and sugar. Serve at once or let sit at room temperature for 1 hour to develop the flavor. To store, cover and refrigerate for up to 3 days.

## TOMATO GRANITA

This savory version of an Italian frozen-fruit dessert offers an interesting contrast to raw oysters.

**Makes about 1 cup (240 ml); enough for 24 oysters**

2 cups (330 g) peeled, seeded, and chopped heirloom tomatoes
1 tablespoon red wine vinegar
2 teaspoons extra-virgin olive oil
½ teaspoon kosher salt
2 drops Worcestershire sauce

In a blender or food processor, combine the tomatoes, vinegar, oil, salt, and Worcestershire and process until smooth. Transfer the mixture to an 8-inch (20-cm) square baking dish. Cover and freeze until firm, stirring twice during the first 2 hours.

Remove from the freezer and scrape the entire mixture with a fork until fluffy. Using a teaspoon or small melon baller, place a small dollop on top of each oyster on the half shell and serve immediately.

For grilled oysters, choose small- or medium-sized, and cook them on a charcoal or gas grill over direct heat. The simplest method is to place unopened oysters on the grill grate and let the heat from the grill pop them open, then add the sauce or butter when serving. At Hog Island, we prefer to shuck the oysters first and add a little sauce or butter to each oyster before putting on the grill.

# GRILLED OYSTERS

12 very fresh raw small or medium oysters

Your favorite sauce or compound butter
(see below or pages 42 or 334–341)

Prepare a medium-hot fire in a charcoal grill or preheat a gas grill to medium-high. Brush the grill grates clean.

To grill the oysters unopened, set them cupped side down (to preserve the liquor) on the grill grate. Cover the grill and cook until the shells pop open and the meat is slightly opaque, 2 to 3 minutes. Carefully watch the oysters as some will not pop open on time.

Using tongs or a grill mitt, carefully remove the hot oysters from the grill. Using an oyster knife, carefully remove the top shells (they will be very hot) and run the knife along the inside of the bottom shell to loosen the oyster from the shell. Top with the sauce or butter and heat through.

Alternatively, start with shucked oysters on the half shell (page 29), top with a sauce or compound butter, and place on the grill. Open a cold beer and wait for the sauce to start bubbling or the butter to melt. Let the oysters sizzle for about 1 minute. Remove from the grill, let cool slightly so you don't burn your mouth, and enjoy!
**MAKES 12 OYSTERS; SERVES 4**

## CHIPOTLE-BOURBON BUTTER

This is a staple at the Hog Island Oyster Bars and was developed by Garret Hamner, a former retail manager.

**Makes about 1 cup (225 g); enough for at least 24 oysters**

¼ cup (55 g) brown sugar, lightly packed
3 tablespoons bourbon
1 cup (225 g) unsalted butter, at room temperature
¼ cup (35 g) garlic cloves, minced
¼ cup (65 g) minced chipotle chiles in adobo sauce, or to taste

In a medium bowl, stir the brown sugar into the bourbon to dissolve. Add the butter, garlic, and chipotle chiles with their sauce and mix well.

On a piece of parchment paper or plastic wrap, pile the butter mixture along the center to form a log about 1 inch (2.5 cm) in diameter. Wrap closed and refrigerate for at least 1 hour.

Follow the instructions above to top each shucked oyster on the half shell with a thin slice of the compound butter before grilling.

## HARISSA BUTTER

**Makes about ⅔ cup (150 g); enough for 24 oysters**

½ cup (115 g) unsalted butter, at room temperature
2 tablespoons harissa paste, homemade (page 341) or store-bought

In a bowl, beat together the butter with the harissa paste. On a piece of parchment paper or plastic wrap, pile the butter mixture along the center to form a log about 1 inch (2.5 cm) in diameter. Wrap closed and refrigerate for at least 1 hour.

Follow the instructions above to top each shucked oyster on the half shell with a thin slice of the compound butter before grilling.

## MENDOCINO MISO BUTTER

This recipe was created by chef B Adamo, head chef at Hog Island Oyster Bar in Larkspur.

**Makes about ⅔ cup (150 g); enough for 24 oysters**

½ cup (115 g) unsalted butter, at room temperature
2 tablespoons white (shiro) or yellow miso paste
1 tablespoon minced fresh chives
1 teaspoon minced garlic
½ teaspoon coarsely ground pepper

In a bowl, beat together the butter with the miso paste, chives, garlic, and pepper. On a piece of parchment paper or plastic wrap, pile the butter mixture along the center to form a log about 1 inch (2.5 cm) in diameter. Wrap closed and refrigerate for at least 1 hour.

Follow the instructions on page 41 to top each shucked oyster on the half shell with a thin slice of the compound butter before grilling.

## CLASSIC BBQ SAUCE

**Makes about 1½ cups (360 ml); enough for 36 oysters**

⅔ cup (165 ml) ketchup
½ cup (120 ml) cider vinegar
¼ cup (55 g) light or dark brown sugar, lightly packed
2 teaspoons pimentón (smoked Spanish paprika)
1 teaspoon ground cumin
1 teaspoon kosher salt
1 teaspoon freshly cracked pepper

In a small saucepan, combine the ketchup, vinegar, brown sugar, pimentón, cumin, salt, and pepper. Bring to a simmer over medium heat and cook while stirring, about 5 minutes. Use now or let cool, cover, and refrigerate for up to 5 days.

Follow the instructions on page 41 to top each shucked oyster on the half shell with 2 teaspoons or so of the sauce before grilling.

---

Invented at Antoine's restaurant in New Orleans in 1899, this classic baked oyster dish was named after John D. Rockefeller, the wealthiest man in America at that time, because of its richness. Antoine's has kept the original recipe secret, but all kinds of interpretations exist. This slimmed-down version omits the original cream sauce but is still packed with flavor.

# OYSTERS ROCKEFELLER

24 small to medium oysters

2 cups (40 g) baby spinach leaves, loosely packed

1½ cups (45 g) watercress sprigs (or an equal amount of spinach), loosely packed

⅓ cup (17 g) celery leaves, loosely packed

2 teaspoons minced green onions

¼ cup (55 g) unsalted butter

1 tablespoon Pernod or other anise-flavored liqueur

Fine sea salt

Fresh lemon juice and hot sauce, to taste

¾ cup (75 g) freshly grated Parmesan cheese

Shuck the oysters (page 29), discarding the flat top shells. In a fine-mesh sieve set over a bowl, drain the oysters, reserving their liquor. Carefully transfer the oyster meat to an airtight container, keeping each oyster intact. Cover and separately refrigerate the oysters and their liquor. Wash the bottom shells thoroughly and set aside.

In a medium saucepan of lightly salted boiling water, blanch the spinach, watercress, and celery leaves until wilted, about 30 seconds. Drain and rinse thoroughly in cold water to stop the cooking and set the bright green color. Add the greens to a food processor along with the green onions and pulse to mince very finely (or mince by hand).

In a medium skillet, melt the butter over medium heat, add the greens mixture, and cook until most of the liquid has evaporated, about 2 minutes. Add the reserved oyster liquor and Pernod and season to taste with salt, lemon juice, and hot sauce. Cook until the liquid is mostly absorbed, about 3 minutes. Set aside.

Preheat the oven to 450°F (230°C). Line a rimmed baking sheet with ⅓ inch (8 mm) or so of rock salt and press the reserved oyster shells into the salt to keep them upright. Place an oyster in each shell and divide the green sauce among them. Top with Parmesan and bake until the sauce is bubbly and the cheese is lightly browned, about 8 minutes. **SERVES 4 TO 6**

Raw oysters in shot glasses topped with sangrita, the tomato-citrus chaser usually served with a shot of tequila, is a fun starter for any gathering, especially outside around the grill in summer. If you can find it, use white wine Worcestershire sauce.

# OYSTER SANGRITA SHOOTERS

2 cups (480 ml) tomato juice

¼ cup (60 ml) fresh orange juice

1 tablespoon fresh lime or lemon juice

1 tablespoon light or dark brown sugar

1 tablespoon olive brine from a jar of green olives

Worcestershire sauce, to taste

Hot sauce, to taste

Fine sea salt and freshly ground pepper

10 shucked small or extra-small oysters (page 29)

In a medium bowl, stir the tomato juice, orange juice, lime juice, sugar, and olive brine. Add a the Worcestershire and hot sauce and season to taste with salt and pepper. Refrigerate for at least 1 hour for the flavors to marry.

Just before serving, taste and adjust the seasonings. Drop an oyster into each of ten 2-ounce (60-ml) shot glasses, fill with sangrita, and throw it back! **MAKES TEN 2-OUNCE (60-ML) SHOOTERS**

Josh Silvers, of Jackson's Bar and Oven in Santa Rosa, has long been one of my favorite chefs and is a wizard with seafood. His recipe for butter-poached oysters is both simple and elegant.

# BUTTER-POACHED OYSTERS

2 tablespoons water

1 cup (225 g) unsalted butter, cut into cubes

1 dozen extra small or small oysters, shucked, liquor reserved (page 29)

1 tablespoon fresh lemon juice

Pinch of kosher salt

1 teaspoon minced fresh chives

Caviar (optional, but very nice)

In a medium saucepan, bring the water to a boil over medium heat. Quickly whisk in the butter, a few cubes at a time, to make an emulsified sauce. Turn the heat to low and whisk in 1 or 2 tablespoons of the reserved oyster liquor. Add the oysters, lemon juice, and a pinch of salt.

Poach the oysters until they just begin to firm, about 2 minutes. Be careful not to overcook. Gently stir in the chives and divide the oysters among 4 small, warm plates. Top with caviar, if using, and serve at once. **SERVES 4**

This is my version of a recipe from my grandmother. It's great with roast turkey, of course, but you could also use it in roulades of sole or to stuff a whole roasted or grilled fish. If you don't have giblets, double the mushrooms.

# CORNBREAD-OYSTER STUFFING
## with thyme and fennel

Giblets from turkey or chicken (optional)

2 cups (480 ml) chicken stock (page 333), turkey stock, or vegetable stock (page 333), plus more as needed

4 tablespoons (55 g) unsalted butter, plus more for baking dish

1 small leek, chopped, both white and green parts (2 cups/180 g)

3 ounces (85 g) cremini mushrooms, chopped (1 cup)

About 6 cups (225 g) cubed day-old cornbread

2 cups (524 g) small shucked (page 29) or jarred raw oysters, liquor reserved

¼ cup (13 g) chopped fresh flat-leaf parsley

1 cup (120 g) chopped walnuts, toasted (page 344)

2 large eggs, beaten

1 teaspoon dried thyme

½ teaspoon crushed fennel seed

1 teaspoon kosher salt

½ teaspoon ground white pepper

1 teaspoon ground nutmeg

Preheat the oven to 350°F (175°C) and butter a 2-quart (2-l) baking dish. If using the giblets, bring the stock to a simmer in a small saucepan, add the giblets, and cook for 15 minutes or until tender. Remove the giblets and chop finely, reserving the stock.

In a large skillet, melt the butter over medium heat. Add the leeks and mushrooms and cook until soft and slightly brown. In a large bowl, combine the reserved stock, vegetables, cornbread, oysters, parsley, walnuts, eggs, thyme, fennel seed, salt, white pepper, and nutmeg and mix well to make a mixture that is moist but not soggy. When squeezed gently, the mixture should just hold together. If necessary, add some of the reserved oyster liquor.

Spread the mixture in the prepared baking dish and bake until heated through and browned and crispy on top, about 45 minutes. **MAKES ABOUT 8 CUPS (500 G); SERVES 4 TO 6**

This classic dish from the Gold Country of California has a rich, if somewhat disputed, history. During the mid-1800s, Hangtown (known as Placerville today) was an important supply base for mining in Northern California. One theory is that it got its colorful name after three desperadoes were hanged there on the same day. According to legend, this dish was requested by each of them as their last meal because bacon, oysters, and eggs were so expensive and hard to come by in the mountains. Today, Hangtown fry is the official dish of both the city of Placerville and the county of El Dorado.

# HANGTOWN FRY

½ pound (225 g) sliced bacon

2 cups (200 g) dry bread crumbs, such as panko (Japanese bread crumbs)

8 large eggs

Kosher salt and freshly ground pepper

12 small, shucked oysters, drained (page 29)

¼ cup (60 ml) heavy cream

1 tablespoon finely chopped fresh flat-leaf parsley

3 tablespoons freshly grated Parmesan cheese

Parsley sprigs, for garnish

In a large skillet over medium heat, fry the bacon until crisp. Transfer to paper towels to drain. Remove all but 3 tablespoons of the bacon fat from the skillet.

Place the bread crumbs in a shallow bowl. In another shallow bowl, beat 2 eggs seasoned with salt and pepper. One at a time, dip the oysters in the beaten eggs and then into the breadcrumbs, turning to coat both sides. Transfer to a plate.

Heat the skillet with the bacon fat over medium heat. Add the oysters and fry, turning once, until they begin to curl, about 2 minutes.

In a bowl, beat the remaining 6 eggs with the cream, chopped parsley, and cheese. Season with salt and pepper. Pour the egg mixture over the oysters in the skillet, reduce the heat to low, and gently scramble the eggs, lifting the oysters so that the eggs surround them.

When the eggs have firmed but are still moist, turn out onto a warm serving plate. Break the bacon into large pieces and place on top with the parsley sprigs. Serve at once. **SERVES 6**

This recipe is from Beth Snow, who is the computer whiz whose help was invaluable in putting this book together. She writes: "This dish was always included at my family's holiday dinners, served alongside roast turkey and all the trimmings. I've adapted this recipe from the original by adding mushrooms and lemon zest." If you can find only large, jarred oysters, cut them in half to use here.

# BETH'S OYSTER GRATIN
## with oyster mushrooms

1 cup (90 g) saltine cracker crumbs

½ cup (25 g fresh; 50 g dried) fresh or dried bread crumbs

½ cup (115 g) unsalted butter, melted

2 cups (524 g) small to medium shucked (page 29) or jarred raw oysters, drained and liquor reserved

3 ounces (1 cup/85 g) chopped oyster or cremini mushrooms

Kosher salt and freshly ground pepper

4 tablespoons (60 ml) heavy cream

1 teaspoon finely grated lemon zest

Preheat the oven to 400°F (205°C). In a medium bowl, mix the cracker crumbs and bread crumbs together. Stir in the melted butter.

In an 8-inch (20-cm) square baking dish, spread an even layer of a little less than ⅓ cup (15 g fresh; 35 g dried) of the crumbs. Cover with half of the oysters and half of the mushrooms. Season with salt and pepper plus 2 tablespoons each of the oyster liquor and the cream. Repeat with another layer of crumbs, oysters, the remaining oyster liquid, the remaining cream, and the lemon zest. Top with the remaining crumbs. Bake until the crumbs on top are lightly browned, about 25 minutes. Serve hot. **SERVES 4 TO 8**

---

Jarred and refrigerated shucked raw oysters are widely available and both cheaper and easier to use than shucking your own. The downside is that they can vary widely in size. You'll get big ones and little ones in the same jar. Cut them, if necessary, into similarly sized bite-size pieces for this recipe. Look for oysters labeled extra smalls or smalls which tend to be a little more uniform in size. Look for Mae Ploy coconut milk; it's my favorite because it doesn't contain any thickeners or stabilizers. And for fish sauce, look for the Red Boat brand.

# CURRIED OYSTER SOUP

1 tablespoon coconut oil or olive oil

3 tablespoons sliced shallots

1 teaspoon Thai yellow curry paste

2 cups (480 ml) fish stock (page 332) or chicken stock (page 333)

One 19-ounce (570-ml) can unsweetened coconut milk, preferably Mae Ploy

1 tablespoon fish sauce

1 teaspoon brown sugar or palm sugar

1 pint (524 g) shucked small or extra-small raw oysters (page 29)

1 cup (85 g) julienned snow peas

1 tablespoon fresh lime juice

In a deep saucepan or soup pot, heat the oil over medium heat. Add the shallots and cook until softened, 1 or 2 minutes. Add the curry paste and cook, stirring constantly, until fragrant.

Add the stock, coconut milk, fish sauce, and sugar and bring to a simmer. Taste and adjust the seasoning. Add the snow peas and oysters with their liquor and cook until the oysters are just beginning to curl, about 2 minutes. Don't overcook.

Stir in the lime juice and ladle into warm bowls to serve. **SERVES 4 TO 6**

This classic New Orleans sandwich is thought to be a version of the sub or hoagy of the Northeast using local ingredients. The origin story goes back to 1929, when a restaurant in the city served free sandwiches to streetcar drivers who were on strike and so were called "poor boys," or "po' boys" in the local dialect. This version of the recipe is known as a "dressed" po' boy because it includes bacon, lettuce, and tomatoes. Use only your best ripe summer tomatoes here. A variation of these po' boys—each of them slightly different—is served at all of the Hog Island Oyster Bars.

# OYSTER PO' BOYS

1½ cups (270 g) yellow or white cornmeal

3 tablespoons unbleached all-purpose flour

2 teaspoons or more Cajun seasoning, homemade (page 341) or store-bought

1½ teaspoons salt

16 small shucked (page 29) or jarred raw oysters, drained

Peanut or vegetable oil, for frying

4 brioche or French bread rolls, split and toasted

4 tablespoons (60 ml) mayonnaise

4 thick applewood-smoked bacon slices, cooked until crisp and drained

2 cups (110 g) shredded iceberg lettuce

2 ripe tomatoes, thinly sliced

4 slices sweet white or red onion (optional)

In a medium bowl, whisk together the cornmeal, flour, Cajun seasoning, and salt. Toss the oysters in the seasoned flour, shake off the excess, and set aside on a plate.

In a large, deep sauté pan or a wide saucepan, heat 2 inches (5 cm) of oil over medium-high heat until it shimmers (350°F/175°C on a deep-frying thermometer). Carefully add the oysters and fry until lightly golden brown, 1 or 2 minutes on each side. Using a slotted spoon or a wire-mesh skimmer, transfer to paper towels to drain.

To assemble the sandwiches, spread the toasted buns liberally with mayonnaise, then top equally with the oysters, bacon, lettuce, tomatoes, and onion (if using). Add the bun tops and consume at once! **MAKES 4 SANDWICHES**

**VARIATION** Substitute an equal amount of large shrimp, scallops, firm white fish pieces, or a combination for the oysters.

Clam steamers are always available at the Hog Island Oyster Bars. Manila clams are a beautiful small clam, farmed by Hog Island, that steams easily and is also delicious raw on the half shell. Calabrian chiles, a staple of Southern Italian cooking, are at once spicy, fruity, and fiery, with a bright, vinegary finish. They are available in many major grocery chains as well as online. Jarred products include whole chiles, sliced chiles, and crushed chiles packed in oil. You can also find them dried and powdered. Spanish chorizo is a cured spicy sausage, unlike Mexican chorizo, which is raw. Together, this recipe highlights a brilliant combination of ingredients.

# CLAM STEAMERS
## with chorizo, greens, and calabrian chile butter

**CALABRIAN CHILE BUTTER**

4 tablespoons (55 g) unsalted butter, at room temperature

1 small clove garlic, finely chopped

3 oil-packed Calabrian chiles in oil, drained and finely chopped

1 tablespoon finely chopped fresh rosemary

1 tablespoon finely chopped shallots

Grated zest of 1 lemon

**CLAM STEAMERS**

¼ cup (60 ml) extra-virgin olive oil

¾ pound (340 g) Spanish chorizo, cut into ¼-inch (6-mm) dice

1 cup (240 ml) water

1 cup (240 ml) dry white wine

3 pounds (1.4 kg) Manila clams, scrubbed (page 32)

1 pound (455 g) braising greens, such as chard, kale, escarole, or radicchio

Fresh lemon juice, to taste

Warm crusty bread, for serving

To make the chile butter, in a small bowl, combine the butter, garlic, chiles, rosemary, shallots, and lemon zest and stir to blend. Cover and refrigerate for at least 1 hour.

To make the steamed clams, in a large, heavy pot, heat the olive oil over medium-high heat. Add the chorizo and cook, stirring occasionally, until cooked through, 4 to 5 minutes. Add the water, wine, and reserved chile butter. Stir to incorporate and simmer for a minute or two. Add the clams, cover, and reduce the heat to medium. Add the braising greens and cook, stirring occasionally, until almost tender, about 4 minutes. Cover and simmer until the clams have opened, 4 to 7 minutes. Look through and discard any clams that haven't opened.

You should have a good amount of broth; if not, add a little water. Add a few drops of lemon juice to brighten the flavors. Ladle the clams, broth, and greens into serving bowls and serve with warm bread for dipping.
**SERVES 4 TO 6**

This dish of clams stuffed with a mixture of bread crumbs, bacon, and chopped peppers is said to have been created in 1917 by Julius Keller, the maître d' at the Casino restaurant at the Tower on Narragansett Bay in Rhode Island. He was asked to prepare something special to impress the guests of an important socialite, Mrs. Paran Stevens. And the rest is history for this famous dish.

# CLAMS CASINO

3 tablespoons olive oil

½ pound (225 g) thick-cut bacon, finely chopped

1 cup (145 g) finely chopped red bell pepper

½ cup (75 g) finely chopped poblano chile

1 tablespoon minced garlic

Fine sea salt and finely ground pepper

⅓ cup (20 g) chopped green onion, including green tops

1 tablespoon fresh lemon juice

⅔ cup (55 g) panko (Japanese bread crumbs)

Coarse salt or rock salt, for baking

30 littleneck clams, scrubbed (page 32)

Preheat the oven to 450°F (230°C).

In a medium skillet, heat 2 teaspoons of the olive oil over medium heat. Add the bacon and sauté until the bacon is brown and nearly crisp, about 4 minutes. Using a slotted spoon, transfer the bacon to a medium bowl. Remove all but 2 tablespoons of the fat.

Add the bell pepper, poblano chile, and garlic to the pan with the bacon fat and season lightly with salt and pepper. Cook, stirring, until the vegetables have softened a bit, about 3 minutes. Add the vegetables to the bowl with the bacon, then add the green onion, lemon juice, and half of the bread crumbs to the bowl. In another small bowl, toss the remaining bread crumbs with the remaining olive oil to lightly coat.

Pour enough coarse salt onto a baking sheet to make a base for the clams. This will prevent them from tipping and losing their juices.

Shuck the clams (page 32), leaving them in the bottom shells and running your knife under the clams to release the meat. Top each clam with about 1 teaspoon of the bacon mixture and then some of the oiled bread crumbs. Nestle each clam into the salt on the baking sheet.

Bake until the bread crumbs are lightly browned and the clam juices are bubbling, about 10 minutes. Let cool for a minute or so before serving. **MAKES 30; SERVES 4 TO 6**

Hog Island founder John Finger decreed that the New England–style clam chowder served at the restaurant needed to be like those he grew up with—including his mom's—with no thickeners, unlike many versions of this dish that use a roux. Because of this, the flavor of the clams is allowed to sing. This creamy classic chowder is served with whole clams in the shell, and plenty of tender potatoes, buttery leeks, and bacon.

# HOG ISLAND CLAM CHOWDER

6 pounds (2.7 kg) small Manila clams in the shell, scrubbed (page 32)

8 to 10 (3 pounds/1.4 kg) Yukon Gold potatoes, peeled and cut into bite-size cubes

2 tablespoons unsalted butter

3 sprigs fresh thyme

½ pound (225 g) thick-sliced bacon, diced

2 large leeks, white part only, thinly sliced and well rinsed

½ small stalk celery, thinly sliced

1 large carrot, peeled and thinly sliced

4 cups (960 ml) heavy cream

Kosher salt and freshly cracked pepper

Chopped fresh flat-leaf parsley, for garnish

Warm crusty bread, for serving

After scrubbing the clams, allow them to drain in the colander in the sink while you prepare the base.

In a large, heavy stockpot, bring 5 to 6 cups (1.2 to 1.4 l) of water to a low boil and cook the potatoes until al dente, or just before fork-tender, about 8 minutes. Drain, reserving the cooking water.

In the stockpot, melt the butter with the thyme over low heat. Add the bacon and cook until it has rendered its fat. Add the leeks, celery, and carrot and cook, stirring, until the vegetables are just beginning to brighten in color, about 3 minutes. Add the potatoes and 4 cups (960 ml) of the cooking water, reserving the rest of the cooking water for other soups or to thin the chowder. (The chowder base can be cooled, covered, and refrigerated for up to 2 days at this stage. Rewarm the refrigerated base before proceeding.)

Increase the heat to medium and add the clams to the stockpot. Cover and simmer until the clams open, 5 to 6 minutes. Pick out and discard any clams that have not opened. (Don't skip this step—unopened clams may spoil the chowder.)

Add the cream and bring the chowder to a simmer. If it is too thick, add some of the reserved potato water. Season to taste with salt. When the chowder is bubbling in the center, it is ready.

Serve garnished with cracked pepper and parsley, with the bread for dipping. Place extra bowls on the table for the discarded shells. **SERVES 6 TO 8**

If you're from the Northeast, you know about clam shacks. Being from the West Coast, it took me a while to discover the delicious fare in these often-ramshackle places. My intro to clam-shack cooking was, of all places, Howard Johnson's, a former chain of restaurants whose heyday was in the 1960s. They served fried Ipswich clams, which I couldn't get enough of. The following recipe is close to the Hojo version.

# CLAM SHACK FRIED CLAMS

1 cup (130 g) corn flour or masa harina

1 cup (125 g) unbleached all-purpose flour

1 teaspoon fine sea salt

½ teaspoon freshly ground black pepper

¼ teaspoon cayenne pepper

Peanut or vegetable oil, for frying

2 cups (480 ml) buttermilk

1½ pounds (680 g) whole belly steamer clams, scrubbed and shucked (page 32)

Lemon wedges and hot sauce, for serving

In a large bowl, combine the flours, salt, and peppers and stir to blend.

Preheat the oven to 250°F (120°C). Line a baking sheet with paper towels and place in the oven.

In a 4 to 5-quart (3.8 to 4.7-l) Dutch oven, heat 2 inches (5 cm) of oil over medium-high heat until it shimmers (360°F/180°C on a deep-frying thermometer).

Pour the buttermilk into a large bowl, add the clams, and stir gently. Using a slotted spoon or a wire-mesh skimmer, carefully scoop up a small batch of clams, allowing the excess buttermilk to drain, then add them to the flour mixture and gently toss to coat evenly. Lift the clams out of the flour mixture, gently shake off excess, and carefully add to the oil. Try to spread them out to keep them from sticking together. Let the clams cook for 15 to 20 seconds without moving them, then gently stir the clams and cook until golden brown, 1 to 1½ minutes more. Use chopsticks or tongs to loosen any clams sticking to the bottom.

Using the slotted spoon or skimmer, transfer the clams to the paper towel–lined baking sheet to drain. Repeat to cook the remaining clams. Serve with the lemon wedges and hot sauce as quickly as possible so the clams don't lose their crunch. **SERVES 4**

This is a recipe from Jose Romo, head chef at the Hog Island Oyster Bar in Napa. It's also a favorite dish of Hog Island CEO John Finger's mom. There are lots of versions in New England, but ground zero for stuffed clams is Rhode Island. There they are called "stuffies," and you can find them in delis and seafood shacks as well as expensive eateries. Bread crumbs are traditionally used but there are lots of recipes that use crushed saltines or Ritz crackers in their place.

# STUFFED CLAMS

6 large quahog clams, scrubbed (page 32)

¾ cup (180 ml) dry white wine

3 slices thick-sliced bacon, preferably peppered, finely diced

1½ cups (190 g) finely chopped white or yellow onion

1½ cups (150 g) finely chopped celery

¾ cup (110 g) seeded and finely chopped red bell pepper

1 tablespoon finely sliced garlic

2 teaspoons smoked paprika

¼ cup (13 g) chopped fresh flat-leaf parsley

1 teaspoon finely chopped fresh oregano

1½ cups (120 g) panko (Japanese bread crumbs), crushed saltines, or crushed Ritz crackers

3 tablespoons unsalted butter, melted

Lemon wedges, for serving

Preheat the oven to 375°F (190°C). In a deep saucepan, combine the clams and wine. Cover and cook over medium-high heat until the clams open, about 5 minutes. Drain in a fine-mesh sieve set over a bowl, reserving the cooking juices. Look through and discard any clams that don't open. Let cool enough to handle and pull the meat from each shell reserving the shells for stuffing. Finely chop the meat and set aside in a large bowl.

In a medium skillet, cook the bacon over medium heat until crisp. Using a slotted spoon, transfer the cooked bacon to paper towels to drain. Add the onion, celery, bell pepper, garlic, and smoked paprika to the pan with the bacon fat and cook until the vegetables are lightly browned, about 6 minutes. Add a couple tablespoons of the reserved cooking juices to the skillet and stir to scrape up any bits on the bottom of the pan.

Add the vegetable mixture to the clams along with the parsley, oregano, and panko. Stir gently to combine just until the mixture holds together. Add more bread crumbs or cooking juices if needed.

Stuff the mixture into the clam shells that held the clam (discarding the other half of shell) or small ovenproof ramekins. Drizzle with melted butter. Put the stuffed shells or ramekins on a baking sheet and bake until lightly browned, 20 to 25 minutes. Serve with lemon wedges to squeeze over. **MAKES 6 LARGE CLAMS**

Renee Erickson, a James Beard Award–winning chef and the co-owner of Sea Creatures sister restaurants in Seattle, created this colorful summer dish. She writes: "I love cooking this in the height of cherry tomato season when tomatoes are super sweet. They are the main star next to the clams here, so they should be very flavorful and full of the great acidity you get with summer tomatoes. This is a great dish to make when camping, as well as on a beach."

# CLAMS with cherry tomatoes, herbs, and crème fraîche

4 tablespoons (60 ml) extra-virgin olive oil, plus more as needed

3 pints (870 g) Sun Gold cherry tomatoes

Kosher salt and freshly ground pepper

4 shallots, peeled and sliced into thin rounds

5 pounds (2.3 kg) Manila clams, scrubbed (page 32)

2 cups (480 ml) dry white wine

Julienned zest of 1 lemon

1 cup (240 ml) crème fraîche

1 tablespoon fresh lemon juice

½ cup (15 g) loosely packed fresh marjoram leaves

½ cup (25 g) loosely packed fresh tarragon leaves

Warm crusty bread, for serving

In large skillet, heat 2 tablespoons of olive oil over medium-high heat until it shimmers. Cooking in batches, add half of the cherry tomatoes to the oil. Do not crowd them. Sprinkle lightly with salt and cook for 1 minute, then stir until they start to blister and break open. Using a slotted spoon, transfer the tomatoes to a bowl. Repeat until all the tomatoes are cooked, adding more oil if necessary to keep the tomato juice in the pan from burning. Cover the bowl with a plate and set aside.

Heat the remaining 2 tablespoons oil over medium heat. Add the shallots and cook until translucent, about 2 minutes. Stir in the clams, then add the white wine. Season lightly with salt and pepper. Cover and steam until the clams are opened, about 5 minutes. Discard any clams that do not open.

Turn the heat off and stir in the lemon zest and crème fraîche and let it melt. Add the cherry tomatoes and their liquid, the lemon juice, and herbs, then gently fold all the ingredients together. Taste for seasoning. Serve hot with crusty bread for dipping in the broth. **SERVES 4 TO 6**

This traditional Italian recipe, found everywhere in Italy, highlights the sea flavor of clams and the delicacy of narrow ribbon pasta. You will also find it made with angel hair pasta but never with Italian-American red sauce. And remember that in Italy, grated Parmesan is never added to this seafood dish. Mussels are a great substitute for the clams in this recipe.

# LINGUINE WITH CLAMS

4 tablespoons (60 ml) extra-virgin olive oil

6 cloves garlic, thinly sliced

4 to 6 oil-packed anchovies

36 littleneck clams (about 3½ pounds/ 1.6 kg or so), scrubbed (page 32)

¼ teaspoon crushed red pepper flakes

½ teaspoon dried oregano

1 cup (240 ml) dry white wine

8 ounces (225 g) dried linguine

⅓ cup (17 g) chopped fresh flat-leaf parsley leaves

Set a large pot of salted water over high heat to boil for the pasta. Meanwhile, in a large skillet over medium heat, heat the olive oil. Add the garlic and cook until softened, 1 to 2 minutes. Add the anchovies and stir until the anchovies break up and dissolve into the oil, about 2 more minutes. Add the clams to the skillet along with the red pepper and oregano. Add about 1 cup (240 ml) water and the wine. Bring to a gentle boil, cover, and cook until clams open, 5 to 7 minutes. Using a slotted spoon or a wire-mesh skimmer, transfer the clams to a bowl. Look through and discard any clams that have not opened.

Increase the heat to high under the pan. Cook until the liquid is reduced by half, about 7 minutes. Meanwhile, remove the meat from the clams, leaving a few for garnish, if you like.

While the clams are steaming, liberally salt the boiling pasta water and add the linguine. Cook, stirring once or twice, until the pasta is al dente according to the directions on the package.

Drain the pasta and add it to the sauce in the skillet. Toss and cook until the pasta is coated with the sauce. Add the shucked clams and parsley and cook 1 minute more to blend the flavors. Serve at once, garnished with the reserved clams in their shells if desired. **SERVES 4**

---

I've visited Vietnam many times, and the food is fabulous, especially at the street stands which is where I first sampled this dish. There are many variations of this savory, brightly flavored recipe, but most of them, like this one, combine tender clams with chili-garlic sauce, onions, and herbs.

# SAIGON CLAMS

2 tablespoons canola or other neutral oil

1 cup (100 g) sliced onions

⅓ cup (75 ml) rice wine, such as sake

2 teaspoons chili-garlic sauce

2 teaspoons palm or light brown sugar

3 pounds (1.4 kg) cherrystone or Manila clams, scrubbed (page 32)

3 tablespoons fresh lime juice

2 tablespoons unsalted butter

1 tablespoon fish sauce

Steamed jasmine rice, for serving

4 generous sprigs fresh Thai basil or cilantro

In a large stockpot, heat the oil over medium-high heat. Add the onions and sauté for a couple of minutes until softened. Stir in the wine, chili-garlic sauce, and sugar, then add the clams. Cover and steam until the clams have opened, about 4 minutes. Look through and discard any unopened or cracked clams. Add the lime juice, butter, and fish sauce, adjusting the flavors to your taste. Stir until the butter melts. Divide the clams and sauce between bowls of steamed rice, top with the sprigs of basil, and serve at once. **SERVES 4**

This recipe is adapted from one by Craig Claiborne, the longtime food editor of the *New York Times*. A great believer in authentic American cooking, in 1976 he called this dish "Americana, pure and simple." He used a lemon mayonnaise but I enjoy serving this with a smoked paprika aioli.

# CLAM FRITTERS
# with smoked-paprika aioli

**SMOKED PAPRIKA AIOLI**

3 large poached garlic cloves (page 345)

1 tablespoon olive oil

⅔ cup (165 ml) mayonnaise

2 teaspoons pimentón (smoked Spanish paprika)

Fresh lemon juice

Kosher salt and freshly ground pepper

**CLAM FRITTERS**

2 large eggs

½ cup (60 g) rice flour

¼ cup (30 g) unbleached all-purpose flour

1 teaspoon baking powder

⅓ cup (75 ml) plain yogurt

¼ cup (60 ml) milk

2 teaspoons grated lemon zest

2 tablespoons finely chopped fresh chives

Pinch of cayenne

Kosher salt and freshly ground pepper

3 dozen Manila clams, scrubbed (page 32), shucked (page 32), and coarsely chopped

Peanut or vegetable oil, for frying

To make the aioli, in a mini food processor, combine the poached garlic, olive oil, mayonnaise, pimentón, and lemon juice and pulse until smooth. Season with salt and pepper. Cover and refrigerate for at least 1 hour or up to 3 days.

Preheat the oven to 250°F (120°C). Line a baking sheet with paper towels.

To make the clam fritters, break the eggs into a bowl and whisk until frothy. Add the flours, baking powder, yogurt, milk, lemon zest, chives, and cayenne. Season with salt and pepper. Mix just until blended. Stir in the clams.

In a heavy skillet, heat ¼ inch (6 mm) oil over medium heat until it shimmers. Working in batches, for each fritter spoon about 2 tablespoons of clam batter into the hot oil. Fry until golden on one side, about 2 minutes, then turn the fritters and continue frying until golden on the second side, about 2 minutes more. Using a wire-mesh skimmer, transfer the fritters to the paper-towel-lined baking sheet and place them in the oven to keep warm. Repeat to cook the remaining batter.

Serve the warm fritters at once, with the aioli. **MAKES ABOUT 16 FRITTERS**

Both Spain and Portugal have many delicious recipes for shellfish with a green sauce. Cilantro-poblano sauce, or *mojo de cilantro*, with its bread crumb topping, illustrates the bright simplicity of southern Mediterranean cuisine. Try it, too, with grilled fish and chicken as well as spooned over sliced fresh mozzarella or goat cheese. Any leftover bread crumbs are delicious sprinkled over pasta.

# CLAMS with cilantro-poblano sauce

**CILANTRO-POBLANO SAUCE**

6 large poached garlic cloves (page 345)

½ poblano chile, seeded and chopped

1 cup (40 g) finely chopped cilantro leaves and tender stems

½ cup (120 ml) extra-virgin olive oil

3 tablespoons white wine vinegar

Fine sea salt and freshly ground pepper

**CLAMS**

2 dozen littleneck or Manila clams, scrubbed (page 32)

½ cup (120 ml) dry white wine

1½ cups (70 g) Garlic-Lemon Bread Crumbs (page 342)

To make the sauce, in a mini food processor, combine the poached garlic, chile, and cilantro and chop finely. Stir in the oil and vinegar, then season to taste with salt and pepper. Use now, or cover and refrigerate for up to 2 days.

To make the clams, position a rack about 6 inches (15 cm) from the broiler and preheat the broiler. Add the clams and wine to a large pot. Cover and cook over medium-high heat until the clams open, 5 to 7 minutes. Look through and discard any clams that haven't opened.

Discard the top shell of each clam, leaving the meat in the bottom. Place the clams on a baking sheet. Spoon a little sauce over each clam and top each with about 1 tablespoon of the bread crumbs.

Place the pan under the broiler until lightly browned and heated through, about 2 minutes. Serve immediately. **SERVES 4 TO 6**

---

In Japan, this simple, fast dish is made with shimeji mushrooms, little white-stemmed, brown-capped mushrooms that grow in clusters. Most Japanese markets carry these fresh, but if you can't find them, use enoki mushrooms or sliced cremini.

# SAKE-STEAMED CLAMS with shimeji mushrooms

3 tablespoons unsalted butter

1½ pounds (680 g) Manila clams, scrubbed (page 32)

1¼ (300 ml) cups water

¼ cup (15 g) shimeji mushrooms

½ cup (120 ml) cooking sake or dry white wine

¼ cup (60 ml) mirin

1 tablespoon chopped green onion, green part only

Freshly grated lemon zest

Toasted sesame oil, preferably hot sesame oil

In a large, deep saucepan, melt the butter over medium heat. Add the clams, water, mushrooms, sake, and mirin. Cover, turn the heat to high, and cook until the clams open, about 5 minutes.

Look through and discard any unopened or cracked clams. Divide the clams between two bowls. Garnish with the green onion, lemon zest, and a few drops of sesame oil. **SERVES 2**

This recipe from Peter Reinhart, the "Gandalf of Pizza," is based on one created by Brian Spangler, chef-owner of Apizza Scholls in Portland, Oregon, for Anthony Bourdain. Clams casino (page 51) is one of the classic recipes using clams. Shellfish and smoked bacon make a delicious combination.

# CLAMS CASINO PIZZA

**GARLIC-HERB BLEND**

Cloves from 1 head garlic, peeled and mashed

4 teaspoons crushed red pepper flakes

1 tablespoon *each* dried oregano, basil, and parsley

1 teaspoon dried marjoram or thyme

½ teaspoon kosher salt

½ teaspoon freshly ground pepper

**CLAM PIZZA**

24 ounces (680 g) sliced bacon

Peter's New York Pizza Dough (page 343), made at least 1 day ahead

Vegetable oil, for misting

Cornmeal, for dusting

8 ounces (225 g) freshly grated Parmesan or Grana Padano cheese

45 Manila or cherrystone clams in the shell, scrubbed (page 32)

½ cup (25 g) chopped fresh flat-leaf parsley, for garnish

To make the garlic-herb blend, in a bowl, combine the mashed garlic, pepper flakes, dried herbs, salt, and pepper. Set aside.

Preheat the oven 400°F (205°C). Lay the bacon slices in a single layer on two 12-by-18-inch (30.5-by-46-cm) baking pans. Cook in the oven until the bacon is about three-quarters cooked, 10 to 15 minutes. Remove from the oven and let cool. Cut the slices in half crosswise. Stack them on a paper towel–lined plate, cover with plastic wrap, and refrigerate until ready to use.

Three hours before baking, remove the dough from the refrigerator. Divide into three 12-ounce (340-g) pieces and form them into tight balls. Lightly mist a baking sheet with vegetable oil. Place the dough balls on top, mist them with vegetable oil, and cover loosely with plastic wrap. Set aside to proof at room temperature for about 3 hours.

One hour before making the pizzas, place a baking stone or steel on the middle rack of the oven and preheat the oven to 550°F (290°C) or as hot as the oven allows.

Make one pizza at a time by stretching the dough to a 14-inch (35.5-cm) diameter. Lightly dust a pizza peel with cornmeal and lay the dough on the peel. Sprinkle one-third of the cheese over the surface, leaving a ½-inch (12-mm) border without cheese. Scatter one-third of the garlic-herb blend on top of the cheese. Place 15 clams on top and drape one-third of the halved bacon slices over the clams. Make sure the pizza slides easily on the peel. If not, add more cornmeal under the pizza.

Slide the pizza onto the preheated stone and bake for 4 minutes. Rotate the pizza 180 degrees and continue baking until the crust is golden brown around the edges and on the bottom, 2 to 4 minutes. The clams will have opened, with the juices dripping over the cheese and into the crust. Transfer the pizza to a cutting board and garnish with one-third of the parsley. Slice and serve. Repeat to make two more pizzas.

**MAKES THREE 14-INCH (35.5-CM) PIZZAS**

In this recipe from Abel Padilla, head chef at the Hog Island Oyster Bar in San Francisco's Ferry Building, raw geoduck is thinly sliced and served as ceviche with a brilliant orange sauce that both "cooks" and flavors the fresh seafood. This is nice served with corn chips, potato chips, or shrimp chips.

# GEODUCK CEVICHE
## with calabrian chile sauce

8 whole Calabrian chiles in oil

4 cloves garlic

2 small stalks celery, finely chopped

½ cup (120 ml) fresh lime juice

1¼ cups (300 ml) grapeseed or other neutral oil

Fine sea salt

3 geoduck siphons (page 32)

Micro cilantro or other greens

Put the chiles, garlic, celery, and lime juice in a food processor and pulse until finely ground. With the machine running, gradually drizzle in the grapeseed oil to create an emulsion. Season to taste with salt.

With a very sharp knife, thinly slice the geoduck siphons. Put the slices into a bowl and drizzle with just enough chile sauce to coat the geoduck. Stir until they are nicely coated and arrange attractively on plates. Garnish with a few sprigs of micro cilantro and serve at once. **SERVES 6 TO 8**

Here, chopped geoduck body is marinated in buttermilk and cooked into crisp, golden brown fritters. Serve it simply with lemon wedges, or with homemade aioli (page 337). This recipe is from chef Abel Padilla of the Hog Island Oyster Bar in San Francisco.

# GEODUCK FRITTERS

1 geoduck body, finely chopped (page 32)

2 cups (480 ml) buttermilk

1 cup (160 g) rice flour

1 tablespoon sweet Hungarian paprika

Kosher salt and freshly ground pepper

Rice bran oil or canola oil, for frying

Lemon wedges, for serving

In a medium bowl, soak the geoduck in buttermilk for 30 to 60 minutes. Drain and form into small 1-inch (2.5-cm) balls or cakes. In a shallow bowl, combine the rice flour, paprika, salt, and pepper. Coat the balls one at a time in the flour mixture, shaking gently to remove excess flour. Transfer them to a plate.

In a heavy pot, heat 2 inches (5 cm) of oil over medium-high heat until shimmering (350°F/175°C on a deep-frying thermometer). Add the balls and cook, turning as necessary, until golden brown, about 3 minutes. You may need to cook them in batches to avoid overcrowding the pan. Using a slotted spoon, transfer the fritters to paper towels to drain. Serve hot, with lemon wedges alongside. **SERVES 4**

Mussels are typically steamed in white wine with other flavorings and served in their savory broth. The famous Belgian dish *moules frites*, accompanies them with a pile of thin French fries served with a little bowl of mayonnaise for dipping the fries. Use the recipe for chips on page 206 to make the fries, but note that if you want a more authentic experience, cut the fries to ¼-inch (6-mm) width and reduce the frying time slightly. Crusty bread is a must to serve alongside for dipping into the broth.

# CLASSIC STEAMED MUSSELS

6 tablespoons (90 ml) unsalted butter or olive oil

1 cup (125 g) finely chopped onions

2 tablespoons finely chopped garlic

2 cups (480 ml) dry white wine

⅓ cup (17 g) chopped fresh flat-leaf parsley

2 teaspoons grated lemon zest

1 teaspoon crushed fennel seeds

Big pinch of crushed red pepper flakes

4 pounds (1.8 kg) mussels in the shell, rinsed and debearded (page 33)

Freshly ground pepper

Crusty French bread, for serving

In a large Dutch oven or other pot, melt the butter over medium heat. Add the onions and garlic and cook, stirring, until translucent, about 3 minutes. Add the wine, parsley, lemon zest, fennel seeds, crushed red pepper, mussels, and a grinding or two of black pepper. Cover tightly and bring to a boil over high heat. Reduce the heat to low and simmer until the mussels open, 4 to 5 minutes. Look through and discard any mussels that don't open.

Divide the mussels and their broth among warm bowls and serve at once, with the bread. **SERVES 4 TO 6**

# MUSSELS COOKED WITH PINE NEEDLES

This dish, known in Southern France as *éclade de moules*, is a showstopper. It originated with fishermen cooking mussels on a beach surrounded by pine forests. It's a no-recipe dish perfect for camping by the sea. You will need a large nail, a thick plank or round of wood, rinsed and debearded mussels (page 33), and a quantity of dry pine needles.

First, pound the nail into center of the wood. Place the wood on sand away from any foliage or objects that could catch fire. Begin standing mussels hinge side up against the nail to keep the ash from getting inside the mussels. Keep stacking the mussels, hinge side up, in concentric circles. Cover the mussels completely with a pile of pine needles and light the needles on fire. Let burn for about 5 minutes; the mussels should be opened and infused with the piney smoke from the needles.

Using a shovel, move the ashes away from the mussels and serve them with French bread and cultured butter and a glass of chilled white wine.

Escabeches have long been used to pickle cooked fish or shellfish, fowl, game meats, and mushrooms. This technique was introduced to Spain, Portugal, and Sicily by the Moorish Arabs, probably in the fourteenth century, and was a delicious way of preserving food pre-refrigeration. Known as *conservas* in Portugal and Spain, you'll see stores totally devoted to offering colorfully labeled cans of various fishes and meats preserved *en escabeche*. This version, known as *mejillones en escabeche,* is delicious served simply speared with toothpicks or on top of crunchy crostini and are also enjoyed in endless ways in appetizers, sides, and main dishes.

# MUSSELS ESCABECHE

3 pounds (1.4 kg) mussels, rinsed and debearded (page 33)

1 cup (240 ml) white wine

1½ cups (360 ml) extra-virgin olive oil

8 cloves unpeeled garlic

Two 2-inch (5-cm) sprigs rosemary

2 bay leaves

· 1 cinnamon stick

½ teaspoon black peppercorns

Peeled zest of half a small lemon, cut into thin strips

¾ teaspoon sweet paprika

½ cup (120 ml) good-quality white or red wine vinegar or sherry vinegar

1 teaspoon honey

1 teaspoon kosher salt, or to taste

Crisp crackers or crostini (page 343) for serving (optional)

Wash the mussels thoroughly and discard any that don't close when you pinch them shut.

In a large pot or Dutch oven, add the wine and mussels, cover, and set over medium-high heat. Cook, stirring, until all mussels have opened, about 6 minutes. Discard any that haven't opened.

Strain the mussels reserving the cooking broth. It's delicious used in sauces and to make rice. If not using right away, freeze in heavy-duty plastic bags to use later. When cool enough to handle, remove the meat from the cooked mussels and set aside in a medium bowl. Discard the shells.

Meanwhile, in a medium saucepan, make the marinade. Combine the olive oil, garlic, rosemary, bay leaves, cinnamon stick, peppercorns, and lemon zest and set over medium-low heat and cook until gently bubbling, about 6 minutes.

Remove the oil mixture from heat, and add paprika, vinegar, honey, and salt and give it a quick stir. Pour the warm marinade over the mussels and stir to combine. Cover the bowl with plastic wrap and let mussels marinate in the refrigerator for at least a day before serving. Can be stored for up to 10 days refrigerated.

Before serving, squeeze the garlic from its skin to enjoy alongside the mussels. **SERVES 4 TO 8**

Craig Claiborne, the longtime food editor of the *New York Times*, called this combination of mussels and cream "the most elegant and delicious soup ever created," and "one of the sublime creations on Earth." It's said to be named after William B. Leeds Sr., a wealthy American tycoon who dined nightly at Maxim's on visits to Paris in the early 1900s. Chef Louis Barthe came from Normandy, and this is his version of a traditional Norman dish. And it really is elegant and delicious—and maybe even sublime.

# BILLI BI MUSSEL SOUP

2 pounds (910 g) mussels, rinsed and debearded (page 33)

⅓ cup (45 g) coarsely chopped shallots

2 sprigs flat-leaf parsley, plus chopped fresh parsley for garnish

1 cup (240 ml) dry white wine, such as pinot grigio or sauvignon blanc

2 tablespoons unsalted butter, cubed

1 bay leaf

2 sprigs fresh thyme or ½ teaspoon dried thyme

Kosher salt and freshly ground pepper

2 cups (480 ml) heavy cream or crème fraîche

1 egg yolk, lightly beaten

Put the mussels in large pot or Dutch oven and add the shallots, the 2 sprigs parsley, wine, butter, bay leaf, and thyme sprigs. Season with salt and pepper. Cover and bring to a boil over medium heat. Reduce the heat to low and simmer, covered, until the mussels have opened, 4 to 5 minutes Look through and discard any mussels that have not opened.

Drain through a fine-mesh sieve set over a bowl, reserving the broth. When cool enough to handle, remove the mussels from their shells (you might save a few for garnish) and set aside.

In a small saucepan, bring the reserved liquid almost to a boil over medium heat. Add the cream and return the mixture almost to a boil, then remove from the heat. Let cool slightly, then whisk in the egg yolk to combine. Return the saucepan to low heat, continue whisking, and let thicken slightly. (Do not boil.)

Taste and adjust the seasoning. To serve, arrange the mussels in large soup dishes and ladle the broth over them. Sprinkle with chopped parsley and enjoy! **SERVES 4 TO 8**

Make this dish a day ahead and then bake at the last minute. Be sure to serve with little cocktail forks or spoons so that you can get every bit of the pesto out of the shell. The basil, cilantro, and mint pesto with ginger and peanuts is a twist on the Mediterranean version that can be used in other dishes calling for traditional basic pesto. In place of the serrano chile, you could substitute a teaspoon or so of Chinese chili-garlic sauce.

# BAKED MUSSELS
## with herb, ginger, and peanut pesto

**HERB, GINGER, AND PEANUT PESTO**

3 cups (120 g) *each* fresh basil and cilantro leaves, lightly packed

1 cup (50 g) fresh mint leaves, lightly packed

¼ cup (35 g) chopped dry-roasted, unsalted peanuts or cashews

3 tablespoons chopped poached or toasted garlic (page 345)

2 tablespoons finely chopped fresh ginger

1 tablespoon toasted sesame oil, or to taste

1 teaspoon seeded and finely chopped serrano chile

Grated zest and juice of 1 lime

½ cup (120 ml) olive or peanut oil

Fine sea salt and freshly ground pepper

**STEAMED MUSSELS**

3 pounds (1.4 kg) fresh mussels, rinsed and debearded (page 33)

1 cup (240 ml) dry white wine

2 tablespoons unsalted butter

3 tablespoons chopped fresh flat-leaf parsley

To make the pesto, in a small saucepan of lightly salted boiling water, blanch the basil, cilantro, and mint leaves for 5 seconds. Drain and immediately plunge them into ice water to stop the cooking and set the color. Drain and squeeze dry. Using a chef's knife and a cutting board, chop the herbs and add them to a blender along with the peanuts, garlic, ginger, sesame oil, serrano chile, and lime zest and juice. Pulse a few times to chop the ingredients and then, with the machine running, gradually add the olive or peanut oil, scraping down the sides as needed, until the mixture is pureed. Season to taste with salt and pepper. Use at once or cover and refrigerate for up to 5 days.

Preheat the oven to 400°F (205°C). Add the mussels, wine, butter, and parsley to a large pot. Cover and cook over high heat until the mussels open, about 4 minutes. Drain over a bowl, reserving the broth. Look through and discard any mussels that don't open.

Remove the top shell from each mussel. Loosen the meat and place mussels in their half shells on a baking sheet on top of a loosely crumpled sheet of aluminum foil or rock salt to keep the mussels from tipping. Add a scant teaspoon of reserved broth to each mussel and then top with a generous teaspoon of pesto. (You can cover the mussels with plastic wrap and refrigerate up to 1 day in advance before baking; remove the plastic wrap before baking.)

Bake until the pesto just begins to "melt" and the mussels are heated through, 4 to 6 minutes. Divide among 6 small serving plates and serve at once. **SERVES 6**

This fresh-tasting recipe from chef B Adamo, head chef at Hog Island Oyster Bar in Larkspur, makes use of spring vegetables like green garlic, leeks, and tender herbs. Look for green garlic, which is harvested before the bulb develops, at farmers' markets. It adds a mild garlic flavor to these steamed mussels and to other dishes. The leeks and herbal liqueur add more green notes to the broth.

# GREEN GARLIC MUSSELS

2 tablespoons unsalted butter

2 cups (180 g) sliced leeks, both white and tender green parts, well rinsed

2 stalks green garlic, minced

½ cup (120 ml) dry white wine

¼ cup (60 ml) Génépy or other herbal liqueur, such as Chartreuse (optional)

½ cup (120 ml) fish stock (page 332)

2 pounds (910 g) mussels, rinsed and debearded (page 33)

½ cup (25 g) mixed fresh herb sprigs, including tarragon, dill, and parsley, chopped

Crusty bread and lemon wedges, for serving

In a large pot, melt the butter over medium heat and sauté the leeks and green garlic until soft but not browned, about 3 minutes. Add the wine and liqueur (if using) and cook to reduce the liquid by half. Add the fish stock and mussels.

Cover and cook until the mussels open, about 4 minutes. Look through and discard any mussels that have not opened.

Add the herbs and serve with the crusty bread and lemon wedges alongside. **SERVES 2**

Versions of this spicy curry are found throughout Thailand and Vietnam. Adjust the sweet, sour, spicy, and salty flavors to make this dish your own. You can substitute laksa paste (page 342) for the red curry paste.

# SPICY THAI RED CURRY MUSSELS

One 13½-ounce (405-ml) can unsweetened coconut milk

⅓ cup (75 ml) fresh lime juice, plus lime wedges for serving

⅓ cup (75 ml) dry white wine

1½ tablespoons Thai red curry paste

1½ tablespoons minced garlic

1 tablespoon fish sauce

1 tablespoon sugar

5 pounds (2.3 kg) mussels, rinsed and debearded (page 33)

2 cups (80 g) fresh cilantro sprigs, chopped

In a large Dutch oven or other pot, combine the coconut milk, lime juice, wine, curry paste, garlic, fish sauce, and sugar and bring to a boil over high heat, stirring occasionally.

Add the mussels, tossing to combine. Cover and cook the mussels, stirring once or twice, until opened, about 4 minutes. Look through and discard any unopened mussels.

Add the cilantro and toss with the mussels. Serve the mussels in their broth, with lime wedges alongside. **SERVES 6**

This is a typical Japanese izakaya (bar food) recipe. Be sure to use very fresh or deep frozen and thawed bay scallops.

# BAY SCALLOPS AND AVOCADO
## with miso dressing

4 tablespoons (60 ml) mayonnaise, preferably Japanese Kewpie-style

2 tablespoons white shiro miso

2 tablespoons dashi (page 334) or chicken stock (page 333)

1 tablespoon sugar

1 pound (455 g) sashimi-grade bay scallops

1 firm-ripe avocado, pitted, peeled, and cut into ½-inch (12-mm) cubes

2 small green onions, sliced thinly on the bias

3 tablespoons cilantro leaves

1 teaspoon sesame seeds, toasted (page 344)

In a large bowl, stir together the mayonnaise, miso, dashi, and sugar until smooth. Taste and adjust the flavor to your liking. Add the scallops, avocado, and green onion and toss gently to coat evenly. Divide the mixture between small plates and garnish with the cilantro and sesame seeds. Serve immediately. **SERVES 4 TO 6**

---

The secret to a good ceviche is to not let the fish "cook" in its citrusy marinade too long, which not only toughens the meat but also covers up the flavor of the fresh seafood. This simple recipe calls for the less-expensive bay scallops, but you could also use halved or quartered sea scallops. Diced firm ripe avocado and/or mango would make a nice addition.

# SCALLOP CEVICHE

1 pound (455 g) bay scallops

1 cup (145 g) cherry tomatoes (about 10), halved or quartered

1 teaspoon seeded and chopped serrano chile, or to taste

½ cup (20 g) chopped fresh cilantro, plus cilantro sprigs for garnish

½ cup (65 g) finely diced red onion

1 cup (240 ml) fresh orange juice

⅓ cup (75 ml) fresh lime juice

1 teaspoon sugar

Fine sea salt and freshly ground pepper

In a large glass or ceramic bowl, combine the scallops, tomatoes, serrano chile, chopped cilantro, red onion, orange juice, lime juice, and sugar and stir to mix well. Season with salt and pepper. Cover and refrigerate for a maximum of 10 minutes.

Spoon the ceviche into attractive glasses, garnish with cilantro sprigs, and serve. **SERVES 6 TO 8**

This rich dish of gratinéed sea scallops is a traditional French first course that is usually served in real scallop shells. But you can serve your coquilles Saint-Jacques (French for "scallops") in any small gratin dishes.

# COQUILLES SAINT-JACQUES

½ cup (25 g) fresh bread crumbs

2 tablespoons freshly grated Parmesan cheese

3 tablespoons unsalted butter, melted

1 tablespoon finely chopped fresh chives

1 tablespoon minced shallot

5 ounces (140 g) white button or cremini mushrooms, finely chopped

Kosher salt and freshly ground pepper

2 tablespoons dry white vermouth or white wine

¾ cup (180 ml) crème fraîche

⅓ cup (75 ml) shrimp stock (page 332) or chicken stock (page 333)

6 large (3 ounces/85 g each) sea scallops, side muscle removed and cut in half horizontally

1 teaspoon fresh lemon juice, or to taste

In a small bowl, combine the bread crumbs, Parmesan, 1 tablespoon of the melted butter, and the chives. Mix well and set aside.

In a small skillet, melt the remaining 2 tablespoons melted butter over medium heat and cook the shallots and mushrooms until they have softened and are just beginning to brown. Season with salt and pepper. Add the vermouth and cook, stirring to scrape up any browned bits on the bottom of the pan. Divide the mushrooms among 6 scallop shells or gratin dishes. Reserve the pan.

Add the crème fraîche and shrimp stock to the reserved pan and cook over medium-low heat until the mixture has thickened a bit, about 3 minutes. Add the scallops and cook until they are firm but still slightly translucent, no longer than 2 minutes. Remove from the heat and stir in the lemon juice. Taste and adjust the seasoning. Spoon the scallop mixture over the mushrooms, dividing the scallops equally between the shells or dishes. Finish the dish now, or set aside for up to 1 hour to finish later.

Position a rack 6 inches (15 cm) from the broiler and preheat the broiler. Sprinkle the reserved bread crumb mixture on top of the scallop mixture, dividing equally. Broil until the topping is golden brown and bubbling. Serve at once.
**SERVES 6**

This simple Thai-inspired salad is a satisfying main course. In place of the scallops, you can substitute other seafood such as lobster, large shrimp, or hot-smoked salmon.

# GRILLED SCALLOP AND ASPARAGUS SALAD
## with spicy lime dressing

**SPICY LIME DRESSING**

¼ cup (60 ml) fresh lime juice

¼ cup (60 ml) fresh orange juice

¼ cup (60 ml) fish sauce

1 teaspoon minced fresh red chile

1 teaspoon minced garlic

2 teaspoons minced fresh ginger

1 tablespoon rice vinegar

5 tablespoons (65 g) sugar

1 tablespoon fresh cilantro leaves, coarsely chopped

Kosher salt and freshly ground pepper

**SCALLOP-ASPARAGUS SALAD**

1 pound (455 g) tender asparagus spears

Olive oil, for coating

Fine sea salt and freshly ground pepper

1¼ pounds (570 g) large fresh sea scallops, side muscle removed

1 tablespoon grated lemon zest

3 cups (120 g) loosely packed mixed fresh herb leaves, such as mint, basil, cilantro, and chervil, and tender lettuce leaves, such as mâche, frisée, or micro greens

1 large ripe avocado, pitted, peeled, and cut into large dice

1 large navel orange, cut into segments (page 345)

Basil oil or extra-virgin olive oil, for garnish (optional)

To make the dressing, in a small bowl, combine the lime and orange juices, the fish sauce, chile, garlic, ginger, vinegar, sugar, and cilantro and stir until the sugar is dissolved. Season with salt and pepper. Let sit for at least 30 minutes before serving for the flavors to develop. Taste and adjust the seasoning.

To make the salad, prepare a medium-hot fire in a charcoal grill or preheat a gas grill to medium-high. Brush the grill grates clean. Coat the asparagus with the olive oil and season with salt and pepper. Grill until crisp-tender and grill-marked, turning occasionally with tongs. Slice diagonally into 2-inch (5-cm) segments and set aside.

Put the scallops in a bowl and lightly coat them with olive oil. Add the zest, season with salt and pepper, and turn gently to coat. Put a grill screen on top of the grill grate, add the scallops, and grill them, turning once, until almost cooked through, about 3 minutes total. Be careful not to overcook. The scallops should still be translucent in the center.

Arrange lettuces, herbs, avocado, and orange segments on plates. Divide the scallops and asparagus between the plates. Drizzle each serving with the dressing, then drizzle some of the basil oil, if using, around the plate. Serve immediately. **SERVES 4**

This makes a beautiful first course. The key with this dish is to use absolutely fresh, dry-packed day-boat scallops (page 34). Pick celery root that are heavy for their size, as these won't have a cavity in the center.

# SCALLOPS with celery root salad

1 large celery root (1 to 1½ pounds/455 to 680 g)

1 cup (240 ml) mayonnaise

¼ cup (60 ml) buttermilk

2 tablespoons *each* whole-grain and smooth Dijon mustard

1 tablespoon fresh lemon juice

2 teaspoons sherry vinegar or brown rice vinegar

Fine sea salt and freshly ground pepper

2 tablespoons olive oil

8 jumbo (under 10 per pound/455 g) dry-packed day-boat scallops, side muscle removed

Big pinch of hot pimentón (Spanish smoked paprika) or cayenne pepper

3 to 4 ounces (85 to 115 g) fresh salmon roe (or sturgeon caviar if you're feeling flush!)

Chervil or dill sprigs, for garnish

Peel, thinly slice, and cut the celery root into julienne. (A mandoline makes this an easier task.) In a pot of boiling salted water, blanch the celery root for 10 seconds, then immediately drain and put into a bowl of ice water to stop the cooking. Drain again and gently roll the celery root on a clean tea towel to dry it off a bit.

In a medium bowl, whisk together the mayonnaise, buttermilk, mustards, lemon juice, and vinegar until smooth. Stir in the celery root to evenly coat, then season with salt and pepper. Cover and refrigerate for at least 1 hour or up to 48 hours.

In a large skillet, heat the olive oil over medium-high heat. Pat the scallops dry with a paper towel, then season with salt and pepper. Sear on both sides until nicely browned, 3 to 4 minutes total. The scallops should be translucent in the center. Slice the scallops in half horizontally, if desired.

To serve, mound the celery root on plates and set the scallops on top. Top with the caviar and chervil sprigs and serve immediately. **SERVES 8**

Sabayon (French) or zabaglione (Italian) is a warm custard sauce that is usually sweetened and served for dessert. But it's equally excellent as a savory sauce, and here it is a delicious accompaniment to scallops. Be sure to ask your fishmonger for fresh day-boat or dry-pack scallops.

# SEARED SCALLOPS
## with roasted-garlic sabayon

**ROASTED-GARLIC SABAYON**

½ cup (120 ml) shellfish stock (page 332) or fish stock (page 332)

3 tablespoons dry white vermouth or white wine

1 tablespoon fresh lemon juice

4 large egg yolks

1 or 2 tablespoons roasted garlic (page 345)

1 tablespoon finely chopped mixed fresh herbs, such as chives, tarragon, and parsley

Fine sea salt and freshly ground pepper

**SEARED SCALLOPS**

12 jumbo (under 10 per pound/455 g) day-boat scallops, side muscle removed

Fine sea salt and freshly ground pepper

3 tablespoons olive oil

2 cups (40 g) baby greens, such as arugula or tat soi, lightly packed

To make the sabayon, in a medium saucepan, bring the stock and wine to a simmer over medium heat. Remove from the heat and stir in the lemon juice. In a medium metal bowl, whisk the egg yolks and garlic until smooth, then very gradually whisk the warm stock mixture into the yolk mixture to temper them.

Place the bowl on top of a pot with about 2 inches (5 cm) of simmering water, making sure the bottom of the bowl doesn't touch the water, and whisk constantly until the mixture has thickened, about 3 minutes. Remove the bowl from the pan and stir in the herbs. Add salt and pepper to taste.

To make the scallops, pat the scallops dry with paper towel and season lightly with salt and pepper. In a large skillet, heat the olive oil over medium-high heat. Sear the scallops on both sides until golden brown, about 3 minutes total. Be careful not to overcook; the scallops should be translucent in the center. Arrange the greens on 4 warm plates. Place the scallops on top, spoon the sabayon over, and serve immediately. **SERVES 4**

We usually think of vanilla in context with sweets but it's also delicious used in savory dishes. Here, we've used it with scallops, but try it with any simply cooked fish or even boneless, skinless chicken breasts.

# SEARED SCALLOPS
## with savory vanilla butter sauce

**VANILLA BUTTER SAUCE**

2 tablespoons unsalted butter

3 tablespoons chopped shallots or green onions, including some green parts

½ cup (30 g) sliced mushrooms

3 cups (720 ml) chicken stock (page 333) or fish stock (page 332)

1 cup (240 ml) dry white wine, such as Chardonnay

⅔ cup (165 ml) heavy cream

One 3-inch (7.5-cm) vanilla bean, split lengthwise

Fresh lemon juice, to taste

Fine sea salt and freshly ground pepper

**SEARED SCALLOPS**

1 pound (455 g) large sea scallops, (8/10 size) side muscle removed

3 tablespoons olive oil

Fine sea salt and freshly ground pepper

Chopped fresh chives, for garnish

To make the sauce, in a medium skillet, melt the butter over medium heat. Add the shallots and mushrooms and cook, stirring, until soft but not browned. Add the stock and wine, increase the heat to high, and cook to reduce the liquid by half, about 5 minutes.

Add the cream and vanilla bean and cook to reduce again to a light sauce consistency. Strain though a fine-mesh sieve set over a bowl, pressing on the solids with the back of a large spoon. Scrape the soft center of the vanilla bean into the strained sauce and discard the bean pod. Season with lemon juice and salt and pepper. Cover and keep warm over a bowl or pan of hot water until serving (up to 2 hours).

To make the scallops, lightly rub the scallops with 1 tablespoon of the olive oil and season lightly with salt and pepper. In a large nonstick skillet, heat the remaining 2 tablespoons of oil over medium-high heat. Add the scallops (in batches if necessary) and sear, turning once, until golden brown on both sides, about 2 minutes. The scallops should be slightly translucent in the center.

To serve, divide the warm sauce among warm plates and divide the scallops between them. Sprinkle with chives and serve immediately. **SERVES 4 TO 6**

I love this combination of rich scallops, salty coppa, peppery cress, and sweet-savory sauce. If dry-packed scallops are unavailable, substitute firm white fish, such as halibut, sablefish, or sea bass. Other cooked vegetables, such as green peas, cubed butternut squash, and diced carrots, could substitute for the corn in this creamy sauce. Puree and strain the sauce again for a velvety smooth finish.

# SEARED SCALLOPS
## with coppa and creamy corn sauce

**CREAMY CORN SAUCE**

2 tablespoons unsalted butter or olive oil

1 cup (110 g) chopped white onion

½ teaspoon mild chile powder, such as ancho

2 cups (480 ml) chicken stock (page 333) or shellfish stock (page 332)

1½ cups (205 g) fresh or frozen corn kernels

⅔ cup (165 ml) heavy cream

2 teaspoons dry sherry

Fine sea salt and freshly ground pepper

Drop of truffle oil (optional)

**SCALLOPS AND COPPA**

12 thinly sliced rounds of dry coppa or slices of prosciutto

12 large sea scallops (about 1½ pounds/ 680 g), side muscle removed

Fine sea salt and freshly ground black pepper

3 tablespoons olive oil

2 cups (60 g) young watercress or upland cress leaves and tender stems

To make the sauce, in a deep saucepan, melt the butter over medium heat and sauté the onion and chile powder until the onions are soft but not brown. Add the stock and corn, cover, and simmer until the vegetables are very soft, about 10 minutes. Add the cream and sherry and bring to a simmer.

Transfer to a blender and blend until very smooth. Strain through a fine-mesh sieve over a bowl, pressing down on the solids with the back of a large spoon. Discard the solids and return the sauce to the pan. Season with salt, pepper, and truffle oil, if using. Keep warm.

To make the scallops and coppa, preheat the oven to 375°F (190°C). Lay the coppa in a single layer on a baking sheet and cook until firm, 3 to 4 minutes. Using a slotted spatula, transfer the coppa to a plate to cool.

Pat the scallops dry with a paper towel, then season lightly with salt and pepper. In a large skillet, heat the olive oil over medium-high heat. Using tongs, add the scallops to the pan and cook until golden brown on the bottom, about 2 minutes. Turn and cook the other side until browned, about 1 minute. Transfer to a plate. The scallops should be slightly translucent in the center.

Arrange the watercress leaves in the center of warm plates and place the scallops on top. Spoon the corn cream around the watercress, place the cooked coppa on top of the scallops, and serve immediately. **SERVES 6**

In parts of Asia, rice porridge is a staple often made to serve at breakfast or to heal what ails you. Known as congee or jook in China and okayu in Japan, it is made by cooking whole, broken, or ground rice grains in a large amount of broth or water to the consistency of porridge. The addition of abalone makes it a special treat. You can use fresh abalone, of course, but frozen, canned, or dried is most often used. If using canned, boil it for a minute or two and then drain to minimize the canned flavor. Dried abalone must be soaked overnight to soften it.

# RICE PORRIDGE with abalone

1 cup (200 g) short-grain rice

8 cups (2 l) fish stock (page 332), shrimp stock (page 332), or water

2 tablespoons peeled and finely julienned fresh ginger

1 tablespoon dark soy sauce

2 teaspoons toasted sesame oil

1 teaspoon sugar

6 ounces (170 g) cleaned fresh abalone (page 35); boiled and drained canned abalone; or dried abalone soaked overnight and drained, cut into thin julienne

⅓ cup (20 g) thinly sliced green onions, including green parts

Flaky sea salt and freshly ground pepper

Put the rice in a small bowl and add enough water to just cover the rice; set aside for 1 hour.

Add the rice-water mixture to a blender, and pulse until finely ground but not gluey. Transfer to a pot, add the stock, and bring to a boil over high heat. Reduce the heat to low, cover, and cook, stirring occasionally, until softened and porridge-like, about 2 hours. Ladle the hot rice mixture into individual large, deep soup bowls.

About 15 minutes before serving, in a bowl whisk together the ginger, soy sauce, sesame oil, and sugar. Add the abalone and toss until evenly coated. Heat a large nonstick skillet or wok over medium heat and quickly stir-fry the abalone until it is just beginning to color, about 2 minutes.

Spoon a couple of tablespoons of the abalone mixture on top of each bowl of porridge and garnish with green onions. Ask your guests to season their serving to taste with salt and pepper. **SERVES 4 TO 6**

I think a simple pan-fried abalone is the best way to appreciate it. It takes some time to tenderize all the slices, but it's an important step—without it, the abalone will be tough and chewy. If you like, garnish the abalone with chopped fresh chives and a sprinkle of flaky sea salt, and serve with aioli (page 337).

# PAN-FRIED ABALONE

1 wild abalone or 8 ounces (225 g) farmed abalones, shucked, cleaned (page 35), and thinly sliced

1 cup (100 g) panko (Japanese bread crumbs)

½ teaspoon smoked paprika

½ teaspoon fine sea salt

⅛ teaspoon freshly ground pepper

2 tablespoons unsalted butter

1 tablespoon olive oil

Lemon wedges, for serving

Using a meat tenderizer or the back of a large metal spoon, gently tap the abalone slices until the texture softens, becoming limp. (Make sure not to pound the abalone as it is not as effective at tenderizing as gentle tapping.)

In a wide, shallow bowl, whisk together the panko, smoked paprika, salt, and pepper. Dredge the abalone slices in the mixture to coat evenly, shaking off any excess. Lay the slices in a single layer on a baking sheet, cutting board, or platter.

In a large frying pan over medium-high heat, melt the butter with the olive oil. Add the prepared abalone slices to the pan in a single layer and cook, turning once, until golden on both sides, about 4 minutes total.

Serve at once, with lemon wedges to squeeze over. **SERVES 4**

I had a dish like this on a trip to Venice in one of those amazing back-alley restaurants. For the mixed seafood, any combination of shelled shellfish (such as clams, shrimp, scallops, mussels, and/or crab) or fin fish (such as cod, halibut, or salmon) can be used.

# SEAFOOD SPAGHETTI CARBONARA

3 tablespoons extra-virgin olive oil

3 ounces (85 g) guanciale or pancetta, finely diced

2 teaspoons freshly cracked pepper, plus more as needed

1¾ cups (175 g) freshly grated Parmesan cheese

1 large egg, plus 3 yolks

2 cups (340 g) mixed seafood (see Note), cut into small pieces

2 tablespoons chopped fresh flat-leaf parsley or basil

Kosher salt

1 pound (455 g) spaghetti or other long pasta

In a medium skillet, heat the olive oil over medium heat. Add the guanciale and cook, stirring occasionally, until lightly browned, 6 to 8 minutes. Add the pepper and cook, stirring until fragrant, 2 minutes more. Transfer the guanciale mixture to a large bowl and let cool. Stir in 1½ cups (150 g) of the Parmesan, the egg, egg yolks, seafood mixture, and parsley. Stir to combine and set aside.

Meanwhile, bring a large pot of salted water to a boil. Add the pasta and cook until al dente, about 10 minutes, or according to package directions. Reserving ¾ cup (180 ml) of the pasta water, drain the pasta and transfer it to the guanciale mixture. Toss, adding pasta water a little at a time to make a creamy sauce. Season with salt and pepper to taste. Serve topped with the remaining ¼ cup (25 g) Parmesan. **SERVES 4**

Bouillabaisse is the most famous dish of Marseille in France's Provence region. A fish stew/soup, there are probably as many variations of this recipe as there are people who make it. Like cioppino (page 88), bouillabaisse was originally a stew made by fishermen using the bony rockfish and other fishes that they were unable to sell to restaurants or markets. The California designation here means that it uses fish and shellfish common to the Golden State. Use what you like.

# CALIFORNIA BOUILLABAISSE
## with rouille

### ROUILLE

⅛ teaspoon crumbled saffron threads

1 teaspoon hot water

1 cup (240 ml) mayonnaise, preferably homemade

¼ cup (40 g) roasted, peeled, and chopped red bell peppers

¼ cup (60 ml) extra-virgin olive oil

1 teaspoon fresh lemon juice

1 to 2 teaspoons chopped garlic

¼ teaspoon cayenne pepper

Fine sea salt

### BOUILLABAISSE

1 cup (240 ml) dry white wine

4 cups (960 ml) fish stock (page 332), shrimp stock (page 332), or chicken stock (page 333), or water

3 pounds (1.4 kg) Manila clams, scrubbed (page 32)

3 tablespoons olive oil

2 leeks, white part only, halved, rinsed, and sliced (about 2 cups/180 g)

1 small fennel bulb, trimmed and diced (about 2 cups/220 g)

4 large cloves garlic, chopped

Two 15-ounce (430-g) cans diced tomatoes with juice, preferably fire-roasted

1 large poblano chile, charred, peeled, seeded, and chopped (page 341)

¾ pound (340 g) small creamer or fingerling potatoes, scrubbed

1¼ pounds (570 g) Pacific rock cod, true cod, or sablefish (black cod) cut into 1½-inch (4-cm) pieces

1 large cooked Dungeness crab, cleaned, cracked, and cut into sections

Fine sea salt and freshly ground black pepper

Lemon wedges, for serving

Garlic Croutons (page 343), for serving

To make the rouille, sprinkle the saffron over the hot water in a cup and let stand for a few minutes. Add to a blender with the mayonnaise, bell peppers, olive oil, lemon juice, garlic, cayenne pepper, and salt and blend until smooth. This is best made at least an hour in advance for the flavors to develop.

To make the bouillabaisse, in a stockpot, bring the wine and stock to a boil over medium-high heat. Add the clams. Cover and shake and cook until the clams have opened, about 3 minutes. Using a slotted spoon, transfer the clams to a bowl and set aside; reserve the stock.

In a large saucepan, heat the olive oil over medium heat and sauté the leeks and fennel just until softened, about 2 minutes. Do not brown. Add the garlic and cook for 1 minute to remove its raw taste. Add the tomatoes, poblano, potatoes, and reserved stock and simmer for a few minutes. Add the cod and crab and cook until just cooked through, about 3 minutes. Be careful not to overcook; the cod should be slightly translucent in the center.

Add the reserved clams and let sit in the broth for a few minutes to reheat. Season with salt and pepper and divide the mixture among four bowls. Place a dollop of rouille in the center for guests to stir in and pass lemon wedges and croutons alongside. **SERVES 6**

Cioppino, a flavorful fish stew, is closely identified with San Francisco. It's believed to have been brought to the city by the bay by early Italian fishermen who emigrated there from Genoa. In place of the Mediterranean fish used in the original dish, it uses local favorites like Dungeness crab and rockfish, plus shrimp and mussels. If you can, use whole crab in the shell; the shell adds flavor. The tomato and red wine stock can be made ahead. Remember to add the various fish and shellfish separately so that you can control their cooking time. Be aware of not overcooking the fish as it continues to cook while sitting in the broth. Hog Island does a variation on this called rustic seafood stew, their version of cioppino, which is one of their staple menu items. Serve with crusty bread and a big glass of the red wine used to make the stew.

# CIOPPINO

¼ cup (60 ml) olive oil

3 cups (330 g) chopped onions

1 cup (140 g) chopped peeled carrot

⅔ cup (65 g) chopped celery or fennel

3 tablespoons chopped garlic

3 cups (495 g) canned whole or diced peeled tomatoes with their juice

6 cups (1.4 l) fish stock (page 332) or chicken stock (page 333)

2½ cups (600 ml) hearty red wine, such as zinfandel, cabernet, or sangiovese

3 large bay leaves

¼ cup (10 g) chopped fresh basil

1 tablespoon chopped fresh oregano

2 teaspoons fennel seeds

½ teaspoon crushed red pepper flakes

Fine sea salt and freshly ground black pepper

1 whole Dungeness crab (about 2 pounds/ 910 g), cleaned and chopped into sections

1½ pounds (680 g) mussels (18 to 24), scrubbed and debearded (page 33)

2 pounds (910 g) rockfish fillets, cut into 1-inch (2.5-cm) cubes

16 medium shrimp (31 to 35 count), peeled and deveined (page 115), shells reserved

8 thick slices sourdough bread, brushed with garlic-infused olive oil and toasted

¼ cup (13 g) chopped fresh flat-leaf parsley

In a large pot, heat the olive oil over medium heat and add the onions, carrot, celery, and garlic. Sauté until the vegetables are lightly browned. Add the tomatoes, stock, wine, bay leaves, basil, oregano, fennel seeds, and crushed red pepper. Bring to a boil over high heat, then reduce the heat to a simmer and cook, partially covered, for 15 to 20 minutes.

Drain in a fine-mesh sieve over a bowl. Discard the solids and return the broth to the pot. Season to taste with salt and pepper. Set aside to use now, or let cool, cover, and refrigerate for up to 5 days.

To finish the cioppino, add the crab and mussels to the broth and cook over medium heat until the mussels open, about 5 minutes. Add the fish and shrimp and cook until the fish is opaque. Look through and discard any mussels that have not opened. Place a sourdough toast in the bottom of each of 8 large, deep bowls and ladle the stew on top. Sprinkle with parsley and serve immediately. **SERVES 8**

This classic saffron-scented dish from Spain is often cooked over a wood or charcoal fire using a special shallow pan. You'll need a 14-inch (35.5-cm) paella pan for this recipe. You can cook this paella on the stove top, as I've done here, or on the grill or in the oven. Paella can contain all manner of meats, including sausage along with fish, shellfish, and vegetables, depending on the whim and budget of the cook. For the rice, look for a short-grain Spanish variety called Valencia, also known as Bomba, or the more widely available Calrose. The goal of making a great paella is to develop the socarrat, a crunchy cooked layer on the bottom of the pan. Once the rice is cooked through, increase the heat under the rice just until you can smell the rice begin to toast. When serving, be sure to scrape up a little of that delicious toasty stuff with each portion.

# PAELLA with clams, shrimp, and chorizo

¼ cup (60 ml) olive oil

½ pound (225 g) Spanish chorizo or other cured garlic sausage, cut into thin rounds

1 white onion, chopped

2 tablespoons sliced garlic

1 cup (150 g) diced poblano or Anaheim chile

2 cups (400 g) Valencia (Bomba) or Calrose rice

½ cup (120 ml) dry white wine

4 cups (960 ml) hot shellfish stock (page 332) or chicken stock (page 333), plus more if needed

¼ teaspoon saffron threads bloomed in 2 tablespoons white wine or water

1 cup (165 g) seeded and diced fresh or drained chopped canned tomatoes

3 or 4 fresh thyme sprigs, or 1 teaspoon dried thyme

1 teaspoon fennel seeds

2 pounds (910 g) Manila or littleneck clams, scrubbed (page 32)

1 pound (455 g) large (16 to 20 count) shrimp, peeled and deveined (page 115)

2 cups (400 g) cooked fresh or frozen giant lima or fava beans

Kosher salt and freshly ground pepper

Chopped fresh flat-leaf parsley, for garnish

Lemon wedges, for serving

In a large paella pan, heat the olive oil over medium-high heat. (You may need to do this over two burners.) Add the chorizo and cook until lightly browned on both sides, about 3 minutes total. Using a slotted spoon, transfer the chorizo to paper towels to drain. Add the onion, garlic, and chile to the pan and sauté until the vegetables just begin to color, about 2 minutes. Add the rice and stir for a minute or two to coat the grains.

Add the wine, stock, saffron mixture, tomatoes, thyme, and fennel seeds and stir gently. Bring to a boil and nestle the clams down in the rice mixture. Cover the pan with aluminum foil and cook until the clams open and the rice is almost tender, about 12 minutes. Nestle the shrimp in the rice mixture and cook, uncovered, until the shrimp are evenly pink, about 2 minutes (they will continue to cook after removed from heat). Add the beans, reserved chorizo, and salt and pepper to taste.

If desired, develop the socarrat: Place the pan over high heat and cook until you smell the rice toasting, about 5 minutes. Do not stir.

Turn off the heat and let the paella rest for at least 5 minutes. Taste and adjust the seasoning. Serve topped with chopped parsley and lemon wedges. Be sure to scrape up a little of the toasty socarrat with each serving. **SERVES 6 TO 8**

# CEPHALOPODS

## squid, octopus

Cephalopods are another part of the mollusk family, which includes cuttlefish, octopus, squid, and nautilus. Their name comes from the Greek for "head with feet," since their arms attach directly to the head. There is growing interest in this family because their population is growing even with climate degradation. We now recognize the need to find alternative sources for food in the future. With dwindling finned fish populations as well as finding new sources of protein that can replace meat from land animals, there is great interest in learning how to cook cephalopods. This chapter explores the many delicious ways you can prepare them.

# SQUID

Squid, well known by its Italian name *calamari*, is a versatile seafood. It is delicious fried, as it is most often encountered in America, but can be prepared in many other ways, whether grilled, braised, or stewed. As many as three hundred or more species of squid are found in all the oceans of the world, even the Antarctic. They are voracious eaters of a wide range of creatures such as krill, small fish, crustaceans, and even other squid.

Although squid have some similarities to octopus, they are completely different animals. Squid (like octopus) have the ability to change colors and camouflage themselves in their environment. While the size of squid can vary widely, most sold for culinary uses are usually no more than 1 foot (30.5 cm) long. Giant squid, the focus of many folklore stories, can reach a length of over 40 feet (12 m).

As a source of human food, squid is popular in Asia and the Mediterranean. It's also an important source of food for many marine mammals, such as the sperm whale, who count squid as part of their primary diet. Squid play a key role in stabilizing the food chain and supporting the ocean ecosystem. Due to their short lifespans and popularity in the diets of many larger predators, squid reproduce rapidly and in abundance, making them a very sustainable food resource in regions where the fishery is well managed. On the West Coast, the California market squid (*Doryteuthis opalescens*) is renowned in Monterey Bay and well managed. On the East Coast the longfin squid (*Doryteuthis pealeii*) fishery is similarly well managed.

## HOW TO CLEAN AND PREPARE SQUID

Rinse the squid thoroughly under cold running water. Holding a squid body firmly in one hand, grasp the tentacles at the base with the other. **1.** Gently but firmly pull the head, which is just above the tentacles, away from the body. As you do this, the soft entrails will come away with it. **2. & 3.** Using a sharp knife, cut the tentacles from the head of the squid. Remove and discard the hard beak from the center of the tentacles and reserve the tentacles. Gently remove and reserve the ink sac, then discard the head. **4.** Peel the purplish membrane away from the body with your fingers and discard. **5.** Pull out the "quill" in the center of the body and discard. Wash the body well in cold running water. Cut the body (tube), flaps, and tentacles to the desired size, or leave whole. When cooking squid there is no in-between. Either you cook them very briefly or else simmer for a long time. Anything in-between results in tough, rubbery, and chewy squid!

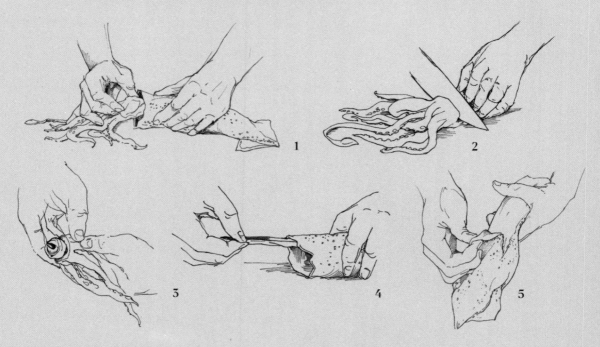

# OCTOPUS

Unlike squid, octopuses have no internal "shell" or quill. Their eight equal-size tentacles have two rows of suckers and, depending on species, can grow very large. The larger an octopus grows, the tougher it becomes, so small ones make for the best eating.

Most of the octopus we buy are already cleaned, cooked, and usually frozen. If you buy frozen, defrost overnight in the refrigerator or in cold water. From a sustainability perspective octopus, like squid, are short-lived and reproduce abundantly. Unlike squid, they are solitary and bottom-dwelling and are caught with traps, jigs, or by bottom trawlers. Trap and jig style fisheries are highly sustainable but bottom trawling can damage seafloor ecosystems.

## HOW TO CLEAN OCTOPUS

If you've caught your own, octopus are easy to clean. **1.** Cut the head off the octopus and then cut the head in half lengthwise. Remove the base where the eyes are and discard. **2.** Cut the tentacles in half lengthwise. **3.** Remove and discard the hard beak in the center of the tentacles. Separate the tentacles and thoroughly wash the head pieces and tentacles in cold water. Cook right away after cleaning.

## HOW TO COOK OCTOPUS

The late A. J. McClane, whom many consider to be one of the best writers on seafood, notes that though many people feel that you must tenderize the octopus before cooking, A.J. McClane felt it was not necessary. He also noted that the Spanish method of dipping the octopus into boiling water a couple of times was the best method to tenderize it. Do this by holding the mantle (head) and dip the body and tentacles into boiling water for several seconds. Lift it out and cool for a couple of minutes. Repeat the dipping and cooling.

To cook the octopus, put it in a large pot with enough water to cover by 2 inches (5 cm). Add aromatics like onion, bay leaf, etc., if you like, along with a couple of teaspoons of salt. Bring the water to a gentle simmer, and cook until a knife can be easily inserted where the head meets the tentacles, about 50 minutes. Remove the octopus and set aside to cool. Octopus can be cooked a day or two ahead. Refrigerate it in the cooking liquid.

### Tips for Tenderizing Octopus

- Add a tablespoon or so of vinegar into the simmering liquid which helps break down the connective tissue in the tentacles.

- Marinate the fresh octopus overnight in whole milk before cooking it.

This pan-seared squid topped with a fresh-herb dressing is my version of a simple and delicious dish served by chef B Adamo, head chef at the Hog Island Oyster Bar in Larkspur.

# HERBED CAST-IRON SQUID

**HERB DRESSING**

½ cup (120 ml) olive oil

½ cup (25 g) finely chopped fresh flat-leaf parsley

⅓ cup (15 g) finely chopped fresh cilantro leaves and tender stems

¼ cup (60 ml) fresh lime juice

2 teaspoons minced garlic

2 teaspoons kosher salt

1 teaspoon finely chopped serrano chile

¼ teaspoon ground cumin

**SEARED SQUID**

1 pound (455 g) cleaned squid (page 94)

Olive oil

Kosher salt

Cilantro sprigs, for garnish

Flaky sea salt, such as Maldon, for garnish

Lime wedges, for serving

To make the dressing, combine the olive oil, parsley, cilantro, lime juice, garlic, salt, chile, and cumin in a small bowl and stir lightly to blend. Set aside.

To make the squid, cut the squid tubes into ½-inch (12-mm) rings and cut the tentacles in half lengthwise. In a large cast-iron pan, add enough oil to cover the bottom of the pan, and heat over high heat until it shimmers. Working in batches if necessary to avoid crowding the pan, lightly salt the squid, add it to the pan, and sear until the edges are slightly crispy and charred, about 2 minutes.

In a medium bowl, combine the squid and the dressing; toss to coat. Serve at once, garnished with cilantro sprigs and flaky salt, with lime wedges alongside. **SERVES 2 TO 4**

This is a nice appetizer to serve as part of a summer grill menu. You can cook the calamari under a hot broiler if you don't want to fire up the grill—but the smoky flavor that charcoal grilling adds is a real plus. The bruschetta toppings are also great tossed with pasta.

# BRUSCHETTA with grilled calamari, tomatoes, and goat cheese

⅓ cup (75 ml) extra-virgin olive oil, plus 3 tablespoons for brushing and drizzling

3 tablespoons fresh lemon juice

3 tablespoons chopped fresh basil

Fine sea salt and freshly ground pepper

1½ pounds (680 g) cleaned small calamari (page 94)

1 pound (455 g) firm, ripe plum tomatoes, halved and seeded

1 small sweet red onion, halved and cut into ¼-inch (6-mm) slices

3 tablespoons coarsely chopped fresh mint

2 tablespoons chopped fresh chives

1 tablespoon mashed roasted garlic (page 345)

Red wine vinegar

4 ounces (115 g) firm aged goat cheese, such as Cabécou or Tome, finely diced

1 Italian or French baguette, cut into ½-inch (12-mm) slices

Small fresh mint leaves and fried capers (page 344), for garnish (optional)

In a medium bowl, whisk the ⅓ cup (75 ml) olive oil, the lemon juice, basil, 1 teaspoon salt, and a few grindings of pepper together. Add the calamari tubes and tentacles and marinate for 1 hour at room temperature. Remove the squid from the marinade and reserve the marinade.

Meanwhile, prepare a medium-hot fire in a charcoal grill or preheat a gas grill to medium-high. Brush the grill grates clean. Using a grill screen, grill the squid tubes and tentacles until they just begin to firm and turn opaque, about 2 minutes. Be careful not to overcook or the calamari will be tough. Cut the tubes crosswise into bite-size rings and the tentacles into bite-size portions. Set aside in a bowl.

Add the tomatoes and onion to the reserved marinade and stir to coat. Drain, discarding the marinade, and then grill the tomatoes and onion just long enough to cook just through. Transfer to a cutting board.

Coarsely chop the tomatoes and onion and add to the calamari along with the mint, chives, garlic, a drizzle of olive oil, and red wine vinegar to taste. Season with salt and pepper. Gently stir in the goat cheese.

Lightly brush the bread with olive oil and grill, turning once, until lightly toasted and grill-marked. Place a heaping tablespoon or two of the calamari mixture on each toast and garnish with a mint leaf and fried capers, if using.
**MAKES 12 TO 16 TOASTS**

In this variation of the tempura recipe on page 129, the prepped squid is fried in tempura batter just like the shrimp and then dipped in a salt and pepper mix using Sichuan peppercorns (also spelled Szechuan). The unique characteristic of Sichuan pepper is that it gives you a numbing sensation in the mouth and tongue.

# FRIED SALT AND PEPPER SQUID

**SALT AND PEPPER SEASONING**

2 tablespoons fine sea salt

1 tablespoon Sichuan peppercorns

**FRIED SQUID**

Peanut or vegetable oil, for frying

1½ cups (190 g) unbleached all-purpose flour

½ cup (65 g) cornstarch

1 large egg

1 cup (240 ml) vodka

1 cup (240 ml) seltzer water

1½ pounds (680 g) cleaned squid, tubes sliced into rings, tentacles halved lengthwise if large

To make the seasoning, in a medium skillet over medium-low heat, combine the salt and Sichuan peppercorns and cook, shaking the pan occasionally, until the peppercorns are fragrant and the salt turns a light brown color. Remove from the heat and let cool to room temperature. Use a mortar and pestle or a spice grinder to grind the cooled mixture. Set aside to use now, or cover tightly and store in a cool, dark place for up to 1 month.

To make the fried squid, position an oven rack in the upper-middle position and preheat the oven to 200°F (90°C). In a large, heavy Dutch oven, heat 2 inches (5 cm) of oil to 375°F (190°C) on a deep-frying thermometer, until it shimmers.

In a large bowl, whisk the flour and cornstarch together. In another large bowl, whisk the egg and vodka together. Whisk the seltzer water into egg mixture.

When the oil reaches 375°F (190°C), pour the liquid mixture into the bowl with the flour mixture and whisk gently until just combined (it's okay if small lumps remain). Submerge half of the squid in the batter. Using tongs and working in batches, remove the squid from batter a few at a time, allowing the excess batter to drip off, and carefully place in the oil.

Fry, stirring occasionally with a chopstick or wooden skewer to prevent sticking, until light brown, 2 to 3 minutes. Using a slotted spoon, transfer the squid to a paper towel–lined plate and sprinkle with the salt and pepper seasoning. To keep warm, place the fried squid on a wire rack set in a rimmed baking sheet and place it in the preheated oven while frying the remaining squid. Serve at once. **SERVES 6 TO 8**

Though squid recipes generally use quick-cooking techniques like grilling, sautéing, and frying, braised squid is one of the most delicious ways to prepare them. Here, a half hour of simmering them with tomatoes and wine yields tender squid to serve over fregola. Often referred to as Sardinian couscous, fregola is couscous's tastier cousin. Both are made from semolina mixed with water, formed into pellets, and dried. But couscous pellets are light and fine, whereas fregola is coarser and rougher. More important, fregola is toasted, which gives it a nutty, wheaty taste.

# BRAISED SQUID
## with tomato, harissa, and fregola

**BRAISED SQUID**

2 tablespoons olive oil or clarified butter (page 345)

1 small yellow onion (6 ounces/170 g), quartered and thinly sliced

4 cloves garlic, thinly sliced

½ cup (120 ml) dry white wine

2 pounds (910 g) cleaned squid, cleaned, tubes cut into ½-inch (12-mm) rings and large tentacles halved (page 94)

One 28-ounce (800-g) can whole peeled tomatoes, preferably San Marzano, crushed by hand

1 cup (155 g) pitted black olives, such as Cerignola

½ teaspoon fennel seeds, crushed

1 small bay leaf

1½ teaspoons harissa paste, homemade (page 341) or store-bought

2 teaspoons finely grated zest

Kosher salt and freshly ground pepper

Small handful minced fresh basil leaves

**FREGOLA WITH PANCETTA AND PECORINO**

1 cup (195 g) fregola

4 tablespoons (55 g) clarified butter (page 345) or unsalted butter

5 ounces (140 g) thinly sliced pancetta, chopped

1 large shallot, finely chopped

2 cloves garlic, very thinly sliced

1 cup (240 ml) chicken stock (page 333) or shrimp stock (page 332)

Kosher salt and freshly ground pepper

½ cup (50 g) freshly grated pecorino cheese

2 tablespoons finely chopped fresh chives

To make the squid, in a large saucepan, heat the olive oil over medium-high heat until shimmering. Add the onion and garlic and cook, stirring, until softened but not browned, about 4 minutes. Add the wine and squid, bring to a simmer, and cook, stirring occasionally, until the alcohol smell has mostly cooked off, about 3 minutes. Stir in the tomatoes, olives, fennel, and bay leaf, and return to a gentle simmer. Cook, stirring occasionally, until the squid is tender, about 30 minutes. Discard the bay leaf. Stir the harissa and lemon zest and season to taste with salt and pepper.

While the squid is braising, make the fregola. In a large pot of salted boiling water, cook the fregola until al dente, 7 to 8 minutes. Drain and set aside.

In large skillet over medium-high heat, melt 2 tablespoons of the butter and cook the pancetta until crisp, about 4 minutes. Using a slotted spoon, transfer to paper towels to drain; reserve the pan. Add the shallot and garlic to the pan and cook, stirring, until the shallot is translucent, about 2 minutes.

Add the fregola to the pan. Stir the fregola and shallot mixture and add the chicken stock. Season with a few turns of freshly ground pepper. Bring the stock to a simmer, turn the heat to low, and cook, stirring occasionally, until the fregola is tender and the stock is almost evaporated, about 3 minutes. Add the remaining 2 tablespoons butter to the fregola and stir to melt. Add salt to taste.

To serve, divide the fregola among bowls and crumble a bit of crispy pancetta over each portion followed by the pecorino cheese, chives, and a few turns of black pepper. Spoon the braised squid alongside the fregola, dividing it between the bowls, sprinkle the squid with basil, and serve at once. **SERVES 4 TO 6**

Frying is one of the best ways to cook tender squid and is the method often used in restaurants. This Italian treatment adds fried chickpeas and lemon slices to the mix for more texture and a bright citrus note. A lovely pesto mayonnaise is the perfect choice for dipping.

# CRISPY CALAMARI
## with pesto mayonnaise

**PESTO MAYONNAISE**

⅔ cup (165 ml) basil pesto, homemade (page 336) or store-bought

1 cup (240 ml) mayonnaise

Fresh lemon juice and hot sauce, to taste

Fine sea salt and freshly ground pepper

**FRIED CALAMARI**

Peanut or vegetable oil, for frying

⅓ cup (40 g) Wondra flour

⅓ cup (45 g) cornstarch

⅓ cup (30 g) chickpea flour

2 cups (480 ml) milk

1 pound (455 g) cleaned calamari, tubes cut into ¼-inch (6-mm) rings and tentacles halved (page 94)

½ cup (80 g) canned chickpeas, drained and rinsed

1 small lemon, cut into thin rounds and seeded

1 tablespoon kosher salt

1 teaspoon pimentón (smoked Spanish paprika) or Aleppo pepper

Upland cress tossed with a little lemon juice and extra-virgin olive oil, for serving (optional)

To make the mayonnaise, in a small bowl, combine the pesto and mayonnaise. Season with a few drops of lemon juice and hot sauce and stir to blend. Taste and adjust the seasoning with salt and pepper.

To make the calamari, in a large Dutch oven, heat 2 inches (5 cm) of oil over medium-high heat until it shimmers (350°F/175°C on a deep-frying thermometer).

In a shallow bowl, whisk the flour, cornstarch, and chickpea flour together. In a large bowl, combine the milk, calamari, chickpeas, and lemon. Drain in a fine-mesh sieve and transfer to the flour mixture, tossing until coated.

Working in batches and using a wire-mesh skimmer, transfer the calamari, chickpeas, and lemon slices to the hot oil and fry until the calamari is golden brown, about 2 minutes. Be careful not to overcook. Transfer to paper towels to drain. Keep warm in a low oven.

In a small bowl, stir the salt and pimentón together and sprinkle over the calamari. Transfer the calamari to a serving platter, quickly toss with the dressed cress, if using, and serve right away, with the pesto mayonnaise on the side. **SERVES 4**

These easy-to-make pancakes are great on their own, but even better when squid is included. Shrimp would be another popular choice. Doenjang is a Korean fermented soybean paste and adds an umami kick, while gochugaru, a bright red Korean chile powder, adds flavorful spice. Both are available in well-stocked markets.

# KOREAN GREEN ONION PANCAKES
## with squid

**DIPPING SAUCE**

3 tablespoons soy sauce

1 tablespoon unseasoned rice wine vinegar

¼ teaspoon gochugaru (Korean red pepper flakes) or pinch of crushed red pepper flakes

1 teaspoon toasted sesame oil

¼ teaspoon grated fresh ginger

¼ teaspoon sugar

¼ teaspoon sesame seeds, toasted (page 344)

**GREEN ONION–SQUID PANCAKES**

½ cup (65 g) unbleached all-purpose flour

½ cup (60 g) white rice flour

2 tablespoons cornstarch

½ teaspoon baking powder

½ teaspoon salt

1 large egg

¾ cup (180 ml) ice-cold water

1 small garlic clove, grated or minced

1 teaspoon doenjang or white (shiro) miso (optional)

½ pound (225 g), cleaned squid, tubes cut into ½-inch (12-mm) rings and tentacles halved (page 94)

3 to 4 tablespoons canola or other neutral oil

3 or 4 green onions, cut into 2-inch (5-cm) pieces, including green parts

To make the dipping sauce, in a small bowl, combine the soy sauce, vinegar, gochugaru, sesame oil, ginger, sugar, and sesame seeds. Taste and adjust the seasoning.

To make the pancakes, in a large bowl, combine the flours, cornstarch, baking powder, and salt; stir with a whisk to blend. In a small bowl, whisk the egg, water, garlic, and optional doenjang together. Add this to the dry mixture and gently whisk until the batter is smooth. Don't overmix. It should be the thickness of thin pancake batter. If too thick, add more water a teaspoon at a time. Stir in the squid.

In an 8-inch (20-cm) nonstick skillet, heat 1 tablespoon of the oil over medium heat. Add one-third of the green onions in a single layer. Spoon one-third of the batter over the onions to cover them evenly. Cook until browned on the bottom. Turn, adding a bit more oil if necessary, and crisp the other side.

Using tongs, transfer the pancake to paper towels to drain. On a cutting board, cut the pancake into quarters. Repeat with the remaining green onions and batter. Serve hot, with the dipping sauce. **MAKES 3 PANCAKES; SERVES 3 TO 6**

Squid takes on a lovely smoky flavor when grilled, but this Thai-inspired recipe can also be cooked under a broiler. It's a refreshing main-course salad on a warm day, or perfect picnic fare when served in individual "to-go" boxes.

# GRILLED SQUID NOODLE SALAD
## with mango, cabbage, and cucumber

1 pound (455 g) baby squid, cleaned (page 94)

¼ cup (60 ml) olive oil, plus more for brushing

Fine sea salt and freshly ground pepper

1 cup (240 ml) Vietnamese Dipping Sauce (Nuoc Cham) (page 338)

6 ounces (170 g) large shiitake mushrooms, stemmed

2 ounces (55 g) thin rice noodles (vermicelli)

Toasted sesame oil, to taste

1½ cups (215 g) diagonally sliced English or Persian cucumber

¾ cup (90 g) finely julienned or sliced carrot

2 cups (140 g) finely sliced green or napa cabbage

1 large mango, peeled, seeded, and cut into large dice

½ cup (25 g) daikon sprouts

⅓ cup (15 g) lightly packed fresh cilantro leaves

¼ cup (13 g) lightly packed fresh mint leaves

Prepare a medium-hot fire in a charcoal grill or preheat a gas grill to medium-high. Brush the grill grates clean. Toss the squid tubes and tentacles in a bowl with the olive oil to lightly coat and a generous sprinkling of salt and pepper. Using a grill screen, grill the tubes and tentacles until they puff and take on a little color, about 1 minute on each side. The tentacles will take slightly longer than the tubes.

Cut the tubes into rings or 1-inch (2.5-cm) pieces and the tentacles into bite-size pieces. In a medium bowl, toss with half of the dipping sauce and set aside. Brush the mushrooms with olive oil, season with salt and pepper, and cook on the grill screen until browned. Cut into thick slices and add to the squid. Toss to combine.

Soak the noodles in hot water to cover until softened, about 15 minutes. Drain, place on a cutting board, and chop a couple of times. Toss with a few drops of sesame oil. Combine the noodles, squid mixture, cucumber, carrot, cabbage, mango, and sprouts. Arrange on small plates or in shallow bowls. Drizzle with the remaining dipping sauce and top with the cilantro and mint leaves. **SERVES 4 TO 6**

This recipe is from Jeremy Sewall of Row 34 restaurant in Boston and Portsmouth. He notes: "Fresh squid is one of my favorites and it loves to be grilled. Marinate for a least an hour, but longer is okay. If you don't have a grill for the squid, you can sauté it as well. If you have everything ready, this dish comes together pretty quickly. If you want to add other seafood like shrimp or mussels to this pasta, they are a great addition. If you do, marinate and grill the shrimp as well."

# RIGATONI with grilled squid, clams, and heirloom tomatoes

### HERB-MARINATED SQUID

1 large shallot, peeled and coarsely chopped

2 cloves garlic

½ cup (25 g) fresh flat-leaf parsley leaves

½ cup (20 g) fresh basil leaves

½ cup (30 g) chopped green onion tops

3 tablespoons fresh lime juice

3 tablespoons rice wine vinegar

1 cup (240 ml) olive oil

1 pound (455 g) squid, cleaned and cut into tubes and tentacles (page 94)

### STEAMED CLAMS

¼ cup (60 ml) extra-virgin olive oil

¼ cup (35 g) minced white onion

1 tablespoon chopped garlic

5 ripe heirloom or beefsteak tomatoes, seeded and finely chopped

¼ cup (60 ml) white wine

1 pound (455 g) Manila clams, scrubbed (page 32)

12 large fresh basil leaves, sliced into thin strips

Fine sea salt and freshly ground pepper

### RIGATONI

1 pound (455 g) rigatoni or favorite pasta

¼ cup (25 g) sourdough crumbs, toasted (page 345)

1 teaspoon crushed red pepper flakes

¼ cup (25 g) grated Parmesan

To make the marinated squid, in a blender, combine the shallot, garlic, parsley, basil, green onion, lime juice, vinegar, and olive oil and puree until smooth. In a medium bowl, combine the marinade and the squid and mix well. Cover and refrigerate for 1 hour.

Prepare a medium-hot fire in a charcoal grill or preheat a gas grill to medium-high. Brush the grill grates clean. Using a grill screen, char the squid tubes and tentacles until cooked almost through. Remove from the grill and let cool slightly, then cut the tubes into thin rounds and the tentacles in half. Set aside.

Bring a large pot of salted water to a boil over high heat.

To make the clams, in a large saucepan, heat the olive oil over medium heat and add the onion and garlic. Cook, stirring, until they begin to color lightly. Add the chopped tomatoes and their juice and bring to a simmer, cooking for about 5 minutes. Add the white wine and clams, cover, and simmer until the clams open. Using a slotted spoon or wire-mesh skimmer, transfer the clams to a large bowl. Discard any clams that haven't opened. Add the reserved squid and basil leaves to the saucepan with the tomato mixture and stir. Season with salt and pepper to taste.

While the clams are cooking, add the pasta to the pot of boiling water and cook until al dente, or according to the package directions. Drain the pasta in a fine-mesh sieve, then add to the squid and tomato sauce. Toss to combine.

Divide the pasta among 4 bowls and top with the clams, bread crumbs, crushed red pepper, and Parmesan. Serve at once. **SERVES 4**

Octopus is a popular seafood all over the Iberian Peninsula, so you will often find it served at tapas bars. Here, it is braised until tender, then coated with a spicy green olive relish. Serve in small dishes or on crostini (page 343). Since baby octopus are used, they are small enough to be included whole. If using larger octopus, cut into bite-size pieces.

# BABY OCTOPUS
## with green olive relish

**GREEN OLIVE RELISH**

1½ cups (230 g) pitted green olives, such as manzanilla or picholine, chopped

¼ cup (60 ml) extra-virgin olive oil

Grated zest and juice of 1 lemon

1 teaspoon drained capers, chopped

½ teaspoon minced garlic

½ teaspoon coarsely ground black pepper

Big pinch of crushed red pepper flakes

**BRAISED OCTOPUS**

2 pounds (910 g) cleaned baby octopus (page 95)

1 cup (125 g) diced onion

½ cup (120 ml) dry white wine

2 small bay leaves

2 large cloves garlic, smashed with the side of a knife

Kosher salt and freshly ground black pepper

Chopped fresh flat-leaf parsley, for garnish

Lemon wedges, for serving

To make the relish, in a small bowl, combine the olives, olive oil, lemon juice, capers, garlic, black pepper, and red pepper flakes and stir to blend. Use now, or cover and refrigerate for up to 5 days.

To make the octopus, in a large saucepan, combine the octopus, onion, wine, bay leaves, garlic, ½ teaspoon salt, and ¼ teaspoon pepper. Bring to a boil, then reduce the heat to a simmer. Cover and cook, stirring often, until the octopus is fork-tender, about 50 minutes. Check occasionally to make sure there is liquid in the pan; if not, add a bit of water.

Let the octopus cool in the broth. Drain, discarding the onion, bay leaves, and garlic cloves. Transfer the octopus to a bowl and stir in enough olive relish to your taste. Season with salt and pepper.

Divide the octopus between small dishes and garnish with parsley. Serve with lemon wedges and any remaining olive relish alongside. **MAKES 12 TAPAS**

In this recipe for a popular Japanese street food, chopped tender octopus, green onion, and ginger are covered in batter and cooked in a special pan. Typically served in paper dishes that resemble little boats, it's a staple food of Japanese festivals and can be found in convenience stores, food trucks, and restaurants all around the country. Takoyaki pans are widely available online, or if you're lucky enough to have an aebleskiver pan used to make Danish pancake balls, you can use that. Octopus is a traditional ingredient, but you can also use shrimp, crab, or mushrooms.

# TAKOYAKI (japanese octopus balls)

**TAKOYAKI SAUCE**

3 tablespoons Worcestershire sauce

1 teaspoon mentsuyu (Japanese noodle base)

¼ teaspoon sugar

1 teaspoon ketchup

**SPICY MAYONNAISE**

2 tablespoons mayonnaise, preferably Kewpie

1 tablespoon fresh lemon juice

1 teaspoon chili-garlic sauce

**TAKOYAKI**

2 cups (480 ml) dashi (page 334)

1 cup (125 g) unbleached all-purpose flour

2 large eggs

2 teaspoons soy sauce

Canola oil, for brushing

4 ounces (115 g) cooked octopus, cut into ½-inch (12-mm) cubes (page 95)

2 small green onions, finely chopped, including green parts

2 tablespoons chopped pickled red ginger

Aonori (dried green seaweed) and dried bonito flakes, for sprinkling (optional)

To make the takoyaki sauce, in a small bowl, combine the Worcestershire sauce, mentsuyu, sugar, and ketchup and stir to combine.

To make the spicy mayonnaise, in another small bowl, combine the mayonnaise, lemon juice, and chili-garlic sauce and stir to combine.

To make the takoyaki, in a large bowl, whisk the dashi, flour, eggs, and soy sauce together. Pour the batter into a small pitcher. Brush a takoyaki pan generously with oil.

Heat the pan over medium heat just until the oil begins to smoke. Add enough batter to fill the cups in the pan halfway full. Add some of the octopus, green onions, and ginger to each cup and fill the cups to the top with more batter. Cook for 1 to 2 minutes, then turn using small tongs, chopsticks, or a wooden skewer. Cook another 3 to 4 minutes, turning constantly until all sides are golden brown.

Place the cooked takoyaki on a plate and drizzle the takoyaki sauce and mayo attractively over them. Sprinkle with aonori and dried bonito flakes. Serve with toothpicks for spearing. **MAKES ABOUT 30 TAKOYAKI**

NOTE Mentsuyu noodle soup base is widely used in Japanese cooking. You will find it at Japanese and other well-stocked markets. Aonori is an edible seaweed that appears in many Japanese dishes, primarily as a seasoning.

Chef Jose Romo of the Hog Island Oyster Bar in Napa simmers fresh octopus until tender, then sears it on the stove top before tossing it with roasted potatoes, caramelized shallots, frisée lettuce, and an olive dressing. If using fresh octopus, buy it cleaned from your fishmonger. To clean it yourself, see page 95. Frozen octopus comes already cleaned. You could also make this dish with store-bought cooked octopus. If using a cooked octopus, skip the cooking instructions below. Marble potatoes are simply baby red, yellow, and/or purple potatoes.

# SEARED OCTOPUS
## with roasted potatoes

**OCTOPUS**

2 to 3 pounds (910 g to 1.4 kg) fresh or frozen octopus, cleaned (page 95)

1 large bay leaf

2 cups (200 g) coarsely chopped celery

1 tablespoon whole black peppercorns

**KALAMATA DRESSING**

½ cup (120 ml) olive oil

⅓ cup (50 g) pitted kalamata olives

2 tablespoons red wine vinegar

1 clove garlic, chopped

Kosher salt and freshly ground pepper

**CARAMELIZED SHALLOTS**

6 ounces (170 g) shallots

Olive oil

¼ cup (60 ml) dry white wine

**ROASTED MARBLE POTATOES**

1 pound (455 g) marble potatoes, halved

Olive oil

Kosher salt and freshly ground pepper

Leaves from 1 head frisée lettuce

Lemon wedges, for serving

Thoroughly defrost the frozen octopus in the refrigerator overnight. For both defrosted and fresh octopus, put it in a large pot with enough water to cover by 2 inches (5 cm). Add the bay leaf, celery, and peppercorns. Bring the water to a gentle simmer, and cook until a knife can be easily inserted into the tentacles, about 50 minutes. Remove the octopus and set aside to cool. Portion the tentacles into 4 to 6 servings.

To make the dressing, in a blender, combine the olive oil, olives, vinegar, and garlic, and process to a smooth puree. Season with salt and pepper. Set aside.

To make the shallots, peel and cut the shallots into sixths. Toss with the olive oil to coat. In a large cast-iron skillet over medium heat, cook the shallots, stirring, until browned on all sides. Add the wine and stir to scrape up any bits on the bottom of the pan. Set aside and let cool.

Preheat the oven to 425°F (220°C).

To make the potatoes, in a bowl, toss the potatoes with the olive oil, salt, and pepper to coat. Place on a baking sheet and roast in the oven until tender, about 10 minutes. To check, make sure you can smash one with a fork. Set aside and let cool.

When the potatoes are done, place a grill pan in the oven to preheat for 5 minutes. Add the octopus to the grill pan and return it to the oven. Roast until it begins to brown. Flip the pieces over and add the potatoes and shallots. Return to the oven and cook until all are nicely browned, a few minutes more. Remove and let cool.

Put the frisée in a large bowl and toss with some of the dressing. Add the octopus, potatoes, and shallots to the bowl and toss gently, adding more dressing if desired. Serve with the lemon wedges. **SERVES 4 TO 6**

# CRUSTACEANS

## shrimp, crab, lobster, crayfish

All crustaceans belong to the enormous family of decapods, meaning ten-limbed. They are believed to have lived on Earth for up to four hundred million years. Their spidery limbs hide delicious, sweet flesh. Crustaceans interestingly can only grow if they periodically cast off their exoskeleton or shell and grow a new, larger one. During this short period of growing a new shell, they become known as "soft shells" and are highly vulnerable. They are delicious at this point and you can eat them shell and all.

# SHRIMP

There are hundreds of species of shrimp around the world. They range from tiny to "colossal" in size, and their shells come in many colors, from the familiar gray, pink, and white to red, yellow, green, blue, and multicolored stripes. This vast group can be divided into two categories: warmwater and cold-water species.

## Warmwater Shrimp

Most of what we consume in this country, where shrimp is by far the favorite seafood, comes from warm waters in the tropics and subtropics.

- **Gulf or Mexican white** (*Litopenaeus setiferus*) **or pink shrimp** (*Farfantepenaeus duorarum*) are the most expensive shrimp, prized for their sweet flavor and firm texture; these are caught wild, though more are being farmed, especially in China. As the name implies, many of these come from the Gulf Coasts of America and Mexico, but a substantial supply reaches us from Peru, Ecuador, and Chile.

- **Gulf brown shrimp** (*Farfantepenaeus aztecus*), also from the American and Mexican Gulf Coasts, are more plentiful, less expensive, and have a stronger flavor than Gulf whites or pinks. They are omnivores, feeding on both algae and the microscopic animals known as zooplankton.

- **Tiger shrimp** (*Penaeus monodon*) are popular in markets today because of their cheaper price. Although native to the Pacific and Indian Oceans, most are farm-raised in Asia and India. The shell is marked with a distinctive black or gray stripe. They survive in fresh or brackish water, and some unscrupulous farmers turn a fast buck by digging out ponds, filling them with water, seeding the shrimp, and because tigers mature quickly, harvesting them and starting a new crop. After a while, the ponds become so polluted they won't support life anymore. The farmer moves on, scooping out a new pond, leaving behind the polluted one. Certainly not all tigers are raised this way, but don't buy them unless your store can vouch that they have been wholesomely and sustainably raised.

- **Rock shrimp** (*Sicyonia brevirostris*) have become more available in recent years, especially in restaurants. They come from the Gulf Coast and, as the name suggests, have shells that are rock hard. As a result, they must be put through rollers that crush the shell so that it can be removed. In the process, the shrimp meat gets a little beaten up, but don't let this dissuade you from buying them; the flavor and texture are delicious. Referred to as "poor man's lobster," they do resemble lobster in both flavor and texture. They cook very quickly so be careful not to overcook them. Rock shrimp are delicious sautéed for pasta or salads and are great in stuffings and fish cakes.

## Cold-Water Shrimp

The icy northern oceans of the world produce several varieties of small shrimp. These are most often caught wild and are sold peeled and cooked as "bay" shrimp or salad shrimp; they are also called shrimp meat. They have a more pronounced iodine flavor, which makes them ideal for salads, shrimp cocktails, and sandwiches.

## California Spot Prawns (*Pandalus platyceros*)

One of the favorite wild shrimp species at Hog Island are California spot prawns. Native to the cold, clean waters of North America's West Coast, spot prawns are still fished primarily by smaller boats using basket traps, which are similar to crab traps (they are also crustaceans after all!). In both British Columbia and the United States, spot prawn fishery is well managed, with some frozen at sea (British Columbia) and the rest sold fresh during the very short May to June season. Due to the short season and the highly regulated take, spot prawns are expensive, but they are so delicious they are worth the higher price for a truly seasonal delight.

# SHRIMP VS. PRAWNS

Jumbo shrimp are commonly referred to as "prawns," but while these two creatures look alike, they are botanically different. Prawns live in fresh water, while shrimp live in salt water. True prawns are not commercially available in the United States, though efforts are being made to farm them.

## BUYING SHRIMP

Shrimp are usually sold by processors and wholesalers according to their size, expressed in number per pound, as in "U 10" (under 10 per pound/455 g), "10–15" (10 to 15 per pound/455 g), and so on. In other words, the higher the number, the smaller the shrimp. The sizes for shrimp per pound in this book are medium (31 to 35 count), large (21 to 30 count), extra-large (16 to 20 count), and jumbo (11 to 15 count).

Purchased shrimp should have a clean, fresh seaweed smell. Any hint of ammonia means that they're old, so don't buy them. Unless you're where you can buy shrimp right off the boat, all commercial shrimp in this country have been frozen. Once out of the water, shrimp deteriorate quickly, and for this reason they are usually processed and flash frozen. Most shrimp are sold with the head removed because that's the first part to go as they age. When it comes to shrimp, don't be fooled by promises of "fresh," and don't be put off by the word *frozen*.

Sodium tripolyphosphate (STPP) is an alkaline salt that shrimp, scallops, and fish fillets are often treated with. It causes seafood to absorb water, which makes the food appear firmer, smoother, and glossier. The added water weight makes seafood cost more. You can tell that shrimp have been soaked with STPP if a milky white liquid develops as you cook them.

## HOW TO PEEL AND DEVEIN SHRIMP

My recommendation is to always buy raw shrimp with the peel on. Peeled shrimp are susceptible to freezer burn and are generally less flavorful. The vein of the shrimp is its intestinal tract and should be removed, as it sometimes contains grit and can be unpleasant in taste.

**1.** For peeled shrimp, simply use a sharp knife to make a shallow cut down the center of the back from the head to the tail and pull out the vein, then rinse the shrimp.

**2.** For unpeeled shrimp, use kitchens shears or sharp scissors to cut the back of the shell down the middle, then gently peel it off. Depending on the recipe you can leave the tail intact or remove it. Reserve the peels to make stock (page 332). **3.** Use a sharp knife to make a shallow cut down the center of the back from the head to the tail and pull out the vein, then rinse the shrimp.

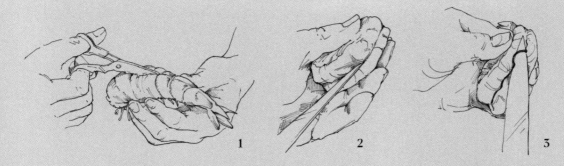

1       2       3

## ABOUT BRINING SHRIMP

Brining works wonderfully well with shrimp and fish in general. I almost always brine raw shrimp before cooking. It doesn't take long, and it adds succulence and a firm texture. You can use the liquid brine in the recipe for Grilled Shrimp with Salsa Verde (page 127) and brine peeled or unpeeled shrimp in it for 5 minutes to 2 hours. Alternatively, use the "dry method" and simply sprinkle peeled raw shrimp with generously with kosher salt and let sit for 10 minutes. With either method, be sure to rinse the shrimp well before you cook them to remove any excess salt.

## HOW TO COOK SHRIMP

Bring a large saucepan of water to a boil. Add the shrimp and immediately turn off the heat. Allow the shrimp to sit in the water until evenly pink, about 2 minutes. Immediately drain the shrimp and submerge them in a large bowl of very cold water. When cool, drain and transfer the shrimp to another large bowl.

# CRAB

There are estimated to be at least forty-five hundred different crab species in the world. They range in size from the tiny pea crab, which, as the name suggests, is about the size of a pea, all the way up to the giant Japanese spider crab, which can measure as much as 12 feet (3.7 m) from claw tip to claw tip. Following are the best-known and most widely available crabs for use in the kitchen.

## Blue Crab (*Callinectes sapidus*)

Its Latin name means "beautiful swimmer," and it is indeed a beautiful blue-green color, which turns red when cooked. It's the most prolific species on the east coast of the United States down to the Gulf of Mexico. The Chesapeake Bay is perhaps the most famous home for these delectable little creatures. Most of the meat comes from the body.

## Soft-shell Crabs

When blue crab molt or shed their shells, which they do annually from April through September, they are known as "soft shell" crabs. They are beloved because you can eat them shells and all. They're best when you buy them alive and quickly sauté or deep-fry them so that the soft shell becomes crispy.

**To clean soft-shelled crab**, remove the face, spongy gills, and intestinal vein from the crab or have your fishmonger do it for you. Rinse well before using.

## Dungeness Crab (*Cancer magister*)

This large crab usually weighs in from 1½ to 4 pounds (680 g to 1.8 kg) and is brown to purple in color before cooking. Named for the small town of Dungeness on the Olympic Peninsula in Washington state, which first began commercially harvesting the delicacy, Dungeness crabs are found on the Pacific coast from Southern California up to Alaska. They yield succulent sweet meat from both the body and the legs and claws. When cooked simply in boiling seawater the shell turns a bright red. It is a favorite of Hog Island. A keeper must be at least 6¼ inches (16 cm) long, and only males are harvested. Their main season is November to the end of April.

### Pacific Red Rock Crab (*Cancer productus*)

This crab is as delicious as the Dungeness but quite a bit smaller, making its body meat more difficult to pick. No doubt this is the reason it is less common in the market. It is widely available on the Northwest Coast of the United States, and it is a favorite of sport fishers.

### Horseshoe Crab (*Limulus polyphemus*)

This crab is aptly named because it does resemble a horseshoe. A living fossil, it traces its roots back at least five hundred million years. Found along the Atlantic Coast, it ranges from Nova Scotia to Mexico's Yucatan Peninsula. It is also found along coasts from Japan to India. They are edible, but most people feel the ratio of meat to shell is too small to make them worth pursuing.

### King Crab (*Paralithodes camtschaticus*)

This giant crab can reach up to 25 pounds (11 kg) and measure up to 10 feet (3 m) across. The meat yield is small, about 25 percent coming from legs and claws. The harvest is focused on males, allowing the females to return to the ocean to provide for the next generation. The meat of this crab is sweet and white, with a bright orange edge.

### Peekytoe Crab (*Cancer irroratus*)

Commonly known as rock, sand, or bay crab, this was a throwaway by-product of lobster fishing in the northeastern U.S. before a brilliant renaming as "peekytoe" made them the darlings of chefs. It is analogous to the renaming of Chilean sea bass from Patagonian toothfish. The new name sounds more inviting. Amazing how just changing a name can make such a difference.

### Portly Spider Crab (*Libinia emarginata*)

The most common type of spider crab, the portly spider crab, is found along the East Coast of the United States. A variety of crabs are referred to as spider crabs because of their long, spindly legs. These include snow crabs, tanner crabs, and queen crabs, all of which are similar in flavor and texture.

### Stone Crab (*Menippe mercenaria*)

The stone crab has large, extremely hard claws that are enjoyed for their firm, sweet, and succulent meat. Harvested in Florida from October 15 to May 15, they are sold frozen the rest of the year. When stone crabs are caught, fishermen twist off one claw and toss them back to grow a new one, which takes about eighteen months. Once cooked, the claws are cracked with a small mallet and served with a dipping sauce.

## HOW TO STORE LIVE CRAB

Live crab doesn't store well. They should be cooked as soon after catching or purchasing as possible. If you do need to store a live crab, cover with a damp towel and refrigerate for no more than 6 hours.

## HOW TO COOK A LIVE CRAB

Fresh-cooked crab is one of nature's treasures. Whether winter Dungeness or summer blue crabs, they can quickly be boiled, steamed, or roasted. Start first by humanely dispatching the crab, in the same way as lobster (page 119).

**Steaming:** This is the preferred method, as steamed crabs retain their tasty juices and don't become water-logged. Bring 1 inch (2.5 cm) of salted water to a boil in a large pot. Put the crab(s) in a steamer basket or insert. Add to the steamer, cover, and cook for 12 minutes for blue crabs and 20 minutes for Dungeness. Using tongs or an oven mitt, remove the crab(s) from the pot and let cool to the touch before cleaning.

**Boiling:** Bring a large pot of salted water to a boil. Add a couple of halved lemons, a bay leaf or two, and some beer or white wine. Add any other seasonings you like; Old Bay is a favorite of many. Add the crab(s), bring the water back to a boil, and cook until the crab(s) have turned bright red. Small blue crabs will take 6 minutes or so, and a large Dungeness will take 8 to 12 minutes. Using tongs or an oven mitt, remove the crab(s) and let cool to the touch before cleaning.

**Roasting:** Preheat the oven to 450°F (230°C). Boil or steam the crab(s) for 5 minutes, let cool, then clean them. Separate into parts or leave whole. Toss the crab with some olive oil or melted butter. Place the crabs in a single layer in a roasting pan and cook until browned and sizzling.

## HOW TO CLEAN AND CRACK COOKED CRAB

**1.** Pull the top shell off with your thumbs. Break off the claws and legs, including the knuckles (the part connected to the claws and legs). **2.** Pull off and discard the feathery-looking gills around the center section of the body. Wash any of the yellow-green tomalley and internal organs away. (We used to eat the tomalley or "butter," but it is not recommended to do so because it's a catch basin for heavy metals.) To easily get the meat out, cut the body section in half, rinse well, and pick out all of the meat with a crab pick. Discard the body shell. **3.** With kitchen shears, cut the claws and knuckles in at least a couple of places. This makes it easier to get at the meat. Pick out the meat and add to the body meat.

## BUYING COOKED CRABMEAT

You can often purchase freshly cooked whole crabs at many fishmongers, which saves you the trouble of having to cook live crabs. You can also often purchase bulk crabmeat at some fishmongers or markets. Several species of crab are available canned or vacuum-packed, which makes life easier when making a recipe that uses already-cooked crab. Just beware, bulk, canned, and vacuum-packed crab is expensive. The big concern in purchasing cooked crabmeat is errant pieces of shell, so be sure to pick it over and discard any you find.

# LOBSTER

Two types of lobsters are commercially available in the United States: clawed and spiny. Both the American and European lobsters have been farmed but not very successfully because they are cannibalistic. What we see in the market are harvested from the wild. As wild stocks have dwindled, farmed has become more important. Climate change is altering the habitat for lobsters, which accounts for their increasing price. When harvested, lobsters have their claws "banded," which makes them both easier to handle and curbs their aggressive behavior. If banded too long, the claw meat will begin to deteriorate.

Unfortunately, lobster has recently been moved to the "Avoid" list by the Monterey Bay Aquarium. The concern is that whales are easily entangled in lobster-fishing gear. It is an important fishery in America and only time will tell if alternative methods can be found to catch lobster. California spiny lobster is considered a good alternative, because the wild-capture fishery is well managed and has little bycatch.

## Spiny Lobsters (*Palinuridae*)

Spiny lobsters, also known as rock lobsters, are typically a warmwater crustacean. They are found off the coast of southern California, near Florida, and in the Caribbean Sea. They are also found in the Mediterranean and near Australia, New Zealand, New Guinea, and some other Pacific islands, as well as along the coast of South Africa.

Spiny lobsters are covered with pointed spines to help protect them from predators. The meat of a spiny lobster is firmer and stringier and not as sweet as that of clawed lobsters. They are less expensive than clawed lobsters but still good to eat.

## Clawed Lobsters: American Lobsters (*Homarus americanus*) and European Lobsters (*Homarus gammarus*)

In North America, the American clawed lobster is found off the coasts of New England and Canada. In Europe, clawed lobsters are found in the eastern Atlantic from Norway all the way to the Mediterranean.

Both American and European clawed lobsters are cold-water varieties that thrive in salt water. American lobsters tend to be reddish brown in color before being cooked, while the European ones are often blue. Both turn bright red after they are cooked.

Most of the meat of clawed lobsters is in the large claws and tail. The claw and tail meat from a Maine lobster is considered to be the sweetest of all lobster meat.

## HUMANELY DISPATCHING A LOBSTER FOR COOKING

Live shellfish, including lobster, should be killed immediately before cooking. Otherwise, harmful bacteria can release toxins in the meat that may cause food poisoning. There is considerable debate about how best to do this.

Some believe that plunging a lobster into boiling water is inhumane. The quickest alternative method is to plunge a sharp knife straight down at the point where the head joins the body. The legs may continue to move a bit after this, but the lobster is in fact dead.

Another method is to put the lobster in the freezer for 30 minutes before putting it headfirst into a pot of boiling water.

# HOW TO STEAM OR BOIL LIVE LOBSTER

To steam a lobster, fill a large stockpot with 3 inches (7.5 cm) of water and put a wire rack in the bottom. Bring the water to a boil. Dispatch the lobster (page 119). Add the lobster to the pot and steam, covered, for 9 to 11 minutes.

Alternatively, to boil a lobster, fill a large pot three-fourths full of water and bring to a boil. Add about 1 tablespoon of salt per quart (960 ml) of water. Dispatch the lobster (page 119). Add the lobster to the pot and cook for 7 to 9 minutes.

Remove the lobster from the pot, drain well, and let cool to the touch.

# HOW TO CLEAN AND CRACK LOBSTER

**1.** Pull the tail away from the head by twisting it. **2.** With sharp kitchen shears, cut the underside of the shell of the tail down the middle. Open the shell and remove the meat. **3.** Remove and discard the long, thin black intestinal vein that runs the length of the lobster and also the lumpy head sac located near the eyes. **4.** Break off the claws and cut them down one side with the shears. **5.** You can also crack the claws with a lobster cracker or nutcracker. Remove the meat from the claws in as large pieces as possible. Cut one side of the leg and remove any meat.

**NOTE** Using a mallet to crack the shells is not recommended, as this can break up the meat and result in a lot of little shell pieces.

1    2

3    4    5

# CRAYFISH

Depending on the region of the United States you're in, you'll hear them called crawfish, crayfish, mudbugs, yabbies, and crawdads. They are all the same freshwater crustacean. Crayfish look like very small lobsters, which they are closely related to, and are usually prepared steamed or boiled.

Crayfish, which can be found globally in rivers, lakes, and swamps, are freshwater crustaceans similar in flavor to lobster and shrimp. While 95 percent of the crayfish eaten in the United States are caught in Louisiana, there are over 500 species of crayfish worldwide and over half of them are native to North America. Out of the 330 kinds of crayfish found in the United States, the most commonly consumed are red swamp crayfish (*Procambarus clarkii*) and white river crayfish (*Procambarus acutus*)—they have nearly identical flavors and can be used interchangeably.

## HOW TO CLEAN CRAYFISH

Crayfish typically live in muddy water and need to be thoroughly cleaned before cooking. Start by washing them repeatedly in clean water. Once the water runs clear, add a couple of handfuls of salt into a basin of water and let them sit for 10 minutes. Soaking longer in salted water will kill them. Drain and rinse them off with fresh water. If the water is still murky, rinse again until it becomes clear.

## HOW TO COOK CRAYFISH

To boil crayfish, heat a large pot of boiling salted water. Add the crayfish and cook just until evenly pink, about 3 minutes. Drain and transfer to a bowl. They will continue to cook after draining.

To steam crayfish, place a large steamer over a pot of gently boiling salted water. Add the crayfish and cook just until evenly pink, 5 to 7 minutes. Remove the steamer and transfer the crayfish to a bowl. They will continue to cook after draining.

## HOW TO REMOVE THE MEAT FROM CRAYFISH

**1.** Once crayfish is cleaned and cooked it's ready to eat or you can remove the tail meat to be used in a recipe.
**2.** After cooking, twist the head away from the tail. Peel the shell from the tail meat and eat or transfer to a bowl to be used in a recipe. If the crayfish are really clean, many love the idea of "sucking the heads" for the tasty treats that they provide.

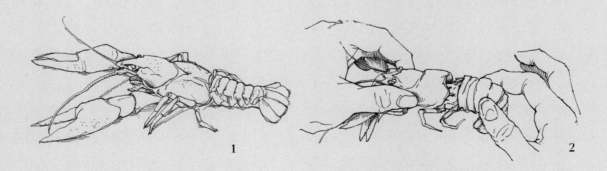

1

2

These Vietnamese-inspired salad rolls are easy to make and a fun choice for a DIY party with friends and family. You could substitute cooked lump crabmeat or other cooked fish for the shrimp. You can also serve these with Coconut-Peanut Sauce (page 338).

# SHRIMP RICE PAPER ROLLS

2 ounces (55 g) thin rice stick noodles (vermicelli)

1 small cucumber

2 firm, ripe avocados, pitted and peeled

Twelve 8-to-9-inch (20-to-23-cm) rice paper rounds

¾ pound (340 g) cooked medium (31 to 35 count) shrimp, peeled, deveined, and halved lengthwise (page 115)

3 tablespoons drained and julienned sweet pickled ginger

¼ cup (15 g) finely sliced green onion, including green parts, or garlic chives

⅓ cup (15 g) loosely packed fresh mint and/or cilantro leaves

2 tablespoons lightly toasted sesame seeds (page 344)

Vietnamese Dipping Sauce (Nuoc Cham) (page 338)

In a bowl of hot water, soften the noodles for 10 minutes; drain. Transfer to a medium saucepan of boiling water and cook the noodles for 1 minute. Drain and rinse in cold water to stop the cooking. Drain again and set aside, covered loosely with plastic wrap.

Peel and seed the cucumber and cut into thin 4-inch- (10-cm-) long strips with a mandoline or a sharp knife. Cut the avocado into long thin slices.

In a bowl of hot water, dip 2 or 3 rice paper rounds until they begin to soften, about 20 seconds. Transfer to a baking sheet.

For each roll, lay a softened rice paper on a clean surface and place about 1 tablespoon of the softened noodles across the bottom third of the round. Top with some cucumber, avocado slices, shrimp, pickled ginger, green onion, and a couple of mint leaves. Sprinkle with sesame seeds.

Roll the bottom of the paper up over the filling and then roll it up gently but firmly, folding in the sides as you go. The paper will seal by sticking to itself. Repeat with the remaining wrappers and filling. Serve the rolls cut in half, with the dipping sauce on the side. **MAKES 12 ROLLS**

This traditional Spanish cold soup is made sumptuous with the addition of shrimp. Note that the base mixture needs to be refrigerated for at least 2 hours or up to 24 hours for the rich flavors to marry and develop. Other cooked fish or shellfish may be substituted for the shrimp or crab.

# WINE COUNTRY GAZPACHO
## with shrimp

1 tablespoon chopped roasted garlic (page 345)

1 cup (55 g) rustic bread cubes, crusts removed before cutting

¼ cup (60 ml) red wine vinegar

⅓ cup (75 ml) extra-virgin olive oil

1 teaspoon cumin seeds, lightly toasted (page 344) and crushed

2 to 3 cups (480 to 720 ml) tomato juice or spicy V-8

2 to 3 cups (480 to 720 ml) shrimp stock (page 332) or fish stock (page 332)

2 pounds (910 g) vine-ripe tomatoes, seeded and chopped

⅔ cup (85 g) finely diced sweet red onion

1 cup (140 g) peeled, finely diced cucumber

½ cup (75 g) finely diced red or yellow bell pepper

½ cup (50 g) finely diced celery

1 teaspoon minced serrano chile

2 tablespoons minced fresh basil

1 tablespoon minced fresh mint

¼ cup (10 g) minced fresh cilantro

Fresh lemon juice or balsamic vinegar

1 teaspoon chipotle in adobo (optional)

Kosher salt and freshly ground black pepper

1 pound (455 g) cooked, peeled, and deveined shrimp (page 115) or cooked crabmeat (pages 117–118)

Sliced firm-ripe avocado and fresh cilantro sprigs, for garnish

In a food processor or blender, combine the garlic, bread, vinegar, oil, and cumin seeds and blend until smooth. Add the tomato juice, stock, tomatoes, red onion, cucumber, bell pepper, celery, serrano chile, basil, mint, cilantro, lemon juice, and chipotle. Blend to your preferred consistency, adding more tomato juice and stock as needed. Taste and adjust the seasoning with salt, black pepper, lemon juice, and/or vinegar. Cover and refrigerate for at least 2 hours or up to 24 hours.

To serve, divide the gazpacho between bowls. Top with the shrimp, dividing equally, then garnish with avocado and cilantro. **SERVES 6 TO 8**

Peppers, tomatoes, chiles, and of course "mother corn," all native to the Americas, were cultivated by Indigenous peoples as a basic part of their diet. These colorful foods come together beautifully in this hearty version of shrimp cocktail. Serve this in a large martini or margarita glass to show off the ingredients, which are roasted or grilled then chopped and combined with cooked pink shrimp and vegetable puree.

# SOUTHWESTERN SHRIMP COCKTAIL

3 plum tomatoes, halved and seeded

4 large tomatillos, husked and rinsed

1 small red onion, quartered

2 jalapeno chiles, halved and seeded

1 large poblano chile, halved and seeded

1 large red or orange bell pepper, halved and seeded

1 large ear corn, husked

3 tablespoons olive oil

Fine sea salt and freshly ground black pepper

1 pound (455 g) extra-large (16 to 20 count) raw shrimp, peeled and deveined (page 115)

½ cup (120 ml) fresh lime juice

⅓ cup (75 ml) fresh orange juice

¼ cup (60 ml) tomato juice

2 teaspoons brown sugar

1½ teaspoons kosher salt

Hot sauce, to taste

**GARNISHES**

2 tablespoons chopped fresh chives or green onion tops finely sliced on the bias

¼ cup (10 g) fresh cilantro leaves

½ cup (28 g) freshly popped unsalted popcorn

One small avocado, pitted, peeled, and cut into 4 fans

Jicama spears (optional)

Preheat the oven to 500°F (260°C) and line a baking sheet with aluminum foil. Brush the tomatoes, tomatillos, onion, chiles, bell pepper, and corn with the olive oil and sprinkle with salt and pepper. Place the vegetables cut side down on the prepared pan. Roast until the vegetables begin to color, removing them as they do. Tomatoes and tomatillos will take about 5 minutes, chiles, peppers, and corn about 8 minutes. Let cool.

Meanwhile, bring a large saucepan of water to a boil. Add the shrimp and immediately turn off the heat. Allow the shrimp to sit in the water until evenly pink, about 2 minutes. Immediately drain the shrimp and submerge them in a large bowl of very cold water. When cool, drain and transfer the shrimp to another large bowl.

Slip the skins off the tomatoes, chiles, and bell peppers. Coarsely chop each vegetable, including the onion and tomatillos, separately. Cut the corn kernels off the cob and set aside. Place half of each vegetable in a blender with the lime juice, orange juice, tomato juice, sugar, and salt. Blend until smooth. You should have about 2½ cups (600 ml). Strain through a medium-mesh sieve set over a bowl, pushing down on the solids with the back of a large spoon. Discard the solids. Season the sauce to taste with hot sauce.

Using drinking glasses or glass bowls, arrange half of the remaining vegetables, including the corn, attractively in each glass. Reserving 4 shrimp, divide the remaining shrimp among the glasses and spoon some of the sauce over. Sprinkle with half of the chives and cilantro, then add a final layer of roasted vegetables and sauce and top each with a shrimp. Sprinkle with the remaining chives and cilantro and finally the popcorn. Finish by inserting avocado fans and spears of jicama, if using, into the cocktails. Serve right away. **SERVES 4**

I first encountered this quesadilla at a little stand in Mexico many years ago on a beach near Manzanillo. Made open-faced with nuggets of shrimp and topped with fresh vegetables, herbs, and melting cheese, it's a perfect summer lunch. Here, I've used the same flavors but simplified this by sandwiching the filling between two tortillas.

# ROCK SHRIMP QUESADILLAS
## with oaxacan cheese and tomatoes

Eight 6-inch (15-cm) corn or flour tortillas

2 teaspoons olive oil

1 cup (100 g) sliced red or yellow onion

4 teaspoons thinly slivered garlic

2 cups (360 g) rock shrimp or coarsely chopped peeled and deveined (page 115) medium (31 to 35 count) shrimp

Hot pepper sauce

¼ cup (10 g) coarsely chopped fresh cilantro leaves

1⅓ cups (220 g) seeded, diced plum tomato

Fine sea salt and freshly ground pepper

Fresh lime juice

2 cups (230 g) shredded melting cheese, such as Jack, Oaxaca, or low-moisture mozzarella

Guacamole (page 341) and cilantro sprigs, for garnish

In a dry nonstick skillet, heat the tortillas over medium heat for a few seconds on each side and then transfer them to a plate. Cover with a clean kitchen towel to keep warm.

Add the olive oil, onion, and garlic to the skillet and sauté until softened. Add the shrimp, season with hot sauce, and sauté 1 minute more. Stir in the cilantro and tomato and season to taste with salt, pepper, and lime juice. Transfer to a bowl and wipe out the pan.

For each quesadilla, spread one quarter of the cheese and one quarter of the filling onto one tortilla, then top with a second tortilla. Add to the skillet over medium heat and cook, turning once, until the cheese is melted and the tortilla is nicely browned.

Cut into wedges and serve immediately, topped with guacamole and cilantro sprigs. Repeat to cook the remaining quesadillas. **SERVES 4**

Brining is a terrific way to add flavor and succulence to shrimp. Here, extra-large shrimp are both brined and marinated, then grilled and serve with a glorious green sauce. They are also excellent served with Poblano Chile Sauce (page 340) instead of the salsa verde.

# GRILLED SHRIMP with salsa verde

**BRINED SHRIMP**

⅓ cup (95 g) kosher salt

⅓ cup (75 g) brown sugar, lightly packed

4 cups (960 ml) cold water

1 pound (455 g) extra-large (16 to 20 count) raw shrimp, peeled and deveined (page 115)

**MARINADE**

¼ cup (60 ml) olive oil

2 teaspoons finely chopped garlic

1 tablespoon chopped fresh flat-leaf parsley

¼ teaspoon crushed red pepper flakes

2 tablespoons dry white wine

Salsa Verde (page 337)

Fresh cilantro sprigs, for garnish

To make the brined shrimp, in a large bowl, combine the salt, brown sugar, and water and stir until the salt and sugar are dissolved. Add the shrimp, cover, and refrigerate for 20 minutes.

To make the marinade, in a small bowl, combine the olive oil, garlic, parsley, red pepper flakes, and wine and stir to blend. Drain the brined shrimp and rinse well. Add to the bowl with the marinade and toss to coat. Cover and refrigerate for up to 1 hour.

Prepare a medium-hot fire in a charcoal grill, or preheat a gas grill to medium-high. Brush the grill grates clean. Place the shrimp on a grill screen, place the screen on the grill grate, and cook the shrimp until evenly pink, about 1 minute on each side. Divide the shrimp between plates and top with salsa verde and cilantro sprigs. Serve warm or at room temperature. **SERVES 4 TO 6**

---

Known in Japan as *chawanmushi*, this is pure comfort food. Eggs, dashi (the basic stock of Japan), chicken, shrimp, and vegetables are combined to create a silky, savory custard that is steamed or baked in a hot-water bath. *Chawanmushi* means "teacup steam," and special cups with lids for this dish are sold in Japanese or other well-stocked grocery stores. Custard cups are a perfect substitute.

# JAPANESE EGG CUSTARDS with shrimp

4 medium (31 to 35 count) raw shrimp, peeled and deveined (page 115)

4 ounces (115 g) boneless, skinless chicken breast, cut into ½-inch (12-mm) cubes

2 teaspoons Japanese soy sauce

3 large eggs

2¾ cups (660 ml) dashi (page 334) or chicken stock (page 333)

¼ teaspoon fine sea salt

½ teaspoon sake (optional)

2 teaspoons peeled and grated fresh ginger

Fresh cilantro or mitsuba (Japanese parsley) leaves

Cut the shrimp in half lengthwise. In a medium bowl, toss the shrimp with the chicken and soy sauce. Divide the shrimp and chicken among four 8-ounce (240-ml) custard cups or ramekins. In a bowl, beat the eggs well and stir in the dashi, salt, and sake. Gently pour the egg custard mixture equally into the cups and skim off any bubbles. Cover each cup securely with aluminum foil. Place the cups in a single layer in a steamer, partially cover, and steam over medium heat until the custards are just firm, 15 to 20 minutes. To serve, remove the foil and top each custard with a little ginger and a cilantro leaf. Serve warm. **SERVES 4**

The following recipe owes much to the Serious Eats website who, to the best of my knowledge, popularized the use of vodka in the batter. When water (in this case seltzer) and flour are mixed, the proteins in the flour form gluten, which provides structure. But too much stirring or too many minutes sitting develops the gluten and makes a heavy batter. Because vodka is about 60 percent water and 40 percent alcohol (which does not combine with protein to form gluten), it keeps gluten formation in check no matter how much you stir or how long you let it sit. This batter yields the impossibly light and crisp tempura coating we all know and love. The same batter is used for the Fried Salt and Pepper Squid on page 99. Hondashi, a brand of instant dashi, is a quick substitute for dashi soup. Look for it in well-stocked markets.

# SHRIMP TEMPURA
## with ginger-soy dipping sauce

**GINGER-SOY DIPPING SAUCE**

¾ cup (180 ml) warm water

2 teaspoons sugar

1 teaspoon instant dashi powder, preferably Hondashi (page 334)

3 tablespoons soy sauce

2 tablespoons mirin

1 teaspoon finely chopped fresh ginger

**SHRIMP TEMPURA**

Peanut or vegetable oil, for frying

1½ pounds (680 g) extra-large (16 to 20 count) shrimp, peeled and deveined (page 115), tails left on

1½ cups (190 g) unbleached all-purpose flour

½ cup (65 g) cornstarch

1 large egg

1 cup (240 ml) vodka

1 cup (240 ml) seltzer water

Kosher salt, for sprinkling

To make the dipping sauce, in a small saucepan over medium-high heat, combine the water, sugar, and dashi powder and bring to a boil. Remove from the heat and stir in the soy sauce, mirin, and ginger. Set aside, or cover and refrigerate for up to 1 week.

To make the tempura, preheat the oven to 200°F (90°C). Line a baking sheet with paper towels and place a large wire rack on another baking sheet.

In a large Dutch oven, heat 2 inches (5 cm) of oil over medium-high heat to 375°F (190°C) on a deep-frying thermometer, or until it shimmers.

While the oil heats, make 2 shallow crosswise cuts about ¼ inch (6 mm) deep and 1 inch (2.5 cm) apart on the underside of each shrimp. This will keep them from curling. In a large bowl, whisk the flour and cornstarch together. In a second large bowl, whisk the egg, vodka, and seltzer water together.

When the oil reaches 375°F (190°C), pour the liquid mixture into the flour mixture and whisk gently until just combined (it's okay if small lumps remain). Add half of the shrimp to the batter. Using tongs, remove the shrimp from the batter a couple at a time, allowing excess batter to drip off, and carefully place them in the hot oil.

Fry, stirring with a chopstick to prevent the shrimp from sticking together. Cook until light brown, 2 to 3 minutes. Using a slotted spoon or spider, remove the shrimp and place them on the wire rack. Sprinkle lightly with salt and transfer to the oven to keep warm.

Return the oil to 375°F (190°C) and repeat with the remaining shrimp. Serve immediately, with the dipping sauce.
**SERVES 4 TO 6**

Southeast Asia flavors are at work here. I adapted this from a trip to Thailand. It is a good example of the "four flavor Gods": sweet, salty, sour, and hot. I've used both shrimp and chicken here but you could use just one or any other protein you like, such as tofu.

# THAI SHRIMP AND CHICKEN MEATBALL SOUP

5 ounces (140 g) dried mung bean or rice noodles, softened according to package directions

½ pound (225 g) extra-large shrimp (16 to 20 count), peeled and deveined (page 115)

½ pound (225 g) boneless, skinless chicken thighs, chopped

3 tablespoons finely chopped green onion, including some green tops

2 tablespoons fish sauce

2 teaspoons minced garlic

1 teaspoon sugar

½ teaspoon freshly ground pepper

8 cups (2 l) ginger chicken stock (page 333) or chicken stock (page 333)

2 tablespoons soy sauce

1 tablespoon brown sugar

2 teaspoons chili-garlic sauce, or to taste

One 2-inch (5-cm) piece fresh ginger, peeled and cut into fine julienne

¼ cup (60 ml) fresh lime juice

¼ cup (10 g) coarsely chopped fresh cilantro

Fried shallots (optional) (page 344)

Prepare the noodles according to the package directions. Drain and set aside.

In a food processor, separately pulse the shrimp and chicken until coarsely chopped. In a large bowl, combine the chopped shrimp and chicken, green onion, fish sauce, garlic, sugar, and pepper. Scoop up a tablespoonful, gently roll into a ball, and set aside. Repeat to use all the mixture.

In a soup pot, combine the stock, soy sauce, brown sugar, chili-garlic sauce, and ginger and bring to a boil. Drop in the meatballs and cook, adjusting the heat to a gentle simmer, until the meatballs are cooked through, about 8 minutes. Taste the broth and adjust the seasoning.

Divide the noodles and lime juice among deep soup bowls, add the meatballs, and ladle the broth over the soup. Top with cilantro and fried shallots (if using) and serve. **SERVES 6**

The name for this beloved traditional Greek appetizer, or meze, comes from the two-handled dish in which it is cooked. It should be served bubbling hot, sometimes with a splash of ouzo. It is delicious and comes together very quickly. Serve with shouts of "*Opa!*"

# GREEK SHRIMP SAGANAKI
## with tomatoes, olives, and feta

3 tablespoons extra-virgin olive oil (preferably Greek), plus more for frying

1 medium red onion, halved and sliced

¼ cup (60 ml) ouzo (optional)

One 14-ounce (400-g) can petite diced tomatoes, drained

Big pinch of crushed red pepper flakes, or to taste

Kosher salt

1 pound (455 g) extra-large shrimp (16 to 20 count), peeled and deveined (page 115) and cut in half lengthwise

½ cup (75 g) pitted kalamata olives, coarsely chopped

2 tablespoons chopped fresh dill

6 ounces (170 g) Greek feta, kasseri, or Halloumi cheese

Flour, for dredging

Good crusty bread for serving

Preheat the oven to 200°F (90°C). In a large skillet over medium-high heat, warm the 3 tablespoons olive oil. Add the onion and cook, stirring occasionally, until lightly browned, about 5 minutes. Deglaze the pan with ouzo, if using.

Add the tomatoes and crushed red pepper flakes, then season with salt. Cook until bubbling, about 3 minutes. Add the shrimp and olives and cook, stirring occasionally, until the shrimp are just cooked through, about 2 minutes. Stir in 1 tablespoon dill. Set aside and cover to keep warm.

Meanwhile, cut the feta into ¼-inch- (6-mm-) thick slices, about 2 inches (5 cm) square. Dredge with flour, shaking off any excess, and set aside.

In a large skillet, heat a thin layer of olive oil over medium heat. Fry the cheese slices in batches, cooking on both sides until golden brown and crusty, about 5 minutes. Drain on paper towels, transfer to a baking sheet, and keep warm in the oven until all the slices are fried.

To serve, transfer the cheese to a warm platter. Spoon the shrimp sauce over the cheese and sprinkle with the remaining 1 tablespoon dill. Serve immediately with crusty bread. **SERVES 4**

Laksa is a popular spicy noodle soup from the Peranakan culture, a merger of Chinese and Malay populations found in Malaysia and Singapore. It combines coconut milk, chicken broth, shrimp, and vegetables with rice noodles and laksa paste, a nut-based coconut curry paste. This paste is gold! Make a big batch and freeze it to keep on hand to use wherever you use curry paste.

# SHRIMP LAKSA SOUP
## with noodles

3 cups (720 ml) chicken stock (page 333) or shrimp stock (page 332)

1 pound (455 g) extra-large (16 to 20 count) shrimp, peeled and deveined, shells reserved (page 115)

3½ cups (840 ml) coconut milk, well stirred

1 cup (230 g) laksa paste (page 342)

3 tablespoons rice wine or sake

1 tablespoon soy sauce

2 tablespoons peanut or other neutral oil

1 small zucchini, cut into long julienne

4 ounces (115 g) thin rice noodles (vermicelli), soaked in warm water for 20 minutes and drained

Fresh lime juice

Fine sea salt and freshly ground pepper

Fresh cilantro leaves, for garnish

2 or 3 green onions, including green parts, sliced on the diagonal, for garnish

In a soup pot, heat the stock to boiling and add the reserved shrimp shells; cover and simmer for 5 minutes. Drain in a fine-mesh sieve over a bowl. Discard the shells and return the stock to the pot. Over medium heat, add the coconut milk to the stock and bring to a simmer. Whisk in the laksa paste. Cover to keep warm.

Using a sharp knife, halve the shrimp lengthwise. In a medium bowl, stir the rice wine and soy sauce together. Add the shrimp and toss to lightly coat. Set aside.

In a wok or large sauté pan, heat the oil over high heat until it shimmers. Working in batches if necessary, add the shrimp and stir-fry just until evenly pink, about 2 minutes. Transfer the shrimp to a bowl.

Add the zucchini and noodles to warmed deep bowls. Top with the shrimp. Season with salt, pepper, and lime juice to taste. Rewarm the stock if necessary, then ladle the hot stock over the noodles and serve immediately, garnished with cilantro leaves and green onions. **SERVES 4 TO 6**

Grits, a Southern staple, is believed to have originated with Native Americans, who stone-ground treated dried corn kernels to make a kind of mush. Shrimp and grits is a historic dish in the Low Country cooking of South Carolina and the Georgia coast.

# SHRIMP AND GRITS

**GRITS**

2½ cups (600 ml) water

1 cup (240 ml) milk

¾ cup (130 g) stone-ground grits

1 cup (115 g) shredded Cheddar cheese

½ cup (50 g) freshly grated Parmesan cheese

3 tablespoons unsalted butter

½ teaspoon kosher salt

**CAJUN SHRIMP**

12 extra-large (16 to 20 count) raw shrimp, peeled and deveined (page 115)

Kosher salt and freshly ground pepper

Cajun seasoning, homemade (page 341) or store-bought

1 tablespoon olive oil

**SAUCE**

½ cup (120 ml) shrimp stock (page 332) or chicken stock (page 333)

1 tablespoon fresh lemon juice

1 tablespoon Worcestershire sauce

2 teaspoons hot sauce

3 tablespoons cold unsalted butter, diced

½ cup (85 g) seeded and finely diced ripe tomatoes, for garnish

2 tablespoons chopped fresh flat-leaf parsley, for garnish

To make the grits, in a medium saucepan, bring the water and milk to a boil over medium heat. Slowly stir in the grits. Reduce the heat to low, cover, and cook for 45 minutes or until the grits are tender and the liquid is absorbed. Remove from the heat and stir in the cheeses, butter, and salt. Cover to keep warm.

To make the Cajun shrimp, season the shrimp lightly with salt, pepper, and Cajun seasoning. In a large skillet, heat the olive oil over medium heat. Add the shrimp and cook, turning once, until just cooked through, about 3 minutes. Transfer to a paper towel-lined plate.

To make the sauce, place the pan back over the heat and add the stock, lemon juice, Worcestershire sauce, and hot sauce. Heat until bubbling. Remove from the heat and whisk in the butter to form a satiny sauce. Add the shrimp and turn to coat.

Divide the cooked grits and place in the center of each of 4 shallow dishes. Place 3 shrimp on top of each portion of grits. Spoon the butter sauce from the pan over the shrimp, top with tomatoes, and garnish with parsley. Serve hot.

**SERVES 4**

Crisp fried rock shrimp cakes and bright green salsa are a brilliant combination. This salsa is also terrific on grilled and roasted fish. The cakes take on extra flavor with the optional dried shrimp. Look for fresh tomatillos in Latino markets.

# ROCK SHRIMP CAKES
## with avocado and tomatillo salsa

1 pound (455 g) raw rock shrimp

¼ cup (60 ml) dry white wine

1 large egg, beaten

1½ cups (120 g) panko (Japanese bread crumbs)

5 tablespoons (75 ml) mayonnaise

1 teaspoon dry mustard

2 tablespoons minced fresh flat-leaf parsley

2 tablespoons minced green onion

2 teaspoons white wine Worcestershire

2 teaspoons ground dried shrimp (optional)

Hot sauce

Kosher salt and freshly ground pepper

2 tablespoons or so clarified butter (page 345) or olive oil

2 cups (80 g) mixed salad greens

Avocado and Tomatillo Salsa (page 338)

Fresh cilantro sprigs, for garnish

Savory sprouts, such as sunflower or daikon, for garnish (optional)

In a large skillet, combine the shrimp and wine and cook over medium-high heat for 1 minute. The shrimp will still be translucent and half-cooked. Drain the shrimp, let cool, and chop coarsely. Wipe out the skillet.

Combine the egg, ½ cup (40 g) of the panko, mayonnaise, mustard, parsley, green onion, Worcestershire, dried shrimp (if using), and hot sauce to taste. Fold in the rock shrimp and their juices. Form into 8 cakes about ¾ inch (2 cm) thick. Put the remaining 1 cup (80 g) panko in a shallow bowl and coat both sides of each cake in panko. Place the cakes on a baking sheet and refrigerate, uncovered, for at least 30 minutes or up to 2 hours.

In the skillet, melt the butter or heat the olive oil over medium heat. Cook the cakes until lightly browned on both sides, about 2 minutes per side.

Divide the salad greens among 4 plates. Top with a shrimp cake, then spoon salsa over each cake. Garnish each with cilantro sprigs and sprouts (if using) and serve at once. **SERVES 4**

According to legend, hush puppies were devised by hunters in the South, who would throw an occasional fritter to their hunting dogs to keep them quiet. These hot, crisp little bites blend cornmeal with crabmeat for an elegant appetizer. They are best served with your favorite mayonnaise-based sauce, such as tartar sauce (page 339) or garlic aioli (page 337), for dipping.

# CRAB HUSH PUPPIES

Peanut or vegetable oil, for frying

2 cups (360 g) yellow cornmeal

1 cup (125 g) unbleached all-purpose flour

2 tablespoons baking powder

2 tablespoons sugar

1 tablespoon salt

1½ cups (360 ml) milk

2 large eggs

1 to 2 tablespoons hot sauce

1 pound (455 g) cooked lump crabmeat, picked over for shell (pages 117–118)

2 tablespoons unsalted butter

3 large green onions, thinly sliced, including some green parts

Preheat the oven to 250°F (120°C). Line a baking sheet with paper towels.

Fill a large, heavy pot with 2 inches (5 cm) of oil and heat over high heat until it shimmers (350°F/175°C on a deep-frying thermometer).

While the oil is heating, in a medium bowl whisk together the cornmeal, flour, baking powder, sugar, and salt. In a small bowl, whisk together the milk, eggs, and hot sauce until blended, then add to the cornmeal mixture and stir until combined. Fold in the crabmeat.

In a small skillet, melt the butter over medium-low heat, add the green onions, and cook until soft. Stir into the batter.

Using two teaspoons and working in batches, carefully add 1 rounded teaspoon of batter per hush puppy to the hot oil and fry, turning occasionally, until golden brown all over and cooked through, 2 to 3 minutes. Using a slotted spoon, transfer to the prepared baking sheet and place in the oven to keep warm. Repeat to fry the remaining batter, returning the oil to 350°F (175°C) between batches. Serve immediately. **MAKES 20 TO 30 HUSH PUPPIES**

This beautifully green soup can be served either hot or cold, but I especially like to serve it cold in summer. It's a wonderfully versatile soup, as broccoli or asparagus can be substituted for some or all of the peas, watercress or spinach for some or all of the romaine, and basil or tarragon for some or all of the mint. If using fresh peas you may want to add a pinch or two of sugar, depending on their maturity. Salmon or trout roe is a colorful and flavorful finishing touch along with the pea shoots.

# GREEN PEA SOUP
## with crab

2 tablespoons olive oil

½ cup (30 g) chopped green onions, including green parts

2 teaspoons chopped garlic

3 cups (about 12 ounces/340 g) fresh or frozen green peas

2 cups (480 ml) chicken stock (page 333) or vegetable stock (page 333)

1½ cups (85 g) finely chopped romaine or other lettuce, lightly packed

3 tablespoons chopped fresh mint

⅔ cup (165 ml) buttermilk

Fine sea salt

Fresh lemon juice and hot sauce, to taste

¼ cup (60 ml) crème fraîche

⅔ cup (90 g) cooked lump crabmeat, picked over for shell (pages 117–118)

2 ounces (55 g) fresh salmon or trout roe (optional)

Tiny pea shoots and/or herb sprigs, such as chervil or tarragon, for garnish

In a large soup pot, heat the olive oil over medium heat and sauté the green onions and garlic until softened, about 3 minutes. Add the peas and stock and bring to a simmer. Cook until the peas are just cooked through. Remove from the heat. Add to a blender and puree. Add the romaine and mint and puree again until smooth. Add the buttermilk and blend until combined. Season to taste with salt, lemon juice, and hot sauce. Press and strain through a medium-mesh sieve set over a bowl, discarding the solids. Cover and refrigerate until chilled, at least 3 hours. Before serving, taste and adjust the seasonings.

To serve, place a tablespoon of crème fraîche in the center of each of 4 large shallow soup bowls. Top each with a rounded tablespoonful of the crab, then top with the optional roe, the pea shoots, and herb sprigs, if using. Ladle or pour chilled the soup around. **SERVES 4**

This rich soup is a meal in a bowl! Serve it in summer, when you can find fresh sweet corn. You can use frozen corn kernels, of course, but you won't have the cobs to make the flavorful stock.

# CRAB AND CORN CHOWDER
## with bacon and wild mushrooms

5 ears sweet corn

2 cups (480 ml) chicken stock (page 333)

4 cups (960 ml) heavy cream

2 tablespoons olive oil

6 ounces (170 g) slab bacon cut into ¼-inch (6-mm) dice

1½ cups (190 g) finely diced onions

1½ cups (135 g) finely diced leeks, white and some tender green parts, well rinsed

¾ cup (75 g) diced celery

1 teaspoon fennel seeds

3 cups (420 g) diced waxy potatoes

2 tablespoons unsalted butter

8 ounces (225 g) wild mushrooms, such as chanterelles or oysters, thickly sliced (about 3 cups)

1 teaspoon fresh thyme leaves, or ½ teaspoon dried

Fine sea salt and freshly ground pepper

3 tablespoons dry or medium-dry sherry

1 pound (455 g) lump crabmeat, picked over for shell (pages 117–118)

2 tablespoons finely chopped fresh flat-leaf parsley

Using a large knife, cut the kernels from the cobs. You should have about 5 cups (725 g). In a large saucepan, combine the cobs, stock, and cream. Bring to a simmer over medium heat and cook for 5 minutes. Remove from the heat.

In a large, heavy soup pot, heat the olive oil over medium-high heat and sauté the bacon until browned and crisp. Using a slotted spoon, transfer the bacon to paper towels to drain. Discard all but 3 tablespoons of fat from the pot.

Add the onions, leeks, celery, and fennel seeds and sauté over medium heat until the vegetables are crisp-tender. Add the potatoes and stir. Remove and discard the cobs from the cream mixture and strain the mixture into the pot with the vegetables. Bring to a simmer and cook until potatoes are barely tender, about 10 minutes. Add the corn kernels and simmer for 2 minutes, then remove from the heat.

In a large skillet, melt the butter over medium heat. Add the mushrooms and sauté until tender. Add the thyme leaves and season with salt and pepper to taste. Add the mushrooms to the soup along with the sherry, reserving the mushroom pan. Taste and adjust the seasoning. If desired, thin with additional stock or cream.

Add the crab to the reserved pan and gently warm over low heat. Divide the crab among warm shallow soup bowls along with the reserved bacon and the parsley. Ladle the soup over and serve immediately. **SERVES 6 TO 8**

Watercress, golden beets, and avocado combine with crabmeat to make a colorful and healthful salad served with a sweet-spicy lime vinaigrette.

# CRAB, AVOCADO, AND GOLDEN BEET SALAD
## with lime vinaigrette

**ROASTED BEETS**

12 small golden beets

2 tablespoons extra-virgin olive oil

Fine sea salt and freshly ground pepper

Juice of 1 lemon

**LIME VINAIGRETTE**

¼ cup (35 g) finely diced shallots

2 teaspoons seeded and diced jalapeño chile

2 tablespoons wildflower honey

⅓ cup (75 ml) fresh lime juice

½ cup (120 ml) extra-virgin olive oil

Fine sea salt and freshly ground pepper

**CRAB SALAD**

2 firm, ripe avocados, halved, pitted, and peeled

Fine sea salt and freshly ground pepper

1 bunch watercress, stemmed

¾ pound (340 g) cooked lump crabmeat, picked over for shell (pages 117–118)

1 tablespoon chopped fresh flat-leaf parsley

1 tablespoon chopped fresh cilantro

½ cup (120 ml) crème fraîche

To roast the beets, preheat the oven to 400°F (205°C). Cut the leaves and stems from the beets (save the greens for another dish). Clean the beets well. Place the beets in a small roasting pan. Add 1 tablespoon of oil and sprinkle with salt and pepper; roll the beets in the pan to coat with oil. Cover with aluminum foil and roast until knife-tender, 30 to 40 minutes.

Carefully remove the foil. Let the beets cool and peel them by rubbing with a paper towel. Cut the beets into ½-inch (12-mm) wedges. Toss them in a medium bowl with the remaining 1 tablespoon olive oil, a generous squeeze of lemon juice, and a sprinkling of salt and pepper. Taste and adjust the seasoning.

To make the vinaigrette, in a small bowl, combine the shallots, jalapeños, honey, and lime juice. Let sit for 5 minutes. Whisk in the olive oil. Season with salt and pepper.

To make the salad, cut each avocado into ⅓-inch- (8-mm-) thick slices and season with salt and pepper. Fan the avocado slices on one side of a chilled platter. Place the beets on the other side and arrange the watercress in the center.

In a large bowl, toss the crab gently with two-thirds of the lime vinaigrette and all of the parsley and cilantro. Pile the crab on the watercress and top with the crème fraîche. Serve, passing the remaining vinaigrette alongside.
**SERVES 4**

Add a note of elegance to deviled eggs by folding lump crabmeat in to the mashed yolks. This dish will brighten any potluck.

# CRAB DEVILED EGGS

4 large hard-boiled eggs (page 344)

¼ cup (60 ml) mayonnaise

2 teaspoons Dijon mustard

1 teaspoon Worcestershire sauce, preferably white

5 ounces (140 g) cooked lump crabmeat, picked over for shell (pages 117–118)

Fine sea salt

Hot sauce, to taste

Fresh lemon juice, to taste

Pimentón (smoked Spanish paprika), for garnish

Cut the eggs in half lengthwise. Remove the yolks from the eggs, making sure not to break the 8 halved whites that remain. Put the yolks in a medium bowl and mash them with a fork. Add the mayonnaise, mustard, and Worcestershire sauce and blend well until smooth.

Fold in the crabmeat, trying to keep the crab pieces as intact as possible. Season to taste with salt, hot sauce, and lemon juice. Spoon the mixture into the egg whites. Garnish with pimentón. Serve or refrigerate for up to 2 hours.

---

This simple dish celebrates one of the real treasures of the Northern California, Oregon, and Washington coasts: Dungeness crab! I think crab from this region is the best, but unfortunately, it's not generally available fresh outside these areas. You can substitute other crab, such as King crab. Fresh mussels, clams, and shrimp can also be substituted or added to the mix. Serve with a big stack of napkins and lots of crusty French bread.

# CRAB IN WINE AND VERMOUTH

1 large (about 3 pounds/1.4 kg) cooked, fresh Dungeness crab, cleaned (pages 117–118)

1½ cups (260 ml) chicken stock (page 333)

⅔ cup (165 ml) vermouth

½ cup (120 ml) dry white wine

½ cup (115 g) unsalted butter, cut into pieces

3 tablespoons thinly sliced garlic

One 1½-inch (4-cm) piece fresh ginger, peeled and cut into thin coins

1½ tablespoons soy sauce

1 tablespoon fresh lemon juice

2 teaspoons sugar

2 teaspoons cornstarch, dissolved in 1 tablespoon cold water

¼ cup (13 g) chopped fresh flat-leaf parsley or a combination of parsley and chives

Freshly ground pepper

Crusty French bread for serving

Crack and separate the crab into sections and set aside. In a large saucepan over medium-high heat, combine the stock, vermouth, wine, butter, garlic, ginger, soy sauce, lemon juice, sugar, and cornstarch mixture. Bring to a simmer then reduce the heat to low, cover, and simmer for about 5 minutes. Add the crab pieces, parsley, and pepper to taste and cook, stirring occasionally, until the crab is warmed through. Divide into large bowls with the broth and serve immediately with the bread alongside. **SERVES 2 TO 4**

The best crab cakes minimize the bread crumbs and maximize the crabmeat. The cakes should just hold together when gently squeezed. Here, they are served with a tarragon aioli, a perfect complement to the delicate taste of crabmeat.

# CRAB CAKES
## with tarragon aioli

**TARRAGON AIOLI**

¾ cup (180 ml) mayonnaise

3 large poached garlic cloves (page 345)

1 tablespoon olive oil

1 tablespoon chopped fresh tarragon

Fresh lemon juice, to taste

**CRAB CAKES**

1 pound (455 g) cooked lump crabmeat, picked over for shell (pages 117–118)

1 large egg, beaten

5 tablespoons (75 ml) mayonnaise

1 tablespoon minced fresh flat-leaf parsley

1 tablespoon minced green onion, including green tops

2 teaspoons Worcestershire sauce, preferably white

Fine sea salt and freshly ground white pepper

Hot sauce, to taste

½ cup (40 g) panko (Japanese bread crumbs), plus more for dusting

2 tablespoons clarified butter (page 345) or olive oil

Fresh tarragon sprigs, for garnish

2 ounces (55 g) fresh salmon caviar, rinsed (optional), for garnish

To make the aioli, add the mayonnaise, garlic, olive oil, and tarragon to a mini food processor and pulse until smooth. Stir in a few drops of lemon juice to taste. Cover and refrigerate for at least 1 hour to let the flavors blend.

To make the crab cakes, gently squeeze the crabmeat to get rid of any excess moisture. In a medium bowl, combine the crabmeat, egg, mayonnaise, parsley, green onion, and Worcestershire. Season to taste with salt, pepper, and hot sauce. Stir in the ½ cup (40 g) panko. Don't overmix. You want the cakes to just hold together and be delicate in texture. Mix in additional panko if the mixture is too moist. (Cook a little tester to make sure). Form into 6 cakes, about 1 inch (2.5 cm) thick. Lightly dust both sides with additional panko.

In a large skillet, heat the clarified butter over medium heat. Add the cakes and cook until lightly browned on both sides, about 3 minutes per side.

Serve the cakes topped with a dollop of aioli and garnished with the tarragon sprigs and the salmon caviar, if using.
**SERVES 6**

There are as many versions of this famous salad as there are cooks who make it. The dressing is not only the common denominator between versions, but it really makes the salad. Here is my version, which can also be made with shrimp or lobster.

# CRAB LOUIS SALAD

**LOUIS DRESSING**

1½ cups (360 ml) mayonnaise

⅓ cup (75 ml) chili sauce, preferably Heinz

3 tablespoons finely chopped green onion, including some green tops

3 tablespoons finely chopped green bell peppers

2 tablespoons fresh lemon juice

1 teaspoon Worcestershire sauce

2 teaspoons chopped fresh flat-leaf parsley, finely chopped

Kosher salt

Cayenne pepper

**CRAB SALAD**

1 small head Bibb or Boston lettuce, leaves torn into bite-sized pieces

3 small, ripe avocados, preferably Hass, halved, pitted, and peeled

1½ pounds (680 g) cooked lump Dungeness crabmeat, picked over for shell (pages 117–118)

2 firm, ripe tomatoes, cut into 6 wedges *each*

3 large hard-boiled eggs (page 344), cut lengthwise into quarters

1 Kirby or Persian cucumber, cut into large dice

6 lemon wedges, for serving

To make the dressing, in a small bowl, combine the mayonnaise, chili sauce, green onion, bell pepper, lemon juice, Worcestershire sauce, parsley, salt, and cayenne pepper and whisk to blend. Season to taste with salt and cayenne. Set aside, or cover and refrigerate for up to 3 days.

To make the salad, divide the lettuce among 6 salad plates. Top each with an avocado half, then spoon the crabmeat into the avocado cavities, dividing it equally. Arrange the tomatoes, eggs, and cucumber around the avocado attractively. Top each salad with a heaping tablespoon of dressing and garnish with a lemon wedge or two. Pass the remaining dressing for guests to add if they desire. **SERVES 6**

# CRAB LOUIS

The origin of Crab Louis has lots of entries. Because of where Dungeness resides, the Northwest—from San Francisco to Vancouver—was its birthplace, probably sometime around the mid-nineteenth century.

Refrigerated railcars made both crab and fresh produce more widely available. And by the early twentieth century, crab with lettuce and other veggies and ingredients made it a delicious luxury dish all over the country. An article in the *Seattle Post-Intelligencer* from the 1930s declared, "A trip to Seattle without a feast of crab à la Louis is like Paris without the Eiffel Tower."

Crab Louis (pronounced *loo-ey*) first appeared in *The Neighborhood Cookbook*, by the Portland Council of Jewish Women, in 1912. It called for simple ingredients: lettuce, hard-boiled eggs, as well as shredded crab meat. The most important part, however, was the Louis dressing. Not just plain mayonnaise, but a zesty, pink concoction that also included ketchup, lemon, chile sauce, and more.

Many claim to having invented it, but James Beard, who ate it growing up in Portland, brought it to national attention.

Crispy sauteéd soft-shell crabs, fresh rolls, and spicy mayonnaise are a combination of flavors and textures that celebrate summer.

# SOFT-SHELL CRAB SANDWICHES
## with chipotle mayonnaise

**CHIPOTLE MAYONNAISE**

1 tablespoon chopped chipotle in adobo

1 large egg

1 teaspoon chopped garlic

1 tablespoon chopped fresh cilantro

½ teaspoon sugar

2 teaspoons fresh lemon or lime juice

½ cup (120 ml) olive oil

Kosher salt

**FRIED SOFT-SHELL CRABS**

4 soft-shell crabs, cleaned (page 118)

½ cup (120 ml) buttermilk

½ cup (65 g) unbleached all-purpose flour

¼ cup (45 g) cornmeal

2 teaspoons kosher salt

½ teaspoon freshly ground black pepper

Big pinch of cayenne pepper

½ teaspoon dried thyme, crushed

1 teaspoon grated lemon zest

Olive oil, for frying

**SANDWICHES**

4 soft Kaiser, onion, or ciabatta rolls, split

1 sweet red or Vidalia onion, sliced into rounds

2 cups (110 g) finely shredded romaine hearts

To make the chipotle mayonnaise, in a blender, combine the chipotle, egg, garlic, cilantro, sugar, and lemon juice and blend until smooth. With the machine running, gradually add the olive oil in a thin stream until emulsified. Season to taste with salt. Thin with water if necessary. Cover and refrigerate for up to 5 days.

To make the crab, preheat the oven to 200°F (90°C). Have ready a baking sheet plus a second baking sheet lined with paper towels.

Marinate the crabs in buttermilk for a few minutes. In a separate bowl, mix together the flour, cornmeal, salt, peppers, thyme, and lemon zest. One at a time, remove the crabs from the buttermilk and dredge them in the seasoned flour.

Add enough oil to cover the bottom of a large, heavy skillet. Heat over medium-high heat. Add the crabs and cook, turning once, until browned and crisp, about 3 minutes on each side. Drain on paper towels and keep warm.

To assemble the sandwiches, spread both sides of each roll liberally with the chipotle mayonnaise. Top the bottom of the roll with onions, lettuce, and crab. Close the rolls and serve immediately. **SERVES 4**

A pungent spice paste gives this coconut-milk-based curry a kick, while lump crabmeat adds richness. Serve it with steamed jasmine rice.

# THAI CRAB CURRY
## with chiles, ginger, and lime leaves

**CURRY PASTE**

2 seeded and chopped serrano or Thai chiles

One 2-inch (5-cm) piece fresh ginger or galangal, peeled and finely chopped

3 cloves garlic, chopped

2 large shallots, chopped

1 tablespoon ground coriander

2 tablespoons grated lime zest

1 stalk lemongrass, tender white parts only, finely chopped

1 teaspoon shrimp paste (optional)

**CRAB CURRY**

2 cups (480 ml) well-stirred full-fat coconut milk

1 pound (455 g) cooked lump crabmeat, picked over for shell (pages 117–118)

2 tablespoons fish sauce

1 tablespoon sugar

3 to 4 fresh makrut lime leaves (optional)

Freshly ground pepper

Steamed jasmine rice, for serving

Fresh cilantro leaves, for garnish

To make the curry paste, in a food processor, combine the chiles, ginger, garlic, shallots, coriander, lime zest, lemongrass, and shrimp paste (if using) and process until smooth. Alternatively, use a mortar and pestle to pound to a paste.

To make the curry, in a large saucepan, bring the coconut milk to a simmer over medium heat. Add the spice paste and stir it into the coconut milk until simmering again. Do not boil.

Add the crab, fish sauce, sugar, and lime leaves, if using, and cook gently until the crab is heated through, about 4 minutes. Add pepper to taste. Taste and adjust the seasoning. Serve over steamed rice, topped with cilantro.
**SERVES 4 TO 6**

A classic treatment for Dungeness crab, here pungent Chinese black bean sauce complements sweet, meaty Maine lobster. Of course, you can substitute one whole Dungeness crab for the lobster and jumbo shrimp make a delicious and quick substitute as well.

# STIR-FRIED LOBSTER
# IN BLACK BEAN SAUCE

One 1 ½-pound (680-g) live Maine lobster

¼ cup (60 ml) peanut or other neutral oil

2 tablespoons black bean sauce

1 teaspoon minced garlic

1 teaspoon minced fresh ginger

2 tablespoons soy sauce

1 tablespoon dry sherry

1 teaspoon sugar

1 cup (240 ml) shellfish stock (page 332) or chicken stock (page 333)

1 tablespoon tapioca starch

¼ cup (60 ml) cold water

2 green onions, sliced on the diagonal, including green parts

Steamed rice, for serving

Dispatch the lobster (page 119). Split the lobsters in half lengthwise and gently crack the claws or use shears to open up the shell. Remove and discard the long, thin dark intestinal vein that runs the length of the lobster and also the lumpy head sac located near the eyes. Using a cleaver, chop the lobster into 1-inch (2.5-cm) pieces. Pick out any shell splinters.

In a large wok, heat the oil over high heat until just beginning to smoke. Add the lobster and stir-fry for 1 minute. Stir in the black bean sauce, garlic, and ginger and stir-fry for 2 minutes. Add the soy sauce, sherry, and sugar and stir-fry for 2 more minutes. Add the stock, cover, and simmer until the lobster meat is opaque, about 5 minutes.

In a cup, mix the tapioca starch with the water and stir into the lobster mixture. Bring to a boil, stir in the green onions, and then remove from the heat. Spoon onto warmed plates, with rice on the side. **SERVES 2**

My favorite way to cook lobster is on the grill. The shells char as the meat cooks, giving the lobster a delicious flavor. Use the roasted garlic butter as suggested here, or try one of the many other compound butters on pages 334 to 335. I also particularly like the Maître d'Hotel Butter.

# GRILLED LOBSTER
## with roasted garlic butter

Two 1¾-pound (800-g) live Maine lobsters

Olive oil, for brushing

Fine sea salt and freshly ground pepper

Roasted Garlic Butter (page 335), melted

Lemon wedges, for serving

Dispatch the lobsters (page 119). Split the lobsters in half lengthwise. Remove and discard the long thin black intestinal vein that runs the length of the lobster and also the lumpy head sac located near the eyes.

Prepare a medium fire in a charcoal grill or preheat a gas grill to medium. Brush the grill grates clean. Brush the lobster shells and tail meat with oil and season the meat with salt and pepper. Place shell side down on the grill grate. Liberally brush with the melted butter, working some of it into the cracked claws. Grill for 2 minutes, then repeat brushing with the melted butter. The shells should begin to char a bit. Move the lobsters to a cooler spot on the grill if necessary and cover the lobster with a metal roasting pan.

Cook just until the meat is opaque, 4 to 5 more minutes. Serve with the remaining melted butter and lemon wedges to squeeze over. **SERVES 2**

---

This beloved Northeast treat is simply a butter-toasted roll filled with lobster salad. You could substitute rock shrimp or bay shrimp for the pricey lobster, or use cooked lump Dungeness crab meat for an equally stunning sandwich. Purists demand a top-split roll or hot dog bun, as this helps to hold the salad in, but a brioche or potato roll is also nice. Toasting the buttered rolls is essential.

# LOBSTER ROLLS

2 to 3 cups (270 to 405 g) chopped, cooked lobster meat (page 120)

⅓ cup (75 ml) mayonnaise

½ cup (50 g) finely diced celery

Fresh lemon juice, to taste

1 tablespoon finely chopped mixed fresh herbs, such as tarragon, and/or chives

Fine sea salt and freshly ground pepper

4 split-top buns or other buns

3 tablespoons unsalted butter, at room temperature

Shredded iceberg lettuce (optional)

In a medium bowl, combine the lobster, mayonnaise, celery, lemon juice, and herbs. Season with salt and pepper.

Open the buns and flatten them, being careful not to break them apart. Spread the insides with the butter. Heat a large cast-iron skillet or griddle over medium heat. Add the buns, butter side down, and toast until golden brown, about 4 minutes.

While the buns are still warm, divide the lobster salad between them, close, and serve at once. You can add the optional lettuce if you want, but a Mainer wouldn't. **MAKES 4 SANDWICHES**

What could be more comforting and delectable than a lobster potpie? This one combines mushrooms and lobster with a rich cream sauce, and is topped with crisp puff pastry. Crabmeat, crayfish tails, or bay shrimp can be substituted for the lobster.

# LOBSTER POTPIES

3 tablespoons unsalted butter

1 yellow onion, finely chopped

2 cloves garlic, minced

½ cup (30 g) finely chopped cremini or stemmed shiitake mushrooms

¼ cup (60 ml) dry white vermouth

2 tablespoons flour, plus more for rolling out pastry

1¾ cups (420 ml) heavy cream

1 pound (455 g) raw or thawed frozen lobster meat, cut into ¾-inch (2-cm) pieces

⅛ teaspoon freshly grated nutmeg

Kosher salt and freshly ground pepper

One 14-oz (400-g) package frozen puff pastry, thawed

1 egg, beaten with 2 teaspoons water

Preheat the oven to 425°F (220°C). In a saucepan, melt the butter over medium-high heat. Add the onion and garlic and cook, stirring, until golden, about 5 minutes. Add the mushrooms and cook until they begin to brown. Add the vermouth and cook until reduced by half, about 2 minutes. Whisk in the 2 tablespoons of flour and cook for 2 to 3 minutes. Add the cream and bring just to a boil. Reduce the heat to medium-low and cook, stirring, until the sauce is lightly thickened, 3 to 4 minutes. Stir in the lobster, nutmeg, and salt and pepper to taste.

Place four 8-ounce (240-ml) ramekins on a baking sheet. Divide the lobster mixture among the ramekins.

On a lightly floured surface, roll the puff pastry into a 14-inch (35.5-cm) square. Cut out four 4½-inch (11-cm) rounds. Brush the edges of the ramekins with the egg wash. Place one round over each ramekin and press the edges to seal. Brush the pastry with the egg wash and bake until golden brown, 20 to 25 minutes. Serve at once.
**SERVES 4**

---

This traditional lobster bisque is rich, creamy, and luxurious, with a hint of sherry and a little heat from cayenne pepper. You can easily transform this into a crab bisque by substituting 1 pound (455 g) of cooked lump crabmeat (pages 117–118) for the lobster.

# LOBSTER BISQUE

2 tablespoons unsalted butter

⅓ cup (45 g) chopped shallots

¾ cup (180 ml) dry white wine

4 cups (960 ml) shellfish stock (page 332)

¼ cup (45 g) long-grain white rice

1 tablespoon tomato paste

1 pound (455 g) cooked lobster, chopped (page 120)

1¼ cups (300 ml) heavy cream

2 tablespoons dry sherry

½ teaspoon salt

⅛ teaspoon cayenne pepper

In a large saucepan, melt the butter over medium heat. Add the shallots and cook until translucent, about 3 minutes. Add the wine, stock, rice, and tomato paste. Bring to a simmer and cook, covered, until the rice is tender, about 25 minutes. Remove from the heat and let cool for several minutes.

Add about two-thirds of the lobster meat to the soup. Working in batches, ladle the soup into a blender and puree until completely smooth. Return the pureed soup to the pan. Add the cream, then gently heat the soup over low heat until it is hot enough for serving. Add the remaining lobster meat. Stir in the sherry, salt, and cayenne pepper. Serve at once. **SERVES 4 TO 6**

Fresh lobster is best cooked and sauced simply. Here, Maine lobster is either steamed or boiled, then removed from the shell, cut into pieces, and served with watercress, orange segments, and a quick aioli.

# LOBSTER WATERCRESS SALAD
## with orange-caper aioli

**ORANGE-CAPER AIOLI**

½ cup (120 ml) mayonnaise

1 tablespoon grated orange zest

1 tablespoon fresh orange juice

2 teaspoons pureed poached garlic (page 345)

1 tablespoon capers, drained, patted dry, and chopped

Kosher salt and ground black pepper

**LOBSTER SALAD**

One 1¾-pound (800-g) live Maine lobster

1 bunch upland cress or watercress

12 orange segments cut from 2 oranges (page 345)

Olive oil, preferably blood-orange oil

Fine sea salt and freshly ground pepper

To make the aioli, in a small bowl, combine the mayonnaise, orange zest, orange juice, garlic, capers and stir to blend. Add salt and pepper to taste. Cover and let sit for 1 hour at room temperature for the flavors to blend, or refrigerate for up to 3 days.

To steam the lobster, fill a large stockpot with 3 inches (7.5 cm) of water and put a wire rack the bottom. Bring the water to a boil. Dispatch the lobster (page 119). Add the lobster to the pot and steam, covered, for 9 to 11 minutes.

Alternatively, to boil the lobster, fill a large pot three-fourths full of water and bring to a boil. Add about 1 tablespoon of salt per quart (960 ml) of water. Dispatch the lobster (page 119). Add the lobster to the pot and cook for 7 to 9 minutes.

Remove the lobster from the pot, drain well, and let cool to the touch. Remove the meat from the shell and cut into attractive pieces.

In a large bowl, gently toss the cress with the orange segments, drizzle with the olive oil, and season with salt and pepper to taste. Arrange attractively with the lobster on 2 plates and drizzle aioli over all. **SERVES 2**

Étouffée (from a French word that means "smothered") is a spicy stew of shellfish served over rice. Both Creoles and Cajuns have their own versions of this iconic dish. Both use a roux for thickening and the "holy trinity" of onion, celery, and bell pepper. This is a great make-ahead recipe. Prepare the sauce, but don't add the crayfish until after reheating the sauce right before serving. Large shrimp can be substituted for the crayfish.

# CRAYFISH ÉTOUFFÉE

6 tablespoons (85 g) unsalted butter

¼ cup (30 g) unbleached all-purpose flour

1 cup (110 g) chopped white onion

¾ cup (75 g) chopped celery

¾ cup (110 g) seeded and chopped green bell pepper

3 large cloves garlic, chopped

1 teaspoon dried thyme

½ teaspoon fennel seeds

1 teaspoon Cajun or Creole seasoning, homemade (page 341) or store-bought

3 cups (720 ml) shrimp stock (page 332)

2 tablespoons tomato paste

1 tablespoon Worcestershire

½ teaspoon hot sauce

1½ pounds (680 g) crayfish tails (page 121)

¼ cup (15 g) finely chopped green onion, including green parts

2 tablespoons finely chopped fresh flat-leaf parsley

Kosher salt and freshly ground black pepper

Cooked white rice, for serving

Lemon wedges, for serving

Melt the butter in a large skillet or Dutch oven over medium heat. Gradually whisk in the flour. Cook, stirring regularly, until the roux is the color of coffee with cream, about 15 minutes. Be careful not to burn it or you'll have to start again. Reduce the heat if you think this is happening.

Stir in the onion, celery, and bell pepper and cook, stirring occasionally, until the vegetables have softened, about 7 minutes. The roux will continue to darken to a café au lait color.

Add the garlic, thyme, fennel seeds, and Cajun or Creole seasoning. Continue to cook and stir 2 minutes more. Stir in the stock, tomato paste, Worcestershire, and hot sauce. Add the crayfish tails and cook until the crayfish are firm and pink, about 8 minutes. Stir in the green onion and parsley and season to taste with salt and pepper. Serve with rice and lemon wedges to squeeze over. **SERVES 4 TO 6**

This Southern party dish can be made with either crayfish or shrimp. A classic rémoulade sauce is the perfect dip for crayfish flavored with a crayfish boil seasoning mixture, such as the one from Zatarain's, a company that dates from 1886 in New Orleans. The brand is currently owned by McCormick, and is widely available.

# PEEL 'N' EAT CRAYFISH
## with rémoulade

**RÉMOULADE SAUCE**

¾ cup (180 ml) mayonnaise

1 tablespoon finely chopped green onion

1 tablespoon cup finely chopped red bell pepper

1 tablespoon drained, coarsely chopped capers

1 tablespoon chopped fresh flat-leaf parsley

2 teaspoons prepared horseradish

1 teaspoon grainy mustard

Hot sauce and fresh lemon juice, to taste

Fine sea salt and freshly ground pepper

**CRAYFISH**

One 3-ounce (85-g) packet crawfish seasoning, preferably Zatarain's Crawfish, Shrimp and Crab Boil

2 pounds (910 g) shell-on crayfish (page 121) or deveined, shell-on shrimp (page 115)

2 teaspoons unsalted butter, melted

To make the sauce, in a small bowl, combine the mayonnaise, green onion, bell pepper, capers, parsley, horseradish, and mustard and stir to blend. Add hot sauce, lemon juice, salt, and pepper to taste. Cover and refrigerate for at least 2 hours or for up to 5 days. Stir in a tablespoon or two of lukewarm water to thin before serving, if desired.

To make the crayfish, follow the directions on the Zatarain's package, and heat a large pot of boiling salted water, then add the boil mixture. Add the crayfish and cook just until evenly pink, about 3 minutes. They will continue to cook after draining. Drain and transfer to a bowl. Add the butter and toss to coat. Serve warm or at room temperature with the rémoulade sauce for dipping. **SERVES 6 TO 8**

# THE SALMON FAMILY

## salmon, trout

The salmon family (Salmonidae) is made up of a broad range of familiar species including trout, char, whitefish, grayling, and of course, salmon. They can be found worldwide, naturally in the cool climates of the Northern Hemisphere and by introduction into the South.

# SALMON

**Almost all salmonids are anadromous, meaning they migrate upstream from the ocean or larger rivers and lakes to reproduce in protected freshwater streams and rivers. The salmonids are among the most popular and sought-after food fishes in the world, and based on archaeological evidence, they have been on human menus for thousands of years.**

The ecological health of wild salmonids varies widely with species. Some species of trout are thriving and expanding their range, while some salmon stocks teeter on the verge of extinction due to habitat loss or degradation.

Salmonids have a life history that is readily adaptable to aquaculture and a few of the trout, salmon, and char have become globally important as farmed fish. In the case of salmonids farmed in land-based, freshwater systems (trout and char), these are considered highly sustainable and often rated as great choices. The ecological impacts of species that are farmed in ocean pens, most notably Atlantic salmon, are complex, and it is important to check the certification ratings of the source farms.

From a culinary perspective, many of the salmonids are similar in taste and texture, and in most of the recipes in this chapter they can be used interchangeably. Most Americans would rank salmon as the most popular finned fish. It's delicious, easy to cook, and the most available of all fresh fish to both the home cook and restaurateurs alike.

Typically, when you buy whole fish in the Salmonidae family, it has already been cleaned and gutted. Any delay in doing this detracts from its fresh flavor.

## Wild Salmon

All commercially available wild salmon is found on the West Coast. The Pacific Ocean is home to six types of salmon, and U.S. and Canadian boats harvest five of them: chinook, coho, pink, sockeye, and chum. To confuse matters, each of these has at least one other name as well as their Latin name. They are listed here by the names you'll most likely see at markets.

**Chinook salmon** (*Oncorhynchus tshawytscha*), also known as king salmon, is considered by many to be the best-tasting of all salmon. They have a high fat content and a correspondingly rich flesh that ranges from white to a deep red color. The red color comes from the pigment found in the crustaceans that the fish eat, mostly shrimp and krill. White king salmon are genetically unable to process this pigment but are coveted in the market as being more delectable.

**Coho salmon** (*Oncorhynchus kisutch*) are sometimes called silver salmon or "silvers" because of their especially silver skin. They have a bright red flesh and a slightly more delicate texture than Chinook salmon but a similar flavor.

**Pink salmon** (*Oncorhynchus gorbuscha*) is the most common Pacific salmon. It has a lighter colored flesh with a low fat content. Because of its low fat content, the flavor is not as robust. Pink salmon are often canned but are also sold fresh, frozen, and smoked. They are sometimes called "humpies," or humpback salmon, because of the distinctive hump they develop on their back when they spawn.

**Sockeye salmon** (*Oncorhynchus nerka)* are noted for their bright red-orange flesh and deep, rich flavor. They are known as "reds," both for their dark flesh color and because they turn deep red as they move upstream to spawn.

**Chum salmon** (*Oncorhynchus keta*) is also called dog salmon for its doglike teeth. It is sometimes marketed as keta salmon, after its species name, because of the negative association of the word *chum*. It is smaller and has a lower fat content than other salmon. Chum is the salmon usually used for canning, though I often smoke it.

## Atlantic salmon (*Salmo salar*)

While the Pacific is home to several species of salmon, the Atlantic has but one, the species known simply as Atlantic salmon. It is no longer commercially available in the wild due to overfishing. Farmed salmon is almost always the Atlantic species. It was chosen primarily because it grows faster, and as a result, requires less feed to get to market size. They are, unfortunately, often fed colorants to deepen the hue of the flesh and depending on the source, antibiotics are used. These are good questions to ask before buying.

# TROUT

Trout, along with salmon, all belong to one very large group, the family Salmonidae. Referred to as salmonids, they are found around the world, not only in streams and rivers, but also in cool temperature lakes and oceans, including the Arctic.

The Salmonidae include "true" trout such as rainbow, brown, cutthroat, Gila, Apache, and golden. Other fish that we also call trout aren't really trout, but are "chars," like the lake, bull, brook, and Dolly Varden.

Though there are many opinions about which is the "best" trout, my vote would be for rainbows, which are an anadromous salmonid (fish that migrate up rivers from the sea to spawn) and very similar to salmon in terms of fight—if you are a fisherman—and eating quality. Rainbows become "steelheads" when they are at sea, even though they are still the same species. Other trout can be found in the ocean as well. Brook trout also often go to sea from northeastern North American streams but return to their home streams in winter. Anadromous brown trout and brook trout (once believed to be the same species) are both called "sea trout" when they are at sea. Anadromous cutthroat *(Oncorhynchus clarkii)* is called "sea-run cutthroat" when at sea. Many Dolly Vardens also turn anadromous.

Trout in whatever form or name is one of the premier game fishes in America. They are often hatchery-reared to seed dwindling populations in the wild, which helps continue their appeal to anglers.

Trout are also successfully farm raised. According to the U.N.-led World Summit on Sustainable Development, around 75 percent of major marine fish stocks are either depleted, overexploited, or being fished at their biological limit. Aquaculture is a way to meet the world's demand for fish without depleting wild stocks and damaging the marine environment. According to the Monterey Bay Aquarium's Seafood Watch Program, freshwater rainbow trout farmed in ponds, raceways, and recirculating systems are considered a "Best Choice" option. Most of the farmed trout in America come from the Magic Valley region of Idaho near Twin Falls, and the largest producer in the world is Clear Springs Foods.

Trout keep very well refrigerated. Like all fish that you are buying, look for clear, firm eyes and moist, slippery skin. Trout scales are so small and delicate that there is no need for scaling, and most are sold already gutted. If you have caught your own, gut immediately and keep well chilled and moist. Like all things in nature, trout's flavor will depend on what it's been eating and where it's been swimming. Trout is a delicate meat, so don't overpower it with strong bold sauces and seasonings.

# HOW TO SCALE A FISH

Holding the fish by the tail, run a scaler or the back of any kitchen knife along its length to lift off the scales; don't forget the back and belly as well as the sides of the fish. Rinse thoroughly. As this can get messy, it might be best to ask your fishmonger to do it for you.

# HOW TO FILLET A SALMON (OR ROUND FISH)

There are many ways to approach filleting a fish, depending on whether it is a flatfish or round fish. For a typical round fish, like salmon or trout: **1.** With a sharp fillet knife, cut close to the head at an angle to prevent losing too much flesh. To leave the head intact, do not cut all the way through. **2.** With the knife held flat, cut along the backbone as a guide, using long sweeping cuts to the tail—this reveals the fillet. Turn the fish over and do the same thing on the other side. You now will have two fillets.

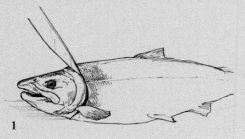

# HOW TO REMOVE PIN BONES

The pin bones are usually found at the thickest part of the fillet, not at the tail end. Run your thumb along the pin bones to make them stand out, and with long-nose pliers, grasp the bones and pull them out.

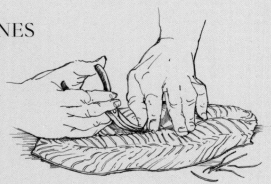

# HOW TO SKIN SALMON AND OTHER ROUND FISH

After removing pin bones, lay the fish flat and grasp the tail. Keeping the knife as close as you can to the skin, make a cut between the flesh and the skin. With your free hand, keeping the skin taut and the knife at a 30-degree angle, using a sawing motion, sliding the knife toward the head to separate the fillet from the skin.

# STOVE-TOP SMOKED SALMON

Smoking salmon on the stove-top produces much of the same flavor and aroma that you can get with a grill. Stove-top smokers are available commercially, or you can make your own by using a wok or a Dutch oven. As with the grilling method, this method works well for other types of fish such as sablefish (black cod), trout, char, or with scallops or shrimp.

## How to make a stove-top smoker

Cover the bottom of large Dutch oven or wok with heavy-duty aluminum foil. Allow for a 4-inch (10-cm) overhang so that you can seal the foil around the edges. Sprinkle a big handful (about ⅓ cup) unsoaked wood chips on the center of the foil. I like fruit woods such as apple or cherry, which have a delicate, almost sweet flavor that is good with fish.

Place a disposable aluminum pie plate on the chips to act as a drip pan and top with a metal steamer basket. The pie plate needs to be at least ½ inch (12 mm) smaller than the Dutch oven or wok to allow for smoke to circulate.

Brush skin-on salmon fillets (the skin adds flavor) with a bit of olive oil and season with salt and pepper. Place the pot or wok over high heat until the chips begin to smoke, about 5 minutes. Make sure you have a kitchen fan running on high. Place the salmon in the steamer basket in a single layer.

Place the lid on the Dutch oven or wok and crimp the edges with the foil overhang. If your wok doesn't have a lid, tent it tightly with foil, crimping the edges as much as you can.

Reduce the heat to medium and cook until the salmon is cooked to the correct degree of doneness, 7 to 10 minutes. This will, of course, depend on the thickness of the fish (or if cooking other fish or shellfish).

Off the heat and in a well-ventilated area, transfer the salmon to a serving platter. If you want a smokier flavor, leave the salmon in the covered smoker or wok for an additional few minutes.

NOTE Instead of using wood chips, you can also tea-smoke the food. This is an old Chinese technique that adds interesting flavors. See the recipe for Tea-Smoked Salmon (page 176).

This is a great dish for spring or early summer when favas, fennel, and citrus are at their best. Salmon season usually begins in late spring, too. All the vegetables requiring blanching could be done a day ahead and refrigerated. The recipe includes directions for smoking your own salmon, however good store-bought hot smoked salmon can be substituted.

# SMOKED SALMON, CITRUS, AND FAVA BEAN SALAD

**HONEY-LEMON VINAIGRETTE**

6 tablespoons (90 ml) rice vinegar

¼ cup (60 ml) fresh lemon juice

2 tablespoons honey

2 tablespoons finely chopped shallots

Pinch of cayenne pepper

¼ cup (60 ml) olive oil

Kosher salt

**SMOKED SALMON SALAD**

Four 5-ounce (140-g) skin-on salmon fillets, preferably wild, pin bones removed

1 heaping tablespoon hardwood chips, such as alder or apple

1 pound (455 g) fava beans in the pod, shelled

1 small head fennel, trimmed (fronds reserved for garnish)

2 to 3 cups (40 to 60 g) young arugula leaves, lightly packed

1 large grapefruit, cut into segments (page 345)

2 large navel oranges, cut into segments (page 345)

1 large lemon, cut into segments (page 345)

To make the vinaigrette, in a small bowl, whisk together the vinegar, lemon juice, honey, shallots, and cayenne pepper. Whisk in the olive oil and season to taste with salt. To store, cover and refrigerate for up to 5 days.

To make the salad, brush the salmon with ¼ cup (60 ml) of the vinaigrette and set aside for up to 30 minutes. Hot smoke the salmon in a stove-top smoker according to the directions on page 165.

In a medium saucepan of boiling salted water, blanch the favas for 1 to 2 minutes. Drain in a colander and plunge them into ice water. Drain and pop the skins off the beans.

Cut the fennel into paper-thin slices, preferably with a mandoline. You should have about 2 cups (200 g).

In a large bowl, toss the fennel, favas, and arugula with ⅓ cup (75 ml) of the vinaigrette and mound attractively on plates. Arrange the citrus segments around the salad. Arrange the salmon on top. Drizzle with the remaining vinaigrette, garnish with the fennel fronds, and serve. **SERVES 4**

Unlike traditional Scandinavian gravlax, which is marinated for a day or two, in this quick version the salmon is cured for just a few minutes and is served with a lemony vinaigrette.

# QUICK SALMON GRAVLAX

½ pound (225 g) salmon fillet, skin on and pin bones removed (page 164), chilled

Kosher salt and freshly ground pepper

3 tablespoons extra-virgin olive oil

Juice of 1 lemon

2 teaspoons coarsely chopped fresh flat-leaf parsley

1 teaspoon coarsely chopped fresh tarragon

1 teaspoon chopped fresh chives

2 teaspoons drained small capers

2 teaspoons cured salmon roe, rinsed

Caperberries, for garnish

Good crackers or sliced black bread, for serving

Using a sharp knife to make long, sawing strokes, cut the salmon on the diagonal into very thin slices, cutting as close to the skin as possible.

Sprinkle each of 4 plates with a little salt and pepper and lay two slices of the salmon neatly on top. Sprinkle with a little more salt and pepper and cover with plastic wrap. Set aside at room temperature for 15 minutes.

In a small bowl, whisk together the olive oil, lemon juice, parsley, tarragon, and chives. Remove the plastic wrap from over the salmon. Drizzle the herb mixture evenly over the salmon. Scatter the capers and salmon roe over the salmon. Garnish with caperberries and serve with crackers or black bread. **SERVES 4**

---

This recipe, which combines both raw and hot-smoked salmon, is a refreshing and delicious way to enjoy raw fish. Make sure to use the freshest fish you can find. Plus, who doesn't like golden, crunchy crostini? (Potato chips also make a great accompaniment.)

# SALMON TARTARE with cucumber

1 cup (140 g) finely diced English cucumber

Fine sea salt

8 ounces (225 g) sushi-quality salmon fillet, skin and pin bones removed (page 164), finely chopped

8 ounces (225 g) hot-smoked salmon fillet, skinned and finely chopped (page 165)

½ cup (120 ml) crème fraîche

6 small cornichons, finely chopped

1 small shallot, minced

¼ cup (11 g) finely chopped fresh chives

2 tablespoons finely chopped fresh dill

1 tablespoon fresh lemon juice

Freshly ground pepper

Crostini, for serving (page 343)

In a fine-mesh sieve, toss the cucumber with 2 teaspoons salt, then let stand for 20 minutes. Rinse under cold running water, drain well, and pat dry with paper towels. Transfer the cucumber to a serving bowl.

Add the fresh salmon, hot-smoked salmon, crème fraîche, cornichons, shallot, chives, dill, and lemon juice and stir gently to combine. Season with salt and pepper. Serve with the crostini. **SERVES 6 TO 8**

You'll have enough vinaigrette and Green Goddess dressing left over to use for other salads. Instead of using the avocados in the dressing, you can garnish the dish with avocado slices when serving.

# GRILLED SALMON SALAD
## with green goddess dressing

**GREEN GODDESS DRESSING**

1 small ripe avocado, pitted, peeled, and chopped

¾ cup (180 ml) buttermilk

¼ cup (60 ml) crème fraîche or sour cream

4 or 5 anchovy fillets packed in oil, drained and chopped

3 tablespoons chopped fresh flat-leaf parsley

3 tablespoons chopped fresh chives

1 tablespoon chopped fresh tarragon leaves

1 tablespoon drained and chopped capers

Fine sea salt and freshly ground pepper

Fresh lemon juice

**GRILLED SALMON SALAD**

4 salmon fillets (6 to 8 ounces/170 to 225 g each and about 1 inch/2.5 cm thick), pin bones removed (page 164)

Olive oil, for brushing

Fine sea salt and freshly ground pepper

4 cups (160 g) loosely packed mixed greens, such as frisée, cress, arugula, and/or mustard

Honey-Lemon Vinaigrette (page 167)

1 avocado, pitted, peeled, and quartered lengthwise

To make the green goddess dressing, in a food processor or blender, combine the avocado, buttermilk, crème fraîche, anchovy fillets, parsley, chives, tarragon, and capers. Pulse a few times to combine. Season to taste with the salt, pepper, and lemon juice. Use right away, or transfer to an airtight container and refrigerate for up to 3 days.

To make the salad, prepare a medium fire in a charcoal grill or preheat a gas grill to medium. Brush the grill grates clean. Generously brush the salmon fillets with oil and season generously with salt and pepper.

In a bowl, toss the salad greens with a little of the lemon vinaigrette, then arrange attractively on plates.

Grill the salmon, flesh side down, until you can lift the fillets with tongs off the grate without sticking, 4 to 5 minutes. Turn the fillets and cook them to the desired doneness, 2 to 3 minutes for medium-rare. If desired, to remove the skin, slide a spatula between the skin and flesh.

Place the fillets on top of the greens. Cut each avocado into thin slices lengthwise, then fan out and place one fan on top of each salmon fillet. Spoon the green goddess dressing over the tops and serve immediately. **SERVES 4**

The soy marinade in this dish works equally well with halibut, cod, or sea bass. The fish can be served hot or at room temperature and is terrific with the accompanying soba noodle salad. It can also be served on its own, with rice and vegetables, or cut into chunks and served over dressed greens as a salad. Roasting the salmon is a quick and easy method, but if you like you can also grill or broil it.

# GINGER-SOY SALMON
## with soba noodle salad

**GINGER-SOY SALMON**

¼ cup (60 ml) soy sauce

¼ cup (60 ml) sake or dry white wine

¼ cup (60 ml) mirin

3 tablespoons finely chopped green onion, including some green parts

3 tablespoons peeled and finely chopped fresh ginger

2 tablespoons sugar

Grated zest and juice of 1 small lemon

Four 5- or 6-ounce (140- or 170-g) wild salmon fillets with skin, pin bones removed (page 164)

Kosher salt

**SOBA NOODLE SALAD**

¼ cup (60 ml) dashi (page 334) or chicken stock (page 333)

2½ tablespoons white (shiro) miso

2 tablespoons seasoned rice wine vinegar

1 tablespoon soy sauce

2 teaspoons toasted sesame oil

⅓ cup (75 ml) canola or other neutral oil

1 tablespoon chopped sweet pickled ginger

Kosher salt

4 ounces (115 g) dried soba noodles

2 cups (280 g) peeled, seeded English or Kirby cucumbers, sliced on an angle

⅓ cup (20 g) green onions, white and green parts, thinly sliced on the diagonal

½ cup (25 g) loosely packed daikon radish (kaiware) or sunflower sprouts (optional)

1 tablespoon toasted sesame seeds (page 344)

Japanese seven-spice powder (Togorashi)

To make the salmon, in a shallow ceramic or glass baking dish, combine the soy sauce, wine, mirin, green onions, ginger, sugar, and lemon zest and juice, stirring to dissolve the sugar. Season the salmon with salt, then add it to the marinade. Refrigerate for at least 2 hours or up to 4 hours. Turn the salmon two or three times.

To make the soba noodle salad, in a blender, combine the dashi, miso, vinegar, soy sauce, and sesame oil. With the machine running, gradually add the oil to form a creamy dressing. Add the ginger and pulse a couple of times to very finely chop and incorporate.

Bring a large pot of salted water to a boil over high heat. Separate the noodles and drop them into the boiling water, stirring once or twice. When the water begins to boil again, add 1 cup (240 ml) of cold water. Repeat this procedure twice, cooking until the noodles are just tender, about 4 minutes. Drain in a colander. Rinse with cold water until completely cooled, tossing gently to remove the surface starch. Drain well.

In a salad bowl, toss the noodles with the dashi dressing, cucumbers, and green onions. Top with the sprouts, sesame seeds, and seven-spice powder.

Preheat the oven to 450°F (230°C).

Remove the salmon from the marinade, letting any excess drip off. Transfer the salmon to a rimmed baking sheet or pan and arrange in a single layer, skin side down. Roast the salmon until it's cooked through but still slightly translucent in the center, 4 to 5 minutes, depending on the thickness of the fillets. Be careful not to overcook.

Alternatively, you can grill the salmon. Prepare a medium indirect fire in a charcoal grill or preheat a gas grill to medium for indirect heat. Brush the grill grates clean. Place the fish, skin side down, on a sheet of heavy aluminum foil and place on the grill. Grill, turning once, until cooked through but slightly translucent in the center, being careful not to overcook.

Divide the noodle salad between plates and top with the salmon. Serve. **SERVES 4**

Salmon cakes are a great way to use up any small pieces left over from filleting salmon. You'll note that I call for the salmon to be both diced and finely chopped. This gives a nice texture to the finished cake. Serve the hot, crispy cakes on a bed of salad greens, topped with the aioli. Mango makes a wonderful base for an eggless aioli and is a terrific partner to these salmon cakes. The aioli is also great with grilled shellfish and other types of fish.

# SALMON CAKES
## with mango aioli

**MANGO AIOLI**

1¼ cups (205 g) ripe mango pulp (2 mangoes, peeled, pitted, and pureed)

½ teaspoon grated lime or lemon zest

2 tablespoons fresh lime or lemon juice

Big pinch of crushed red pepper flakes

1 teaspoon minced poached garlic (page 345) or roasted garlic (page 345)

¼ cup (60 ml) olive oil

Honey, to taste

Fine sea salt and freshly ground white pepper

**SALMON CAKES**

5 ounces (140 g) salmon fillet, skin and pin bones removed (page 164), cut into ¼-inch (6-mm) dice

5 ounces (140 g) salmon, fillet, skin and pin bones removed (page 164), very finely chopped

3 ounces (85 g) shrimp, cut into ¼-inch (6-mm) dice

⅔ cup (55 g) panko (Japanese bread crumbs), plus more if needed

1 egg white, beaten

2 tablespoons finely diced red and/or yellow bell pepper

1 tablespoon finely chopped green onion

2 teaspoons finely grated lemon zest

2 teaspoons mayonnaise, plus more if needed

2 teaspoons drained and chopped capers

½ teaspoon seeded and minced jalapeño chile, or to taste

Fine sea salt and freshly ground black pepper

Olive oil, for frying

4 cups (160 g) mixed salad greens, dressed lightly with extra-virgin olive oil and lemon juice, for serving

To make the aioli, in a blender, combine the mango pulp, lime zest, lime juice, red pepper flakes, and garlic and blend for a few seconds. With the machine running, gradually pour in the olive oil to form an emulsion. Season to taste with honey, salt, and pepper. Use now, or cover and refrigerate for up to 3 days.

To make the salmon cakes, in a medium bowl, combine the two cuts of salmon, the shrimp, half of the panko, the egg white, bell pepper, green onion, lemon zest, mayonnaise, capers, and jalapeño. Season with salt and pepper. It should just hold together and not be too dense and heavy. Add more panko or mayonnaise if needed. Divide the mixture and pat to form into 8 cakes, each about ¾ inch (2 cm) thick.

Put the remaining panko in a shallow bowl and season with salt and pepper. Dredge the salmon cakes in the seasoned panko. Cook now, or refrigerate, uncovered, for up to 4 hours.

In a large skillet, add enough oil to coat the bottom of the pan. Heat over medium heat until shimmering. Add the cakes and cook, turning once, until golden brown, about 3 minutes per side.

Divide the salad greens between plates and top each with a salmon cake. Serve immediately with a dollop of aioli.
**SERVES 8**

I go fishing in Alaska each summer and catch beautiful salmon, halibut, sablefish (black cod), and rockfish. Part of the catch is always smoked for later eating. My favorite is salmon, but any hot-smoked fish could be used here.

# SMOKY SALMON AND POTATO CHOWDER

3 thick slices bacon, diced

2 tablespoons unsalted butter

3 cups (270 g) thinly sliced leeks, white and some light green parts, well rinsed

Fine sea salt and freshly ground pepper

⅓ cup (75 ml) dry white vermouth or white wine

¼ teaspoon hot pimentón (Spanish smoked paprika)

3 cups (720 ml) fish stock (page 332), chicken stock (page 333), or vegetable stock (page 333)

1 cup (240 ml) water

¾ pound (340 g) fingerling potatoes, cut into ¼-inch- (6-mm-) thick rounds

½ teaspoon fennel seeds, crushed

1 cup (240 ml) crème fraîche

1 small bunch spinach, stemmed (about 2 cups/40 g loosely packed)

12 ounces (340 g) hot-smoked salmon fillet (page 165), skinned and cut into 2-inch (5-cm) chunks

Smoked or peppery extra-virgin olive oil, for garnish (optional)

In a large, heavy pot over medium-high heat, cook the bacon until brown and crisp, about 5 minutes. Using a slotted spoon, transfer to paper towels to drain.

Spoon off all but 1 tablespoon of bacon fat from the pot. Add the butter and melt over medium heat. Add the leeks and season with salt and pepper. Sauté until the leeks are soft but not browned, about 5 minutes. Stir in the vermouth and pimentón and simmer until the liquid is almost evaporated, about 3 minutes. Stir in the stock, water, potatoes, and fennel seeds and cook until the potatoes are just tender, about 15 minutes.

Stir in the crème fraîche until smooth. Taste and adjust the seasoning. Divide the spinach among 4 warmed bowls, add the smoked salmon and ladle the soup over. Sprinkle with the cooked bacon and a drizzle of smoked olive oil (if using) and serve immediately. **SERVES 4**

Fresh corn makes a delicious sauce for any fish or white meat like pork or chicken. This is an easy to prepare recipe and best when sweet summer corn is available. Any firm white fish you like can be substituted.

# PAN-ROASTED SALMON
## with seared corn sauce

3 tablespoons unsalted butter

2½ cups (365 g) fresh corn kernels (from 2 large ears)

1 cup (125 g) finely chopped onion

¼ teaspoon chipotle or other pure chile powder, or to taste

1½ cups (360 ml) chicken stock (page 333) or shrimp stock (page 332)

⅔ cup (165 ml) heavy cream

1 tablespoon dry sherry (optional)

1 tablespoon vegetable oil

Fine sea salt and freshly ground pepper

Four 6-ounce (170-g) salmon fillets, pin bones removed (page 164)

Fresh herb sprigs, such as basil, tarragon, or chervil

2 tablespoons rinsed salmon roe (optional)

In a large skillet, melt 2 tablespoons of the butter over medium-high heat. Add ½ cup (75 g) of the corn kernels and cook, stirring often, until they begin to brown on the edges. Using a slotted spoon, transfer the corn to a bowl. Add the onion, the remaining 2 cups (290 g) corn, and the chile powder to the pan and cook until the onion softens, about 3 minutes. Add the stock, cream, and sherry (if using), and continue to cook over medium heat until the mixture just begins to thicken and the vegetables are very soft, about 6 minutes.

Transfer the contents of the pan to a blender and puree until very smooth. Drain in a fine-mesh sieve set over a bowl, pressing on the solids with the back of a large spoon. Discard the solids and return the sauce to the pan. Season with salt and pepper to taste. Set the sauce aside and cover to keep warm.

In a large nonstick skillet, melt the remaining 1 tablespoon butter over medium heat. Season the salmon generously with salt and pepper. Place the salmon skin side down in the pan. Cook until the skin is lightly browned and beginning to crisp, about 4 minutes. Turn and cook on the other side for 2 minutes.

Place the salmon on warm plates. Spoon the warm sauce around and top with reserved browned kernels. Garnish with herb sprigs and salmon roe (if using). **SERVES 4**

Tea-smoking, best known for the famous Chinese dish tea-smoked duck, lends itself to many other preparations. Here, black or oolong tea adds an aromatic note to smoked salmon. You can use a commercial stove-top smoker or make your own using a wok (for more information on stove-top smoking, see page 165).

# TEA-SMOKED SALMON
## with cucumber salad

**BRINED SALMON**

1 tablespoon brown sugar

1 tablespoon kosher salt

⅓ cup (75 ml) mirin

⅔ cup (165 ml) water

One 2-inch (5-cm) piece fresh ginger, peeled and chopped

Four 6-ounce (170-g) salmon fillets, skin and pin bones removed (page 164)

**TEA-SMOKING MIXTURE**

½ cup (110 g) brown sugar

½ cup (100 g) white rice

¼ cup (4 g) black or oolong tea leaves

2 whole star anise

**CUCUMBER SALAD**

1 pound (455 g) English, Kirby, or Armenian cucumbers

2 teaspoons kosher salt

¼ cup (60 ml) rice vinegar

1 tablespoon fresh lime or lemon juice

2 teaspoons sugar

2 teaspoons toasted sesame oil

Pinch of cayenne pepper

½ small red onion, halved and thinly sliced

Sesame seeds, toasted (page 344)

2 cups (80 g) young tender frisée leaves or 2 cups (200 g) finely sliced fennel

To brine the salmon, combine the sugar, salt, mirin, water, and ginger in a bowl and stir until the sugar and salt have dissolved. Place the salmon in a single layer in a bowl and pour the brine over. Cover and refrigerate for up to 1 hour.

To smoke the salmon, line a wok with aluminum foil, fitting it tightly. To make the tea-smoking mixture, in a bowl, stir together the brown sugar, rice, tea leaves, and star anise. Add the tea-smoking mixture to the prepared wok. Remove the salmon from the brine and place it in a bamboo steamer basket or on a wire rack large enough to hold the salmon at least 2 inches (5 cm) above the tea mixture. Heat the wok over medium heat until the mixture begins to smoke. Cover, reduce the heat to low, and smoke the salmon for 10 to 12 minutes. Turn off the heat and let it smoke for another 6 to 8 minutes. The salmon should be cooked to medium-rare at this point.

To make the cucumber salad, peel, halve, and scoop the seeds out of the cucumbers. Cut them into ¼-inch (6-mm) diagonal slices and place them in a fine-mesh sieve set over a bowl. Add the salt and toss. Place a heavy pot on top to weight down the cucumber and let drain for 30 minutes. Rinse and pat dry with paper towels.

In a medium bowl, whisk the vinegar, lime juice, and sugar together until sugar is dissolved. Whisk in the sesame oil and cayenne. Taste and adjust the seasoning. Add the cucumber and onion and toss to coat. Garnish with sesame seeds.

Arrange the frisée on plates and top with the cucumber salad. Top each with a fillet of smoked salmon and serve at once. **SERVES 4**

Salmon is a perfect candidate for sous vide cooking, as it remains tender and moist thanks to this treatment. Sous vide—French for "under vacuum"—has been used for decades in commercial kitchens but has become popular with some home cooks in recent years. It's a precise method of cooking vacuum-packed (or in the case of the home kitchen, food sealed in heavy-duty, zip-top freezer bags) food slowly and evenly in low-temperature water that is circulated with the aid of a small machine. It enables you to cook anything to an exact degree of doneness and then hold it for a time before serving. If a crusty, browned surface is wanted, the food is removed from the bag and given a quick sear in a skillet or on a hot grill. The brine in this recipe helps season the fish and keeps it firm while cooking.

# SOUS VIDE SALMON
## with creamy polenta

**SALMON**

¼ cup (70 g) kosher salt

¼ cup (55 g) firmly packed brown sugar

4 cups (960 ml) cold water

Four 6-ounce (170-g) salmon fillets, pin bones removed (page 164)

Kosher salt and freshly ground pepper

3 tablespoons olive oil

**CREAMY POLENTA**

1 cup (145 g fresh; 135 g frozen) fresh or frozen corn kernels (about 1 large ear)

2 tablespoons unsalted butter

1 tablespoon finely chopped shallot

3½ cups (840 ml) chicken stock (page 333) or shrimp stock (page 332), plus more if needed

¾ cup (135 g) polenta

Kosher salt and freshly ground pepper

¼ cup (25 g) freshly grated Parmesan or Asiago cheese

Fresh basil sprigs, for garnish

To make the salmon, preheat a sous vide water bath to 118°–122°F (48°–50°C) with a circulator.

In a medium bowl, mix the salt, sugar, and water together, stirring until the salt and sugar have dissolved. Add the salmon to the brine and refrigerate for 30 minutes. Remove the salmon from the brine and pat dry with paper towels. Season very lightly with salt and pepper.

Put the fillets in a 1-gallon (3.8-l) plastic bag and add 2 tablespoons of the olive oil to prevent the fillets from sticking together. Press out as much air as you can from the bag and seal. Place the bag in the heated water bath for at least 25 minutes.

Meanwhile, make the polenta. Put the corn kernels in a food processor or blender and process until coarsely pureed. Set aside. In a medium saucepan, melt the butter over medium heat and sauté the shallot until translucent, about 2 minutes. Add the stock and bring to a boil. Very gradually whisk in the polenta in a thin stream and stir until the mixture returns to a boil. Stir in the pureed corn.

Reduce the heat and simmer, stirring occasionally, for 10 to 12 minutes or until the mixture is smooth and cooked to your liking. If you prefer a softer texture cook for a few minutes more, adding a bit more stock and being sure to stir to prevent sticking and burning. Season to taste with salt and pepper. Remove from the heat and cover to keep warm.

Remove the salmon from the water bath and remove from the bag. In a large nonstick skillet, heat the remaining 1 tablespoon olive oil over high heat. Sear the salmon, flesh side down, until a nice crust forms, about 1 minute.

Stir the cheese into the polenta. If it has thickened, add a bit more stock, stirring to loosen. Divide the polenta among 4 shallow soup bowls. Place a salmon fillet on top of each serving and garnish with basil sprigs. Serve.
**SERVES 4**

Plank-roasting is a Native American cooking technique that allows salmon to be cooked by indirect heat and at the same time to be flavored by the wood on which it is grilled. In this recipe, the salmon is given a light cure to add a spicy note to the dish.

# PLANK-ROASTED CURED SALMON

1 plank untreated cedar, oak, or alder, large enough to hold the salmon in a single layer

2 cups (480 ml) dry white wine

¼ cup (50 g) sugar

2 tablespoons kosher salt

2 teaspoons coriander seeds

2 teaspoons fennel seeds

15 whole black peppercorns

3 bay leaves

⅓ cup (17 g) snipped fresh dill

Eight 4-ounce (115-g) salmon fillets, pin bones removed (page 164)

Olive oil, for brushing

Soak the plank in water for at least 1 hour.

To cure the salmon, in a medium saucepan, combine the wine, sugar, salt, coriander seeds, fennel seeds, peppercorns, and bay leaves. Bring to a boil over high heat, then reduce the heat and simmer for 2 minutes. Remove from the heat, add the dill, and let cool completely.

Place the salmon fillets in a baking dish large enough to hold them in a single layer. Pour the curing mixture over the fillets and let the salmon cure for 30 minutes, turning once or twice. Take care not to let the curing time exceed 30 minutes, or the surface of the salmon can toughen. Remove the salmon from the cure and drain. It's okay if some of the spices or dill adheres to the salmon. Lightly brush the salmon with olive oil.

Prepare a medium fire in a charcoal grill or preheat a gas grill to medium. Remove the plank from the water and place on the grill; close the lid. Heat until the plank begins to smoke and crackle a bit, about 3 minutes. Turn the plank over and place the salmon, skin side down, on the plank. Close the lid and grill until the salmon is just cooked through, about 8 minutes depending on the thickness of salmon.

Transfer the plank with the salmon to a heatproof platter, or carefully remove the salmon from the plank and transfer it directly to a warmed platter. Serve hot or at room temperature. **SERVES 8**

## PLANK-GRILLING

Grilling on a wooden plank is a lot like using a pan, except this technique will produce delicious smoke and wood flavors. Start with a clean, untreated piece of wood about 1 inch (2.5 cm) thick and long and wide enough to hold the item you are going to cook. Typically, cedar is used but you can also use alder, oak, maple, cherry, or apple. Cooking-quality wood planks can be found on online or in many specialty food stores.

Wood burns so the plank needs to be soaked/submerged in water for at least an hour first. It is a good idea to have a spray bottle filled with water to tamp down any fire if it does begin to burn. To prevent the fish from sticking to the board, very lightly brush it with cooking oil on the side where you put the fish. Once on the plank, there is no need to turn. Be sure you close the lid of the grill so that any smoke can waft around the fish for flavor. Because it's an indirect cooking method, cooking will take longer.

Once the fish is done, you can remove the whole plank and fish with a pair of mitts. I like serving it on the board, but you can also slide the fish off onto a platter. You can get more than one use out of each plank if it hasn't burned significantly. Be sure to give it a good scrubbing before using it again.

Baking at a low temperature ensures that the salmon will be very moist but still cooked through, though it will look rare. You can also use this technique with other meaty, oily fish such as tuna. This recipe sounds complicated but it really isn't. The sauce can be made ahead of time and reheated, and simple sautéed spinach can be substituted for the chard. It's one of my favorites and goes well with softer red wine like pinot noir.

# SLOW-COOKED SALMON
## with red wine sauce and butter-braised chard

### RED WINE SAUCE

3 cups (720 ml) chicken stock (page 333) or shellfish stock (page 332)

1½ cups (360 ml) fruity dry red wine, such as pinot noir or merlot

¼ cup (35 g) minced shallots

2 tablespoons red wine vinegar

2 cloves garlic, minced

1 large sprig thyme, or 1 tablespoon dried thyme

2 tablespoons unsalted butter, at room temperature

Kosher salt and freshly ground pepper

### SALMON AND SHIITAKES

Four 6-ounce (170-g) salmon fillets, pin bones removed (page 164)

3 tablespoons olive oil

Fine sea salt and freshly ground pepper

1 tablespoon toasted sesame oil

6 ounces (170 g) stemmed and sliced or quartered shiitake mushrooms

2 teaspoons soy sauce

### SWISS CHARD

1 pound (455 g) young Swiss chard, thick stems removed

1 tablespoon olive oil

2 tablespoons unsalted butter

Fine sea salt and freshly ground pepper

Fresh lemon juice, to taste

Preheat the oven to 275°F (135°C). Line a baking sheet with parchment paper.

To make the red wine sauce, in a heavy skillet, bring the stock, wine, shallots, vinegar, garlic, and thyme to a boil over medium-high heat. Cook, stirring, until the liquid has reduced to about ¾ cup (180 ml) and is nicely thickened, about 12 minutes. Whisk in the butter in small bits until melted. Season to taste with salt and pepper. Strain through a fine-mesh sieve into a bowl and cover to keep warm.

Brush the salmon with 2 tablespoons of the olive oil and season with salt and pepper. Place the salmon on the prepared baking sheet and bake until the salmon is firm and a little white collagen appears on the bottom of the fish, 12 to 15 minutes. The white collagen is the indicator that the fish is done, even though it will look rare. You can check by using the sharp point of a knife carefully inserted in the center. Be careful not overcook the fish. You want to retain as much fat and collagen in the fish.

Wipe out the skillet then add the remaining olive oil and the sesame oil. Over medium-high heat, warm the oil until shimmering. Add the mushrooms and cook, stirring occasionally, until lightly browned but still holding their shape, 4 to 5 minutes. Add the soy sauce and salt and pepper to taste. Transfer to a bowl and cover to keep warm.

To make the chard, bring a pot of lightly salted water to a boil. Add the chard and blanch for 1 minute. Drain. Wipe out the skillet then add the olive oil and butter. Melt over medium-high heat until it begins to brown. Add the chard and cook, stirring, for 1 or 2 minutes. Season to taste with salt, pepper, and lemon juice.

To serve, place a mound of chard off-center on each of 4 warm plates. Slide a metal spatula in between the salmon and its skin, leaving the skin behind. Place the salmon on the chard and then top with the mushrooms. Spoon the sauce over the mushrooms and salmon and serve immediately. **SERVES 4**

Smoked trout is available packaged and refrigerated in many supermarkets. The maple vinaigrette and dried fruit are a sweet complement to the smoky trout. Hot-smoked salmon (page 165) or smoked mackerel can be substituted for the trout.

# SMOKED TROUT SALAD
## with maple vinaigrette

**MAPLE VINAIGRETTE**

2 tablespoons maple syrup

2 tablespoons apple cider vinegar

2 teaspoons finely chopped shallot

1 teaspoon Dijon mustard

5 tablespoons (75 ml) walnut oil

Fine sea salt and freshly ground pepper

**SMOKED TROUT SALAD**

1 small tart-sweet apple, such as Fuji, Gala, or Cosmic Crisp, quartered, cored, and cut into ¼-inch- (6-mm-) thick slices

4 large handfuls mixed young salad greens, such as arugula, spinach, cress, mâche, frisée

1 cup (50 g) salad sprouts, such as sunflower or mustard (optional)

1 smoked trout (10 ounces/280 g), skinned, boned, and broken into bite-size pieces (page 165)

¼ cup (35 g) golden raisins or dried tart cherries

3 tablespoons slivered almonds, toasted (page 344)

Fine sea salt and freshly ground pepper

To make the vinaigrette, in a small saucepan, warm the maple syrup over low heat. Whisk in the vinegar, shallot, and Dijon mustard. Whisking constantly, slowly drizzle in the walnut oil to form a light emulsion. Season with salt and pepper to taste. The vinaigrette can be made in advance, covered, and refrigerated for up to 3 days.

To make the salad, in a large serving bowl, combine the apples slices with 2 or 3 tablespoons of the vinaigrette and toss gently to coat. Add the greens, sprouts, trout, raisins, and almonds. Drizzle with some of the vinaigrette and toss to combine. Season with salt and pepper and serve, passing any remaining vinaigrette at the table.
**SERVES 4**

This recipe is a gift from my grandmother. Use any fresh herbs you have on hand. You can substitute thinly sliced pancetta for the bacon. This would be a good time to pull out your fish grilling basket if you have one; it will make it much easier to turn the fish and transfer them to and from the grill.

# GRILLED TROUT with herbs and bacon

1 tablespoon chopped fresh mint

1 tablespoon chopped sage fresh leaves

2 teaspoons grated lemon zest

2 whole trout (10 to 12 ounces/280 to 340 g), cleaned and boned (page 164)

Olive oil, for brushing

Fine sea salt and freshly ground pepper

4 slices thin bacon or pancetta

Lemon wedges, for serving

Prepare a medium fire in a charcoal grill or preheat a gas grill to medium. Brush the grill grates clean.

In a small bowl, combine the mint, sage, and lemon zest. Open the trout like a book; lay it flat on a cutting board, flesh side up. Brush with olive oil and season generously with salt and pepper. Sprinkle the herb mixture over the trout and fold it closed.

Wrap the fish with the bacon and brush lightly with olive oil. Using a grilling basket if you have one, gently place the fish on the hot grill. Cover the grill and cook about 8 minutes, turning once, or until it measures 140°F (60°C) on an instant read thermometer. Remove the basket from the grill and plate the fish, or carefully slide a large spatula or fish turner underneath the fish to transfer it to a plate. Serve with lemon wedges to squeeze over. **SERVES 2 TO 4**

Farmed fresh trout, one of the success stories for sustainable aquaculture, are generally available in most markets. This recipe pairs delicately flavored trout with a creamy white wine and balsamic vinegar sauce. Other white fish fillets, such as sole or flounder, can be substituted for the trout.

# PAN-FRIED TROUT with balsamic butter sauce

**BALSAMIC BUTTER SAUCE**

1 tablespoon olive oil

2 teaspoons finely chopped shallots

⅓ cup (75 ml) dry white wine or dry white vermouth

⅓ cup (75 ml) chicken stock (page 333) or fish stock (page 332)

3 tablespoons white balsamic vinegar

⅓ cup (75 ml) heavy cream

3 tablespoons unsalted butter

Fine sea salt and freshly ground white pepper

**PAN-FRIED TROUT**

8 trout fillets, from 4 trout (page 164)

Fine sea salt and freshly ground pepper

1 cup (180 g) cornmeal

2 tablespoons unsalted butter

2 tablespoons olive oil

2 tablespoons chopped mixed fresh herbs, such as chives and chervil

To make the sauce, in a small saucepan, heat the olive oil over medium heat and add the shallots. Cook and stir until translucent, about 2 minutes. Add the wine, stock, and vinegar. Raise the heat to medium-high and cook to reduce the liquid by half, 5 to 7 minutes.

Add the cream and cook, stirring occasionally, until the sauce has thickened, 4 to 5 minutes. Strain through a fine-mesh sieve set over a bowl. Return the sauce to the pan and reduce the heat to low. Whisk in the butter 1 tablespoon at a time; the sauce will thicken and take on a satiny sheen. Season to taste with salt and pepper. Set over a pan of warm water to keep warm for up to 2 hours.

To make the trout, season the fillets liberally with salt and pepper. Put the cornmeal in a large, shallow bowl and dredge the fillets to coat evenly; shake to remove any excess.

In a large skillet, melt the butter with the olive oil over medium heat. Carefully add the fillets to the pan and cook until golden brown, about 2 minutes on each side.

Using a metal spatula, transfer 2 fillets to each of 4 warm plates. Spoon the sauce over and around the fish, garnish with a sprinkling of herbs, and serve immediately. **SERVES 4**

Agrodolce is a Mediterranean sweet and sour onion topping that can also be used as a marinade for fish such as trout, a preparation known as escabeche. The topping can be made a day or two in advance and stored covered in the refrigerator, then reheated for serving.

# FRIED TROUT AGRODOLCE (sweet and sour)

1 cup (240 ml) extra-virgin olive oil

2 large white onions, sliced (about 5 cups/ 500 g)

5 large cloves garlic, thinly sliced

2 bay leaves

1 teaspoon black peppercorns

1⅓ cups (315 ml) white wine vinegar

½ cup (120 ml) fresh orange juice

⅓ cup (50 g) golden raisins

⅓ cup (45 g) pine nuts, toasted (page 344)

2 tablespoons honey

Fine sea salt and freshly ground pepper

8 trout fillets, from 4 trout (page 164)

1 cup (125 g) unbleached all-purpose flour

2 large eggs, beaten with 1 tablespoon water

1½ cups (120 g) panko (Japanese bread crumbs)

In a large skillet, heat ½ cup (120 ml) of olive oil over medium-low heat. Add the onions, garlic, bay leaves, and peppercorns and cook gently, stirring occasionally, until the onions are soft and golden, about 25 minutes.

Stir in the vinegar, orange juice, raisins, pine nuts, and honey. Raise the heat to medium and simmer until lightly thickened, 8 to 10 minutes. Season with salt and pepper. Set aside.

Wipe out the skillet. Rinse the trout fillets and pat them dry with paper towels. Put the flour, eggs, and panko in three separate shallow bowls. Dip the fish first in the flour, then the egg, and finally the panko, making sure that fish is evenly coated. Season generously with salt and pepper.

In a large, deep sauté pan, heat the remaining ½ cup (120 ml) of olive oil over medium heat until shimmering. Working in two batches, fry the fish, turning once, until golden, about 2 minutes on each side.

Serve 2 fillets on each of 4 warm plates, with a big dollop of the agrodolce mixture on top of the fillets. **SERVES 8**

# OTHER FINNED FISH

sablefish (black cod), catfish, rockfish, cod, lingcod, tilapia, chilean sea bass, grouper, branzino, shad

This isn't a scientific category but a group of species that use similar cooking techniques and whose flesh is also similar after cooking. It is a huge category of creatures found in both salt water and fresh water. The fish in this chapter are the ones you'll find most commonly in the American market. From a sustainability perspective, whether farmed or wild, all of these species can be good options. But because of the range and diversity, it's important to check for the approval of a certifying organization.

# SABLEFISH (BLACK COD)

Sablefish (*Anoplopoma fimbria*)—also known as black cod (though it is not a member of the cod family), butterfish, and gindara in Japan—is a richly-flavored fish with a high oil content and a buttery texture. It inhabits shelf and deep-sea waters (up to 5,000 feet/1,524 m) from central Baja California to Japan and the Bering Sea. Sablefish are extremely long-lived, some reaching over ninety years of age. For this species, life begins with winter spawning along the continental shelf at depths greater than 3,300 feet (1,006 m). It is a favorite sport fish in Alaska. It averages 8 to 10 pounds (3.6 kg to 4.5 kg) but can grow up to 40 pounds (18 kg).

Monterey Bay Aquarium rates sablefish as a "Best Choice" fish for the table. One of its great virtues is that it is nearly impossible to overcook. Even if you leave it in the pan or oven a little too long, it will still be moist and tender because of its high fat content. For those who love the overfished Chilean sea bass (which is actually Patagonian toothfish), sablefish is a great substitute. It takes well to many cooking techniques, including sautéing, baking/roasting, grilling, and steaming and is superb smoked. It's also a delicious fish for sushi and can replace the endangered yellowfin and bluefin tuna. You'll often find frozen sablefish in cryovac-packaged portions, which is very similar in taste and texture to fresh sablefish.

# CATFISH

Catfish is not beautiful, but it is good eating. Its thick, slippery skin must be removed before cooking, so fillets in the market are usually sold without the skin. Catfish are plentiful in the wild but can have a muddy taste since they are bottom feeders. Most farmed catfish don't have this problem, as they are grown in concrete-lined ponds that can be more easily cleaned. Catfish is regional delicacy in the South, served with such traditional side dishes as grits and hush puppies. Farm-raised catfish are listed as a "Best Choice" from Seafood Watch at the Monterey Bay Aquarium and are very sustainable.

# ROCKFISH

Most rockfish (*Sebastes*) are caught along the Pacific Coast. These deepwater fish range from Baja in the south all the way to the Bering Sea in the north. Over fifty Pacific species are marketed under a variety of names, such as Pacific snapper, red snapper, kelp bass, quillback, chilipepper, golden eye, canary, and vermilion. Many of the names result from their widely varied and brilliant skin colors, which range from deep reds to vibrant oranges, blues, and yellows.

Most rockfish are excellent for eating both whole and filleted and are a great alternative for halibut and tilapia in most recipes. Their flesh is tender, flaky, and mild in flavor and good for almost all cooking methods except grilling, as they tend to stick to the grill grates. If you are serving a whole fish, be sure to cut off the very sharp spiny fins before cooking or cutting into the fish.

# SNAPPERS

When it comes to snappers (*Lutjanus*) and rockfish, there is a great deal of confusion around terminology. Both live on or around reefs or rocky structures, both are often nonmigratory, and both present similarly in the market as fillets (light, firm, and mild). However, snappers (there are dozens of species) are usually from warmer, more tropical waters like the Gulf of Mexico, the South Atlantic, and the Sea of Cortez. Snappers are often associated with coral reefs, and the red snapper (*Lutjanus campechanus*) is wildly popular in the Gulf Coast region as "snapper on the halfshell."

# COD

Cod (Gadidae), a delicious, white-fleshed fish, is arguably the most important fish in human history. Fishers on both sides of the Atlantic have been catching this fish forever. Cod was an important part of the Native American diet, and it's probable that it was being harvested in Scandinavia's coastal waters before written historical records began. The search for cod propelled the Vikings to sail the Atlantic and establish outposts in Iceland, Greenland, and Newfoundland.

There are ten codfish families, with more than 200 species. Almost all live in cold salt water in the northern hemisphere. Historically, commercial fishermen have searched for five types of cod and cod-like fish: Atlantic cod, haddock, pollock, whiting, and hake.

**Atlantic cod** (*Gadus morhua*) is the most famous and commercially important of them all, having supported the food economies of northern Europe and New England for centuries. Today, this species is in recovery from this long history, but there are signs that better management is speeding up their restoration.

**Haddock** (*Melanogrammus aeglefinus*) shares a similar North Atlantic range and is also very popular. Unlike cod, which was salted for long preservation, haddock is more commonly smoked or consumed fresh.

**Pollock** (*Pollachius pollachius*) is also native to the North Atlantic, but until recently, was not as prized as cod and haddock. Today, due in part to its relative abundance, pollock is used more widely. Fish and chips and surimi (crab substitute) are commonly made from pollock.

**Whiting** (*Merlangius merlangus*) is another cod-like species that has grown in importance and popularity with the decline of Atlantic cod and haddock. It is native to the Northeast Atlantic and is a common species in Scandinavian fisheries.

**Hake** (Merlucidae family) are found in the cold waters of both the Pacific and the Atlantic and in both hemispheres. Hake features prominently in Argentina, where it is known as *merluza*.

A sixth type of fish, Pacific cod (*Gadus macrocephalus*), has been added to the list. Marketed as true cod, it's a smaller version of the Atlantic cod and is found off of Alaska.

Cod are prolific breeders, able to produce three million eggs in a spawning. They are also voracious and greedy feeders, but even they were no match for the alpha predator: humans.

The collapse of cod fisheries in the North Sea and the Grand Banks off the Northern United States and Canada was due to both overfishing and the development of mechanical harvesting techniques that took a huge harvest. You can still buy cod, of course, but even though it is a delicious, white-fleshed fish that lends itself to almost any cooking technique, it no longer dominates the market. All of the cod-like fish can be used interchangeably.

# LINGCOD

From Alaska to Baja, the lingcod (*Ophiodon elongatus*) holds a special place on West Coast fishing boats, menus, and tables. As the largest, most aggressive fish of the rocky, near-shore environment, anglers from ancient times to present love catching and eating lingcod.

Neither a ling nor a cod (but with similarities to both), they are members of the greenling family and are endemic to the West Coast. From a conservation angle, the lingcod is relatively abundant and the fishery is well managed, and there are both recreational and commercial hook-and-line fisheries. As a culinary species, they are prized for their firm, mild, cod-like meat and are prepared in a wide variety of methods from ceviche to fish tacos. Pro-tip: If you can acquire a whole lingcod, their cheeks are large, meaty, and delicious, and grilled lingcod collars prepared with a miso-sake marinade are every bit as tasty as more traditional yellowtail or black cod collars. This is a favorite species at the Hog Island Oyster Bars.

# TILAPIA

Tilapia (*Cichlidae family*) is a more affordable substitute for almost any mild, firm whitefish. Buy it from a reputable source. This is a fish that definitely tastes like what it eats. As a result, farmed tilapia tastes better than wild tilapia because the latter feeds on algae. It's a versatile fish to prepare. Most of the cooking techniques work: baking, broiling, sautéing, pan-searing, or steaming. Grilling or deep-frying tilapia is not recommended because the meat can be too chewy if you overcook it.

# CHILEAN SEA BASS

One of the most delicious fish is the Chilean sea bass (*Dissostichus eleginoides*), a deepwater species caught in southern oceans near Antarctica. It came to prominence in the late 1980s when a smart fishmonger changed its name from Patagonian toothfish to Chilean sea bass. Its creamy white flesh and mild flavor made it the darling of chefs all over America. It was and is incredibly versatile and hard to overcook.

But toothfish mature and reproduce slowly, making them vulnerable to overfishing. The lucrative returns from fishing brought pirates into the fray. Illegal catches were higher than legal ones by the 1990s and fisheries were edging towards collapse. The food service industry began to have second thoughts about serving Chilean sea bass, and more than seven hundred U.S. chefs joined forces with environmental groups for the now legendary "Take a Pass" campaign.

Recognizing the problem, the Australian Fisheries Management Authority instituted strict regulations and mounted a collaborative effort twenty years or so ago to eliminate illegal, unregulated, and unreported toothfish fishing and to devise new methods to reduce seabird bycatch. This was joined by a broad group of industry, conservation groups, and national governments.

Fast forward to today, and the Monterey Bay Aquarium Seafood Watch program has upgraded more than half of all Chilean sea bass fisheries from "Avoid" to "Best Choice" or "Good Alternative."

What does this mean for consumers? If you buy Chilean sea bass, make sure that it's from a fishery approved by the Marine Stewardship Council (MSC) and/or Seafood Watch. If a seller can't vouch for its origin, don't buy or consume it. A good alternative is sablefish (black cod), page 188.

# GROUPER

Grouper (Serranidae family) is one of the most popular species of bottom fish, highly sought after by both sportsmen and diners. Their aggressive nature, fighting ability, and the fact that they can grow to a very large size puts them in the trophy category.

The largest is the Atlantic goliath grouper (*Epinephelus itajara*), at nearly 900 pounds (408 kg). The name *grouper* is a general term applied to a large group of related sub-species (at least 100) that share similar traits, like salmon. Cooks like them because they are firm-fleshed with a mild flavor, making them a blank canvas for many preparation techniques as well as saucing and flavoring. Various species can be found from New England to South America, but Florida has the biggest population.

# BRANZINO

This Mediterranean or European sea bass is most commonly sold by its Italian name, branzino (*Dicentrarchus labrax*). A round, nonoily, warm-to-temperate-water fish, it's found predominantly in the North Atlantic and Mediterranean Sea. Similar in size and taste to American stripers, it is in fact a different species than the popular recreational fish striped American sea bass (*Morone saxatilis*), found in the eastern United States.

Though they exist in the wild, most branzino found in the market is farm-raised. Commercial farming is well established around the Mediterranean but there are concerns about environmental impacts in such a relatively small body of water. Demand is increasing in the United States and most branzino farming here is done in indoor recirculating systems. Seafood Watch lists fish raised in indoor recirculating aquaculture systems (RAS) as "Good" or "Best Choices." To make sure that any branzino is sustainably sourced just ask your fishmonger!

# SHAD

The Latin name of this fish translates to "most delicious of herrings." Shad (*Alosa sapidissima*) spends most of its time in salty waters but, like salmon, swims upriver in the spring to spawn. It is found on the east coast of North America from Canada to Florida, but is concentrated between Connecticut and North Carolina. It was introduced to the West Coast in the 1870s.

Shad has a large roe sac often called lobes, which is a celebrated spring delicacy (page 220). The fish itself has a substantial number of bones for its small size, but those who love it think its flavor outweighs the inconvenience of dealing with the bones. Shad is often smoked, grilled whole, baked, or deep-fried, but I like to poach them (see method on page 232) and remove the meat from the bones to use in fish cakes or salads. American shad are not farmed.

## OTHER FINNED FISH

**Striped bass** (*Morone saxatilis*), also known as stripers or rockfish, is a native of the East Coast. Like salmon, it swims upstream from salt water to fresh water to spawn. A most sought-after species, it has a subtly sweet flavor and takes well to most cooking methods, especially grilling and baking in a salt crust. Stripers have been introduced into lakes all over the United States, and farmed stripers are available in markets throughout the year.

**Orange roughy** (*Hoplostethus atlanticus*), although it's now more difficult to find, can substitute for almost any mild, firm whitefish when cooked correctly. It has a slightly different texture than halibut, but it has a mild, delicate flavor, and its moist, large-flaked meat stays intact even after the fish is cooked. Deep-frying or grilling is not recommended. The sustainability varies, according to Monterey Bay Aquarium, by individual species and where and how it is caught.

This recipe is from Jamie Burgess, head chef at The Boat Oyster Bar at Hog Island Oyster Farm in Marshall, California. You could serve this with a crunchy veggie slaw and roasted-pepper puree or with your favorite bowl of ramen. Smoked sablefish is also great for other fish cakes, such as the Salmon Cakes recipe on page 172, and can be used to make a beautiful warm dip, per Jamie!

# SMOKED SABLEFISH

2 tablespoons fennel seeds

1 tablespoon coriander seeds

½ teaspoon black peppercorns

1 small bay leaf, broken into small pieces

¼ cup (70 g) kosher salt

1 tablespoon dried oregano

½ teaspoon crushed red pepper flakes

⅓ cup (75 g) lightly packed dark brown sugar

2 pounds (910 g) sablefish (black cod) fillets

Olive oil, for rubbing

In a small dry skillet over medium heat, combine the fennel seeds, coriander seeds, peppercorns, and bay leaf. Cook, stirring often, just until fragrant. Transfer to a plate to cool.

In a spice grinder or using a mortar and pestle, grind the fennel seed mixture with the salt, oregano, and red pepper flakes to a powder. Transfer to a small bowl, add the sugar, and stir to blend.

Pat the fillets dry with paper towels. Line a baking sheet with plastic wrap, including enough to double back over the fish. Lay the fillets, skin side down, on the plastic wrap. Sprinkle with a thin layer of spice mixture and rub it into the flesh. Cover with the remaining mixture in a thick layer. Cover with the plastic wrap.

Refrigerate for 3 hours; the spice mixture should appear wet at this point. Rinse the fillets, leaving any residual rub on the flesh. Gently pat dry with paper towels. Lay the fillets, skin side down, on a large wire rack set on a baking sheet and refrigerate for at least 4 hours or preferably overnight.

Preheat a smoker to 190°F (90°C). Turn the fillets skin side up and rub the skin with olive oil. Place on the grill grate skin side down and smoke until the internal temperature is 140°F (60°C) on a meat thermometer, about 2 hours, depending on the thickness of the fish. This can also be done on a stove-top smoker (page 165).

Transfer the fillets to a wire rack and let cool. Can be stored in the refrigerator, covered, for up to three days.
**SERVES 6**

Baking fish in an aluminum foil packet with aromatic ingredients is not only a healthy way to cook, but locks in an abundance of flavor. This technique lends itself well to virtually any meaty fish, and I particularly like cod and halibut. This can be done in a regular or wood fired oven, on a grill, or nestled right down in the dying coals of a grill or campfire. These are also known as hobo packs, which goes back to the Great Depression when those knights of the road, "hobos," cooked a whole meal in a single container, usually a coffee can over an open fire. If you like, instead of baking, try cooking the packets over an open fire or on a charcoal or gas grill.

# BAKED SABLEFISH
## with tomatoes and capers

3 tablespoons extra-virgin olive oil

Four 5-ounce (140-g) skinless sablefish (black cod) fillets

Fine sea salt and freshly ground pepper

8 thin lemon slices (from 1 lemon)

8 sprigs fresh thyme

12 cherry or grape tomatoes, halved

2 cloves garlic, very thinly sliced

3 tablespoons coarsely chopped fresh basil and/or flat-leaf parsley

2 tablespoons drained capers

Cut four 12-inch (30.5-cm) squares of heavy-duty aluminum foil. Lay the foil sheets out in a single layer and brush with 1 tablespoon of the olive oil.

Preheat the oven to 400°F (205°C). Pat the fillets dry with paper towels and sprinkle both sides with salt and pepper. Arrange the fillets, skin side down, on the bottom half of each foil square and slide 1 lemon slice under each fillet and place another on top. Arrange 2 thyme sprigs on top of each fillet.

In a small bowl, combine the tomatoes, garlic, basil, and capers and season with salt and pepper. Spoon the tomato mixture over the fillets, dividing it equally, then fold the foil over each fillet, tenting it slightly, and crimp the edges together tightly to firmly seal.

Place the packets on a baking sheet and bake until the fish is just cooked through, 8 to 10 minutes (depending on the thickness of the fish). Though it's a little tricky to check for doneness, you can remove one packet and carefully open it, taking care not to lose any of the juices. Remember that the fish will continue to cook off heat as it sits.

Packets can also be cooked on a covered hot grill or directly on coals until the fish is just cooked through, 8 to 10 minutes (depending on the thickness of fish). Though it's a little tricky to check, you can remove one packet and carefully open, taking care not to lose any of the wonderful juices. Remember that it will continue to cook off heat as it sits.

Carefully open each packet, reserving the juices, discard the thyme, and serve. **SERVES 4**

This is one of my favorite recipes using sablefish. You can substitute any firm white fish, such as cod or halibut, for the sablefish, and any wild or domestic mushroom you like can be substituted for the chanterelles.

# SABLEFISH
## with chanterelles and parsley sauce

**PARSLEY SAUCE**

1 large clove garlic

2 cups (100 g) fresh flat-leaf parsley leaves with tender stems, lightly packed

1 cup (40 g) basil leaves, lightly packed

½ cup (120 ml) extra-virgin olive oil

Fine sea salt and freshly ground pepper

**SABLEFISH**

Four 5-to-6-ounce (140-to-170-g) sablefish (black cod) fillets

Fine sea salt and freshly ground pepper

2 tablespoons unsalted butter

1 tablespoon extra-virgin olive oil

¼ cup (60 ml) dry white vermouth or dry white wine

2 tablespoons fresh lemon juice

**CHANTERELLES**

2 tablespoons unsalted butter

1 tablespoon extra-virgin olive oil

8 ounces (225 g) chanterelles, quartered

1 tablespoon minced shallots or green onion

Fine sea salt and freshly ground pepper

1 teaspoon finely grated lemon zest

To make the sauce, bring a pot of salted water to a boil, add the garlic, and cook for 1 minute. Stir in the parsley and basil and blanch for 10 seconds. Drain in a medium-mesh wire sieve and immediately plunge into ice water to preserve the color and flavor. Drain again and squeeze as much water out of the greens as you can. Transfer the garlic and greens to a food processor or blender and puree until smooth. With the machine running, gradually add the olive oil and puree until smooth. Season to taste with salt and pepper. Transfer to a bowl.

To make the sablefish, preheat the oven to 425°F (220°C). Season the fish with salt and pepper. In a large ovenproof skillet, melt the butter with the olive oil until the butter has stopped foaming. Add the fish and cook until nicely browned on the bottom. Using a metal spatula, turn the fish over, place the pan in the oven, and cook until the fish is opaque and flakes when a fork is inserted, 4 to 5 minutes. Transfer the fish to a plate, cover, and keep warm.

Add the vermouth and lemon juice to the pan, increase the heat to high, and cook to reduce the liquid until syrupy, while scraping up any browned bits from the bottom of the pan. Stir the liquid into the parsley sauce.

To make the chanterelles, while the fish is roasting, heat a large skillet over high heat and melt the butter with the olive oil. Add the mushrooms and let them sit and sear for several seconds, then cook until they release their juices. Add the shallots and salt and pepper to taste and continue to cook until the juices have evaporated and the mushrooms are lightly browned but still holding their shape. Stir in the zest and taste for seasoning.

Spoon a generous portion of the sauce onto 4 warmed plates. Place fish on top and top with the mushrooms. Serve immediately. **SERVES 4**

A filling and complex blend of sablefish, coconut milk, curry paste, and rice noodles. Finned fish, such as salmon or halibut, or shellfish, such as shrimp and scallops, could be used in place of the sablefish. Look for fresh lime leaves, coconut milk, and Thai curry pastes in well-stocked markets; my favorite brand for coconut milk and curry paste is Mae Ploy.

# SABLEFISH COCONUT CURRY
## with vermicelli

4 ounces (115 g) thin rice noodles (vermicelli)

1 tablespoon canola oil

1 white onion, thinly sliced (about 2 cups/200 g)

1 tablespoon Thai green curry paste, or more if you like it spicier

5 cups (1.2 l) chicken stock (page 333) or vegetable stock (page 333)

2 cups (480 ml) well-shaken coconut milk

3 large fresh makrut lime leaves, bruised

2 tablespoons fish sauce

2 teaspoons chili-garlic sauce

1 tablespoon palm or brown sugar, or to taste

¼ cup (60 ml) fresh lime juice

1 pound (455 g) sablefish (black cod) fillet, skinned, boned, and cut into 2-inch (5-cm) pieces

3 cups (60 g) baby spinach leaves, loosely packed

¼ cup (15 g) diagonally sliced green onions, including green parts

Fresh Thai basil and/or cilantro sprigs, for garnish

In a medium bowl, soak the rice noodles in hot water until softened, at least 15 minutes or according to package directions.

Meanwhile, in a large soup pot heat the canola oil over medium heat. Add the onion and cook, stirring, until just softened, about 3 minutes. Add the curry paste and cook for 1 minute, then add the stock, coconut milk, makrut lime leaves, fish sauce, chili-garlic sauce, and sugar and bring to a simmer. Stir in the lime juice and cod and cook until the fish is just cooked through and opaque, about 5 minutes. Taste and adjust the seasoning.

Drain the noodles and divide among deep soup bowls along with the spinach leaves. Ladle the hot soup over and top with the green onions and Thai basil. **SERVES 4 TO 6**

The Mediterranean flavors of this dish pair well with the richness of sablefish. This recipe also works well with all kinds of meaty, firm-fleshed white fish, such as cod, halibut, salmon, or trout.

# SABLEFISH with tomatoes, pine nuts, and olives

2 tablespoons extra-virgin olive oil

4 skinless sablefish (black cod) fillets (about 5 ounces/140 g each)

Fine sea salt and freshly ground pepper

2 cloves garlic, thinly sliced

¾ cup (180 ml) shrimp stock (page 332) or chicken stock (page 333)

¼ cup (60 ml) dry white wine, such as sauvignon blanc

2 cups (270 g) grape tomatoes, halved (or quartered if large)

½ cup (75 g) pitted and slivered green olives, such as Castelvetrano

½ teaspoon chopped fresh rosemary

1 tablespoon unsalted butter, at room temperature

½ cup (65 g) pine nuts, lightly toasted (page 344)

1 tablespoon chopped fresh chives

Lemon wedges for serving

In a large nonstick skillet, heat the olive oil over medium-high heat. Add the fish, season generously with salt and pepper, and cook until lightly browned and crusty on both sides, about 5 minutes. Transfer the fish to a plate and set aside.

Add the garlic to the skillet and cook, stirring, until fragrant, about 1 minute. Add the stock and wine and bring to a boil. Cook until reduced by half, about 2 minutes. Add the tomatoes and olives. Bring to a simmer and cook, stirring occasionally, until the tomatoes begin to soften, about 2 minutes. Stir in the rosemary. Remove from the heat and whisk in the butter.

Divide the fillets between 4 shallow soup bowls. Stir the pine nuts and chives into the sauce and adjust the seasoning with salt and pepper. Spoon the sauce around the fish and serve immediately. **SERVES 4**

If you are from the South, you know catfish. Once considered food for the poor, it has been become widely popular for its versatility and sweet flavor. In fact, it is the most eaten American fish. Like fried chicken, cheese grits, and sweet tea, fried catfish is a quintessential Southern soul food. Cole slaw makes a great accompaniment.

# SOUTHERN FRIED CATFISH

1½ cups (360 ml) buttermilk

½ teaspoon hot sauce

2 pounds (910 g) skinned catfish fillets

½ cup (90 g) yellow or white cornmeal

½ cup (65 g) unbleached all-purpose flour

2 teaspoons kosher salt

1 teaspoon freshly ground pepper

¼ teaspoon garlic powder

⅛ teaspoon cayenne pepper

Peanut or vegetable oil, for frying

Tartar Sauce (page 339) or ketchup, for serving

In a small bowl, whisk the buttermilk and hot sauce together. Place the fillets in a single layer in a 13-by-9-inch (33-by-23-cm) baking dish; pour the buttermilk mixture over the fish. Cover and refrigerate for at least 4 hours or up to 8 hours, turning once or twice.

Preheat the oven to 225°F (110°C). Line a baking sheet with paper towels and top with a large wire rack.

In a shallow dish, combine the cornmeal, flour, salt, pepper, garlic powder, and cayenne and stir with a small whisk to blend. Using a metal spatula, remove one fillet at a time from the buttermilk mixture, letting the excess buttermilk drip off. Dredge the fillet in the cornmeal mixture to coat evenly, shaking off the excess. Repeat with all the remaining fillets.

In a large sauté pan or cast-iron skillet, heat 1½ inches (4 cm) of the oil until it shimmers (360°F/180°C on a deep-frying thermometer). Working in batches, transfer the fish to the oil and fry until golden brown, about 2 minutes on each side. Transfer the first batch of fried fish to the pan with the wire rack and place it in the oven to keep warm. Repeat to fry the second batch.

Serve at once, with tartar sauce. **MAKES 6 TO 8 SERVINGS**

Fish tacos, which trace their origin to Baja California, are wildly popular in the United States these days. In this recipe, the cabbage slaw and citrus salsa can be made ahead of time and the fish grilled at the last moment. Any firm-fleshed white fish, such as cod, halibut, sablefish, or tilapia can be used in place of the rockfish.

# GRILLED ROCKFISH TACOS
## with citrus salsa and cabbage slaw

**CABBAGE SLAW**

2 cups (190 g) finely shredded green cabbage

½ cup (45 g) thinly sliced red bell pepper

⅓ cup (30 g) thinly sliced red onion

2 tablespoons finely sliced mint leaves

2 tablespoons olive oil

1 tablespoon seasoned rice wine vinegar

Kosher salt and freshly ground pepper

**CITRUS SALSA**

2 small navel oranges, cut into segments (page 345)

1 small lime, cut into segments (page 345)

1 teaspoon chopped fresh cilantro

½ teaspoon seeded and minced serrano chile

1 teaspoon seasoned rice wine vinegar, or to taste

2 teaspoons olive oil

Kosher salt and freshly ground pepper

**CILANTRO CREMA**

½ cup (120 ml) Mexican crema, crème fraîche, or sour cream

1 tablespoon chopped fresh cilantro

Fresh lime juice, to taste

Kosher salt and freshly ground pepper

**ROCKFISH TACOS**

⅓ cup (75 ml) olive oil

1 tablespoon ancho or New Mexico chile powder

1 tablespoon fresh lime juice

Kosher salt and freshly ground pepper

Four 4-ounce (115-g) rockfish fillets

Eight 6-inch (15-cm) corn tortillas

To make the slaw, in a medium bowl, combine the cabbage, bell pepper, red onion, mint, olive oil, and vinegar. Gently toss and then season with salt and pepper. Use now, or cover and refrigerate for up to 24 hours.

To make the salsa, in a small bowl, combine the citrus segments, cilantro, chile, vinegar, and olive oil. Toss to combine. Season with salt and pepper.

To make the crema, in a small bowl, mix the crema and cilantro together. Season with lime juice, salt, and pepper.

To make the tacos, prepare a medium fire in a charcoal grill or preheat a gas grill to medium. Brush the grill grates clean.

In a small bowl, whisk the olive oil, chile powder, and lime juice together. Season with salt and pepper. Brush the mixture liberally on the fish fillets, place the fillets on the grill, and cook until cooked through and opaque.

When the fish is done, heat the tortillas on the grill until warm. For each serving, place 2 warm tortillas on a plate. Top with the slaw, a portion of the grilled fish, a heaping tablespoonful or two of the salsa, and a spoonful of the crema.
**SERVES 4**

The Chinese are experts at steaming fish, and this simple recipe illustrates that technique. Here we are using a bamboo steamer. You'll need a plate that fits comfortably in the basket. Serve this classic dish from Taiwan with steamed baby bok choy and rice.

# STEAMED ROCKFISH with ginger

1 whole rockfish (12 to 16 ounces/340 to 455 g), cleaned and scaled (page 164)

One 1-inch (2.5-cm) piece ginger, peeled and cut into coins, plus one 3-inch (7.5-cm) piece, peeled and julienned

2 tablespoons Chinese cooking wine, such as Shaoxing rice wine

3 tablespoons light soy sauce

2 tablespoons dried fermented black beans, soaked for 30 minutes and drained

3 green onions, sliced

¼ cup (60 ml) peanut or canola oil

Place half the ginger coins on a 12-inch (30.5-cm) heatproof plate and place the fish on top of the coins, making sure they are under the fish. Put the remaining ginger coins inside the cavity of the fish; set aside.

Pour water to a depth of 1 inch (2.5 cm) into a large sauté pan or wok and bring to a boil. Put the bottom of a bamboo or metal steamer basket on top. The water should not touch the basket. Place the plate with the fish in the steaming basket. Cover the pan with aluminum foil and steam until cooked through, about 15 minutes. To test for doneness, open the foil, and using a sharp small knife check that the fish is opaque throughout.

Using a kitchen towel and tongs, transfer the plate to a cooling rack. Pour off the excess liquid. Drizzle the fish with the wine and soy sauce and scatter the julienned ginger, black beans, and green onions over the fish. Pour the oil into a saucepan over high heat and heat until just starting to smoke. Drizzle the hot oil over the fish and serve. **SERVES 2**

---

This recipe, from chef Jamie Burgess of The Boat Oyster Bar at Hog Island Oyster Farm in Marshall, combines briefly marinated rockfish with crisp vegetables and avocado. Perfect on a hot day by the water.

# SPICY ROCKFISH CEVICHE with cucumber

1 cup (140 g) chopped cucumber

2 small serrano chiles, halved lengthwise

1 small bunch fresh cilantro, chopped, plus more for garnish

½ cup (120 ml) fresh lime juice

½ cup (120 ml) fresh navel orange juice

Finely grated zest of 2 lemons

Kosher salt and freshly ground pepper

2 pounds (910 g) rockfish fillets

1 large plum tomato, seeded and diced

½ English or Persian cucumber, cut into ⅛-inch (3-mm) half-moons

½ small red onion, thinly sliced

2 small jalapeño chiles, seeded and diced

1 ripe avocado, pitted, peeled, and diced

Broken tostadas or tortilla chips

In a blender, combine the cucumber, serranos, the small bunch of cilantro, lime and orange juice, and lemon zest; blend until smooth. Drain through a fine-mesh sieve set over a bowl for 20 minutes. Stir but don't press down on the solids, then discard the solids. Season the marinade with salt and pepper. Cut the fish into bite-size pieces. Add the fish to the marinade and mix gently to coat the fish. Cover and refrigerate for at least 1 hour, stirring once or twice.

Season the fish mixture with salt and pepper, then stir gently. Gently stir in the tomato, cucumber, red onion, and jalapeño. Using a slotted spoon, transfer the fish to individual bowls. Top with the avocado and garnish with cilantro. Serve with the tostadas alongside. **SERVES 6 TO 8**

In this classic dish from the Mexican state of Veracruz, Pacific red snapper (a type of rockfish) is cooked in a savory sauce of tomatoes, olives, raisins, and capers. Any other firm-fleshed sustainable white fish, such as halibut, Pacific cod, or tilapia, can also be used here.

# "RED SNAPPER" VERACRUZ STYLE

One 28-ounce (800-g) can diced tomatoes (preferably fire-roasted), drained and juices reserved

¼ cup (60 ml) extra-virgin olive oil

1 cup (125 g) finely chopped white onion

3 large cloves garlic, finely chopped

½ teaspoon hot pimentón (Spanish smoked paprika) or other pure ground chile

2 small bay leaves

2 tablespoons chopped fresh flat-leaf parsley

1 teaspoon dried Mexican oregano

¼ cup (40 g) chopped pitted green olives

2 tablespoons raisins

2 tablespoons drained capers

Fine sea salt and freshly ground pepper

Four 5-ounce (140-g) rockfish fillets

2 limes, cut into wedges

3 pickled jalapeño chiles, sliced into rounds (optional)

Cooked medium shrimp (page 116) and fresh cilantro sprigs, for garnish (optional)

In a medium bowl, using a potato masher or your hands, crush the tomatoes to a coarse puree.

In a large skillet, heat the olive oil over medium-high heat. Add the onion and cook until lightly browned. Add the garlic and pimentón and stir for 1 minute. Add the pureed tomatoes, bay leaves, parsley, and oregano. Simmer until the sauce thickens, about 3 minutes. Add the olives, raisins, capers, and reserved tomato juices. Simmer, stirring occasionally, until the sauce thickens again, about 5 minutes. Season to taste with salt, pepper, and more pimentón, if you like. Use now, or cover and refrigerate up to 24 hours.

Preheat the oven to 425°F (220°C). Spread ⅓ cup (75 ml) of the sauce in a glass baking dish. Arrange the fish in a single layer on top. Season generously with salt and pepper. Squeeze a wedge of lime over the fish. Spoon the remaining sauce over. Bake, uncovered, until fish is just opaque in the center, about 10 minutes depending on the thickness of the fish. Transfer the fish and sauce to warm plates. Garnish with pickled jalapeños and the shrimp and cilantro (if using). Serve with the remaining lime wedges. **SERVES 4**

The culinary technique of blackening hails from Louisiana and was made popular by famed New Orleans chef Paul Prudhomme. Coated with Cajun seasoning, foods develop a distinctive flavor by being cooked over high heat in a cast-iron skillet. Because the fish in this recipe is dipped in melted butter, then cooked in a dry skillet, it can create lots of smoke, so be sure you have good ventilation.

# BLACKENED RED SNAPPER
## with cheese grits

**CHEESE GRITS**

2 cups (480 ml) chicken stock (page 333)

2 cups (480 ml) water

2 teaspoons kosher salt, plus more for seasoning

1 cup (170 g) stone-ground yellow grits

2 tablespoons unsalted butter at room temperature

⅓ cup (30 g) freshly grated Parmesan cheese, plus more for garnish (optional)

**BLACKENED RED SNAPPER**

Four 5-to-6-ounce (140-to-170-g) skinless red snapper, catfish, or other white fish fillets

2 tablespoons extra-virgin olive oil

2 tablespoons unsalted butter, melted

2 tablespoons Cajun seasoning, homemade (page 341) or store-bought

Hot sauce, to taste

Thinly sliced green onions and lemon wedges, for serving

To make the grits, in a large saucepan, bring the stock, water, and salt to a boil over high heat. Slowly add the grits in a steady stream, whisking constantly to prevent any lumps. Bring to a boil again and continue to whisk. Turn the heat to low and simmer, stirring occasionally, until the grits are tender and thickened, 30 to 45 minutes. Stir in the butter and the ⅓ cup (30 g) of cheese. Taste and adjust the seasoning. Cover and keep warm over low heat.

While the grits cook, prepare the fish. Pat the fish fillets dry with paper towels. In a small bowl, use a small whisk to mix the olive oil and melted butter together. Brush the fish on both sides with the oil mixture, reserving the remaining mixture. Sprinkle the Cajun seasoning over both sides of the fillets to completely coat. Let the fish sit at room temperature for 20 minutes.

In a large cast-iron skillet, heat the remaining reserved oil mixture over medium-high heat. Add the fish fillets and cook, turning once, until the spices are darkened and aromatic and the fish flakes easily with a fork, 2 to 4 minutes per side.

Divide the grits among 4 serving dishes and garnish with more cheese, if desired. Place the fish on top and garnish with the hot sauce, green onions, and lemon wedges. **SERVES 4**

Fish and chips is a British national dish and a staple at Tony's Seafood, which is part of the Hog Island family. Use a thick cut of a white-fleshed fish, such as cod, haddock, or pollock. The chips are fried once to blanch them, then the fish are fried in the same pot, and finally the chips are fried a second time in the same pot to a golden brown.

# BEER-BATTERED FISH AND CHIPS

**BEER BATTER**

7 tablespoons (50 g) cornstarch

5 tablespoons (40 g) unbleached all-purpose flour

1 teaspoon baking powder

Fine sea salt and freshly ground pepper

⅔ cup (165 ml) cold stout beer, or diluted using half sparkling water

**CHIPS**

2 pounds (910 g) russet (baking) potatoes

Peanut or vegetable oil, for frying

**FISH**

Four 7-ounce (200-g) cod, haddock, pollock, or other thick white fish fillets

Fine sea salt and freshly ground pepper

2 tablespoons unbleached all-purpose flour

Malt vinegar or apple cider vinegar, for sprinkling

Tartar Sauce (page 339) or Sauce Gribiche (page 337), for serving

Lemon wedges, for serving

To make the batter, in a shallow bowl, combine the cornstarch, flour, baking powder, salt, and pepper. Using a small whisk, gradually add the beer, mixing until you have a thick, smooth batter. Cover and refrigerate for 1 hour.

To make the chips, cut the potatoes lengthwise into ½-inch- (12-mm-) thick planks, then each plank again into ½-inch- (12-mm-) thick chips. Place in a colander and rinse under cold running water. Drain thoroughly and pat dry with paper towels.

In a large Dutch oven or deep fryer, heat 2 inches (5 cm) of oil over medium-high heat until it shimmers (350°F/175°C on a deep-frying thermometer). Working in batches, cook the potatoes until limp, about 2 minutes. Using a wire-mesh skimmer, transfer the potatoes to paper towels to drain. Set aside to finish cooking later.

Preheat the oven to 250°F (120°C). Line a baking sheet with paper towels.

To cook the fillets, return the oil to 350°F (175°C). Pat the fillets dry with paper towels then season lightly with salt and pepper. Put the flour in a shallow dish. Dredge each fillet in the flour and shake off the excess. This is for a light dusting that ensures the batter will stick. Working in batches, coat each fillet in the batter then carefully lower into the hot oil and fry until batter is crisp and golden, about 5 minutes. Using a wire-mesh skimmer, transfer to the paper towels to drain. Place the pan in the oven to keep warm.

Bring the oil to 375°F (190°C) on a deep-frying thermometer and cook the blanched chips until golden and crisp, about 5 minutes.

Divide the fish and chips among warm plates. Serve with malt vinegar to sprinkle on the chips and the tartar sauce and lemon wedges for the fish. **SERVES 4**

This recipe uses the classic three-step method for coating fish for frying. You can also use this same technique for classic fried shrimp or oysters, simply substitute the same amount of large peeled and deveined shrimp or oysters for the fish. Serve with your favorite sauce, such as Tartar Sauce (page 339) or Sauce Gribiche (page 337).

# PANKO-FRIED FISH

½ cup (65 g) unbleached all-purpose flour

2 eggs beaten with 1 tablespoon water

1 cup (80 g) panko (Japanese bread crumbs)

¾ teaspoon kosher salt

½ teaspoon pimentón (Spanish smoked paprika)

¼ teaspoon granulated garlic

¼ cup (25 g) freshly grated Parmesan (optional)

Peanut or vegetable oil, for frying

1¼ pounds (570 g) cod, haddock, or halibut fillets cut into strips or bite-size pieces

Preheat the oven to 200°F (90°C). Line a baking sheet with paper towels and place a large wire rack on top of a second baking sheet. Put the flour in a shallow bowl and the egg mixture in a second shallow bowl. In a third shallow bowl, combine the panko, salt, pimentón, and garlic; stir with a small whisk to blend.

Dredge one piece of fish in the flour to coat on both sides, then dip in the egg, and then into the panko. Transfer the fish to a plate. Repeat until all fish is coated.

In a large, deep sauté pan over medium heat, heat ½ inch (12 mm) of oil over medium-high heat until it shimmers (350°F/175°C on a deep-frying thermometer). Working in batches and being careful not to crowd the pan, fry the fish until golden brown. Transfer to paper towels to drain, then place on the wire rack on the second baking sheet. Transfer the pan to the oven to keep warm. Repeat to cook all the fish. Serve immediately. **SERVES 4**

# DEEP-FRYING TIPS

- Use a neutral-flavored oil with a relatively high smoke point, such as canola, peanut, grapeseed, and corn oil.

- The sweet spot for frying is 350°F to 375°F (175°C to 190°C). At this temperature, the surface of the oil will shimmer, but the oil will not smoke. Use a deep-frying thermometer to be sure. If the oil is under 350°F (175°C), the food will absorb some of the oil and be greasy when done; if it's over 375°F (190°C), the outside of the food will be cooked before the inside is done.

- Cold food into hot fat is best. When cold food hits the hot fat, there is an immediate crisping of the surface, which helps to retard the absorption of oil. It won't make the food impervious to the oil, but it does help to make the food less greasy.

- Cut food into similar-size pieces so they'll fry at the same rate.

- To help bread-crumb coatings dry and adhere, let breaded food sit on a rack, refrigerated, for up to 30 minutes before frying.

- Fry in small batches to prevent the oil temperature from dropping too low, which can lead to greasy food.

- Let the oil come back up to frying temperature between batches.

- Briefly drain fried food on paper towels or a wire rack.

- Season food immediately after frying so the seasoning adheres to the hot food.

- If not eating right away, transfer each batch of fried food to a preheated 200°F (90°C) oven to keep it hot and crisp.

Tilapias have a mild, slightly sweet flavor which makes them a blank canvas for cooking and saucing. This "blank canvas" quality and moderate price makes them very attractive. They are farmed throughout the world and feed on algae and other aquatic plants. In this recipe, they are quickly grilled, then served with a warm sabayon flavored with fresh tarragon.

# GRILLED TILAPIA
## with herb sabayon

1 cup (240 ml) dry white wine

½ cup (70 g) minced shallots

1 teaspoon white wine vinegar

4 large egg yolks

3 tablespoons water

2 tablespoons finely chopped fresh tarragon

Fine sea salt and freshly ground white pepper

Four 7-to-8-ounce (200-to-225-g) tilapia fillets

2 tablespoons canola oil

Fresh tarragon sprigs, for garnish

Prepare a medium-hot fire in a charcoal grill, or preheat a gas grill to medium-high. Brush the grill grates clean.

In a small, heavy saucepan, combine the wine, shallots, and the vinegar. Bring to a boil over high heat and cook until the liquid is reduced to 2 tablespoons, about 6 minutes. Remove from the heat. Use now, or set aside for up to 4 hours.

In a medium metal bowl, whisk the egg yolks and water together. Set the bowl over a saucepan with about 4 inches (10 cm) of barely simmering water. Do not let the bowl touch the water. Whisk constantly until the mixture is light and foamy, about 2 minutes. Whisk in the reserved wine reduction and the chopped tarragon and whisk constantly until the mixture is thick and creamy. Season with salt and pepper. Remove from the heat and keep warm over the hot water in the saucepan.

Brush the fish with oil and sprinkle generously with salt and pepper. Place on the grill and cook until slightly charred and just barely opaque in center, about 3 minutes per side. Transfer to warm plates, spoon the warm sabayon over the fish, garnish with tarragon sprigs, and serve immediately. **SERVES 4**

This recipe for fish sliders is adapted from a dish served at the Hog Island Oyster Bar in San Francisco and created by chef Abel Padilla. While this recipe calls for lingcod, you can use any firm white fish you like from the large cod family (page 189). The cabbage-apple slaw is a crunchy, fresh complement to the sautéed fish.

# LINGCOD SLIDERS
## with napa cabbage–apple slaw

**CABBAGE-APPLE SLAW**

⅓ head small napa cabbage, cored and thinly sliced

½ small red onion, thinly sliced

1 apple, such as Fuji, cored and cut into matchsticks

⅓ cup (75 ml) apple cider vinegar

3 tablespoons mayonnaise

1 teaspoon sugar, or to taste

Fine sea salt and freshly ground pepper

**LINGCOD SLIDERS**

1 pound (455 g) lingcod fillet, cut into 4 even pieces

Kosher salt and freshly ground pepper

Olive oil

4 slider rolls, such as Acme's pain de mie rolls or King's Hawaiian sweet rolls

½ cup (120 ml) tartar sauce, homemade (page 339) or store-bought

To make the slaw, in a large bowl, combine the cabbage, onion, apple, vinegar, mayonnaise, and sugar. Toss gently to mix. Season with salt and pepper and toss again.

To make the sliders, season the fish pieces with salt and pepper. In a large, heavy skillet, add enough oil to cover the bottom. Heat over medium heat. Add the fish and cook, turning once, until golden brown on both sides, 4 to 5 minutes total.

To assemble, split the slider buns in half and smear a small amount of tartar sauce on the bottom half of each. Add a piece of fish, top with slaw and the top bun, and serve. **MAKES 4 SANDWICHES**

Ras el hanout is a fragrant spice blend—often including cinnamon, cardamom, nutmeg, anise, ginger, turmeric, and pepper—that is used in many Moroccan dishes. Here it adds spicy aroma to a sweet and tangy onion jam that is spread over silky cod fillets before baking. You can easily substitute monkfish, halibut, or rockfish fillets using this preparation. The recipe makes a bit more jam than you'll need, so you can use it with other seafood dishes or with chicken or pork.

# BAKED COD with ras el hanout onion jam

**SWEET ONION JAM**

2 tablespoons olive oil

2 large yellow onions, diced

1 teaspoon fine sea salt

1 teaspoon ras el hanout

¼ teaspoon freshly ground pepper

2 tablespoons packed light brown sugar

1 tablespoon fresh lemon juice

1 tablespoon apple cider vinegar

**BAKED COD**

Four 6-ounce (170-g) skinless cod
or other white fish fillets

Fine sea salt

½ teaspoon ras el hanout

Chopped fresh flat-leaf parsley leaves,
for garnish

Lemon wedges, for serving

To make the jam, in a medium heavy-bottomed saucepan over medium heat, warm the olive oil. Add the onions, salt, ras el hanout, and pepper, stirring to combine. Cook, stirring, until the onions start to release their liquid, about 2 minutes. Reduce the heat to low, cover, and cook, stirring occasionally, until the onions are very soft, about 30 minutes.

Remove the lid and add the brown sugar, lemon juice, and apple cider vinegar to the onions. Increase the heat to medium-low and cook, stirring occasionally, until the mixture is golden brown and reaches a jammy consistency, 15 to 20 minutes. Toward the end of cooking, stir often to avoid the jam sticking or burning. You should have about 1 cup (240 ml) jam. Set aside while you make the cod. The jam can be made up to 2 weeks in advance and stored in an airtight container in the refrigerator.

To make the cod, season both sides of each fillet with salt. Arrange the cod fillets in an ovenproof dish just large enough to hold them in one layer. Sprinkle the top of the fillets evenly with the ras el hanout. Refrigerate for 30 minutes. Preheat the oven to 375°F (190°C).

Spread about ⅔ cup (165 ml) of the onion jam on top of the cod fillets, dividing it evenly between the fillets. Bake until cooked through, about 12 minutes. Garnish with parsley and serve with lemon wedges alongside to squeeze over. **SERVES 4**

This is a recipe adapted from one by Chris Peterson, the sausage "king" at Willowside Meats in Santa Rosa, California. Serve in your favorite recipe that uses sausage, such as grilled or pan-fried with onions and peppers or in a sandwich roll. The bulk sausage mixture is also good as a filling for raviolis.

# SEAFOOD SAUSAGES

½ pound (225 g) cod or other firm fleshed white fish, patted dry and chopped

½ pound (225 g) shrimp, peeled, deveined, and chopped (page 115)

2 egg whites

2 cups (480 ml) heavy cream

1 teaspoon kosher salt

½ teaspoon freshly ground pepper

¼ cup (20 g) panko (Japanese bread crumbs)

2 tablespoons chopped fresh flat-leaf parsley

1 tablespoon chopped fresh chives

1 tablespoon chopped green onion

Big pinch *each* of cayenne pepper and pimentón (smoked Spanish paprika)

In a food processor, combine the cod and shrimp and pulse to grind. Add the egg whites, pulse briefly, then add the cream, salt, and pepper and continue pulsing until combined. The mixture should have a little texture. Transfer the mixture to a large bowl and stir in the panko, parsley, chives, green onion, cayenne, and pimentón.

Using a pastry bag or a large plastic freezer bag with one corner cut off, pipe the seafood mixture into a long log on a large piece of plastic wrap. Roll the plastic wrap up tightly in a long sausage shape about 1 inch (2.5 cm) in diameter. Twist to form 4 to 6 links. Knot or tie the ends of each link snugly with cooking string.

Bring a large pot of water to a simmer over high heat. Add the sausage links, reduce the heat to medium-low, and cover. Cook for 8 minutes, then turn off the heat and let stand (the sausages will continue to cook) for another 5 minutes, covered. Alternatively, steam the sausages in a covered steamer over simmering water for about 12 minutes. Using tongs, remove the sausages from the pot, remove and discard the plastic wrap and strings, and serve.

Sausages can be made 2 days ahead and stored refrigerated. Also, using a zip-top freezer bag, they can be stored frozen for up to 2 months. **MAKES 4 TO 6 SAUSAGES**

Annato seeds, the basis for achiote paste, are used extensively in Mexican and Caribbean cuisines. This is a classic preparation in Mexico's Yucatan state. The achiote paste contributes not only a bright orange-red color, but also a subtle flavor. You can buy prepared achiote paste in Latino markets, but the recipe below is fast and easy to make. Sea scallops can be substituted for the sea bass.

# ACHIOTE-GRILLED SEA BASS AND CITRUS SALAD

**ACHIOTE PASTE**

2 tablespoons finely ground annato seeds (sometimes labeled as achiote)

2 tablespoons chopped fresh garlic

1 tablespoon pure chile powder, such as ancho

1 tablespoon olive oil

2 teaspoons honey

2 teaspoons dried oregano, preferably Mexican

1 teaspoon whole allspice berries (about 5), toasted and ground (page 344)

1 teaspoon salt

½ teaspoon ground cinnamon

⅓ cup (75 ml) or so fresh orange or tangerine juice (enough to make a smooth paste)

**CITRUS SALAD**

¼ cup (60 ml) fresh orange or grapefruit juice

1 tablespoon sherry vinegar, or to taste

2 teaspoons peeled, finely chopped fresh ginger

Pinch of cayenne pepper

3 tablespoons olive oil

Honey, to taste

Fine sea salt and freshly ground pepper

1 tablespoon finely chopped fresh mint

2 oranges, cut into segments (page 345)

1 grapefruit, cut into segments (page 345)

2 limes, cut into segments (page 345)

**SEA BASS**

Six 5-ounce (140-g) sea bass fillets or other firm-fleshed white fish

2 cups (80 g) mixed young salad greens, such as arugula, watercress, frisée, etc.

Cilantro sprigs and avocado slices for garnish (optional)

To make the achiote paste, in a blender, combine the annato seeds, garlic, chile powder, olive oil, honey, oregano, allspice, salt, and cinnamon. With the machine running, gradually add the orange juice to make a very smooth paste. Set aside or transfer to an airtight container and refrigerate for up to 5 days.

To make the citrus salad, in a blender, combine the orange juice, vinegar, ginger, and cayenne and puree. With the machine running, gradually add the olive oil to form a light emulsion. Season to taste with honey, salt, and pepper. Stir in the mint. Pour the mixture over the citrus segments and add honey to taste. Season to taste with salt and pepper, and stir gently to combine.

Smear the achiote paste on both sides of the sea bass and marinate for at least 15 minutes.

Prepare a medium-hot fire in a charcoal grill or preheat a gas grill to medium-high. Brush the grill grates clean. Grill the fish, turning once, until just cooked through and nicely grill marked, about 7 minutes depending on the thickness of the fillet. Be careful not to overcook.

To serve, arrange the greens and citrus salad attractively on plates and place the fillets on top of the salad. Garnish with cilantro and avocado (if using), and serve immediately. **SERVES 6**

The idea for this sprang from the desire to make a hearty fish dish that could go nicely with red wine. Any hearty fish could be used here, such as halibut, sea bass, or swordfish. Ask your butcher to cut the ham hocks into pieces.

# PAN-SEARED SEA BASS
## with ham hocks and savory red wine sauce

**SAVORY RED WINE SAUCE**

2 tablespoons olive oil

2 cups (220 g) chopped onions

1 cup (140 g) peeled, chopped carrot

1 cup (100 g) chopped celery

3 ounces (85 g) cremini mushrooms, chopped (about 1 cup)

4 large cloves garlic, unpeeled

2 pounds (910 g) smoked ham hocks, cut into 2-inch (5-cm) pieces

2 cups (480 ml) hearty red wine

2 cups (480 ml) beef stock or chicken stock (page 333)

4 cups (960 ml) water

2 large bay leaves

2 whole cloves

1 teaspoon cracked black peppercorns

1 tablespoon balsamic vinegar

2 tablespoons unsalted butter, at room temperature

**PAN-SEARED SEA BASS**

1 tablespoon unsalted butter

2 teaspoons olive oil

Six 6-ounce (170-g) sea bass or grouper fillets, skin on

Fine sea salt and freshly ground pepper

To make the sauce, in a Dutch oven or other large, heavy pot, heat the olive oil over medium heat. Add the onions, carrot, celery, mushrooms, and garlic and cook until lightly browned. Add the ham hocks, wine, stock, water, bay leaves, cloves, and peppercorns. Bring to a boil, then reduce the heat to low and simmer, partially covered, until the meat is very tender and falling off the bone about 2 hours. Periodically skim off any scum or froth that rises to the surface.

Remove from the heat. Using tongs, transfer the ham hocks to a plate to cool to the touch. Pull the meat off the bones in small pieces, discarding the bones and any fat or gristle. Set the meat aside. In a medium-mesh sieve set over a bowl, strain the stock. Discard the solids. Skim the fat from the surface of the stock, or refrigerate overnight and then remove and discard the solidified fat on the surface.

Add the stock to a large, heavy saucepan (you should have about 3 cups/720 ml), add the balsamic vinegar, and cook over high heat to reduce to ⅔ cup(165 ml). Whisk in the butter. Taste and adjust the seasoning. Add the shredded ham. Set aside and keep warm to use now, or let cool, cover, and refrigerate for up to 24 hours. Warm gently to reheat before serving if refrigerated.

To make the fish, in a large, heavy skillet, melt the butter with the olive oil over high heat until the butter stops foaming. Season the fish with salt and pepper on both sides and add to the pan skin side down. Lower the heat to medium and cook until the edges of the fish begin to turn opaque, about 4 minutes. Turn and continue to cook until just opaque all the way through, about 4 minutes more.

Place the fish on warm plates and spoon the sauce around. **SERVES 6**

This is a recipe from Hog Island friend Bryan Rackley and executive chef Brian Wolfe of Kimball House in Decatur, Georgia. They note that the cheeks of Gulf grouper are the best part of the fish; they are also plentiful and inexpensive. The size of grouper cheeks varies greatly, and larger fish can have cheeks upwards of 8 ounces (225 g). Cheeks are firm, flavorful, and more forgiving to cook than fillets. Save the leftover salsa for chips and such. Lingcod, yellowtail, or sablefish cheeks may be used in place of grouper cheeks.

# BRAISED GROUPER CHEEKS
## with green tomato salsa verde

**GREEN TOMATO SALSA VERDE**

4 large green tomatoes, chopped

1 bunch green onions, coarsely chopped

3 ripe jalapeño chiles, seeded if you prefer less spice

Olive oil, for drizzling

Kosher salt

1 cup (130 g) pumpkin seeds

3 guajillo chiles, seeded and stemmed

10 cloves garlic, smashed

¾ tablespoon freshly ground pepper

¾ tablespoon ground cumin

½ tablespoon ground coriander

½ tablespoon fennel seeds, ground

2 allspice berries, ground

1½ cups (360 ml) beer

1½ cups (360 ml) water

Leaves from ½ bunch fresh cilantro, coarsely chopped

Grated zest and juice of 1 large lime

**GROUPER CHEEKS**

Six 6-to-8-ounce (170-to-225-g) grouper cheeks

Fine sea salt

Olive oil

Warm, cooked rice, preferably Carolina Gold

Fresh cilantro leaves, for garnish

Flaky sea salt, such as Maldon, for garnish

Lemon wedges, for serving

To make the salsa verde, drizzle the tomatoes, green onions, and jalapeño with olive oil and toss to coat. In a large cast-iron skillet, char the vegetables, stirring occasionally, until they are darkened (but not burned), aromatic, and tender. Season to taste with salt.

Add the pumpkin seeds, guajillo chiles, garlic, pepper, cumin, coriander, fennel, and allspice to the pan and continue to cook, being careful not to burn the garlic, until nicely caramelized and aromatic. Add the beer and water. Simmer gently, uncovered, for 10 minutes, then taste and adjust the seasoning. Remove from the heat and let cool. Working in batches, if necessary, add to a blender with the cilantro, lime zest, and juice and process to a slightly chunky sauce.

Clean the grouper cheeks of any silver skin or cartilage. Pat dry with paper towels and sprinkle lightly with salt. In a large cast-iron skillet, heat the olive oil over medium-high heat, add the cheeks, and sear until crusty and golden brown on the bottom, about 2 minutes. Using a metal spatula, turn the cheeks over carefully. Add the green tomato salsa verde to nearly cover the cheeks, bring to a gentle simmer, and cook until the fish is tender, about 7 minutes.

Serve the cheeks and salsa verde over the cooked rice. Garnish with cilantro and a sprinkle of flaky salt. Pass lemon wedges for squeezing over the fish. **SERVES 6**

This may be the simplest recipe in the book, but also one of the most satisfying. Serving the fish whole makes an impressive presentation.

# ROASTED WHOLE BRANZINO

4 small branzino (1 pound/455 g each), scaled and cleaned (page 164)

Extra-virgin olive oil, for brushing

Fine sea salt and freshly ground pepper

2 lemons, thinly sliced, plus lemon wedges, for serving

4 cloves garlic, thinly sliced

2 tablespoons capers, drained and chopped

1 small bunch fresh flat-leaf parsley

1 small bunch fresh thyme

Preheat the oven to 450°F (230°C). Lightly oil a baking sheet.

Make 3 shallow, diagonal slits on each side of each fish, taking care not to cut too deep. Pat the fish dry with a paper towel. Brush the interior and both sides of each fish liberally with olive oil and generously sprinkle with salt and pepper inside and out. Line the cavity of each fish with a few slices of the lemons, some of the garlic, ½ tablespoon of the capers, and a few sprigs of parsley and thyme. Place the fish on the baking sheet.

Roast until just cooked through, 15 to 20 minutes. Pierce the flesh with the point of a small sharp knife to make sure its cooked through. Transfer to 4 serving plates and serve with the lemon wedges. **SERVES 4**

One of the easiest and most flavorful ways to prepare a whole fish, the salt crust serves as a vehicle for sealing in flavor and juices. Traditional recipes call for mixing the salt with egg whites to form a kind of plaster, but I don't find this necessary. Leave the head and tail on the whole fish, but remove the gills. The scales are left on, as they both add flavor and make it easier to scrape off the salt. Serve with sautéed greens of your choice.

# BRANZINO BAKED IN A SALT CRUST

One 3-pound (1.4-kg) whole fish, such as branzino, rockfish, or striped bass, gutted but not scaled, gills removed

8 cups (2.3 kg) kosher salt

Extra-virgin olive oil, for drizzling

Lemon wedges, for serving

Preheat the oven to 450°F (230°C). Rinse the fish well and pat dry with paper towels.

Spread about 1 cup (290 g) of the salt in a baking dish big enough to snugly hold the fish. The tail and head can extend beyond the edge of the dish if necessary. Place the fish on top of the salt and pour the remaining salt over to completely cover the fish. Place the dish in the oven and bake until an instant-read thermometer inserted in the thickest part reads 135°F (57°C), about 40 minutes.

Remove from the oven. Brush away as much salt as you can, making sure that the salt won't get on the exposed flesh when you remove the skin. With a sharp, flexible knife, carefully scrape away the skin from the top fillet and discard. With two large spoons, remove the top fillet in neat pieces (as much as you can) and place on two warm plates. With the spoons, carefully remove the center bones and discard. Remove the bottom fillet in neat pieces and place on two additional warm plates.

Serve immediately, with olive oil and lemon wedges to drizzle over. No other seasoning is needed. **SERVES 4**

Look for deboned shad in the market, as removing the bones at home is painstaking. Here, this delicate fish is coated in melted butter, quickly broiled, and simply served with lemon wedges.

# BROILED SHAD with butter and lemon

6 tablespoons (85 g) unsalted butter, cut into small pieces

2 pounds (910 g) boned shad fillets, skin on

Fine sea salt and freshly ground pepper

1 large lemon, cut into wedges

Preheat the broiler to the highest heat. In a baking pan just large enough to hold the fillets in a single layer, melt the butter over low heat on the stove top. Rinse the shad fillets in cold water and pat dry with paper towels. Dip the fillets into the butter and turn to coat on both sides.

Broil the fish skin side down about 4 inches (10 cm) from the heat source, basting a few times with the butter in the pan, until the fish flakes easily with a fork, 6 to 8 minutes. Don't turn the shad over, and take care not to let it burn. Season with salt and pepper to taste and serve in the baking pan, with lemon wedges alongside. **SERVES 4**

---

Shad roe is a delicacy that's available only during the spring, so make the most of it when it's available. Coating the roe sacs with buttermilk and flour, frying them in bacon fat until crisp, and serving them with bacon and lemon segments is one of the best ways to enjoy this food. Nothing else is needed.

# SHAD ROE with bacon and lemon

Four 5-ounce (140-g) lobes shad roe (2 sets)

1½ cups (360 ml) buttermilk

4 slices thick-cut bacon

1 cup (125 g) unbleached all-purpose flour

Fine sea salt and freshly ground pepper

1 tablespoon olive oil

2 tablespoons minced shallot

1 tablespoon unsalted butter

1 small lemon, segmented (page 345), plus lemon wedges for serving

2 tablespoons sherry vinegar

3 tablespoons finely chopped fresh flat-leaf parsley

Add the shad roe lobes to a small bowl and pour the buttermilk over the lobes to cover the lobes. Let sit at room temperature for 1 hour.

In a large skillet over medium-low heat, cook the bacon, turning once, until browned and crisp, 5 to 8 minutes. Transfer to paper towels to drain, reserving the fat in the pan. Tear the bacon into large pieces. Set aside.

Add the flour to a shallow bowl and season with salt and pepper.

In the same skillet, heat the olive oil in the bacon fat. Remove the roe lobes from the buttermilk, allowing the excess to drip back into the dish. Dredge the lobes in the seasoned flour and add to the skillet. Turn the heat to medium-high and cook, turning once, until browned and crisp, 5 to 6 minutes total. Set aside and keep warm.

Lower the heat to medium, add the shallot to the skillet and cook, stirring, until softened, about 1 minute. Add the butter, some of the lemon segments, the sherry vinegar, and parsley and cook about 1 more minute or until the sauce is bubbling. Season lightly with salt and pepper.

Pull off and discard the thin connective tissue between the sacs of roe and place the roe on warm plates. Spoon the pan sauce over the roe and top with the bacon and additional lemon wedges. Serve right away. **SERVES 4**

# HALIBUT AND OTHER FLATFISH

## halibut, sole, flounder, monkfish

The world of flatfish is vast. They start out life with an eye on either side their head, like a round fish. As they mature, they start to swim on one side only and one eye moves over onto the dark skin side of the body. At this point, they hang out on the seabed and feed on whatever edible creatures swim by. Because they don't have to chase their food, their flesh is delicate and without much muscle. They have a simple bone structure, which is great for people who are nervous about bones (page 225 for how to fillet a flatfish). The fish in this chapter are flatfish that you'll encounter in the market. Note that monkfish and dogfish are not true flatfish but are included in this chapter because their flesh when cooked is similar to flatfish.

# HALIBUT

Halibut are the largest members of the "right-eyed" flounder family, so called because they lie on the seafloor on their left side of their bodies and have both eyes looking up from the right side.

The types commonly encountered in North America are the California halibut (*Paralichthys californicus*), Atlantic halibut (*Hippoglossus hippoglossus*), and the giant Pacific halibut (*Hippoglossus stenolepis*), which can weigh more than 400 pounds (181 kg). Halibut are predatory hunters that camouflage themselves in sandy seafloor habitats and explode up to ambush smaller fish passing by. This lifestyle makes them a firm, muscular fish, and they are prized for both flavor and texture. From a sustainability perspective, halibut require close attention with regard to capture method. Because they are bottom dwellers, some fisheries use bottom dredging, which can be very damaging to seafloor ecosystems. Hook-and-line fisheries, however, can be very sustainable and earn a "Best Choice" score with Seafood Watch. Hog Island Oyster Company works exclusively with small, hook-and-line fishers to source all of its California halibut. Atlantic halibut are also farmed, and depending on aquaculture practices, can be a great choice too.

An excellent eating fish, its meat is firm, white, and low in fat, with a mild, sweet flavor. Available both fresh and frozen, it takes to all standard preparation methods, including baking, broiling, grilling, deep-frying, and panfrying. Just be careful not to overcook it, or it can dry out and fall apart. Halibut's tender texture and clean flavor make it also a great choice for sushi, sashimi, and crudo. Any of the firm whitefish, such as sole, flounder, dogfish shark, or tilapia can be substituted.

# SOLE AND FLOUNDER

Sole (*Solea solea*) has a mild, delicate, and subtly sweet flavor. The most popular varieties in the market are Dover sole and lemon sole. Their clean-tasting flavors make them popular with chefs and food lovers. Panfrying and baking are the usual cooking methods. For example, European flounder (*Platichthys flesus*) is a flatfish with a meaty, firm texture and mildly sweet flavor. It doesn't do well on the grill because its tender flesh tends to stick to the grill grates and fall apart. Panfrying, broiling, and poaching are the preferred cooking methods for this fish.

Soles are part of the large family of flatfishes, which includes brill, dab, halibut, flounder, and turbot. Flounder is often marketed as sole. In fact, English sole, petrale sole, Dover sole, and lemon sole are all flounders. The point is that the names of flatfish often have very little to do with the species themselves; many go by more than one name, and most of them are called by a different name elsewhere.

The European Dover sole is widely acclaimed by chefs for its sweet, buttery taste and firm, meaty texture. It is easy to prepare and simple to debone. Pacific Dover sole was so named to boost its popularity, but it lacks the thickness and firmness of true Dover sole, which is better for cooking but also much more expensive.

## Pacific Sand Dabs (*Citharichthys sordidus*)

These small flounders generally weigh in at less than a pound (455 g) and measure just 6 to 8 inches (15 to 20 cm). Their natural territory stretches from the tip of Baja California to the Bering Sea, but sand dabs are considered a San Francisco delicacy, regularly found in restaurants.

Related to other popular flatfish—including Dover, English, petrale, and rex sole, it is the smallest of them all. Sand dabs have a moist, tender texture and a sweet, mild taste. Pacific sand dabs are considered a sustainable choice by Seafood Watch. The flavor of sand dabs is mild and sweet, very similar to sole.

Sand dabs are generally sold fresh and whole. Ask a fishmonger to clean them for you, if possible, and eat them within a day or two of buying or catching them. You can bread and panfry the fish (page 208). Alternatively, broil them simply with a little butter, salt, and pepper. Their bones are easily removed at the table.

# MONKFISH

Monkfish (*Lophius piscatorius*) is a scary-looking creature with a huge head and razor-sharp teeth. Don't let that put you off, however. Monkfish has a delicious flavor reminiscent of lobster, resulting in its nickname "poor man's lobster." Its firm flesh is delicately sweet.

Monkfish are found in the Northwest Atlantic and are usually sold as deboned and deveined tail fillets in most American markets. However, some fishmongers and markets will sell whole fish and even the head, which contains edible meat in the cheeks and liver—a delicacy in Japan and sushi restaurants in America.

Take care when cooking this fish, as it is very lean and tends to dry out if overcooked. Before cooking monkfish, make sure to remove the tan or gray membrane surrounding the fillets if it hasn't already been removed by your fishmonger. It's harmless but has a chewy texture and will shrink when cooked. Monkfish can be prepared using almost any cooking method, and its firmness makes it a great choice for soups and stews. It holds up well to panfrying, grilling, roasting, and baking.

## OTHER FLATFISH

**Turbot** (*Scophthalmus maximus*) is a flatfish similar to a halibut, and is native to the Northeast Atlantic region. It is also widely farmed in Europe, where it is considered a more sustainable option than wild capture. Turbot is a good substitute for almost any mild, firm whitefish. It has a subtly sweet flavor. Because of its delicate meat, gentle wet-heat cooking methods such as steaming, poaching, or cooking en papillote work best.

**Fluke** (*Paralichthys dentatus*) is a tender fish making it a great choice for raw fish dishes such as crudo, sushi, and sashimi. However, I don't recommend it for grilling or broiling because the tender meat can dry out during cooking. It substitutes well for other flatfish such as sole.

**Dogfish Shark** (*Squalus acanthias*), also known as sand shark or cape shark, lives on both the East and West Coasts and is found in many of the world's oceans. One of the most abundant shark species, it is harmless to humans. Its firm yet flaky meat is sweet and relatively high in fat, which makes it very moist. And, it has no bones, only cartilage. It's often not labeled as shark because of the negative opinion that many consumers have about shark. Dogfish shark is not a flatfish but is included here because it's a good substitute for halibut. It is excellent for grilling and smoking and makes a great chowder. The British often use it for fish and chips.

## HOW TO FILLET A FLATFISH

Remove the head and viscera of the fish (usually your fishmonger does this). **1.** Starting with the dark side up, use a long flexible filleting knife and cut down the center of the fish to the bone. **2.** Using the tip of the knife, remove the fillet from the backbone right to the edge of the fish with long sweeping strokes. Repeat on the second half of the dark side. **3.** Turn the fish over and remove the two fillets and the white side in the same way.

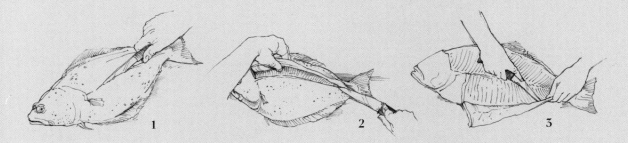

1          2          3

In this recipe from chef B Adamo, head chef of the Hog Island Oyster Bar in Larkspur, raw halibut is served in a puree of fennel, apple, and cucumber, with slices of avocado and pear. Serve this subtle-tasting and refreshing appetizer before a summer meal.

# HALIBUT CRUDO
# with fennel, green apple, and avocado

One 4-ounce (115-g) sushi-grade halibut or fluke fillet

½ small fennel bulb, trimmed

½ small green apple, peeled and cored

½ small Persian cucumber

1 tablespoon fresh lime juice, or to taste

Fine sea salt and freshly ground pepper

1 small firm, ripe avocado, pitted, peeled, and sliced

1 small pear, peeled, cored, and sliced

1 small serrano chile, very thinly sliced

3 tablespoons coarsely chopped fresh cilantro

Extra-virgin olive oil, for drizzling

Cut the halibut into small, bite-size pieces. In a food processor, combine the fennel, apple, cucumber, and lime juice and blend to a smooth puree. Season to taste with salt and pepper.

In a shallow serving bowl, layer the fish with the avocado and pear slices. Pour the fennel mixture around the edges of the layered food. Garnish with the chile, cilantro, a pinch of salt, and a drizzle of olive oil. Serve at once. **SERVES 4**

# THE CRUDO WORLD

*Crudo* is the Italian and Spanish word for "raw," and it refers to a dish of raw protein, usually fish or shellfish, usually coated with olive oil or a citrus-based sauce. Here are some similar variations of this dish:

**Carpaccio:** Raw fish or meat, thinly sliced or pounded super thin. Thinly sliced vegetables also are also served as carpaccio.

**Tartare:** Raw meat or seafood that's minced or finely diced and bound with some sort of sauce, dressing, and/or other seasonings.

**Sashimi:** A Japanese dish of raw fish that usually isn't marinated or sauced.

**Ceviche:** Raw seafood that's marinated in citrus juice to cure, or "cook" it. Found all over Latin America, its ingredients vary by locale.

**Tiradito:** A Peruvian dish of thinly sliced raw fish marinated for a short time in an acidic dressing that cures it for just a few minutes.

**Poke (pronounced poh-kay):** A raw-fish salad served as an appetizer in Hawaiian cuisine; it is commonly made with yellowfin tuna.

This recipe was inspired by chef Gustavo Arana Dagnino of Warike Restobar in Santa Rosa, California. Peruvian ceviche, also known as tiradito, differs from Mexican ceviche in that it uses a marinade called tiger's milk, made with the super-hot ají limo chile. The fish also spends a shorter amount of time marinating in this version of ceviche. Look for ají limo chile paste and the Peruvian garnishes in Latino markets or online. Be sure to use sashimi-grade white-fleshed fish.

# PERUVIAN CEVICHE
## with leche de tigre

### TIGER'S MILK MARINADE

¾ cup (180 ml) fresh lime juice

½ cup (120 ml) fish stock (page 332)

1 tablespoon chopped celery

¼ cup (60 ml) crushed ice

3 tablespoons chopped white fish, such as halibut, fluke, or flounder

1 tablespoon chopped green onion, white part only

1 tablespoon chopped fresh cilantro

1 teaspoon chopped garlic

¼ teaspoon ají limo chile paste or finely chopped jalapeno chile (optional)

½ teaspoon fine sea salt, or to taste

### FISH

6 ounces (115 g) halibut, fluke, or flounder, cubed

½ teaspoon fine sea salt, or to taste

¼ teaspoon finely diced habanero chile (optional)

2 tablespoons thinly sliced red onion

### GARNISHES (OPTIONAL)

Camote (boiled and sliced sweet potato)

Choclo (cooked corn kernels)

Cancha (Peruvian fried corn nuts)

Small sprigs of cilantro

To make the marinade, in a blender, combine the lime juice, fish stock, celery, and crushed ice and blend on high speed until liquefied. Add the chopped fish and blend until smooth. Add the green onion, cilantro, garlic, and ají limo chile and blend for 10 seconds. Strain through a fine-mesh sieve into a bowl, then return it to the blender and blend again. Add the salt.

To make the fish, in a medium bowl, mix the halibut cubes, salt, and the marinade. Add the habanero (if using) to the bowl with the halibut and give a quick stir. Don't let the fish remain in the marinade more than a few minutes; any longer and the marinade may turn the fish mushy.

Divide the ceviche among martini glasses in a mountain shape, placing the red onion on top. Decorate the marinated fish with *camote*, *choclo*, and/or *cancha* (if using). Scatter the cilantro over the top and serve. **SERVES 2 TO 3**

This is a recipe from chef B Adamo, head chef of the Hog Island Oyster Bar in Larkspur. Hog Island is dedicated to using local hook-and-line-caught halibut. This is a traditional risotto, embellished with a nice piece of buttery, fresh halibut.

# HALIBUT with lemon risotto

2 quarts (2 l) fish stock (page 332) or shellfish stock (page 332)

6 tablespoons (90 ml) extra-virgin olive oil

6 tablespoons (85 g) unsalted butter

1 medium onion, diced

3 large cloves garlic, minced

2 cups (400 g) Arborio or other risotto rice

½ cup (120 ml) dry white wine

½ cup (50 g) freshly grated Parmesan cheese

¼ cup (13 g) chopped fresh flat-leaf parsley

Finely grated zest and juice of 1 small lemon

Kosher salt and freshly ground pepper

1 pound (455 g) skinless halibut fillet, divided into 4 portions

½ cup (45 g) lightly packed pea shoots tossed with a squeeze of lemon juice

Lemon wedges, for garnish

In a deep saucepan, bring the stock to a simmer. In another heavy saucepan, over medium heat, add half the olive oil with 2 tablespoons of the butter. When the butter melts, add the onions and garlic and cook, stirring, until softened but not brown, about 3 minutes. Add the rice and stir until very lightly toasted, about 4 minutes.

Add 3 cups (720 ml) of the hot stock and the wine to the rice and continue cooking and stirring until the liquid is mostly absorbed. Continue adding stock about 1 cup (240 ml) at a time and stirring until it's mostly absorbed each time. After 6 cups (1.4 l) of the stock has been added and absorbed, start tasting the rice. Continue stirring and adding stock in ½-cup (120-ml) increments until the rice is tender but still has a bit of texture. It should be creamy, not stiff. Stir in 3 tablespoons butter, the Parmesan, parsley, and the lemon zest and juice. Season with salt and pepper. Remove from the heat and cover to keep warm.

Season both sides of the halibut lightly with salt and pepper. Heat the remaining 3 tablespoons of oil in a skillet over medium-high heat. Add the halibut and lightly brown on both sides, being careful not to flip too soon so it does not stick to the pan. Lower the heat and add the remaining 1 tablespoon of butter to melt and coat the fish.

Divide the risotto between 4 warm pasta bowls. Top each with a portion of fish and garnish with pea shoots and lemon wedges. Serve at once. **SERVES 4 TO 6**

Larb (or laab or laap) is a refreshing Thai-Lao salad, typically made with ground chicken, beef, lamb or pork with lots of assertive fresh herbs and lime juice. I use white fish here, but raw (called "green") shrimp can be substituted in part or wholly. A key ingredient is the Thai toasted rice powder, which is available at well-stocked markets or online. But it's easy to make your own with the recipe on page 342. Don't skip it.

# SEAFOOD LARB

1 pound (455 g) firm white fish fillets, such as halibut, haddock, striped bass, snapper, or rockfish, preferably skin on

Fine sea salt and freshly ground pepper

1 tablespoon canola oil, plus more as needed

1 teaspoon hot chile powder, preferably Thai or Lao, or red chile flakes

2 tablespoons fish sauce

3 tablespoons freshly squeezed lime juice

2 teaspoons sugar

⅓ cup (40 g) finely slivered red onions or shallots

2 tablespoons thinly sliced green onions, including green parts

3 tablespoons torn fresh cilantro leaves

12 torn fresh mint leaves, plus more for serving

2 tablespoons toasted rice powder, store-bought or homemade (page 342)

Butter lettuce leaves, for serving

Cucumber spears, for serving

Lime wedges, for serving

Chopped roasted peanuts, for serving

Sticky rice (page 342) or glutinous rice, for serving (optional)

Pat the fish dry with paper towels and season on both sides with salt and pepper. Heat the oil in a large nonstick skillet over medium-high heat. Working in batches if necessary, cook the fillets skin-side down until nicely browned on the bottom, then flip and cook just until done. The time will vary depending on the thickness of the fish. Add more oil if needed for a second batch. Transfer the fish to a cutting board. Remove the skin if desired, then chop the fish into bite-size chunks.

Transfer the fish to a serving bowl and gently stir in the chile powder, fish sauce, lime juice, sugar, red and green onions, cilantro, mint, and rice powder. Mix gently but thoroughly. Taste and adjust seasonings. The mixture should be tangy, salty, and pleasantly spicy.

Spoon onto a serving plate and surround with lettuce leaves, and cucumber spears, lime wedges, and peanuts. If using sticky rice, pinch some off, mold it into a small ball and dip it into the larb, scooping up a little of each ingredient. Or scoop the larb into the lettuce leaves. **SERVES 4 TO 6**

Court bouillon (French for "quick broth") is a clear, aromatic stock that is traditionally used for poaching seafood. Wine, lemon juice, or vinegar are used interchangeably. Cod or any other firm-fleshed white fish may be substituted for the halibut. Instead of the béarnaise or hollandaise sauce, you can substitute any of the compound butters on pages 334 to 335.

# POACHED HALIBUT IN COURT BOUILLON

2 cups (480 ml) dry white wine

3 cups (720 ml) water

1 small onion, chopped

1 small carrot, peeled and chopped

1 stalk celery, chopped

1 teaspoon black peppercorns, crushed

Pinch of ground cloves

2 teaspoons kosher salt

Four 5-ounce (140-g) halibut fillets

Béarnaise Sauce (page 340) or Blender Hollandaise Sauce (page 339)

Flaky sea salt

2 teaspoons chopped fresh chives

Lemon wedges, for serving

To make the court bouillon, in a large, heavy saucepan combine the wine, water, onion, carrot, celery, peppercorns, cloves, and salt. Bring to a boil over high heat, then reduce the heat to low so the mixture barely simmers. Cover and cook for 20 minutes.

Add the halibut, cover, and continue to cook at a bare simmer, until the halibut is poached and just cooked through, 5 to 7 minutes. (Use a stove top diffuser if you can't get the heat low enough.)

Using a slotted spoon, divide the fish between four warm plates. Spoon some of the court bouillon over the fish and top with some of the béarnaise sauce. Sprinkle the fish with the flaky salt and chives and serve with lemon wedges alongside. **SERVES 4**

This dish combines steamed halibut with oyster mushrooms and chard, all bathed in a pungent coconut-milk curry flavored with yellow or green curry paste. Thai curry pastes are widely available in specialty foods stores and most well-stocked markets.

# STEAMED HALIBUT
## with thai curry cream sauce and chard

**THAI CURRY CREAM**

2 tablespoons olive oil

3 ounces shiitake mushrooms, stemmed and chopped (1 cup/85 g)

⅓ cup (20 g) chopped green onion, including green parts

1 tablespoon chopped garlic

1 tablespoon peeled, chopped fresh ginger

2 tablespoons green or yellow Thai curry paste

2 cups (480 ml) shellfish stock (page 332) or fish stock (page 332)

1½ cups (360 ml) well-stirred coconut milk

¾ cup (180 ml) dry white wine

½ cup (120 ml) heavy cream

1 teaspoon finely grated lime zest

2 teaspoons fresh lime juice

Fine sea salt and freshly ground white pepper

**STEAMED HALIBUT**

Six 5-ounce (140-g) portions halibut, cut ¾ inch (2 cm) thick

Fine sea salt and freshly ground black pepper

2 teaspoons grated lime zest

12 to 16 large chard leaves, tough center rib removed

2 tablespoons olive oil

6 ounces (170 g) oyster mushrooms, sliced (about 2 cups)

⅔ cup (40 g) thinly sliced green onions, including green parts

½ cup (120 ml) fish stock (page 332) or mushroom stock

⅓ cup (75 ml) dry white wine

Cilantro sprigs and fried shallots (page 344), for garnish

To make the curry cream, in a large, heavy saucepan, heat the olive oil over medium heat and cook the mushrooms, green onion, garlic, and ginger until just beginning to color. Stir in the curry paste and continue to cook and stir for 2 minutes more. Add the stock, coconut milk, wine, and cream. Raise the heat to high and cook until the liquid is reduced by half and is a light sauce consistency, 5 to 7 minutes.

Strain the curry cream through a fine-mesh sieve set over a bowl, pressing down on the solids with the back of a large spoon. Return the curry cream to the saucepan, discarding the solids. Stir in the lime zest and juice and season to taste with salt and pepper. Cover and set aside to keep warm.

Season the halibut lightly with salt, pepper, and lime zest and set aside. In a medium pot of lightly salted boiling water, blanch the chard leaves for 5 to 10 seconds. Immediately plunge them into ice water to stop the cooking. Drain the leaves and pat them dry with paper towels. Wrap each portion of halibut in leaves to cover each portion of fish as completely as you can.

In an ovenproof skillet large enough to hold fish in one layer, heat the olive oil over medium heat. Add the mushrooms and green onions and cook, stirring, until the mushroom liquid has evaporated and they are just beginning to color.

Place the wrapped fish portions on top of the mushroom mixture and add the stock and wine. Cover, place in the oven, and cook until the fish is opaque throughout.

Using a spatula, transfer the fish and mushrooms to warm plates, dividing them equally. Pour the curry sauce around the fish and mushrooms. Garnish with cilantro sprigs and fried shallots and serve. **SERVES 6**

A variation of the marinated and seared fish served all around the Mediterranean. It's perfect for a picnic or alfresco meal since it's all made ahead. Any firm fish, such as tuna or swordfish, could be used here. In the Mediterranean, rich, oily mackerel is often served like this.

# PAN-SEARED HALIBUT
## with mediterranean marinade

**MEDITERRANEAN MARINADE**

⅔ cup (165 ml) extra-virgin olive oil

⅓ cup (35 g) finely diced oil-packed sun-dried tomatoes, drained

⅓ cup (50 g) pitted and finely diced black olives, such as niçoise or Kalamata

2 tablespoons salt-packed capers, rinsed and coarsely chopped

2 tablespoons finely chopped chives or green parts of green onion

Finely grated zest and juice of 1 large lemon

Fine sea salt and freshly ground pepper

**PAN-SEARED HALIBUT**

1½ pounds (680 g) halibut cut into 2-inch (5-cm) pieces

Fine sea salt and freshly ground pepper

1 cup (125 g) unbleached all-purpose flour

Extra-virgin olive oil, for frying

Lemon wedges, for serving

Small, fresh basil leaves, for garnish

To make the marinade, in a glass or ceramic bowl, combine the olive oil, sun-dried tomatoes, olives, capers, chives, and the lemon zest and juice. Season with salt and pepper to taste. Let sit for at least 1 hour at room temperature before using for flavors to develop.

To make the halibut, season the fish liberally with salt and pepper. Put the flour in a shallow bowl, then dredge the halibut in the flour to coat lightly. Shake off any excess. In a large, deep sauté pan, heat 1 inch (2.5 cm) of olive oil until it shimmers (350°F/175°C on a deep-frying thermometer). Working in batches, fry the fish, turning once, until golden brown on both sides, about 5 minutes total. Using a spatula, transfer the fish to paper towels to drain.

Place the fillets in a single layer in a glass or ceramic baking dish and pour the marinade over. Turn the fillets to coat on both sides. Let stand for at least 1 hour. Can be made up to 4 hours ahead. Refrigerate and cover. Allow to return to room temperature before serving.

Garnish with basil leaves and serve with lemon wedges alongside. **SERVES 4**

Oven-frying gives fish a crisp, delicate crust with a minimum of fat. The recipe calls for pure powdered chile, which uses a single type of chile like ancho, rather than chili powder, which is a blend of spices. Serve these crispy, tender fish sticks with lemon wedges and creamy tartar sauce.

# OVEN-FRIED CORNMEAL-CRUSTED FISH STICKS

¾ cup (180 ml) buttermilk

2 teaspoons grated lemon zest

¼ cup (60 ml) fresh lemon juice

5 tablespoons (75 ml) olive oil

2 tablespoons minced shallots or green onion, white part only

1 tablespoon chopped fresh thyme, or 1 teaspoon dried

3 teaspoons kosher salt

4 teaspoons pure chile powder, such as ancho or Chimayó

⅔ cup (65 g) freshly grated Parmesan

½ cup (90 g) yellow cornmeal

½ cup (40 g) panko (Japanese bread crumbs)

3 tablespoons minced fresh flat-leaf parsley and/or basil

1 cup (125 g) unbleached all-purpose flour

2½ pounds (1.2 kg) halibut, cut evenly into 1-inch- (2.5-cm-) thick sticks

Lemon wedges, for serving

Tartar Sauce (page 339), for serving

Preheat the oven to 450°F (230°C). Lightly oil a baking sheet.

In a bowl, whisk together the buttermilk, 1 teaspoon of the lemon zest, the lemon juice, 3 tablespoons of the olive oil, the shallots, thyme, 2 teaspoons of the salt, and 2 teaspoons of the chile powder.

In another shallow bowl, combine the Parmesan, cornmeal, panko, parsley, the remaining 1 teaspoon lemon zest, the remaining 1 teaspoon salt, and the remaining 2 teaspoons chile powder. Place the flour in a third shallow bowl.

Dredge the fish in the flour to lightly coat on both sides, shaking off the excess. Dip the fish into the buttermilk mixture and then into the cornmeal mixture to completely and evenly coat. Arrange the fish on the prepared pan, allowing space between each piece. Drizzle with the remaining 2 tablespoons olive oil over and bake until the fish is crisp and opaque throughout, 8 to 10 minutes.

Serve immediately, with lemon wedges and tartar sauce for dipping. **SERVES 6 TO 8**

These "dumplings" are a classic French recipe. Traditionally, they are made with pike, but they can be made with any nonflaky white fish, such as sole. Here, they are served covered with a creamy shrimp sauce and topped with fresh chives.

# SOLE QUENELLES
## with creamy shrimp sauce

**SOLE QUENELLES**

1 pound (455 g) boneless sole fillets (page 225)

½ teaspoon fine sea salt

Big pinch *each* of ground white pepper and ground nutmeg

3 egg whites, lightly beaten

2 cups (480 ml) heavy cream

**CREAMY SHRIMP SAUCE**

1 cup (240 ml) shellfish stock (page 332)

¼ cup (60 ml) dry vermouth

2 teaspoons minced shallot

¾ cup (180 ml) heavy cream

4 tablespoons (55 g) cold unsalted butter, diced

Kosher salt and freshly ground white pepper

½ cup (85 g) diced cooked shrimp (page 115) or crayfish tails (page 121)

Chopped fresh chives, for garnish

To make the quenelles, check the sole for any stray bones, then add to a food processor. Add the salt, pepper, and nutmeg. With the machine running, add the egg whites one at a time through the feeder tube until the mixture is very fine and slightly sticky. Spoon it into a medium bowl.

In a deep bowl, using a whisk or an electric mixer, beat the 2 cups (480 ml) of cream until thickened and soft peaks form. Using a rubber spatula, gradually fold it into the fish mixture, making sure each spoonful has been completely absorbed before adding the next. Cover the bowl tightly with plastic wrap and refrigerate for at least 4 hours or up to overnight.

Bring a wide pan with 2 inches (5 cm) of lightly salted water to a boil, then reduce the heat to a bare simmer. Using two tablespoons dipped into the hot water, use one to take a generous scoop of the mousse and use the second spoon's concave side to shape the mousse into an egg-shaped oval. Slip the quenelle into the simmering water. Repeat for each quenelle.

Poach the quenelles until slightly firm and springy to the touch, 6 to 8 minutes. Flip them over and cook on the second side until cooked through, about 3 minutes longer. Transfer the quenelles to a plate and let cool, draining off any excess water that seeps out. Place the quenelles in a shallow baking dish in one layer. Use now, or cover and refrigerate for up to 2 days.

Make the sauce before serving. In a small saucepan, combine the stock, vermouth, and shallot. Bring to a boil over high heat and cook until the liquid has reduced by half. Add the cream and boil again until the sauce has thickened slightly. Strain the sauce through a fine-mesh strainer set over a bowl. Return the strained sauce to the pan, and whisk in the butter one piece at a time to make a very creamy sauce. Taste and adjust the seasoning and stir in the shrimp. Keep the sauce warm over a pan of hot water.

Preheat the oven to 400°F (205°C). Add the sauce to the baking dish with the quenelles; it should come halfway up the sides of the quenelles. Bake until the quenelles are warm through and the sauce is bubbling, about 20 minutes. Serve the quenelles and the sauce divided among warm plates and garnished with chives. **SERVES 6**

Part of the big flounder family, petrale is a delicious fish and a San Francisco favorite. Any sole or other flatfish could be used here. The fillets can vary in size quite a bit in the market, so choose ones that are about the same size to make cooking and portioning easier.

# PETRALE SOLE with green peppercorn sauce

**GREEN PEPPERCORN SAUCE**

1 tablespoon olive oil

3 tablespoons finely chopped shallots

1 cup (240 ml) chicken stock (page 333)

⅔ cup (165 ml) heavy cream

¼ cup (60 ml) Cognac or brandy

2 tablespoons dry white wine

1 teaspoon grainy Dijon mustard

2 tablespoons green peppercorns in brine, drained

½ teaspoon chopped fresh thyme

Fine sea salt and ground white pepper

**PAN-FRIED SOLE**

1 cup (160 g) rice flour

2 tablespoons unsalted butter

2 tablespoons olive oil

1¼ pounds (570 g) petrale sole fillets

Fine sea salt and ground white pepper

Upland cress or watercress, for garnish

To make the sauce, in a heavy saucepan, heat the olive oil over medium-high heat. Add the shallots and cook until softened but not browned, about 2 minutes. Add the stock, raise the heat to high, and bring to a boil, using a wooden spoon to scrape up any browned bits from the bottom of the pan. Cook to reduce to about ¼ cup (60 ml), about 6 minutes. Add the cream, Cognac, wine, mustard, and green peppercorns and cook until thickened, about 4 minutes. Stir in the thyme and season with salt and pepper to taste. Set aside and keep warm over hot water.

Put the rice flour in a shallow bowl. In a large skillet, melt the butter with the olive oil over medium heat. Dredge the sole fillets in the flour and sauté, turning once, until golden on both sides, about 4 minutes total. Season with salt and pepper. Serve, topped with the green peppercorn sauce and garnished with cress. **SERVES 4**

---

Serve these pan-fried San Francisco favorites simply, with steamed and buttered new potatoes tossed with chopped fresh parsley.

# SAND DABS with lemon-caper vinaigrette

**LEMON-CAPER VINAIGRETTE**

1 lemon, segmented (page 345) and diced

1½ tablespoons drained capers, coarsely chopped, with 2 teaspoons caper juice reserved

1 tablespoon chopped fresh flat-leaf parsley

2 teaspoons minced shallot

6 tablespoons (90 ml) extra-virgin olive oil

Kosher salt and freshly ground pepper

**PAN-FRIED SAND DABS**

1 cup (125 g) unbleached all-purpose flour

Kosher salt and freshly ground pepper

Big pinch of pimentón (smoked paprika)

2 tablespoons extra-virgin olive oil

2 pounds (910 g) sand dabs, about 4 ounces (115 g) each

To make the vinaigrette, in a small bowl, combine the lemon, capers, caper juice, parsley, and shallot. Gradually whisk in the olive oil. Season to taste with salt and pepper.

Put the flour in a shallow bowl, add a big pinch of salt, pepper, and pimentón, and stir with a small whisk to blend. Heat 2 large skillets over medium-high heat. Add 1 tablespoon of oil to each skillet and swirl to coat the bottom. Dredge the sand dabs in the seasoned flour to coat evenly. Shaking off the excess, transfer to a plate. Add the coated fish to the skillets and reduce the heat to medium. Panfry on both sides until golden brown, about 3 minutes per side, depending on the thickness. Place on warm plates and top with the vinaigrette. Serve. **SERVES 4**

This recipe from chef B Adamo, head chef of Hog Island Oyster Bar in Larkspur, was inspired by her Italian grandmother and features caponata, a sweet and savory cooked eggplant relish. She notes, "My nonna used to make caponata every year with her home-grown vegetables and serve it with fish fillets and pasta or sometimes pork or chicken cutlets. As a kid, I especially loved the sweet and savory flavors of this dish."

# PETRALE SOLE CAPONATA

**CAPONATA**

1 large globe eggplant

Fine sea salt and freshly ground pepper

Olive oil

½ yellow onion, diced

2 stalks celery, diced

½ red bell pepper, seeded and diced

1 large clove garlic, minced

16 small cherry tomatoes, halved

1 tablespoon drained capers

3 tablespoons red wine vinegar

1 teaspoon sugar

Kosher salt and freshly ground pepper

**PAN-FRIED SOLE**

1 pound (455 g) petrale sole fillets

Kosher salt and freshly ground pepper

1 cup (125 g) unbleached all-purpose flour

1 large egg beaten with 1 tablespoon water

1 cup (80 g) panko (Japanese bread crumbs)

3 tablespoons clarified butter (page 345), or 1 tablespoon unsalted butter and 2 tablespoons olive oil

Torn fresh basil leaves and chopped fresh flat-leaf parsley, for garnish

To make the caponata, cut the unpeeled eggplant into 1-inch (2.5-cm) square pieces. In a medium bowl, season the eggplant with salt and pepper and toss with enough olive oil to just coat.

In a large skillet, heat enough olive oil to just cover the bottom over medium-high heat. Add the eggplant and cook, stirring, until it is just beginning to brown. Using a slotted spoon transfer the eggplant to a bowl.

Reduce the heat to medium and add 1 tablespoon of olive oil to the pan. Add the onion, celery, and bell pepper and cook, stirring occasionally, until tender, about 5 minutes. Add the garlic and cook, stirring, for 2 minutes. Toss in the cherry tomatoes and cook, stirring, until the tomatoes just begin to split. Stir in the capers, vinegar, and sugar. Return the eggplant to the pan and simmer for 4 minutes to let the flavors marry. Season with salt and pepper. Taste and adjust the seasoning.

To make the sole, line a baking sheet with paper towels. Pat the petrale fillets dry with paper towels and season with salt and pepper. Put the flour in a shallow bowl. Put the egg mixture in a second shallow bowl. Put the panko in a third shallow bowl.

Gently dredge the fillets in the flour until coated evenly then shake off the excess flour. One at a time, dip the floured fillets in the egg and then in the panko to evenly coat. Transfer the coated fillets to a plate.

In a large skillet, heat the clarified butter over medium heat. Working in batches, cook the breaded fillets until golden brown, about 4 minutes. Turn and brown on the other side. Using a spatula, transfer the fillets to the paper-towel-lined baking sheet to drain.

Serve the fillets with a generous scoop of caponata on top, garnished with basil and parsley. **SERVES 4**

This classic recipe makes good use of quick-cooking flounder, sole or other small flatfish fillets. The toasted almond–butter sauce comes together quickly. Browning the butter adds a depth of flavor. If you leave out the almonds and capers this becomes a meunière sauce, another French classic. This illustrates the Pan-Deglazing Sauce (page 340), which is a simple classic sauce you can make with any pan-sautéed fish.

# FLOUNDER AMANDINE

1 cup (240 ml) milk

1 cup (125 g) flour, preferably Wondra

2 teaspoons pimentón (Spanish smoked paprika)

1½ pounds (680 g) boned and skinned flounder or sole fillets (page 225)

Kosher salt and freshly ground pepper

½ cup (115 g) unsalted butter

½ cup (50 g) sliced almonds

2 tablespoons fresh lemon juice

2 tablespoons chopped fresh flat-leaf parsley

1 tablespoon drained and rinsed capers (optional)

Big pinch of flaky sea salt, such as Maldon

Put the milk in a shallow dish. In a second shallow dish, combine the flour and pimentón and stir with a small whisk to combine. Generously season the fish with salt and pepper. One at a time, dip the fillets into the milk and then dredge in the seasoned flour to coat, shaking off the excess. Transfer each coated fillet to a plate.

In a large skillet, melt half of the butter over medium heat until it stops foaming. Working in two batches, add the fish in a single layer and cook on each side until golden, about 4 minutes total. Using a metal spatula, transfer the fillets a warm serving platter. Wipe out the pan with paper towels and repeat to cook the remaining fillets.

Add the remaining half of the butter to the same skillet and melt over medium heat, swirling the skillet so that the butter melts evenly. Cook until the butter begins to turn golden brown and smell nutty, about 3 minutes. Add the almonds and cook until they are lightly browned, about 3 minutes more. Stir in the lemon juice, parsley, capers (if using), and flaky salt.

Spoon the butter and almond sauce over the fillets and serve immediately. **SERVES 6**

This makes an attractive roulade that can then be sauced with whatever sauce you like. Here, I'm suggesting a white wine butter sauce. You could use any other thin fish, such as trout or salmon fillets.

# STEAMED BACON-STUFFED SOLE

6 slices thick-cut bacon, finely diced

½ cup (70 g) finely chopped shallots or green onions, white parts only

3 tablespoons pine nuts or chopped almonds, lightly toasted (page 344)

2 teaspoons finely grated lemon zest

⅓ cup (17 g) finely chopped fresh flat-leaf parsley

1 tablespoon finely chopped fresh mint leaves

Fine sea salt and freshly ground pepper

12 large romaine lettuce leaves of equal size

12 sole fillets, about 4 ounces (115 g) each

White Wine Butter Sauce (page 340) or Vinegar-Cream Sauce (page 341)

In a large skillet, cook the bacon over medium heat until browned and crisp. Transfer the bacon to paper towels to drain. Remove all but 2 tablespoons of fat from the pan. Add the shallots and cook until just beginning to color. Using a slotted spoon, transfer the shallots to a medium bowl and stir in the bacon, pine nuts, lemon zest, parsley, and mint. Season to taste with salt and pepper and set aside.

In a medium pot of lightly salted boiling water, blanch the romaine leaves for 10 seconds. Immediately plunge them into ice water to stop the cooking and set the color. Drain in a fine-mesh sieve and pat dry with paper towels.

Pat the sole fillets dry with paper towels. Divide the bacon mixture to cover each evenly. Roll each fillet up to enclose the filling and then roll in a blanched romaine leaf. Lightly oil a steamer basket and place the rolls in a single layer, seam side down. Add to a steamer with gently steaming water in the bottom. Cover the steamer and cook until the rolls are firm, 10 to 12 minutes. You can make a small incision on the underside to check if the fish is opaque throughout.

While the rolls are steaming, make the sauce and keep warm. To serve, divide the rolls among warm plates and spoon the sauce over. Serve immediately. **SERVES 6**

Thinly sliced raw monkfish topped with flavored olive oil, arugula, and shavings of Parmesan is an elegant starter for a dinner party. Tuna, sea bass, salmon, or sea scallops could be substituted for the monkfish. Any raw fish preparation demands the freshest and best quality, from a reputable fishmonger. You can also dress the raw fish slices with Ponzu Sauce (page 339).

# MONKFISH CARPACCIO

One 8-to-10-ounce (225-to-280-g) solid piece monkfish tail

Lemon- or orange-infused olive oil, such as McEvoy or "O"

1 tablespoon finely chopped fresh chives

Flaky sea salt, such as Maldon

Freshly ground pepper

1 cup (20 g) young or wild arugula

Fresh lemon juice, to taste

⅓ cup (35 g) shaved Parmesan or pecorino cheese

Crusty bread or crostini (page 343), for serving

Wrap the fish tightly in plastic wrap into a cylindrical shape. Freeze until firm but not frozen, about 2 hours.

Remove from the freezer, unwrap, and cut into very thin slices (similar in thickness to smoked salmon) with a sharp, long-bladed knife. Arrange 4 slices attractively in one layer on each of 4 chilled plates. Press on them slightly to flatten. Drizzle the oil over the fish and sprinkle with the chives, flaky salt, and a little pepper.

In a medium bowl, toss the arugula with a little of the olive oil and lemon juice to taste. Season with salt and pepper. Arrange on top of the fish and scatter the cheese shavings over. Serve with good crusty bread. **SERVES 4**

---

The lobster-like flavor and texture of monkfish is seductive topped with a warm, lemony sauce. It is also terrific with buttery Blender Hollandaise Sauce (page 339) or Béarnaise Sauce (page 340). This is an easy recipe with big results.

# MONKFISH with dijon-lemon sauce

Dijon-Lemon Sauce (page 339)

Four 6-to-8-ounce (170-to-225-g) monkfish fillets, each at least 1½ inches (4 cm) thick

Kosher salt and freshly ground pepper

2 tablespoons unsalted butter

2 tablespoons olive oil

Preheat the oven to 400°F (205°C). Make the dijon-lemon sauce then set aside and keep warm over a pan of hot water.

Cut the monkfish fillets into slices about 1 inch (2.5 cm) or so thick. Lightly sprinkle both sides with salt and pepper. In a large ovenproof skillet, melt the butter with the olive oil over medium-high heat. Place the larger pieces of fish in the pan first. Cook for 1 minute, then add the smaller (tail-end) pieces. Cook for another 2 minutes, then turn. Transfer the pan to the oven and roast until opaque throughout, 6 minutes or so. Test with the point of a small knife. It should be tender and opaque all the way through.

Transfer the fish to a large, warm platter. Pour any juices from the skillet into the sauce. Spoon the sauce onto 4 warm plates and arrange the fish on top. Serve at once. **SERVES 4**

# BIG, MEATY FISH

## swordfish, tuna, mahi mahi, sturgeon

These large, meaty species are included together in this chapter because they generally handle, cook, and result in dishes that have similar textures and flavors. This is not a scientific grouping but a culinary grouping. Most recipes are interchangeable among the species. From a sustainability and fisheries management angle, this is an extremely broad category and hard to do justice in a couple of paragraphs. Mahi and smaller tuna are often great choices because they grow quickly and reproduce in abundance. Albacore is especially important on the West Coast for this reason.

# SWORDFISH

In the 1990s, the North Atlantic swordfish (*Xiphias gladius*) was severely overfished. Thanks to a 1999 international plan, this stock has been rebuilt, and today, North Atlantic longline-caught swordfish is one of the most sustainable seafood choices. Swordfish are wide-ranging and also available from Pacific waters as well. Monterey Bay Aquarium lists Pacific swordfish as a good alternative.

Swordfish is almost always sold as steaks, and the meat is so firm that many non-fish eaters will gladly eat it. Its firm texture makes swordfish excellent for grilling and skewering and helps prevent the steaks from falling apart on the grill grate. It takes well to marinades and sauces; just be careful not to overcook it.

Swordfish is now a sustainable seafood choice, though it does have an elevated level of methylmercury since it's at the top of the feeding chain. The FDA advises that this can be of concern to young children, pregnant and nursing women, and women of childbearing age. Therefore, these groups should avoid eating swordfish regularly.

Swordfish steaks with a simple olive oil–based marinade are made for the grill. Keep the skin on, which helps to keep the grilled steaks intact. When serving, remove the skin, as it's not edible. Swordfish is also an excellent fish to poach or stew. It won't fall apart and is a nice replacement for tuna in salad. Shark or tuna are good substitutes.

# TUNA

Tuna (*Thunnus*) are powerful pelagic fish that are found in tropical to temperate oceans around the world. Here are the seven most-common species:

## Atlantic Bluefin Tuna (*Thunnus thynnus*)

Atlantic bluefin tuna are streamlined fish that live for up to twenty-five years and can grow to lengths of 9 feet (2.7 m) and weigh more than 1,500 pounds (680 kg). They are a popular sport fish and a top choice for sushi, sashimi, and steaks. Unfortunately, they have been heavily overfished, in large part due to the popularity of sushi dishes.

## Southern Bluefin (*Thunnus maccoyii*)

Southern bluefin tuna, like the Atlantic bluefin, is a large, fast, streamlined species. It is found throughout the oceans in the Southern Hemisphere. Like Atlantic bluefin, this species has been greatly overfished.

## Albacore Tuna/Longfin Tuna (*Thunnus alalunga*)

These relatively smaller tuna are found throughout the Atlantic and Pacific Oceans and the Mediterranean. They run about 4 feet (1.2 m) and 88 pounds (40 kg). Albacore tuna is commonly sold canned and is usually called "white" tuna. Albacore are fished in several ways, including by trollers, which use a series of lures towed slowly behind a vessel. This is more eco-friendly than using longlines, which can result in a significant amount of bycatch.

## Yellowfin Tuna (*Thunnus albacares*)

This is the species you'll find in canned tuna, often designated as "chunk light." They are typically caught in purse seine nets, which can cause the death of many other fish as well as dolphins. Improvements to the nets in recent times have reduced this bycatch issue.

## Bigeye Tuna (*Thunnus obesus*)

The bigeye tuna looks similar to the yellowfin, but, as its name suggests, it has larger eyes. Found in warmer tropical and subtropical waters in the Atlantic, Pacific, and Indian Oceans, it grows to 6 feet (1.8 m) long and can weigh up to 400 pounds (181 kg). Unfortunately, like other tunas, it is overfished.

### Skipjack Tuna/Bonito (*Katsuwonus pelamis*)

Skipjacks are a smaller tuna that grows to about 3 feet (0.9 m) and weighs up to about 40 pounds (18 kg). They are wide-ranging, living in tropical, subtropical, and temperate oceans. Skipjack is sold fresh, dried, salted, canned, and smoked, as well as raw for use in sushi, sashimi, and poke. Dried and smoked, it is used to make bonito flakes, a key ingredient in dashi (page 334).

### Little Tunny (*Euthynnus alletteratus*)

Also known as mackerel tuna, little tuna, bonita, and false albacore, this fish is found in tropical to temperate waters. The little tunny grows to about 4 feet (1.2 m) in length and weighs up to 35 pounds (16 kg). Commercially, it is used for bait to catch other sharks and marlin. It is not commonly eaten because it has a fairly strong fishy taste. It's a popular game fish, however, because it's a hard fighter.

### Sushi-Grade Tuna

For any recipes in this book calling for sushi-grade tuna, ask your local fishmonger for a block of *saku*, which is tuna with the blood line removed, cryovacked, and frozen. It's what most of us get in sushi restaurants. Sushi-grade fish differs from other fish in that it's fresher and comes from species that are least susceptible to bacteria and parasites. Since sushi-grade fish is specifically intended for raw consumption, it's managed differently to avoid potential transference of bacteria and parasites. Generally, it is caught quickly, bled immediately on capture, and gutted very soon after. Fish intended for sushi is frozen thoroughly, usually at 0°F (-20°C) for 7 days. It can also be flash frozen at -35°F (-37°C) for at least 15 hours. This is done in accordance with FDA regulations (page 23). It is important to know that every fish cannot be sushi grade; a reputable fishmonger is vital.

# MAHI MAHI

Also called dorado or dolphinfish, mahi mahi (*Coryphaena hippurus*) is a saltwater fish that can be found in tropical and subtropical waters. It has a mild, sweet flavor and dense flesh similar to swordfish. This fish is best on the grill because it holds up well, but be careful not to overcook as it tends to flake. Any of the recipes in this book for swordfish or tuna can be substituted with mahi mahi. The arrabbiata sauce (page 339) makes a nice base for this fish.

This beautiful fish has a tall, flat-topped head, particularly in males, giving it a squared appearance. It has iridescent blue-green scales along its back and yellow scales on its sides and underbelly. Mahi mahi are popular targets for commercial fishermen, but because they grow rapidly and reach sexual maturity quickly, they have stable populations and are not endangered. Notoriously difficult to catch, mahi mahi are known for their spectacular leaps when line-caught. Though it is also known as dolphinfish, it has no relation to the dolphin. The word *mahi* translates to "strong" in Hawaiian, and the doubling of the word emphasizes the strength of this fish.

# STURGEON

There are at least two dozen species of sturgeon (Acipenseridae), the most famous of which come from Russia. They are long-lived, up to 150 years, and have a firm texture and a scallop-like flavor. The real glory of sturgeon, however, is its roe or caviar, a truly luxurious food.

A great sport fish, especially in California, it is becoming scarce because of pollution and habitat destruction and is now being farm-raised extensively. In California, the upper Sacramento River is a hot spot for farming. The French also are a source for farm-raised sturgeon. Grilled, broiled, or pan-seared, sturgeon works well with any of the compound butters on pages 334 to 335. They are also excellent smoked. Any of the grilled or seared recipes in this chapter can be adapted to use sturgeon.

Swordfish is one of the easiest fish to grill because of its firm, meaty texture. And it holds up to robust flavors, like the green olives, capers, anchovies, and garlic that accompany this easy recipe. Oranges help brighten the overall dish.

# GRILLED SWORDFISH
## with green olives and oranges

**GARNISH**

2 navel oranges, cut into segments and juice reserved (page 345)

Kosher salt and freshly ground pepper

**GREEN OLIVE RELISH**

1 cup (155 g) pitted green olives, such as Cerignola, pitted and coarsely chopped

3 oil-packed anchovies in olive oil, drained and chopped

2 tablespoons chopped fresh flat-leaf parsley

2 tablespoons olive oil

1 tablespoon capers, drained and chopped

1 small clove garlic, very thinly sliced

¼ teaspoon crushed red pepper flakes

Kosher salt and freshly ground pepper

**GRILLED SWORDFISH**

Four 5-to-6-ounce (140-to-170-g) skin-on swordfish fillets

Olive oil, for brushing

Kosher salt and freshly ground pepper

To make the garnish, combine the citrus segments and juice in a small bowl and season very lightly with salt and pepper. Set aside.

To make the relish, in a small bowl, combine the olives, anchovies, parsley, olive oil, capers, garlic, and crushed red pepper. Stir to mix then season with salt and pepper. Set aside.

To make the swordfish, prepare a medium-hot fire in a charcoal grill or preheat a gas grill to medium-high. Brush the grill grates clean.

Pat the fish dry with paper towels. Lightly brush the fillets on both sides with olive oil, then season with salt and pepper. Place the fish on the grill grate and cover the grill. Cook, turning once, until the swordfish looks opaque throughout when pierced with the tip of a sharp knife, about 6 minutes total. Be careful not to overcook.

Remove the skin and transfer the fillets to individual plates. Top each with a generous spoonful of the green olive relish and add orange segments and some of the juice around the edges of the fish. Serve immediately. **SERVES 4**

This recipe from chef Jose Romo of Hog Island Oyster Bar in Napa is a testament to not wasting anything in the kitchen. The marrow in fish, as well as other animals, is in the center of the vertebrae. To get the spine, you'll want to start with a fish that weighs 25 pounds (11.3 kg) or more. Fillet the meat off the fish and save it for one of the other recipes in this book. Once all the meat is off, chop off the head and tail with a cleaver and save that to make fish stock.

# FISH BONE MARROW
## with grilled bread

1 large fish spine from a swordfish, halibut, or tuna

Fine sea salt and freshly ground pepper

Rustic bread, sliced and brushed with oil for grilling

Fried capers (page 344), for serving

Lemon wedges, flaky sea salt, and chopped fresh chives and parsley, for serving

Prepare a medium fire in a charcoal grill or preheat a gas grill to medium. Brush the grill grates clean.

Carve out the silver skin in between the spine; it's okay if it has some meat on the bones, it becomes a tasty treat. Cut the vertebrae into 2-inch (5-cm) sections. Season generously with salt and pepper.

Place the spine pieces on the grill and cook until the marrow is bubbling and soft, about 7 minutes. While the marrow is cooking, grill the bread lightly on both sides.

Place on plates with the spine points pointing upward. Serve with marrow spoons or picks to remove the marrow. Garnish with fried capers, flaky sea salt, chopped chives, and parsley. **SERVES 2**

---

# FISH COLLARS

You may have heard the sweetest meat is that right next to the bone, and this is most definitely true of fish. Fish collars and bones prove this axiom, and they also honor the concept of using as many parts of the fish as possible.

The fish collar, which includes both bone and cartilage, runs from top to bottom behind the head and includes delicious rich meat along the belly. The cut is anchored to the collarbone, but once cooked, it separates nicely, with no smaller bones to navigate. Fish collars have long been popular in Asia.

They aren't beautiful, but if you have big enough fish, one collar makes a delicious serving for one. Good sources are tuna, swordfish, sturgeon, and mahi mahi, as well as larger yellowtail, lingcod, and halibut. Brush a little soy-based marinade on them, such as the marinade for the Ginger-Soy Salmon on page 170, and grill over a hot fire or under the broiler.

---

The method used in this recipe can be used with any firm-fleshed fish. You can also experiment with the other pesto recipes that are in this book. Be creative!

# PROSCIUTTO-WRAPPED SWORDFISH
## with kale pesto

8 thin slices prosciutto

Four 5-ounce (140-g) swordfish fillets, about 1 inch (2.5 cm) thick

Kosher salt and freshly ground pepper

1 cup (240 ml) kale pesto (page 336)

3 tablespoons olive oil

1 tablespoon minced shallot

½ cup (120 ml) dry white wine

½ cup (120 ml) fish stock (page 332) or chicken stock (page 333)

2 tablespoons unsalted butter, at room temperature

Preheat the oven to 400°F (205°C). Lay two slices of prosciutto side by side on a flat surface. Put one piece of swordfish crosswise on the prosciutto and season lightly with salt and pepper.

Generously coat the top side of the fish with the pesto and wrap the prosciutto securely around the fish. Repeat with remaining fish.

Add the olive oil to a skillet large enough to hold the fish fillets in one layer and heat over medium-high heat. Add the fish and cook, turning once, until lightly browned on both sides. Transfer the pan to the oven and cook another 4 minutes, or just until the fish is done. Remove the fish to warm plates.

Add the shallots to the pan, adding oil as needed, and cook over medium heat until softened but not brown, about 2 minutes. Pour in the wine and stock, increase the heat to high, and bring the mixture to a boil. Reduce the liquid until it becomes syrupy, and then whisk in the butter. Season with salt and pepper, then pour the sauce over the fish. Serve immediately. **SERVES 4**

Ceviche is served throughout Mexico and Central and South America. This recipe for tuna ceviche has its roots in Chile. It's gorgeous served in martini or margarita glasses so you can see all the vibrant colors of the green onion, tomatoes, mango, and avocado.

# AHI TUNA CEVICHE
## with mango and avocado

1¼ pounds (570 g) sushi-grade ahi tuna (page 249), cut into ⅓-inch (8-mm) dice

1 tablespoon olive oil

2 tablespoons coarsely chopped fresh cilantro

1 teaspoon minced fresh oregano

1 teaspoon seeded and minced serrano chile

1 large avocado, pitted, peeled, and cut into ⅓-inch (8-mm) dice

1 mango, peeled, pitted, and cut into ⅓-inch (8-mm) dice

½ cup (85 g) seeded and diced ripe plum tomatoes

¼ cup (15 g) green onion, cut into thin diagonal slices, including green parts

½ cup (120 ml) fresh lime juice

Fine sea salt and freshly ground pepper

Tortilla chips, for serving

Fresh cilantro sprigs, for garnish

Put the tuna in a medium glass or ceramic bowl and toss gently with the olive oil, cilantro, oregano, and chile. Use now, or cover and refrigerate for up to 2 hours.

To serve, add the avocado, mango, tomatoes, and green onion to the tuna. Add the lime juice and toss gently. Season with salt and pepper. Divide among glasses. Insert a chip in each and top with the cilantro sprigs. Serve immediately.
**SERVES 6**

Poke, which means "to cut into pieces" and is pronounced "poh-kay," is a favorite Hawaiian preparation. Before refrigeration was available on the islands, salt was added to raw seafood as a way of preserving and keeping fish fresh. Other sushi-grade fish, such as salmon, char, or halibut can be used in this recipe. Serve with tortilla chips, rice crackers, shrimp chips or on rice. Alternatively, the raw fish can be dressed with Ponzu Sauce (page 339) in place of the soy sauce mixture.

# AHI TUNA POKE

1 pound (455 g) sushi-grade tuna (page 249)

2 small green onions, thinly sliced, white and green parts

3 tablespoons soy sauce

2 teaspoons toasted sesame oil

½ teaspoon chili-garlic sauce or a big pinch crushed red pepper flakes

1 small avocado, pitted and diced

2 teaspoons furikake, homemade (page 326) or store-bought, or sesame seeds, toasted (page 344)

Seaweed salad, store-bought, or Pickled Cucumber, Wakame, and Sesame Salad (page 327)

Tortilla chips, rice crackers, or shrimp chips, for serving

Carefully cut the tuna against the grain into ¾-inch (2-cm) planks and then into ¾-inch (2-cm) cubes. Place in a large bowl and add the green onions.

In a small bowl, combine the soy sauce, sesame oil, and chili-garlic sauce. Whisk to blend.

Pour the soy sauce mixture over the fish mixture and toss gently to combine. Add the avocado and toss gently to combine. Sprinkle the furikake over the fish, toss again gently. Serve immediately or cover and refrigerate up to 1 hour. Serve with the seaweed salad and chips/crackers. **SERVES 4**

These little bites of rice with tuna, salmon, and prosciutto look like beautiful little Christmas ornaments and are simple to make. They make a good starter for a dinner party. For a neater presentation, cut the tuna into a log shape before thinly slicing crosswise.

# TAMARI-ZUCHI RICE BALLS

**RICE BALLS**

6 cups (1.2 kg) prepared Sushi Rice (page 343)

4 ounces (115 g) sushi-grade tuna (page 249), thinly sliced

3 ounces (85 g) thinly sliced smoked salmon

2 ounces (55 g) very thinly sliced prosciutto di Parma or Serrano ham

**GARNISHES (OPTIONAL)**

Wasabi

Hot mustard

Mashed umeboshi (Japanese salt-cured plum)

Drained small capers

Japanese soy sauce (shoyu)

Divide the rice into 30 portions. Cut the tuna, salmon, and prosciutto *each* into 10 uniform 1½-inch (4-cm) square or round pieces.

Place a rice portion (about a rounded tablespoon) on a small piece of plastic wrap (about 8 inches/20 cm square) and twist the ends together tightly to form a ball. Untwist the rice ball, lay a slice of tuna on top and use the plastic wrap to twist the rice and tuna again into a ball. This helps set the tuna in place around the rice. Do the same using smoked salmon in some and prosciutto in others, using only one piece of tuna, salmon, or prosciutto for each rice ball.

Arrange the balls attractively on a plate. If you like, garnish the tuna with a little dot of wasabi, the smoked salmon with the hot mustard, and the prosciutto with the umeboshi and capers. Serve with small dishes of soy sauce to dip the balls in before eating. **MAKES 30 BITE-SIZED BALLS**

# ALBACORE TUNA PREPARATION

Chef John Lyell of Tony's Seafood in Marshall, California, one of the Hog Island restaurants, learned this preparation method from chef Keiko Takahashi. It is based on the Japanese tataki method, in which the outside of the fish is seared and the inside is left rare. According to the chef, this was always done with bluefin, but it works really nicely with Oregon albacore tuna. He writes this in a conversational style much like Laurie Colwin in her two collections of essays *Home Cooking* and *More Home Cooking*, which I love and encourage you to seek out. This is a cross between a crudo and a Japanese *tataki*. It assumes that you know a bit about Japanese cooking.

**Step one: Prepare the mother sauce**
There are many recipes in Japanese cuisine that involve the "mother sauce." It is simple: equal parts low-sodium soy sauce, mirin, and sake. For one albacore loin, 1 cup (240 ml) of each should be more than enough. Put these ingredients in a pot and simmer for 5 minutes. Allow to cool completely.

**Step two: Prepare the fish**
Your loin fillet should be trimmed and filleted. We will be slicing thick, so you will be able see the full shape of the fillet, if that makes sense. With bluefin, we would cut perfect rectangular prisms out of a loin and utilize the scrap elsewhere. I like to trim the bones and belly from the albacore and leave the natural shape intact.

**Step three: Gently poach the fish**
Prepare a bowl of ice water. In saucepan half full of salted water, add a healthy dose of sake—1 part sake to 3 parts water. Bring to a simmer over medium heat. Using tongs, add the loin fillet to the saucepan and cook for 5 seconds maximum while turning the fillet to cover all sides. Immediately transfer to the ice bath. We are not cooking the fish, merely "searing" the outside. The ice bath prevents any carryover cooking. The goal is to see a sliver of cooked flesh on the outside when the loin is sliced. Doing this also opens the fillet up to the marinade, which is the last step.

**Step four: Marinate the fish**
Remove the tuna from the ice bath and submerge it in the mother sauce. Set aside, refrigerated, for 1 hour before slicing. Slice into ¼-inch- (6-mm-) thick slices (or thinner if you like). Serve with the typical wakame salad, fresh herbs, daikon, kyuri (Japanese cucumber) and avocado. There are many garnish variations, so make it your own!

The key to success with tuna burgers is to handle the fish carefully and don't over season, over handle, or overcook it. You can grill these burgers (preferably using a hinged grill rack or a grill screen), but searing them on the stove top gives you more control over the level of the heat. And it's a good idea to chop the tuna by hand, as using a food processor can overprocess it. You can top these with whatever burger garnishes you like, such as lettuce or pea shoots, thinly sliced radishes, or sliced tomatoes, or even Cabbage-Apple Slaw (page 211).

# TUNA BURGERS
## with sriracha mayonnaise

**SRIRACHA MAYONNAISE**

½ cup (120 ml) mayonnaise, preferably Kewpie

1 teaspoon sriracha, or to taste

½ teaspoon grated lime zest

Big pinch of brown sugar

**TUNA BURGERS**

1 pound (455 g) sushi-grade tuna (page 249)

2 tablespoons finely chopped fresh cilantro

2 tablespoons finely chopped green onion

2 tablespoons panko (Japanese bread crumbs)

1 teaspoon minced fresh ginger

1 teaspoon soy sauce, or to taste

½ teaspoon toasted sesame oil

¼ teaspoon freshly ground pepper

2 tablespoons canola oil

4 hamburger buns, split and toasted

Burger garnishes of your choice

To make the mayonnaise, in a small bowl, combine the mayonnaise, sriracha, lime zest, and brown sugar and stir to blend well. Taste and adjust the seasoning.

To make the burgers, using a sharp knife, cut the tuna into ¼-inch (6-mm) dice. In a medium bowl, combine the tuna, cilantro, green onion, panko, ginger, soy sauce, sesame oil, and pepper. Stir gently, just until blended; do not overmix. Divide the mixture into 4 parts and gently press into patties about ¾ inch (2 cm) thick. Cover and refrigerate for at least 20 minutes.

In a large skillet, heat the canola oil over medium heat until shimmering. Add the burgers and cook, turning once, until nicely browned on both sides, about 4 minutes total for medium-rare.

Spread the buns with the sriracha mayonnaise, add the tuna burger and any garnishes of your choice. **SERVES 4**

The fillet of tuna, seared on the outside and rare in the center, is sliced, then coated with a miso-flavored vinaigrette and plated with greens and wedges of avocado.

# SESAME-CRUSTED SEARED TUNA
## with avocado salad and sesame-miso vinaigrette

**SESAME-MISO VINAIGRETTE**

2 tablespoons white (shiro) miso

2 tablespoons canola or other neutral oil

2 tablespoons soy sauce

1 tablespoon rice vinegar

1 tablespoon fresh lime juice

2 teaspoons honey

1 teaspoon toasted sesame oil

1 teaspoon peeled, minced fresh ginger

**SESAME-CRUSTED TUNA**

¼ cup (40 g) sesame seeds

1 teaspoon fine sea salt

½ teaspoon freshly ground pepper

1 sushi-grade ahi tuna fillet (about 1 pound/455 g)

2 tablespoons canola oil or other neutral oil

1 avocado, halved, pitted, and peeled

4 to 6 handfuls mixed baby greens

To make the vinaigrette, in a blender, combine the miso, canola oil, soy sauce, vinegar, lime juice, honey, sesame oil, and ginger and blend until smooth and thickened. Taste and adjust the seasoning. Use now, or cover and refrigerate for up to 3 days.

To make the tuna, in a small bowl, combine the sesame seeds with the salt and pepper. Coat both sides of the tuna with the sesame seed mixture, pressing gently to adhere.

In a large skillet, heat the oil over high heat until it shimmers but is not smoking. Add the tuna and sear for 1 minute on each side for rare, 2 minutes on each side for medium-rare. Transfer the tuna to a cutting board and let it rest for at least 5 minutes.

Slice the tuna across the grain into ½-inch- (12-mm-) thick strips. Slice each avocado half lengthwise into 4 equal wedges.

In a large bowl, toss the greens lightly with some of the vinaigrette and divide among 4 plates. Arrange the avocado and tuna slices on top, dividing equally. Serve, with the remaining vinaigrette alongside. **SERVES 4**

Poaching in olive oil is a delicious way to add flavor and is superior to poaching in water. It keeps the protein moist and succulent. This is excellent served over a salad, such as the Niçoise salad at the right, or used in an upgraded tuna sandwich.

# OLIVE OIL–POACHED TUNA

1 pound (455 g) ahi tuna, cut evenly into a slab about 1½ inches (4 cm) thick

About 3 cups (720 ml) extra-virgin olive oil, plus more as needed

2 tablespoons sliced garlic

1 bay leaf

1 strip lemon zest (about ¾ by 2 inches/ 2 by 5 cm)

2 teaspoons fine sea salt

½ teaspoon crushed red pepper flakes

Freshly ground black pepper

Set a wire rack on a baking sheet. Trim and discard any skin, bones, or dark blood spots from the tuna.

In a heavy saucepan combine the oil, garlic, bay leaf, zest, salt, crushed red pepper, and black pepper and heat to 140°F (60°C). on a deep-frying thermometer. Add the tuna; it should be submerged, but if not, add more olive oil. Return the temperature to 125°F (52°C). Maintain this heat until the fish has whitened and shows a few beads of protein, about 8 minutes. Using a wire-mesh skimmer, transfer the tuna to the wire rack. Use now, or tightly cover in plastic wrap and refrigerate for up to 2 days. Let come to room temperature before serving.

Strain the oil through a fine-mesh sieve set over a bowl and reserve the oil to use in other dishes, such as for sautéing. **MAKES 1 POUND (455 G); SERVES 4**

---

Za'atar is a Middle Eastern spice blend made from ground spices, herbs, and sesame seeds. It is often used in dips and marinades, but is also great on fish, grilled meats, and roasted vegetables. It is available at most well-stocked markets, but also quite easy to make. The ingredients and proportions of the spice blend can vary, as individual cooks create their own signature flavors. This recipe is from chef B Adamo, head chef of Hog Island Oyster Bar in Larkspur.

# ZA'ATAR-SEARED ALBACORE TUNA

Four 4-ounce (115-g) fillets albacore tuna

½ cup (100 g) za'atar (page 341)

Extra-virgin olive oil, plus more for drizzling

1 small fennel bulb, trimmed and very thinly sliced

1 small grapefruit, cut into segments (page 345)

1 small, firm-ripe avocado, pitted, peeled, and sliced

Fresh lemon juice, for serving

Flaky salt, such as Maldon, for sprinkling

Coat the albacore on both sides with the za'atar. In a large skillet, heat enough oil to cover the bottom of the pan over medium heat. Add the albacore and sear until golden brown on both sides, about 6 minutes total.

Divide the fennel, grapefruit, and avocado between the plates, arranging it attractively. Top with the fish. Sprinkle the fish with a little lemon juice and salt, drizzle with olive oil, and serve. **SERVES 4**

Olive oil–poaching yields a very moist and flavorful fish. The sweet and spicy lime citronette adds a bright citrus note to this classic summery Mediterranean salad.

# NIÇOISE SALAD
# with olive oil–poached tuna

**LIME CITRONETTE**

1 tablespoon minced red onion or shallot

1 tablespoon tequila

1 tablespoon honey

1 teaspoon grated lime zest

⅓ cup (75 ml) fresh lime juice

½ teaspoon seeded, minced serrano chile

3 tablespoons extra-virgin olive oil

Fine sea salt and freshly ground pepper

**NIÇOISE SALAD**

½ pound (225 g) haricots verts (French green beans) or baby Blue Lake green beans

½ pound (22 g) small fingerling or new potatoes (about 12), scrubbed

2 small Little Gem lettuces, halved

1½ cups (220 g) tiny Toy Box tomatoes, preferably in different colors

1 tablespoon drained, rinsed large capers, or 8 drained caperberries)

Olive Oil–Poached Tuna (page 264)

2 large hard-boiled eggs, cut into quarters (page 344)

¼ cup (40 g) Cerignola, niçoise, or other meaty olives

Flaky sea salt and freshly ground pepper

To make the lime citronette, in a small bowl, whisk together the red onion, tequila, honey, lime zest, lime juice, and chile. Gradually whisk in the olive oil to make an emulsion. Season to taste with salt and pepper.

To make the salad, blanch the green beans in boiling salted water just until crisp-tender. Shock in a bowl of ice water to stop the cooking. Drain.

Put the potatoes in a large saucepan of salted boiling water. Reduce the heat to a simmer, cover, and cook until just tender, about 10 minutes. Drain and let cool to the touch. Cut the potatoes in halves or quarters depending on size and add to a medium bowl. Add some of the citronette and toss to lightly coat the warm potatoes.

Arrange the lettuce, potatoes, green beans, tomatoes, capers, and tuna (broken into large chunks) attractively on 4 plates. Drizzle the remaining citronette over and finish with the eggs and olives. Season with flaky salt and pepper and serve. **SERVES 4**

Chimichurri's origins are foggy. Some claim it originated with an Irishman named Jimmy McCurry or a British meat man named Jimmy Curry, while others say it's a mangled version of the phrase "give me the curry." All we know for sure is that this tangy, vibrant Argentinian sauce is a revelation with grilled fish and meat.

# GRILLED MAHI MAHI
## with chimichurri

Four 6-ounce (170-g) mahi mahi fillets, at least 1 inch (2.5 cm) thick

Olive oil, for brushing

Kosher salt and freshly ground pepper

Chimichurri Sauce (page 337)

Lemon wedges, for serving

Prepare a hot fire in a charcoal grill, or preheat a gas grill to high. Brush the grill grates clean.

Brush the fillets well on all sides with olive oil and then sprinkle generously on all sides with salt and pepper.

Place the fillets on the grill and cook until the fillets release easily from the grill grate when an edge is lifted with a metal spatula, about 4 minutes. Flip the fillets over and grill for another 3 minutes until the flesh is firm and opaque, but moist in the center, about 3 minutes. Serve topped with a spoonful or two of the chimichurri sauce, with the lemon wedges alongside. **SERVES 4**

---

Also known as kebabs, this simple but colorful recipe could be adapted to any firm flesh fish or shellfish. You can also cook them on a charcoal or gas grill.

# GRILLED MAHI MAHI BROCHETTES

1 pound (455 g) mahi mahi fillets, cut 1¼-inch (3-cm) cubes

8 baby onions, peeled and blanched

½ large yellow bell pepper, seeded, stemmed and cut into 1½-inch (4-cm) squares

8 firm grape or cherry tomatoes

3 tablespoons unsalted butter

2 tablespoons lemon juice

Kosher salt and freshly ground pepper

Big pinch smoked paprika

Alternately thread the fish, onions, bell pepper, and tomatoes on 4 metal or wood skewers (soaked for at least 30 minutes). Melt the butter and lemon juice together in a small pan and season with salt, pepper, and paprika. Brush the brochettes with this mixture.

Heat a stovetop grill pan over medium-high heat and grill the brochettes on all sides until nicely marked and the fish is cooked through, about 8 minutes. Brush occasionally with the butter mixture.

Serve on warm plates with any remaining butter lemon mixture drizzled over. **SERVES 4**

This "steak" of the fish world brings together a delicious mix of salty tart flavors. If you can't find sturgeon, any firm-fleshed fish, such as halibut, sea bass, mahi mahi, or swordfish will do.

# PAN-SEARED STURGEON with
## pancetta, capers, and lemon

2 tablespoons olive oil

4 ounces (115 g) pancetta, cut into ¼-inch (6-mm) dice

Six 5-ounce (140-g) sturgeon fillets

Fine sea salt and freshly ground pepper

¼ cup (30 g) unbleached all-purpose flour

3 tablespoons minced shallots

1 tablespoon minced garlic

1 cup (240 ml) fish stock (page 332) or shellfish stock (page 332)

½ cup (120 ml) dry white wine

2 tablespoons fresh lemon juice

2 tablespoons unsalted butter

⅔ cup (120 g) seeded and diced ripe tomatoes

3 tablespoons drained capers

2 tablespoons minced fresh flat-leaf parsley

In a large skillet, heat the olive oil over medium heat. Add the pancetta and cook until lightly browned. Using a slotted spoon, transfer the pancetta to a bowl.

Liberally season the sturgeon with salt and pepper, then dust with the flour. Add the fillets to the skillet over medium-high heat and cook, turning once, until golden brown on both sides and cooked through, about 8 minutes total depending on thickness. (Unlike salmon, sturgeon must be thoroughly cooked through; check with the point of a knife). Using a slotted metal spatula, transfer the sturgeon to a plate; cover and keep warm.

Return the skillet to medium heat and add the shallots and garlic. Cook, stirring, until translucent, about 2 minutes. Add the stock, wine, and lemon juice, raise the heat to high, and cook, stirring, until reduced to a light sauce consistency. Remove from the heat, whisk in the butter to form a light emulsion, then stir in the tomatoes, capers, parsley, and reserved pancetta. Season with salt and pepper.

Divide the fish and sauce between warm plates and serve at once. **SERVES 6**

# LITTLE FISH

## sardines, anchovies, herring, smelt (whitebait), mackerel

The world of little fish is really the basis for all life in the ocean, since they serve as food for fish farther up the food chain. For cooks, they are a source of deep savory flavors and can be used to enhance many types of dishes. The little fishes of the sea form a fundamental ecological link between the microscopic world of plankton and the world of large ocean predators like sharks, marine mammals, and bigger fishes. Because they are on so many menus, the little fish have evolved to reproduce rapidly and in vast numbers, making them incredibly abundant. The largest migration of biomass on Earth is thought to be that of a stock of sardines, moving in the billions around the coast of South Africa! These huge numbers, along with their accessibility, nutritional value, and deliciousness have made little fishes an important part of human diets as well. All the little fish in this chapter can be found from highly sustainable wild fisheries and are rated as "Best Choices" by monitoring programs. The challenge for these smaller fish species and the ecosystems they support is their harvest for fish meal (to be used in finfish aquaculture feeds) and as fish-oil supplements.

# SARDINES, ANCHOVIES, HERRING, AND SMELT

Max Bonem, in an article in *Food & Wine* magazine, helped us understand the differences between little fishes. The confusion arises because all are small, oily, saltwater fish sold primarily in tins. In markets they are usually positioned next to each other and as a result are regularly confused for each other, particularly sardines and anchovies.

## Sardines

This group of small, oily fish was once found in great abundance around the island of Sardinia, hence their name. A member of the Clupeidae family (which also includes herring), there are up to twenty different species classified as sardines or pilchards. Sardines are up to 7 inches (18 cm) in length. Sardines have a gentle, less intense flavor than anchovies. Sardines are legendary in the Monterey Bay for their boom or bust appearances. John Steinbeck's book *Cannery Row* documents this and is also a great read.

## Anchovies

Like sardines, these are a small, oily fish found in the Mediterranean, as well as further north to Scandinavia. It is estimated that there are more than 140 species of anchovies, all of which are members of the Engraulidae family. When the anchovy runs occur in Northern California, it's a great cause for celebration.

Anchovies are smaller than sardines, generally just a couple of inches (5 cm) up to 5 inches (13 cm) in length.

Anchovies epitomize the now-common term of **umami**. What gives them their intense flavor is the curing process, in which the small fish are very often dried first in salt and then packed in tins with good olive oil.

**Smelt (Whitebait)** is a name given to several types of small fish, such as sardines and anchovies. For culinary purposes they are interchangeable.

## Herring (Culpea)

Herring are another important forage fish found in northern oceans around the world. As with sardines and anchovies, herring occur in huge numbers, grow quickly, and are generally considered a best choice seafood. They are enjoyed smoked, pickled, and cooked fresh.

## HOW TO CLEAN AND FILLET SMALL FISHES

**1.** Cut off the head and tail. **2.** Cut the fish in half lengthwise and remove the innards. **3.** Lift out the spine and scrape the meat lightly with a knife to remove any small bones. Rinse the fish well under cold running water.

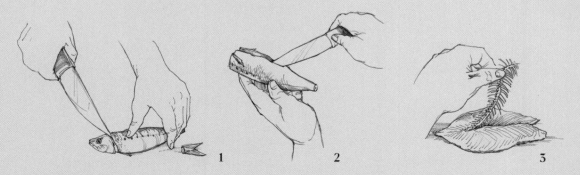

1          2          3

# MACKEREL

Mackerel are a very large group of pelagic fishes belonging to the Scombridae family, which includes tuna. Different species inhabit most of the oceans, including the Atlantic, Pacific, and Indian Oceans.

We find mackerel in the market in many different sizes, from small "finger-size" to larger fish. It's an often confusing world of naming fish, because names are used interchangeably, such as "mackerel" and "bonito," which are the same family. This chapter focuses on smaller mackerel. When purchasing the smaller fish, make sure they are from sustainable fisheries; for larger fish, look for line-caught. Here are some of the most commonly consumed species:

## Atlantic Mackerel (*Scomber scombrus*)

This small fish is considered a smart seafood choice, as their populations have high numbers and sustainable management practices. It is the most commonly used mackerel in Mediterranean conservas. Any hot, dry method of cooking works well with mackerel, including grilling, baking, roasting, panfrying, and smoking. It has an oily, full-flavored flesh that stands up well to heat.

## Sierra Mackerel (*Scomberomorus sierra*)

This variety of Spanish mackerel is commonly encountered in the Eastern Pacific from Baja California to South America. Like other mackerel, they reproduce abundantly and are taken by hook-and-line, making them a sustainable choice.

## Cero Mackerel (*Scomberomorus regalis*)

This fish has several different names, including painted mackerel, pintado, cero mackerel, and kingfish. It lives along the coast of North and South America and ranges throughout the Caribbean.

## King Mackerel (*Scomberomorus cavalla*)

An important commercial fishery exists for king mackerel, and it's also caught as a sport fish. They can weigh up to 100 pounds but most are around 30 pounds. It is a delicious fish, but because it can contain relatively high levels of mercury, the FDA recommends that pregnant women and children avoid it. Others should consume it only occasionally.

## Wahoo (*Acanthocybium solandri*)

Wahoo is a highly sought-after game fish that can swim quickly and powerfully. It is a difficult fish to land, and can weigh up to 150 pounds. In Hawaii, this species is known as ono.

The grape leaves add flavor and help keep the sardines from sticking to the grill or burning. A grill screen can be useful here. You can use this technique with any small fresh fish like anchovies, herring, small trout, or flatfish.

# GRILLED SARDINES in grape leaves

8 fresh sardines, cleaned and scaled, heads on or off (page 272)

Kosher salt and freshly ground pepper

8 thin slices lemon, seeded and halved

8 large bottled grape leaves, rinsed

Extra-virgin olive oil, preferably garlic-flavored, for brushing

Flaky salt, such as Maldon, for serving

Lemon wedges, for serving

Prepare a hot fire in a charcoal grill, or preheat a gas grill to high. Brush the grill grates clean. Alternatively, preheat a broiler.

Season the fish inside and out with salt and pepper. Place 2 sliced lemon halves in the cavity of each fish. Lay out a grape leaf, dull side up. Place a fish across the leaf near the stem end. Tuck the stem inside the cavity and wrap the leaf tightly around the fish. Repeat with the remaining fish.

Brush the wrapped fish generously with olive oil. Place on the grill or broil 4 inches (10 cm) from the heat source until a skewer easily enters the thickest part, about 7 minutes. The grape leaf should char a little, which adds flavor. Serve sprinkled with the flaky salt with lemon wedges alongside. **SERVES 4**

---

This dish is from a tapas bar I visited in Barcelona. It was served warm and with crisply fried sardines, topped with a little mound of the tomato-caper mixture.

# FRIED SARDINES with tomato-caper topping

**FRIED SARDINES**

1 pound (455 g) fresh filleted sardines, skin on

1½ cups (190 g) all-purpose flour

1 tablespoon kosher salt

2 teaspoons ground pepper

2 teaspoons paprika

Peanut or vegetable oil, for frying

**TOMATO-CAPER TOPPING**

1 cup (165 g) seeded, peeled, diced tomatoes

3 tablespoons finely chopped red onion

1 tablespoon capers, drained and rinsed

2 anchovy fillets, rinsed and chopped

1 teaspoon finely grated lemon zest

1 tablespoon chopped fresh parsley

2 tablespoons extra-virgin olive oil

Kosher salt and freshly ground pepper

Sherry vinegar

**GARNISH (OPTIONAL)**

Mint or basil sprigs, lemon wedges and shaved manchego cheese

Wash the sardines thoroughly and set aside. In a shallow bowl, mix the flour, salt, pepper, and paprika together.

To make the topping, in a separate bowl mix the tomatoes, onion, capers, anchovy, lemon zest, parsley, and olive oil. Season to taste with salt, pepper, and a few drops of vinegar. Set aside.

Add ¼-inch oil to a heavy sauté pan and place over medium-high heat. Dredge the sardines in the seasoned flour. Cook, turning once, until golden brown and crisp. Arrange on individual plates and top with a little dollop of the tomato caper mixture. Serve immediately with garnishes. **SERVES 4 TO 6**

White anchovies, or *boquerones en vinagre*, are one of Spain's most traditional tapas. Often served simply on crusty bread or potato chips, they are utilized in all sorts of other ways including with pasta or rolled with goat cheese. They are nothing like regular cured canned anchovies; they are milder, with a more delicate flavor enhanced by the brightness of vinegar, lemon, and garlic. The commercially available version is perfectly fine, but if you want to take it up a notch and make your own using fresh anchovies, here's a recipe. Make them ahead as they need to marinate for two days.

# HOMEMADE WHITE ANCHOVIES IN VINEGAR (boquerones)

1 pound (455 g) fresh anchovies, cleaned (page 272)

Fine sea salt

¾ cup (180 ml) white wine vinegar, or a combination of white wine and sherry vinegars

3 tablespoons fresh lemon juice

1 teaspoon finely chopped garlic

½ cup (50 g) thinly sliced sweet red onion

¼ cup (13 g) chopped fresh flat-leaf parsley

Extra-virgin olive oil to cover

Place the anchovies in a single layer in a glass or ceramic baking dish just large enough to fit them all. Sprinkle them lightly with salt. Pour the vinegar over the fillets, submerging them completely, then cover with plastic wrap and refrigerate for at least 2 days. The fish will turn white from the acid in the vinegar.

Drain and discard the liquid. Pour the lemon juice evenly over the anchovies and sprinkle them with the garlic, red onion, and parsley. Drizzle enough olive oil over the fillets to cover. Serve now, or place in an airtight container and refrigerate for up to 2 weeks. **MAKES 1 POUND (455 G)**

This is a recipe from chef/owner Stuart Brioza of State Bird Provisions and the Anchovy Bar in San Francisco. He is a long-time friend of the Hog Island Oyster Company. Make sure the anchovies are exceptionally fresh, and start this two days before you want to use them. Use these as you would any other boquerone.

# LIME-PICKLED ANCHOVIES, AKA 'CALIFORNIA BOQUERONES'

1¾ cups (420 ml) water

¾ cup (180 ml) plus 2 tablespoons fresh lime juice

6 tablespoons (105 g) kosher salt

1 garlic clove, thinly sliced

1 jalapeño chile (including seeds), thinly sliced

10 whole fresh basil leaves

1 pound (455 g) fresh anchovies (each 3 to 4 inches/7.5 to 10 cm long)

About ¼ cup (60 ml) grapeseed oil

1 pound (455 g) small heirloom tomatoes, preferably golf-ball size, quartered

Fine sea salt and freshly ground pepper

Extra-virgin olive oil, for drizzling

Small, fresh basil leaves, for garnish

In a straight-sided 1-quart (960-ml) container, combine the water, lime juice, and salt and stir until the salt dissolves. Add the garlic, jalapeño, and basil and stir briefly. Cover and refrigerate while you clean the anchovies.

Set the anchovies on a bed of crushed ice to keep them cold as you work. Working with one anchovy at a time, use a sharp knife to cut just behind the gills to remove the head. Insert the tip of the knife into the opening and nudge out the reddish black blob (the guts).

Starting from the opening, slit open the belly, stopping just before the small fin about 1 inch (2.5 cm) from the tail. Use the sharp edge of the knife blade to gently scrape one side of the exposed rib cage to remove the red viscera, then slice off the thin band of flesh you've pulled from the belly to create a straight edge. Flip the fish and do the same to the other side of the rib cage. Put the anchovy back on the bed of ice and repeat with the remaining anchovies.

Fill a large mixing bowl with water and add a tray of ice cubes. One by one, hold the anchovies under the water, use your thumb to gently rub the skin in the direction of the head to dislodge the scales, and gently rub the open belly to remove any lingering viscera. When the water gets murky, drain it and replace with fresh water and more ice cubes. Remove the anchovies from the water, shake gently, and add them to the brine. Cover with plastic wrap pressed against the surface of the brine and refrigerate for 2 days.

One by one, remove the anchovies from the brine. Hold each anchovy with your thumb against the belly and your forefinger against the back and very gently pinch along the length of the fish just to help the backbone release from the flesh. Gently open the fish like a book, grab the backbone at the top, and lift it to remove it and the tail in one piece. Put the anchovy, flesh side down, in a small, flat airtight container in which all will fit snugly (about 4 by 4 by 1½ inches/10 by 10 by 4 cm), stacking them in several layers. Pour in just enough of the grapeseed oil to cover. If not serving immediately, refrigerate for up to 1 week.

To serve, drape the tomato pieces with an anchovy. Sprinkle lightly with salt and pepper, drizzle with olive oil, garnish with basil leaves, and serve. **MAKES ABOUT 40 ANCHOVIES**

There are many variations of pickled herring. This is a traditional Scandinavian approach. Note that this takes 36 hours to brine and pickle so plan ahead. Fresh sardines, anchovies, or small fresh mackerel can be substituted for the herring. Salted herring, which is available from specialty food stores and online, can also be substituted for fresh herring. It has a higher salt content than fresh herring, so it should be soaked overnight in water or milk to cover, then drained. If using salted herring, skip the salting-overnight step and go directly to making the brine.

# PICKLED HERRING ROLLMOPS
## with crème fraîche and pumpernickel

½ cup (145 g) kosher salt

1 pound (455 g) fresh or frozen herring fillets, scaled and filleted (page 272)

3 cups (720 ml) malt vinegar or white wine vinegar

⅓ cup (75 g) brown sugar

1 small dried red chile

4 allspice berries

3 small bay leaves

½ teaspoon black peppercorns

½ teaspoon fennel seed

½ cup (50 g) thinly sliced red onion

About 24 pickled gherkins

About 24 toothpicks

Sliced dense dark bread, such as pumpernickel, for serving

1 cup (240 ml) crème fraîche or sour cream, for serving

Fresh dill sprigs, for garnish

In a saucepan, bring 3 cups (720 ml) water and the salt to a boil over high heat, stirring until the salt is completely dissolved. Set aside to cool completely.

Meanwhile, arrange the herring flesh side up in a single layer in a 9-by-13-inch (23-by-33-cm) glass baking dish. Pour the cooled salt water over the herring; they should be submerged. Cover and refrigerate for 24 hours.

In a large saucepan, combine the vinegar, sugar, chile, allspice, bay leaves, peppercorns, and fennel seed, to a large saucepan and bring to a boil over high heat. Reduce the heat to low and simmer for 5 minutes. Cool.

Strain and rinse the herrings and pat dry. Lay them on a cutting board skin side down. Arrange a few slices of red onion and a gherkin on top of each herring. Roll them up and secure with toothpicks or cocktail picks. Place them in a glass container with a lid and pour the cold spiced vinegar over to cover. Cover and refrigerate for at least 12 hours and up to 5 days.

To serve, remove the herring from the pickling liquid and place on squares of pumpernickel bread. Place a small dollop of crème fraîche on top and garnish with a dill sprig. **SERVES 6**

These tiny fish—which are eaten whole—are served all over the Mediterranean and are especially popular along the Loire River in France. The most popular preparation is this, called *friture*, where the fish are quickly fried and served with aioli and lemons. Whitebait, also known as smelt—and in America, often affectionately known as "fries with eyes"—must be absolutely fresh, so this is where you must rely on a good fishmonger. They are also sold frozen if you can't find fresh. Other small fish are often substituted.

# FRIED WHITEBAIT

1 pound (455 g) whitebait (smelt, small sardines, or small mackerel)

1½ cups (190 g) unbleached all-purpose flour

1 tablespoon kosher salt

2 teaspoons freshly ground pepper

2 teaspoons paprika

Olive or canola oil, for frying

Aioli (page 337), chopped fresh flat-leaf parsley, and lemon wedges for serving

Rinse the whitebait thoroughly under cold running water and set aside in a colander to drain. In a shallow bowl, mix the flour, salt, pepper, and paprika with a small whisk until blended.

In a large, deep sauté pan, heat 1 inch (2.5 cm) of oil over medium-high heat until shimmering (375°F/190°C on a deep-frying thermometer).

Dredge the whitebait in the seasoned flour to coat evenly and transfer to a plate. Working in batches, transfer to the hot oil and fry until golden brown and crisp, about 3 minutes.

Using a wire-mesh skimmer, transfer the fried whitebait to paper towels to drain. Repeat to cook the remaining fish.

Sprinkle with the parsley and serve at once with the aioli and with lemon wedges to squeeze over. **SERVES 6 TO 8**

Adapted from a recipe by Barton Seaver, noted chef and educator who helped to create an online course called Seafood Literacy, this recipe teaches not only how to cook seafood but also how to maintain its sustainability. "En saor" is an Italian method for preserving oily fish with a sweet and sour vinaigrette not unlike escabeche. In Venice, it's a popular appetizer typically made with sardines.

# MACKEREL "EN SAOR"

1½ pounds (680 g) fresh small mackerel fillets, skin on

Fine sea salt

¾ cup (180 ml) extra-virgin olive oil

1 small onion, finely sliced

1 small red bell pepper, seeded and finely diced

1 small eggplant, cut into ½-inch (12-mm) dice (about 2 cups/160 g)

3 tablespoons pine nuts or slivered almonds

2 heaping tablespoons raisins, preferably golden

⅓ cup (75 ml) white wine vinegar

1 tablespoon brown sugar

Freshly ground pepper

Crusty baguette slices or crostini (page 343), for serving

Lightly salt the mackerel on both sides and set aside for 10 minutes.

In a large skillet, heat ¼ cup (60 ml) of the olive oil over medium heat. Place the fish in the pan skin side down and cook without turning until lightly browned, then turn the fillets to finish cooking, about 2 minutes. The fish should be opaque all the way through. Arrange attractively in a rimmed dish.

Return the skillet to medium-high heat. Add the remaining ½ cup (120 ml) of olive oil to the pan. Add the onion, bell pepper, and eggplant and cook until the vegetables have softened and are just beginning to brown. The eggplant will have absorbed much of the olive oil. Stir in the pine nuts and raisins and cook a few more minutes.

Stir in the vinegar and sugar and season with salt and pepper and additional sugar, if desired. Pour the mixture over the fish. Let cool, then cover and refrigerate overnight to allow the flavors to develop. Before serving, let the fillets sit at room temperature for about 1 hour.

Serve with the baguette slices. **SERVES 4 TO 8**

This is a simple way to cook mackerel that yields a delicious result and makes a wonderful first course. Top it with any of the compound butters found in the back of the book (pages 334 to 335). Some favorites are miso butter, mustard-tarragon butter, and 'nduja butter. This method can also be used for other small fish family members (sardines, anchovies, etc); simply adjust the cooking time for the thickness of the fish. Have your fishmonger clean the fish and remove the backbones without cutting them in half.

# BROILED MACKEREL
## with butter and green onions

3 tablespoons olive oil

2 tablespoons finely chopped green onion, including some green parts

2 tablespoons fresh lemon juice

½ teaspoon kosher salt

A few grindings of pepper

2 fresh mackerel, ¾ pound (340 g) each

2 tablespoons unsalted butter

2 tablespoons canola or other neutral oil

Softened compound butter of your choice (pages 334 to 335)

Preheat the broiler. In a shallow baking dish large enough to hold the fish in a single layer, combine the oil, green onion, lemon juice, salt, and pepper. Add the fish, flesh side down, and let sit at room temperature for 15 minutes. Turn the fish over and let sit another 15 minutes.

In a small saucepan, melt the butter with the oil over low heat. Brush the broiler pan with 1 tablespoon of the butter mixture.

Remove the mackerel from the marinade and arrange on the pan, skin side down. Broil, basting from time to time with the remaining butter-oil mixture, and without turning, until the fish are light golden in color and the flesh flakes easily with a fork, about 10 minutes.

Transfer to a platter or plates, top with some of the compound butter, and serve at once. **SERVES 2**

I've spent a lot of time in Japan and appreciate the delicacy and simplicity of the cuisine. This is an adaptation of a recipe from Namiko Chen's website, *Just One Cookbook*. It's one of the simplest recipes you can make and a great introduction to mackerel. Sake and salt are used here tenderize and flavor the fish, but don't let it marinate for longer (or less) than 20 minutes. Serve with steamed rice, miso soup, and a crisp green salad.

# BAKED MACKEREL
## with daikon, soy, and lemon

2 fresh mackerel fillets, about 5 ounces (140 g) each

2 tablespoons sake

½ teaspoon kosher salt

2 tablespoons peeled and finely grated daikon radish

1 teaspoon soy sauce, preferably Japanese

2 lemon wedges, for serving

In a medium bowl, combine the mackerel and sake and turn the mackerel to coat. Transfer the mackerel to paper towels and pat dry, then transfer to a baking sheet lined with parchment paper. Sprinkle the mackerel with the salt on both sides and let it sit at room temperature for exactly 20 minutes.

Meanwhile, position an oven rack in the center of the oven and preheat to 425°F (220°C).

Pat the fish dry again on both sides with paper towels. Place the fish skin side down and bake until the flesh is golden brown, 15 to 20 minutes.

In a small bowl, mix the shredded radish and soy sauce. Serve with the fish, with the lemon wedges alongside.
**SERVES 2**

# CANNED, TINNED, AND JARRED FISH

anchovies, tuna, sardines, and more . . .

In America, canned fish has traditionally been thought of as food for the poor. Though prized in Europe, especially around the Mediterranean, when folks there immigrated to America, inexpensive tinned fish was a remembrance of their earlier life. These days, food lovers and home cooks have learned that fish in a tin (or jar) deserves a place on restaurant menus as well as in their pantry. If you have ever been to Portugal or Spain, you'll remember stores completely devoted to the sale of tinned and jarred fish (called conservas). There you will find a wide variety of fishes including sardines, mackerel, crab, octopus, squid, and more.

# CANNED, TINNED, AND JARRED FISH

Canning, tinning, and jarring fish, which has been in practice for hundreds of years, may have been born from necessity but is now experiencing a renaissance with home cooks and restaurants alike. With sustainability and fair practices in mind, the general consensus is that tinned fish and shellfish are packed with flavor, convenient, budget-friendly, and shelf-stable. They are also endlessly versatile with all different types of seafoods and flavor profiles available—you could make an entire meal out of a pile of toasted crostini and a few varieties of tinned fish.

## Canned Oil- and Salt-Packed Anchovies

Anchovies are typically sold in small tins or jars and are packed in oil, which most of us are familiar with.

Salt-packed anchovies are available at Mediterranean markets or online, and their flavor and texture are worth the extra cost. Rinse them under running water, then separate each into 2 fillets, discarding the spine and any fins or tail pieces. Use as you would oil-packed.

Pizza and anchovies are a match made in heaven. In fact, one of the classic pizzas wouldn't be the same without them. Pizza marinara is made with just tomatoes and anchovies (often no cheese) as the topping. I think when they are "melted" into sauces they shine, such as in the Spaghetti Alla Rustica (page 294). And of course, they are the key to a great Caesar Salad (page 291).

## Boquerones

These are white anchovies that are ubiquitous in tapas bars in Spain. They are delicate and typically packed in a combination of oil and vinegar. You'll find them tinned and also refrigerated in sealed plastic containers in good delicatessens, but if you want to make your own, see the recipe on page 275.

## Canned Tuna

Americans are very familiar with canned tuna. It comes in a variety of styles: chunk, solid-pack, with or without oil, and more. In my opinion, the very best canned tuna comes from the Mediterranean, and oil-packed is without question better than water-packed.

There are several issues, however, around eating canned tuna. Among them is the fact that dolphins are often sacrificed with large-scale harvesting. Also, the presence of mercury is of concern. There are several producers who have taken these issues on, and I suggest researching companies to find out what their practices are. For what it's worth, my favorite brand/producer of tuna is Tonnino, specifically labeled Ventresca, which comes from the belly of the fish. They both test for mercury and follow dolphin-safe practices.

## Sardines and More

Many people have grown up with canned sardines, which you may or may not like. There are so many interesting ways to use them, other than on saltine crackers. Many other tinned fish have become widely available, such as octopus, mackerel, squid, cockles, and herring. Included are some recipes to get you started.

My favorite "surf and turf!" This is a classic Spanish nosh any time of day. You'll see it displayed in delis and restaurants everywhere. Often, it's just the toast with tomatoes but this is a more luxurious version.

# TOMATO TOASTS
## with serrano ham and boquerones

2 large, very ripe tomatoes

2 tablespoons extra-virgin olive oil, preferably Spanish, plus more for drizzling

Fine sea salt

4 thick slices rustic bread

4 thin slices Serrano ham or prosciutto

4 boquerones, homemade (page 275) or store-bought

Manchego cheese, for shaving

Cut the tomatoes in half and gently squeeze to remove the seeds. Using a box grater-shredder set over a large bowl, shred the cut sides of the tomatoes on the large holes of the grater until all the flesh is shredded. Discard the skin.

Add the 2 tablespoons of olive oil to the shredded tomato in the bowl and season to taste with salt. Toast the bread lightly on both sides under a hot broiler about 6 inches (15 cm) from the heat source.

Spoon the tomato mixture over the toasts. Place a slice of ham and a boquerone on top of each. Shave a little Manchego over, drizzle with olive oil, and serve. **SERVES 4**

---

The key to this dish is using oil-packed tuna from Spain or Italy. This top-quality tuna is mixed with the mashed eggs yolks along with capers and mayonnaise, which gives the stuffing maximum flavor. The white anchovy on top of each stuffed egg brings these appetizers to a new level.

# TUNA-STUFFED EGGS
## with boquerones

6 large hard-boiled eggs (page 344), peeled and halved lengthwise

½ cup (80 g) imported oil-packed tuna, drained and finely flaked

2 tablespoons mayonnaise

1 tablespoon fresh lemon juice

2 tablespoons drained and chopped small capers

Fine sea salt and freshly ground pepper

12 boquerones, homemade (page 275) or store-bought

2 tablespoons finely chopped fresh flat-leaf parsley and/or mint

¼ teaspoon pimentón (Spanish smoked paprika)

Put the egg yolks in a medium bowl and mash with a fork. Add the tuna, mayonnaise, lemon juice, and capers and stir to mix thoroughly. Season to taste with salt and pepper.

Spoon the yolk mixture into the egg whites, mounding it to fill. Arrange an anchovy on top of each egg and sprinkle with parsley and pimentón. **MAKES 12 STUFFED EGGS**

This Caesar dressing is a bit unconventional (it uses tofu), but no one will know, I promise. It also avoids using raw egg, which the traditional dressing uses, but the anchovies give it all the flavor and umami of a classic Caesar. It's topped with homemade croutons, which are far better than anything you'll find in a store. You can also add cooked shellfish, such as shrimp, lobster, or scallops. Very thinly sliced watermelon radishes add a burst of bright color.

# JOHN'S CAESAR SALAD

**TOFU CAESAR DRESSING**

6 ounces (170 g) silken tofu

½ cup (50 g) freshly grated Parmesan cheese

¼ cup (60 ml) vegetable stock (page 333), chicken stock (page 333), or water

6 to 8 oil-packed anchovy fillets, drained

1½ tablespoons olive oil

1 tablespoon Dijon mustard

1 tablespoon grated lemon zest

1 tablespoon fresh lemon juice

2 teaspoons chopped fresh garlic

2 teaspoons white wine or cider vinegar

Fine sea salt and freshly ground pepper

**SALAD**

2 large hearts romaine lettuce

2 cups (40 g) tender frisée lettuce leaves, lightly packed

1 small fennel bulb, trimmed and sliced paper thin

Garlic Croutons (page 343)

¼ cup (25 g) freshly shaved Parmesan cheese

To make the dressing, add the tofu, Parmesan, stock, anchovy fillets, olive oil, mustard, lemon zest, lemon juice, garlic, and vinegar to a blender and blend until smooth. Season with salt and pepper and more lemon juice or anchovy.

To make the salad, cut the romaine hearts attractively and combine with the frisée and fennel in a large bowl. Toss with some of the dressing to generously coat. Add the croutons and toss again. Arrange attractively on chilled plates with a scattering of shaved Parmesan on top, passing additional dressing alongside. **SERVES 4**

Bagna cauda ("warm bath"), an ancient concoction from Italy, is a warm olive oil, garlic, and anchovy sauce that you dip raw vegetables, crusty bread, or almost anything into. It couldn't be simpler to make, and you can adjust the ingredients to suit your taste.

# BAGNA CAUDA

¾ cup (180 ml) extra-virgin olive oil

3 tablespoons unsalted butter

2 teaspoons minced garlic

8 to 10 oil-packed anchovy fillets, finely chopped

Fine sea salt and freshly ground pepper

Sliced crusty bread and crudités (raw, bite-size vegetables) for dipping

In a small, heavy saucepan, combine the olive oil, butter, garlic, and anchovies. Cook over low heat, stirring with a wooden spoon to mash and dissolve the anchovies, until the butter is melted. Add salt and pepper to taste.

Serve warm, set over a candle warmer if possible, with sliced bread and raw vegetables for dipping. **SERVES 4 TO 6**

---

This Provençal puree of anchovies with garlic and olive oil can be spread on toast or served as a dip. It's terrific served with wine or cocktails.

# ANCHOÏADE

10 whole salt-packed anchovies, rinsed, filleted (page 272), and coarsely chopped, or 20 oil-packed anchovy fillets, drained and coarsely chopped

3 cloves garlic, chopped

1 teaspoon tomato paste

2 tablespoons unsalted butter, at room temperature

½ cup (120 ml) extra-virgin olive oil

2 teaspoons red wine vinegar, or to taste

Freshly ground pepper

Eight ¾-inch- (2-cm-) thick slices French bread, toasted or grilled

Chopped fresh flat-leaf parsley, for serving

In a food processor, combine the anchovies, garlic, and tomato paste and pulse until smooth. Blend in the butter. Transfer the mixture to a small bowl and stir in the olive oil, a few tablespoons at a time, until incorporated. Stir in the vinegar and season to taste with pepper.

To serve, spread the anchoïade on the toasted bread and sprinkle with the parsley. **SERVES 4**

In Italy, this sauce is traditionally served with vitello tonnato, a classic dish of cold braised and sliced veal. I think it's also delicious tossed with pasta, as here, as well as used a dipping sauce for raw vegetables. If you are concerned about raw egg yolks, use one that has been coddled or even hard-boiled.

# TUNA "TONNATO" PENNE

¾ cup (180 ml) extra-virgin olive oil

1 teaspoon minced garlic

One 6½-ounce (185-g) can oil-packed tuna, undrained

1 large egg yolk

4 anchovy oil-packed fillets

3 tablespoons fresh lemon juice

⅓ cup (75 ml) heavy cream

⅓ cup (75 ml) chicken stock (page 333)

3 tablespoons drained and chopped capers

⅓ cup (17 g) minced fresh flat-leaf parsley, plus more for garnish

Kosher salt and freshly ground white pepper

1 pound (455 g) penne, rigatoni, or other medium-shaped pasta

To make the sauce, in a blender or food processor, combine half the olive oil, the garlic, the tuna with its oil, egg yolk, anchovies, and lemon juice and process briefly to puree. Pour into a small bowl and gradually stir in the cream and stock. Stir in the capers and parsley. Add salt and pepper to taste.

Bring a large pot of salted water to a boil over high heat. Add the pasta and cook until al dente, or according to the package directions. Drain, reserving 1 cup (240 ml) of the pasta water, and put the pasta in a heated serving bowl. Add the tuna sauce and toss quickly, adding a bit of reserved cooking water as needed to make a creamy sauce.

Serve immediately, garnished with the parsley. **SERVES 4 TO 6**

This simple recipe has its roots in the flavorful cooking of Sardinia. Don't be afraid of using all the anchovies, even if you don't like anchovies! They add a deep umami richness, and you won't even know they're there. Feel free to add whatever else you have on hand, like drained capers, chopped olives, or drained and chopped oil-packed sun-dried tomatoes.

# SPAGHETTI ALLA RUSTICA

½ cup (120 ml) olive oil

3 cloves garlic, slightly crushed

6 oil-packed anchovy fillets, chopped

1 tablespoon chopped fresh oregano leaves, or 1½ teaspoons dried

Fine sea salt

Pinch of crushed red pepper flakes

½ pound (225 g) spaghetti

3 tablespoons chopped fresh flat-leaf parsley

2 tablespoons grated lemon zest

½ cup (50 g) freshly grated pecorino cheese

In a small skillet, heat the olive oil over low heat and fry the garlic until lightly brown. Remove and discard the garlic, add the anchovies to the oil and cook until they dissolve into a paste. Stir in the oregano, salt to taste, and the crushed red pepper. Set aside and keep warm.

Bring a large pot of salted water to a boil over high heat. Add the pasta and cook until al dente, or according to the package directions. Drain, reserving 1 cup (240 ml) of the pasta water, and put the spaghetti in a heated serving bowl. Add the anchovy mixture, parsley, and lemon zest and toss quickly, adding a bit of reserved cooking water as needed to make a creamy sauce. Serve immediately, topped with the cheese. **SERVES 4**

---

This recipe comes from John Burkhard, longtime master of the traveling oyster bars at Hog Island. He notes, "I grew up eating this dish, thinking it was some odd recipe my mother learned while flying for Pan Am. Turns out it is classic Sicilian comfort food."

# TUNA SPAGHETTI

1 cup (240 ml) extra-virgin olive oil

1 yellow onion, diced

2 cloves garlic, chopped

½ teaspoon crushed red pepper flakes

One 7-ounce (200-g) jar or can imported tuna in olive oil, undrained if desired

One 28-ounce (800-g) can crushed tomatoes

1 bay leaf

½ teaspoon dried oregano, crushed

Kosher salt

½ pound (225 g) spaghetti, linguini, or bucatini

Freshly grated dry Jack, pecorino, or Parmesan cheese, for garnish

To make the sauce, in a heavy, medium saucepan, heat the olive oil over medium heat. Add the onion and garlic, reduce the heat to low, cover, and cook, stirring occasionally, until the onion is translucent, about 5 minutes. Add the crushed red pepper and tuna (with oil if desired), stir, and cook for about 2 minutes more. Add the tomatoes, bay leaf, and oregano. Simmer, stirring occasionally, until the flavors develop, about 20 minutes. Season with salt to taste.

Bring a large pot of salted water to a boil over high heat. Add the pasta and cook until al dente, or according to the package directions. Drain, reserving ½ cup (120 ml) of the pasta water.

Return the spaghetti to the cooking pot, add half the sauce and the pasta water, and cook over medium heat for about 1 minute, tossing the spaghetti with the sauce. Serve in warm bowls with the remaining sauce on top, sprinkled with grated cheese. **SERVES 4**

A specialty of Provence, the name of this sandwich means "bathed bread." In this version, a split baguette is filled with salad ingredients and canned fish. The loaf is then wrapped in plastic and weighted down to make it moist and compact. It should be made ahead and is perfect for picnics because it travels well.

# PAN BAGNAT

3 plum tomatoes, thinly sliced crosswise

Kosher salt

One 5-ounce (140-g) can oil-packed tuna, drained

½ small red bell pepper, seeded and chopped

⅓ cup (75 ml) extra-virgin olive oil

1 tablespoon Dijon mustard

1 baguette, split (16 to 20 ounces/ 445 to 570 g)

½ cup (25 g) celery leaves or thinly sliced fennel

4 thin slices sweet red onion

1 small Persian cucumber, thinly sliced lengthwise

2 large hard-boiled eggs (page 344), thinly sliced crosswise

6 oil-packed anchovies, drained

8 oil-cured black olives, pitted and chopped

4 large fresh basil leaves, torn

Freshly ground pepper

Put the tomato slices in a colander, sprinkle liberally with salt, and set aside to drain for 30 minutes. Spread out on paper towels and pat dry.

In a small bowl, break up the tuna with a fork and stir in the bell pepper. In another small bowl, whisk the olive oil and mustard together.

Scoop the insides from the bread loaf, leaving a half inch (12 mm) or so, and reserve for another use. Place the tomato slices evenly in the bottom of the bread and then top with the celery leaves, onion, and cucumber. Spread the tuna mixture over the top, then top with the egg slices, anchovies, olives, and basil. Pour the dressing evenly over the ingredients and season with salt and pepper. Cover with the top of the bread, pressing lightly to compact.

Wrap the sandwich tightly in plastic wrap and place on a baking sheet. Top with another baking sheet and weigh it down with a cast-iron skillet. Refrigerate for at least 4 hours or up to overnight. Slice the sandwich into quarters to serve. **SERVES 4**

You probably already have most of the ingredients you need to make this Sicilian-inspired dish, which was adapted from a recipe by Mark Bittman. The anchovy-Parmesan bread crumbs are the perfect final touch. You can substitute any canned fish, such as mackerel, herring, or smoked oysters, for the sardines.

# BUCATINI with sardines and bread crumbs

Kosher salt

2 tablespoons extra-virgin olive oil

1½ cups (165 g) chopped onions

1 teaspoon finely chopped garlic

Freshly ground pepper

Grated zest and juice of 1 small lemon

2 tablespoons drained capers

Two 3.75-ounce (105-g) cans oil-packed sardines

½ pound (225 g) long pasta, such as bucatini

½ cup (25 g) chopped fresh flat-leaf parsley, plus more for garnish

1 cup (80 g) Anchovy-Parmesan Bread Crumbs (page 343)

Set a large pot of salted water over high heat and bring to a boil.

In a large skillet, heat the olive oil over moderate heat. Add the onions and garlic to the pan, sprinkle with salt and pepper, and cook, stirring occasionally, over moderate heat until softened, about 5 minutes. Add the lemon zest and juice, capers, and sardines; cook, stirring occasionally, until just heated through, about 2 minutes. Set aside.

Add the pasta to the boiling salted water and cook until al dente according to the directions on the package. Reserve ½ cup (120 ml) of the pasta water and drain the pasta.

Add the drained pasta to the skillet with the sardine mixture and toss gently to combine, trying to keep the sardines whole. Add the parsley, and some of the reserved pasta water, if necessary, to make a smooth sauce. Taste and adjust the seasoning.

Serve in a large warm pasta bowl, garnished with more parsley and the bread crumbs. **SERVES 4**

This is a recipe contributed by Sallie Miller and Gwen Gunheim of Miracle Plum, a food and wine emporium in Santa Rosa, California. They do a lot of creative recipes with tinned fish, and this is a delicious example. They note that this recipe makes more pickled fennel than you'll need, but you'll find yourself putting it on everything!

# TARTINES
## with octopus and pickled fennel

**PICKLED FENNEL**

1¼ pounds (570 g) fennel bulbs, trimmed

1 tablespoon fresh dill weed

1 tablespoon yellow mustard seeds

¼ teaspoon crushed red pepper flakes, or to taste

2 teaspoons fennel seeds

1½ cups (360 ml) rice vinegar

1½ cups (360 ml) water

1 tablespoon kosher salt

1 tablespoon sugar

**TARTINES**

4 thick slices crusty bread

Two 4-ounce (115-g) cans octopus, drained

Freshly ground black pepper

To make the pickled fennel, cut the fennel bulbs in half lengthwise and cut out the core. Thinly slice using a mandoline or a chef's knife. In a large, clean glass jar, combine the dill weed, mustard seeds, crushed red pepper, fennel seeds, and the fennel.

In a small saucepan, combine the vinegar, water, salt, and sugar and bring to a boil, stirring to dissolve the salt and sugar. Pour over the fennel and spices in the jar. Let cool to room temperature, then cover and refrigerate for at least 8 hours or up to 2 weeks.

To assemble the tartines, top each slice of bread with some of the octopus. Use a slotted spoon to remove some of the pickled fennel from the pickling liquid, then heap it generously on top. Season with black pepper to taste, cut each slice of bread in half, and serve. **SERVES 4**

# OTHER GIFTS FROM THE SEA

caviars and roes, bottarga, salt cod, sea urchins (uni), seaweed and sea vegetables

There has never been a better time to explore the many, sometimes less-appreciated, culinary gifts from the sea. Some of these are thought of as delicacies and others as oddities, but all trace their heritage as food resources in times when nothing was wasted. The curing of fish during times of abundance, along with roes and other organs, was and is a way of valuing those food resources to the fullest. Similarly, seaweeds have also long been a part of a nutritious coastal diet. They are seasonally abundant and can be dried for use year-round. Most of the foods in this chapter are also considered highly sustainable, as they are either by-products of existing fisheries or from species that grow and reproduce rapidly.

# CAVIARS AND ROES

Caviar is generally understood to be the eggs or roe of sturgeon, with a distinctive European heritage associated with affluence, wild sturgeon, and the briny waters of the Black and Caspian Seas of Central Asia.

Today those wild species are threatened with degraded waters and overfishing, and the fisheries lack the transparency to be considered a sustainable choice. However, there is now a thriving domestic aquaculture industry for white sturgeon and well-managed caviar, which, while still expensive, can be widely found. Many other roes are enjoyed around the world as well—both fresh- and saltwater. These include roe from salmon (*ikura*), trout, whitefish, paddlefish, flying fish (*tobiko*) and many more. Some of these alternative "caviars" are quite affordable and obtained from both aquaculture and well-managed wild fisheries.

# BOTTARGA

Known as "poor man's caviar," bottarga is the salted, pressed, and dried roe of either the tuna (*tonno*) or the gray mullet (*muggine*). It is a specialty of Sardinia and Sicily, but similar processes exist in many parts of the world and probably go back before recorded time.

In the United States, the Anna Maria Fish Company in Florida is famous for its bottarga, which it produces using traditional methods. The fat roe sack is salted and massaged by hand over several weeks to eliminate air pockets. The roe is then pressed using wooden planks and stone weights, then sun-dried for one to two months.

Bottarga can be shaved, sliced, chopped, or grated, and just a little of this strongly flavored ingredient can provide much flavor to many dishes. Probably the most popular dish using it is spaghetti with bottarga (page 313), made with grated or finely chopped bottarga, olive oil, crushed red pepper, and chopped parsley. Also try topping a salad of savory greens with shaved bottarga, or grating it into scrambled eggs.

Bottarga should be kept in an airtight container in the fridge to maintain its flavor.

# SALT COD

Salt cod has a history as old as civilization itself in Europe (especially in Portugal, Spain, and Italy), Scandinavia, North America (especially in Newfoundland and New England), and Africa. It remains a diet staple in the diet in many of these locations. Salt cod is called *morue* in French, *bacalao* in Castilian Spanish, *bacalhau* in Portuguese, and *baccalà* in Italian.

Fresh cod was originally salted and dried to preserve the fish before the time of refrigeration, allowing it to last for long periods of time without spoiling or changing in quality. When Christianity mandated meatless meals on certain days in medieval times, the demand for fish skyrocketed. For the poor who lived far from the sea, this meant eating dried cod.

Salt cod comes in several forms, including whole fish, which they vaguely resemble in their dried form. It should be white or ivory in color, without soft spots or discoloration. You can also buy salt cod in small 1-pound (455 g) wooden or waxed paper boxes, which often contain both thin strips and some center or middle-cut chunks. The former is fine for recipes calling for the fish to be flaked or pureed, and the thicker ones can be used for recipes calling for large pieces. I try to look for what are called "middles," large thick pieces that give me the ability to use the cod in any form, from purees to steaks.

## HOW TO PREPARE SALT COD

Salt cod must be soaked to remove the salt. Depending on its thickness and salt concentration, this will usually take at least 24 hours or up to 48 hours. Simply cover it in cold water, place it in the refrigerator, and change the water three or four times a day. To determine if it's desalted enough, take a little bite.

Salt cod can vary in quality, so it's best to buy it from someone who knows what to look for. In Spain, Portugal, and Italy chefs rely on special suppliers to both procure and desalt it.

# SEA URCHINS (UNI)

These spiky, slow moving little sea creatures are common in salt water throughout the world. A The easiest way to describe one is as a "ball of spines," though they have been called the "hedgehogs of the sea." They look like a pincushion filled with needles and appear in a wide variety of colors, shapes, and sizes. There are thought to be more than 950 species, some with incredibly long, thin spines, while others have short thick nubs. Contrary to conventional wisdom, most sea urchins don't sting people and aren't poisonous or venomous. It can be painful, however, if a spine pokes through your skin.

Sea urchins have been used as a source of food by many cultures for generations. They are traditionally eaten in Japanese, Mediterranean, Italian, Chilean, Native American, and New Zealand cultures. The big majority of the sea urchin coral consumed in the United States comes from urchins caught off the California coast.

The edible part of the sea urchin is known as uni in Japan. The five small, orange-colored portions of meat inside the urchin are sometimes mistaken for roe, but in fact are the gonads, or sex organs, that produce roe, sometimes referred to as corals or tongues.

Sea urchins spend their lives foraging for food, and they are voracious eaters. They move about by undulating their spines and shooting water through their tubed feet. In recent years, purple sea urchins have exploded in California, covering the ocean floor in what divers describe as a "purple carpet." They voraciously devour kelp, so much so that the lush forests of seaweed that hugged the coastline are almost gone.

Kelp forests are crucial for the ecosystem for a broad range of marine life, and their demise threatens the ecology of the entire California coast. Warming waters due to climate change and lack of predators such as sea otters are encouraging the urchins' growth.

The flavor of uni is said to be unique, but it does taste of the sea in the same way as oysters do. It combines sweet and salty and also has a definite umami flavor. Its texture is creamy and luxurious, similar to foie gras.

Uni is best eaten simply. I like it with a squeeze of lemon (preferably Meyer), a drizzle of peppery olive oil, and a light sprinkling of flaky sea salt. The idea is to enhance the flavors of the corals without masking their natural ocean flavors. The French serve uni with good butter and crusty bread; they also add it to soufflés and omelets. In Japan, it is simply served on top of seasoned rice, on sushi, or in *chawanmushi* (Japanese egg custards, page 127). In Italy, sea urchin is tossed with buttered spaghetti and lemon.

## HOW TO PREPARE UNI

You'll need gloves, a towel, kitchen shears, and a teaspoon. With gloves on, turn the sea urchin upside down to expose the mouth. **1.** Holding it in a towel for stability, pierce a hole near the perimeter of the shell with the shears. Cut a 3-inch (7.5-cm) circle in the shell. **2.** Using the spoon, lift up the circle and discard it along with the star-shaped chewing organ known as Aristotle's lantern. Pour out all the liquid and "black stuff," which is partially digested food such as seaweed and other organic matter. **3.** Carefully scoop out the orange-colored corals (the uni). Gently rinse them in a bowl of ice water and, with your fingers, remove any "black stuff" still clinging to the corals (uni). The ice water also helps to firm them up.

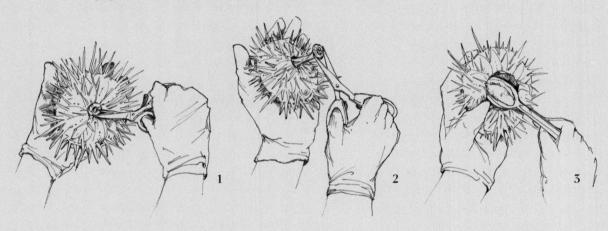

## HOW TO EAT UNI

Typically, when you buy sea urchin it is packed in a lovely wooden box and is always refrigerated. It is best eaten as soon after harvest as possible.

One of the best ways to enjoy uni is by itself, which will give you the full-on sensation of a briny custard, but you can also combine it with other foods:

- Spread it on warm buttered toast.

- Serve it over hot rice or pasta, especially squid ink pasta!

- Dip it in a mixture of soy sauce and wasabi.

- Spread it over medium-rare steak.

# SEAWEED AND SEA VEGETABLES

Seaweed in various forms has been eaten by humans for as long as we've documented such things. In Japan, Korea, and our own East Coast, for example, they are typically used in salads and soups. Extracts from seaweeds have long been used in Japan to prepare and preserve fish and meat. Powdered seaweed can be used to improve the human digestion of beans and as a flavor enhancer since it is a natural source of glutamic acid. It is becoming more and more popular in America as we discover its nutritional and ecological value. Hog Island is increasingly involved in both harvesting seaweed from their gear and their pilot project in Humboldt Bay to farm seaweed.

In addition to providing food for humans, seaweed helps to clean the sea, providing oxygen through photosynthesis. It also helps to prevent erosion and is a home for many organisms.

All kinds of fish, plankton and diatoms exist by eating seaweed, which is at the bottom of the food chain. Seaweed acts as a nursery for many sea creatures.

On top of all that, seaweed removes carbon dioxide, a key greenhouse gas, from the air by absorbing it into its leaves. Large seaweed forests help prevent erosion by keeping sand and rocks from drifting away. Areas with seaweed are more stable than those that lack it. But seaweed can become diseased and float away if it encounters too much pollution, and strong storms can loosen holdfasts if the seaweed is not healthy.

Because of its high nitrogen content, for centuries seaweed has been used as a fertilizer by farmers living close to the sea. And of course, it is itself a source of sustainable and delicious nutrition. Seaweed is used in many of the cuisines of Asia in several different forms. Here are some of the most commonly found varieties of seaweed and their culinary uses.

## Nori

This red seaweed is most familiar to food lovers in the form of thin dark-green sheets that can be eaten as a snack or used to wrap sushi rolls (it turns dark green when it's dried). It is also a main ingredient in furikake (page 326). Because nori absorbs moisture easily, it should be stored airtight. Most nori sold in the market today has been toasted. This will be indicated on the package. If it hasn't been toasted, it's a good idea to do it by simply passing the sheets briefly over an open gas flame or at hot burner on your stove. Nori comes cut in many different sizes, from full-size sheets to needle-thin shreds.

## Kombu

Kombu is the main ingredient in dashi, a clear, flavorful stock that is a cornerstone of Japanese cuisine. This brown kelp is usually sold dried and in wide strips. A variety of foods are made from kombu, including shio kombu, which is made by simmering kombu with soy sauce. Packed with umami and rich in calcium and dietary fiber, it is an excellent seasoning for fish.

## Wakame

Wakame is a brown kelp with a very slightly sweet flavor. It is used to make seaweed salads and is added to miso soup. It is available either dried or salted, in the form of strips. The salted variety is sold packaged and refrigerated. Dried wakame must be soaked before using.

## Dulse

Dulse is a reddish seaweed from the cold waters of the northern Atlantic and northern Pacific Oceans ,where it grows attached to rocks. First harvested in Scotland and Iceland over a thousand years ago, dulse has a soft, leathery texture and a taste reminiscent of bacon. Sold in dry flakes, shredded, or ground into a powder, dulse is used in soups and baked into chips.

# SOURCES FOR SEA VEGETABLES

## Ocean Harvest Sea Vegetables

**seaweedmermaid.com**

This company's wild-harvested seaweed is ethically sourced from California's Mendocino Coast, rinsed in ocean water, and dried by the sun. This hand processing maximizes the seaweed's essential minerals and nutrients.

## Rising Tide Sea Vegetables

**loveseaweed.com**

This company's current product line includes seventeen locally harvested and produced items. In addition to selling direct to the public via their website, they sell through a variety of local and regional specialty foods stores.

## Maine Coast Sea Vegetables

**seaveg.com**

Their products include seaweeds, teas, and seasonings.

## Atlantic Sea Farms

**atlanticseafarms.com**

This Maine-based company sells a wide variety of prepared foods, including Sea Kraut, Seaweed Salad, Sea (Kim) Chi, and ready-cut kelp.

## Pacific Harvest

**pacificharvest.co.nz**

Based in New Zealand, their products are harvested around the world.

These little pancakes, classically served with caviar, are easy to make, especially if you used baking powder instead of yeast, as in this recipe. Here, they are topped with smoked salmon, crème fraîche, good caviar, and sprigs of dill.

# BLINI with smoked salmon and caviar

**BLINI**

⅔ cup (80 g) unbleached all-purpose flour

⅓ cup (40 g) buckwheat flour

1 teaspoon kosher salt

½ teaspoon baking powder

¾ cup (180 ml) plus 2 tablespoons milk

1 large egg

2 tablespoons unsalted butter, melted

**TOPPINGS**

4 ounces (115 g) thinly sliced smoked salmon, cut in blini size pieces

½ cup (120 ml) crème fraîche

2 ounces (55 g) caviar (whatever type you can afford!)

Fresh dill sprigs, for garnish

To make the blini batter, in a bowl, whisk together the flours, salt, and baking powder. In a small bowl, whisk the milk, egg, and 1 tablespoon of butter together. Pour the milk mixture into the flour mixture and whisk until smooth.

In a large skillet, add the remaining 1 tablespoon of butter and warm over medium heat. When the butter stops foaming, drop the batter, 1 tablespoon at a time, into the skillet. Cook until bubbles form in the blini, 1½ to 2 minutes. Flip the blini and continue cooking until browned on the second side, about 1 minute more. Using a metal spatula, transfer the blini to paper towels to drain. Repeat with the remaining batter.

To serve, place a piece of smoked salmon on each blini, then top with crème fraîche, a small spoonful of caviar, and a sprig of fresh dill. **MAKES ABOUT 20; SERVES 6**

This simple but elegant toast is something you might find on a Scandinavian smorgasbord. It's also nice as a passed hors d'oeuvre. Smoked salmon can substitute for caviar.

# CAVIAR TOASTS

½ cup (120 ml) crème fraîche

2 tablespoons diagonally sliced green onion, including some green parts

Kosher salt and freshly ground pepper

2 large hard-boiled eggs (page 344)

4 slices sandwich bread or brioche, thinly sliced

2 tablespoons unsalted butter, at room temperature

2 ounces (55 g) caviar or roe of your choice

1 tablespoon minced fresh chives

In a small bowl, combine the crème fraîche and green onion and season to taste with salt and pepper. Stir until smooth and spreadable. Chop the eggs and set aside.

Toast the bread until light golden brown, then butter one side of each slice. Spread the buttered side of each slice of toast with crème fraîche, then top with an even layer of chopped egg. Evenly dot the caviar on top of the chopped egg and sprinkle with the chives. Slice the toasts in halves on the diagonal. Serve at once. **SERVES 4**

We tend to think of custards as being sweet but they are also delicious savory, and this pretty starter is ideal for an elegant dinner party. Smoked salmon could be used in place of the salmon roe. The custards can be baked up to 4 hours ahead and served at room temperature or reheated in a hot-water bath.

# PARMESAN CUSTARDS with salmon roe

½ cup (120 ml) heavy cream

½ cup (120 ml) milk

¼ cup (25 g) freshly grated Parmesan

1 teaspoon dry sherry

⅛ teaspoon fine sea salt

Pinch of freshly ground white pepper

1 large egg

1 large egg yolk

2 ounces (55 g) fresh salmon or trout roe

Microgreens (optional)

In a small saucepan over medium-high heat, combine the cream, milk, Parmesan, sherry, salt, and pepper. Cook until bubbles appear around the edges of the pan. Remove from the heat, cover the pan, and let the cream steep for 30 minutes.

Preheat the oven to 250°F (120°C). Pour the cream mixture through a fine-mesh sieve set over a large measuring cup or small bowl. Using the back of a tablespoon, gently press the mixture through the sieve; discard any solids. Whisk in the egg and yolk until blended. Pour the custard into six 2-ounce (60-ml) ovenproof ramekins.

Set the cups in a small roasting pan. Pour enough boiling water into the pan to reach halfway up the sides of the cups. Transfer the pan to the oven and bake the custards until just set (or until it barely jiggles), about 45 minutes. Remove the pan from the oven and let the custards cool in the water bath for 5 minutes. Remove the custards from the pan. Top them with roe and microgreens (if using). Serve warm. **SERVES 6**

---

Salmon or trout roe is flavorful, colorful, and much more affordable than sturgeon caviar. It adds a delicate crunch to this luxurious pasta dish.

# PASTA with salmon caviar and smoked salmon

1 pound (455 g) long pasta, such as spaghetti, bucatini, linguini

4 tablespoons (55 g) unsalted butter

1 tablespoon minced shallot

½ cup (120 ml) crème fraîche, plus more for garnish

2 tablespoons chopped fresh flat-leaf parsley

2 teaspoons chopped fresh tarragon, or 1 teaspoon dried

Freshly ground pepper

4 ounces (115 g) thinly sliced smoked salmon, cut into ½-inch (12-mm) ribbons

4 ounces (115 g) rinsed salmon roe

¼ cup (11 g) chopped fresh chives

Bring a large pot of salted water to a boil over high heat. Add the pasta and cook until al dente, or according to the package directions. Drain, reserving ½ cup (120 ml) of the pasta water.

While the pasta is cooking, in a large skillet, melt the butter over medium heat. When the foam subsides, reduce the heat to medium-low, add the shallot, and cook, stirring, until translucent, about 2 minutes. Add the ½ cup (120 ml) of crème fraîche, the parsley, and the tarragon. Stir in about ¼ cup (60 ml) of the reserved pasta cooking water and season with pepper. Add the pasta and toss well. Add up to 2 more tablespoons of the reserved cooking water if the pasta seems too dry. Remove from the heat. Add the smoked salmon and three-fourths of the roe and toss gently. Serve in shallow bowls, garnished with the remaining roe, dollops of crème fraîche, and chives. **SERVES 4 TO 6**

This classic Greek and Turkish dip is made from salted cod or carp roe. You can find the roe refrigerated in Greek and Middle Eastern markets and online. It typically comes in 10-ounce (280-g) jars and is a bright red. This dish is best served the day it is made. Versions vary from cook to cook, some favoring the use of just bread, while some use potatoes and others use both. It makes an elegant first course to serve with warm pita bread.

# TARAMOSALÁTA with warm pita breads

One 10-ounce (280-g) jar tarama (cod roe)

¼ cup (35 g) minced sweet onion

3½ cups (160 g) fresh bread crumbs from a loaf with crusts removed, plus more if needed

2 tablespoons fresh lemon juice, plus a few drops to taste

¾ cup (180 ml) extra-virgin olive oil, plus more if needed

Hot sauce, to taste

Green olives, preferably Greek or Castelvetrano

Finely chopped fresh flat-leaf parsley, for garnish

Warm mini pita breads and crudites (bite-size raw vegetables), including cucumber, for serving

Place the tarama in a medium bowl and cover with cold water. Gently break up any lumps with your fingers. Let sit for 30 minutes.

Using a fine-mesh sieve set over a bowl, gently press the tarama with the back of a large spoon to remove as much water as possible. Discard the water. In a food processor or blender, combine the tarama, onion, and bread crumbs. With the machine running, gradually add the 2 tablespoons of lemon juice and the ¾ cup (180 ml) of oil in a thin, steady stream until the mixture has the texture of thick cream. Add a little water if it's too thick or more bread crumbs if it's too thin. Season to taste with more lemon juice and hot sauce. For a more mellow flavor, add more olive oil.

Sprinkle with parsley and serve with the warm pita and the crudités (if using). **SERVES 6 TO 8**

Bottarga is sold as whole roe lobes or already grated. As with hard cheeses, optimal flavor comes from buying whole pieces and grating it yourself. Make sure to peel off the pellicle, or outer membrane covering the sac, before grating or slicing bottarga. Wrapped well in plastic, bottarga can be stored refrigerated for months.

# SPAGHETTI with bottarga

2 ounces (55 g) mullet bottarga (about 1 whole lobe)

½ cup (120 ml) extra-virgin olive oil

2 cloves garlic, lightly crushed

¼ teaspoon crushed red pepper flakes

Kosher salt

12 ounces (340 g) long pasta, such as spaghetti, spaghettini, or linguine

1 cup (50 g) fresh flat-leaf parsley, loosely packed, chopped

Grated zest of 1 lemon

1 tablespoon fresh lemon juice

¼ cup (25 g) grated pecorino cheese

Cut the lobe shallowly down its length and peel away and discard the pellicle. Using a Microplane, grate the bottarga into a shallow bowl.

In a large skillet, combine the olive oil and garlic. Cook over medium heat, stirring, until the garlic is golden brown on all sides, about 5 minutes. Remove and discard the garlic. Add the crushed red pepper and continue to cook, stirring constantly, until fragrant, about 30 seconds.

Remove the skillet from the heat and add all of the grated bottarga. Stir until combined with the olive oil. Set aside.

Meanwhile, in a deep pot over high heat, bring a large pot of salted water to a boil. Add the pasta and cook until al dente according to the package directions. Just before the pasta is done, scoop out 1 cup (240 ml) of the pasta cooking water. Add ½ cup (120 ml) to the skillet with the olive oil mixture and stir with a wooden spoon to combine.

Drain the pasta and add it to the skillet. Stir and toss the pasta over medium heat until the sauce has thickened and evenly coats the pasta, about 1 minute. Add more pasta water if needed to adjust the consistency of the sauce to your liking.

Stir in the parsley, lemon zest, and juice. Taste and adjust the seasoning. Serve at once in warm serving bowls, garnished with the cheese. **SERVES 4**

Cod-stuffed peppers are a traditional dish of Spain. This is a contemporary twist with the addition of a rich garlic cream that mimics aioli. True piquillo peppers come from the small northern Spanish region of Navarra, and take their name from their distinctive, narrow, triangular shape—*piquillo* means "beak" in Spanish. Piquillo's sweetness gives way to a sneaky heat. They can be found in most well-stocked markets.

# COD-STUFFED PIQUILLO PEPPERS
## with garlic cream and chanterelles

### SALT COD FILLING

10 ounces (280 g) salt cod

⅔ cup (165 ml) half-and-half, plus more if needed

⅛ teaspoon freshly grated nutmeg

2 tablespoons extra-virgin olive oil, plus more for frying

Fine sea salt and freshly ground pepper

Fresh lemon juice

### GARLIC CREAM

1 large head garlic, cloves separated and peeled

¼ cup (60 ml) chicken stock (page 333) or vegetable stock (page 333), plus more as needed

3 tablespoons heavy cream

3 tablespoons extra-virgin olive oil

Fine sea salt and freshly ground pepper

Sherry vinegar, to taste

### PEPPERS AND CHANTERELLES

8 small canned piquillo peppers, drained, rinsed, and patted dry

Olive oil

6 ounces (170 g) small chanterelle or oyster mushrooms

2 tablespoons finely chopped shallots

Fried parsley or basil sprigs (page 344), for garnish

To make the filling, put the salt cod in a large bowl of cold water to cover and soak for 24 hours or up to 3 days, changing the water at least 2 times each day. Drain and shred with your fingers, removing any bones, skin, or dark spots.

Preheat the oven to 375°F (190°C). Lightly oil a 1-quart (960-ml) baking dish.

In a food processor or blender, combine the shredded cod and the ⅔ cup (165 ml) half-and-half. Process until a very thick paste is formed, adding more half-and-half if needed. With the machine running, add the nutmeg then the olive oil a little at a time to make a smooth paste. Season with salt, pepper, and lemon juice to taste. Cover and refrigerate the paste for at least 20 minutes to firm it up.

Meanwhile, make the garlic cream. In a small saucepan of boiling water, blanch the garlic for 30 seconds, then drain. Repeat this process 2 more times. In a blender, combine the garlic, the ¼ cup (60 ml) of stock, and the cream and puree until smooth. With the machine running, gradually add the olive oil in a steady stream to form a light emulsion. Season to taste with salt, pepper, and a drop or two of sherry vinegar. Thin with a little more stock, if desired.

Using a pastry bag or spoon, stuff the peppers with the salt cod mixture. Place the stuffed peppers in the prepared dish and bake until heated through, about 15 minutes.

While the peppers bake, in a medium skillet, heat a drizzle of olive oil over medium-high heat and sauté the mushrooms and shallots until the mushrooms are lightly browned and the juices have evaporated but are still holding their shape. Season with salt and pepper.

To serve, spoon the garlic cream onto 4 warm plates. Place 2 stuffed peppers on top of the garlic cream on each plate and scatter one-fourth of the mushrooms around. Top with fried parsley and serve immediately. **SERVES 4**

Don't be put off by the idea of using "raw" salt cod in a salad. It's a tradition in Spain and other parts of the Mediterranean. This dish is called *remojon* in Spanish. The salt cod isn't really raw, since it's been thoroughly salted and dried. Once it's been soaked and desalted it is used as is, without further cooking, for this unusual and interesting first-course salad. This recipe is adapted from Nancy Harmon Jenkins, who is an important authority on Mediterranean cooking.

# SALT COD, ORANGE, AND BLACK OLIVE SALAD

1 pound (455 g) salt cod

2 large navel oranges and 1 large lemon, cut into segments (page 345)

⅓ cup (50 g) pitted black olives, coarsely chopped

1 small red onion, very thinly sliced

¼ cup (60 ml) extra-virgin olive oil

2 teaspoons honey

1 tablespoon sherry vinegar

2 teaspoons chopped fresh mint

3 cups (60 g) tender young savory greens, such as frisée, arugula, and cress, lightly packed

Red chile threads, for garnishing (optional)

Put the salt cod in a large bowl of cold water to cover and soak for 24 hours or up to 3 days, changing the water at least 2 times each day. Drain and shred with a fork, removing any skin, bones, or brown spots.

Put the citrus segments in a bowl and cut into ½-inch (12-mm) pieces, capturing all of the juices. Add the olives, onion, olive oil, honey, vinegar, and shredded cod and gently toss to combine. Let sit for at least 30 minutes to let the flavors develop. Taste and adjust the seasoning. Stir in the mint.

To serve, arrange the greens attractively on plates and mound the salad on top. Garnish with red chile threads (if using). **SERVES 6**

This recipe is adapted from one of the most important series on cooking from the '60s and '70s, the Time-Life *Foods of the World: Cooking of Spain and Portugal*. This series opened up many of us to the extraordinary variety of flavors that exist in global cuisines. Make the bread crumbs from day-old rustic bread with the crusts removed.

# SALT COD CAKES
## with poached eggs and romesco sauce

1 pound (455 g) salt cod

2 cups (90 g) fresh bread crumbs

¾ cup (180 ml) olive oil

¼ cup (10 g) chopped fresh cilantro leaves and tender stems

1 tablespoon chopped fresh flat-leaf parsley

1 teaspoon chopped fresh mint

2 tablespoons chopped fresh chives

2 tablespoons sweet paprika

1 teaspoon salt

¼ teaspoon freshly ground pepper

2 cloves garlic, halved lengthwise

6 large parsley sprigs

6 large eggs, poached (page 344)

Romesco Sauce (page 338)

Lemon wedges, for serving

Put the salt cod in a large bowl of cold water to cover and soak for 24 hours or up to 2 days, changing the water at least 2 times each day. Drain, rinse, and place in a large pot with enough cold water to cover the fish by ½ inch (12 mm) or so. Bring to a boil over high heat. Drain, cover with fresh water, and bring to a boil again. Reduce the heat and simmer slowly, uncovered, until the flesh flakes easily when prodded gently with a fork, about 10 minutes. Drain thoroughly and let cool.

Meanwhile, in a large bowl, combine the bread crumbs and ½ cup (120 ml) of olive oil. Using a wooden spoon, beat and mash the mixture until the bread has absorbed all the oil.

Remove and discard any skin, bones, and brown spots from the cod. Shred the fish finely with your fingers and place in a medium bowl. Add the herbs, paprika, salt, pepper, and mashed bread mixture and beat vigorously with a wooden spoon until the ingredients are thoroughly combined. With moistened hands, shape the mixture into 6 flat round cakes, about ¾ inch (2 cm) thick.

In a large skillet, heat the remaining ¼ cup (60 ml) of oil over medium heat. Add the garlic and cook, stirring frequently, until golden, about 3 minutes. Using a slotted spoon, remove and discard the garlic. Add the cod cakes to the oil and cook, turning once, until golden brown on both sides. Using a slotted metal spatula, transfer to a warm platter.

Garnish with parsley, top each cake with a poached egg and a small spoonful of romesco sauce, and serve immediately with lemon wedges to squeeze over. **MAKES 6 CAKES; SERVES 6**

Brandade is the French name for this salt cod dish. It's a puree of salt cod, olive oil, and sometimes potatoes and is considered a comfort food. One of my favorite ways of serving this rich dish is as a warm salad: Place a heaping tablespoonful or two of the gratin on a plate and then surround it with young salad greens dressed with a simple honey-lemon vinaigrette (page 167). The gratin can be made a day or two ahead and stored in the refrigerator and then baked just before serving. Add at least 10 minutes to the baking time if baking it cold. You can also bake the gratin in individual ramekins if you like; cut the baking time to 15 minutes or so.

# SALT COD GRATIN (brandade)

**SERVES 6 TO 8**

1 pound (455 g) center-cut salt cod

2 cups (480 ml) milk

½ cup (120 ml) water, or more as needed

8 large cloves garlic

2 bay leaves

4 whole cloves

1 teaspoon fresh or ½ teaspoon dried thyme

3 large fresh sprigs flat-leaf parsley

½ pound (225 g) boiling potatoes, peeled and quartered

⅓ cup (75 ml) extra-virgin olive oil, plus 2 tablespoons to oil the baking dish

⅓ cup (75 ml) heavy cream (optional)

Kosher salt and freshly ground pepper

Freshly grated nutmeg

Lightly toasted baguette slices, for serving

Put the salt cod in a large bowl of cold water to cover and soak for 24 hours or up to 3 days, changing the water at least 2 times each day.

In a large saucepan, combine the milk, ½ cup (120 ml) water, the garlic, bay leaves, cloves, thyme, and parsley sprigs. Drain the soaked salt cod and add to the pan. The liquid should completely cover the cod; if not, add more water. Over medium-high heat, bring the cod just to a simmer. Immediately remove from the heat, cover, and let sit for at least 30 minutes to cool.

Preheat the oven to 450°F (230°C). Lightly oil a 6-cup (1.4-l) baking dish with 2 tablespoons olive oil.

Bring a medium saucepan of lightly salted water to a boil. Add the potatoes, reduce the heat to medium-low, and simmer until very tender, 12 to 15 minutes. Drain and set aside.

Drain the cod in a fine-mesh sieve set over a bowl, reserving the poaching liquid. Discard the bay leaves, cloves, and parsley sprigs. Using a fork, flake the fish, discarding any skin, bones, or brown spots.

In a food processor or blender, combine the cod, potatoes, ½ cup (120 ml) of reserved poaching liquid, the ⅓ cup (75 ml) of olive oil, and the heavy cream, if using. Process, scraping down the sides of the bowl as needed, until very smooth and fluffy, at least 3 minutes. Taste and adjust the seasoning with salt, pepper, and nutmeg.

Add the mixture to the prepared pan and bake until puffed and lightly browned, 20 to 25 minutes. You can also place the dish under the broiler for the last minute or two to brown. Serve immediately, with plenty of toasted baguette slices to scoop up the gratin.

This innovative salad from chef B Adamo, head chef at the Hog Island Oyster Bar in Larkspur, takes advantage of both seaweed and uni. If uni is not available to you, salmon roe makes an interesting substitute.

# HEIRLOOM TOMATO, UNI, AND WAKAME SALAD

¼ cup (11 g) dried wakame seaweed

4 ripe heirloom tomatoes, cut into attractive pieces

1 firm-ripe avocado, pitted, peeled, and sliced or diced

2 small Persian cucumbers, sliced or diced

½ small sweet red onion, thinly sliced

Juice of 1 large orange

1 tablespoon honey

¼ cup (60 ml) unseasoned rice vinegar

1 tablespoon toasted sesame oil

¼ cup (60 ml) olive oil

4 fresh uni (sea urchin corals), cleaned (page 304)

½ cup (25 g) microgreens of your choice

Flaky sea salt, such as Maldon, for sprinkling

In a small bowl, soak the wakame in cold water to cover for 10 minutes. Drain well.

Arrange the tomatoes, avocado, cucumbers, onion, and drained wakame on 4 plates.

In a small bowl, whisk the orange juice, honey, rice vinegar, and oils together well. Drizzle over the salads. Top with the uni and microgreens and a little flaky sea salt. Serve at once. **SERVES 4**

---

Uni has a rich "taste of the sea" flavor. It goes best with something that mellows the flavor a bit, like pasta or rice. Serving it with an easily made horseradish cream is another favorite. This is a recipe with Nordic roots, and it's unique because it is served in the sea urchin shells.

# UNI with horseradish cream

½ cup (120 ml) crème fraîche

2 tablespoons heavy cream

2 to 4 teaspoons freshly grated horseradish or store-bought prepared horseradish

1 to 2 teaspoons fresh lemon juice

1 teaspoon soy sauce

Kosher salt and freshly ground pepper

4 fresh uni (sea urchin coral), cleaned and shells reserved (page 304)

Chopped fresh chives and chive flowers, for garnish

In a deep bowl and using a whisk, beat the crème fraîche and heavy cream together until thickened but not yet in soft peaks. Fold in 2 teaspoons of horseradish, 1 teaspoon of lemon juice, the soy sauce, and salt and pepper to taste. If desired, stir in 1 or 2 more teaspoons of horseradish and/or 1 more teaspoon of lemon juice. Add salt and pepper to taste. Cover and refrigerate for at least 1 hour or up to 1 week. Remember that the horseradish will get hotter the longer it sits.

Spoon the horseradish cream into the cleaned sea urchin shells and top with the uni. Garnish with chives and chive blossoms. **SERVES 4**

This is an innovative spaghetti variation utilizing uni and salmon roe. Furikake is a Japanese seasoning mix typically made with toasted sesame seeds, nori, salt, sugar. It varies from region to region and can also include anything from bonito flakes, crushed red pepper, dried egg yolk, miso powder, shiitake powder, poppy seeds, and more. Typically, it's used to season rice.

# SPAGHETTI with uni and ikura

6 ounces (170 g) fresh uni (sea urchin corals), about 8 to 10, cleaned (page 304)

⅓ cup (75 ml) crème fraîche

Kosher salt

8 to 10 ounces (225 to 280 g) long pasta, such as spaghetti or bucatini

1 tablespoon extra-virgin olive oil, plus more for drizzling

2 cloves garlic, minced

1 small shallot, minced

½ teaspoon chopped oil-packed Calabrian chile or a big pinch of crushed red pepper flakes

½ cup (120 ml) dry sake or white wine

Freshly ground pepper

1 or 2 teaspoons grated lemon zest

1 ounce (28 g) rinsed salmon roe, or to taste

2 tablespoons minced fresh chives, for garnish

A sprinkle of furikake, homemade (page 326) or store-bought (optional)

Set aside 4 uni to use as garnish. In a blender, combine the remaining uni and the crème fraîche and blend until completely smooth. Set aside.

Bring a large pot of salted water to a boil over high heat. Add the pasta and cook, stirring occasionally, until almost al dente, or according to the package directions.

Meanwhile, in a large skillet, heat 1 tablespoon of oil over medium heat. Add the garlic and shallot and cook, stirring, until translucent, about 2 minutes. Add the chile and stir until combined. Add the sake and cook until the liquid is reduced to a scant 2 tablespoons, about 1 minute. Remove from the heat and stir in pepper and lemon zest to taste.

Drain the pasta, reserving about ½ cup (120 ml) of the pasta water. Add the pasta to the skillet with the garlic-shallot mixture. Scrape the uni puree into the skillet and add a tablespoon or two of pasta water. Cook over medium-high heat, stirring constantly, until the sauce develops a creamy consistency and the pasta is fully cooked, about 1 minute. Add more pasta water to thin the sauce if necessary. Season with salt and pepper.

Divide the pasta among warm serving bowls and drizzle each portion with more extra-virgin olive oil. Garnish each with one uni and some salmon roe and sprinkle with the chives and furikake (if using). Serve at once. **SERVES 4**

---

Known in Japan as temaki, hand rolls are another shape for sushi. There are two styles: one is cone shaped and the other a simple cylindrical roll. Use whatever shape you like.

# UNI MINI HAND ROLLS

¼ cup (60 ml) soy sauce

1 tablespoon wasabi, or to taste

1 cup (205 g) prepared Sushi Rice (page 343)

3 sheets nori, cut into 12 rectangles

6 tongues fresh uni (sea urchin coral), cleaned (page 304)

1 ounce (28 g) rinsed salmon roe (optional)

In a small bowl, whisk together the soy sauce and wasabi. Place about 1 tablespoon sushi rice in the center of a nori rectangle. Place a small piece of uni on top of the rice. Wrap the nori around the rice and uni. Repeat to make 12 hand rolls. Serve with the soy sauce mixture for dipping. Add some salmon roe, if using. **MAKES 12 ROLLS**

Chirashizushi, which comes from the Japanese word *chirashi*, meaning "to scatter," consists of rice with a variety of toppings, including pieces of tuna or salmon sashimi, uni, squid, cucumber, shredded omelet, boiled prawns, and shiitake mushrooms. It can be found throughout the Japanese archipelago, and it's so ubiquitous that it is often seen in grocery stores, food courts, and even convenience stores. Chirashizushi is often included as a bento box component, but its versatility and colorful, decorative appearance means it's often served for special occasions. For Westerners, its appeal is that there is no rolling involved as is done for maki sushi, making it much easier for the novice sushi maker.

# CHIRASHI SUSHI

**MUSHROOMS**

8 fresh shiitake mushrooms, thinly sliced

Toasted sesame oil

**OMELET STRIPS**

2 large eggs

½ teaspoon sugar, or 1 teaspoon mirin

½ teaspoon cornstarch or potato starch

1 teaspoon cold water

1 teaspoon canola or other neutral cooking oil

**WAKAME**

⅓ cup dried wakame, cut into 2-inch (5-cm) lengths

1 teaspoon soy sauce

**TUNA**

½ pound (225 g) sushi-grade tuna (page 249), thinly sliced or cubed

¼ teaspoon wasabi (optional)

2 tablespoons soy sauce

**FOR ASSEMBLY**

Sushi Rice (page 343)

½ cup (40 g) julienned Kirby cucumber

4 large cooked and peeled shrimp (page 115), halved lengthwise (optional)

1 ounce (28 g) rinsed salmon roe (optional)

2 tablespoons daikon sprouts (kaiware)

1 tablespoon shredded nori

1 teaspoon toasted sesame seeds (page 344)

A sprinkle of furikake, homemade (page 326) or store-bought (optional)

To make the mushrooms, in a skillet, sauté the mushrooms with sesame oil until lightly browned. Set aside.

To make the omelet strips, in a medium bowl, beat the eggs and sugar together with a whisk. In a cup, mix the cornstarch with the water until dissolved, then beat into the egg mixture. Heat a small nonstick skillet, add the oil, and pour in the egg mixture to make the omelet. Cut the omelet into thin strips and set aside.

To make the wakame, in a medium bowl of cold water, soak the wakame until soft, 6 to 8 minutes. Drain well and add the 1 teaspoon soy sauce, or to taste. Set aside.

Put the tuna in a small bowl and stir in the wasabi (if using). Add the 2 tablespoons soy sauce and marinate for a few minutes. Set aside.

To assemble, divide the rice among individual bowls. Top with equal amounts of the shiitakes, omelet strips, wakame, cucumber, and shrimp. Place the tuna on top of the shrimp, and garnish with salmon roe (if using). Garnish with the daikon sprouts, nori, sesame seeds, and furikake (if using), and serve at once. **SERVES 4**

This is one of the classic Japanese dishes to serve alone or as a starter for a meal.

# MISO SOUP
## with tofu and wakame

¼ cup (11 g) dried wakame

4 cups (960 ml) Kombu Dashi (page 334)

2 to 3 tablespoons aka (red) or shiro (white) miso

6 ounces (170 g) firm tofu, drained, rinsed, and cut into ½-inch (12-mm) dice

2 green onions, thinly sliced, including green parts

Put the wakame in a bowl, cover with cold water, and soak until soft, about 10 minutes. Rinse well to remove the salt. Cut away any hard ribs, then slice the wakame into 1-inch (2.5-cm) pieces.

In a medium saucepan, bring the dashi just to a boil over medium-high heat. Whisk in the miso until dissolved, then reduce the heat to low. Do not allow the soup to return to a boil. Add the tofu and simmer for about 1 minute.

To serve, divide the wakame and green onions among 4 soup bowls, then fill each bowl with hot soup. **SERVES 4**

---

This sandwich may have been my first introduction to seaweed aside from nori-wrapped sushi. Look for whole leaf dulse, which tastes like bacon. You may not need to use bacon again for your BLT! This is also very cool done open face.

# DLTA: DULSE, LETTUCE, TOMATO, AND AVOCADO SANDWICHES

Toasted sesame oil

2 large pieces whole-leaf dulse

Mayonnaise

2 slices whole-grain bread, toasted

1 lettuce leaf

Fresh ripe tomato slices

Avocado slices

In a skillet, heat a drizzle of sesame oil over medium heat. Fry the dulse, pressing down with a metal spatula and turning frequently until crisp and yellow-green, about 1 minute. Using tongs, transfer to paper towels to drain, pat dry, and let cool to a deep red color.

Spread the mayo on the toasted bread and top with the lettuce, crispy dulse, tomato slices, and avocado slices. Eat. **SERVES 1**

These are quite easy to make and have myriad uses beyond a crunchy snack to serve with drinks: Cut or crumble them over any raw or cooked fish, rice or noodle dishes, and soups, even softly scrambled eggs. Seaweed chips are widely available in food stores now but making your own is cheaper and lets you flavor them to your taste. The recipe here can be used for either dulse or nori seaweed. Like nori, dulse comes in many shapes from flakes to whole leaf. Be sure to use the whole leaf dulse.

# SEAWEED CHIPS

4 nori sheets (toasted or untoasted) or ¾ ounce (21 g) whole leaf dulse

Kosher or fine sea salt

Toasted white sesame seeds (page 344)

Toasted sesame oil, for brushing

Onion powder, garlic powder, curry powder, pure chile powder, such as chipotle, or furikake (page 326), optional

Preheat the oven to 325°F (165°C). Cut the seaweed into bite-size squares or triangles.

Brush the seaweed lightly with the sesame oil on both sides with a pastry brush. Place the pieces on a sheet pan in a single layer.

Sprinkle with a bit of salt and sesame seeds and a pinch of one of the spice powders, if desired. (Be stingy in using the powders; you still want to be able to taste the seaweed.)

Bake until the chips are dry and crispy, about 10 minutes. Let cool. Use now, or store in an airtight container for up to 3 days. **MAKES ABOUT 1 CUP CHIPS**

---

Furikake is an all-purpose seaweed seasoning mix that Japanese typically use on rice and also to garnish sushi or onigiri and on salads. It's my favorite topping for popcorn and is great for garnishing simply cooked fish and shellfish. You can buy it already made but fresh, homemade furikake is better. Most furikake is not vegan or vegetarian because it usually contains *katsuobushi*, or dried bonito tuna flakes, which is also a key ingredient in dashi (page 334). This recipe is vegan. The nori used here is snack-size seasoned nori that has been flavored with soy sauce and sugar. It is widely available in well-stocked markets.

# FURIKAKE

4 tablespoons (11 g) nori flakes or shreds

3 tablespoons black sesame seeds

3 tablespoons white sesame seeds

1 tablespoon dulse flakes (optional)

1 tablespoon soy sauce or tamari sauce

1 teaspoon mirin

½ teaspoon sugar

½ teaspoon toasted sesame oil

Preheat the oven to 250°F (120°C). Line a baking sheet with parchment paper.

In a small bowl, combine the nori flakes, black and white sesame seeds, dulse (if using), soy sauce, mirin, sugar, and sesame oil. Spread the mixture evenly on the prepared pan and bake for 15 to 20 minutes, stirring every 5 minutes. Let cool completely, then store in an airtight container for up to 3 months. **MAKES ABOUT ¾ CUP**

This is a classic Japanese dish to serve as a refreshing appetizer or as a side dish to accompany main courses. Be sure to let it chill for at least 1 hour before serving. Look for Persian or Japanese cucumbers, which are smaller and less seedy, for this salad.

# PICKLED CUCUMBER, WAKAME, AND SESAME SALAD

1 pound Persian or Japanese cucumbers, cut into ⅛-inch- (3-mm-) thick slices

2 teaspoons kosher salt

¼ cup (11 g) dried wakame seaweed, cut into 1-inch (2.5-cm) lengths

2 tablespoons rice vinegar

1 tablespoon sugar

2 teaspoons soy sauce, preferably ususkuchi soy sauce (see Note)

½ teaspoon toasted sesame oil

Toasted white sesame seeds (page 344), for garnish

In a small bowl, toss the cucumbers with the salt to coat. Let sit for 15 minutes to draw the water out of the cucumbers.

At the same time, put the wakame in a small bowl and add water to cover. Let sit for at least 10 minutes to rehydrate.

Meanwhile, make the dressing. In a small bowl, combine the rice vinegar, sugar, soy sauce, and sesame oil and whisk to blend until the sugar dissolves.

Drain and squeeze as much of the water as you can out of both the cucumbers and the wakame. Add to a medium bowl and toss with the dressing. Cover and refrigerate for at least 1 hour. Taste and adjust the seasoning. Serve topped with sesame seeds. **SERVES 6 TO 8**

**NOTE** Ususkuchi soy sauce is much lighter in color than regular soy sauce but a bit saltier. It's available in Japanese markets and online.

Chef Mariko Wilkinson grew up in West Marin in the San Geronimo Valley and was the chef at the Boat Oyster Bar at Hog Island Oyster Farm in Marshall for five years. Her time spent there coincided with her discovery of the bounty of this area, including wild seaweed. This recipe is a nod to *tsukemono*, which are Japanese-style pickles, which are brined with wakame. These pickles can be enjoyed alongside fish and rice, alone as a snack, or with barbecued oysters.

# PICKLED CARROTS
## with wakame and miso

2 tablespoons dried wakame

½ cup (120 ml) warm water

½ cup (120 ml) seasoned rice vinegar

¼ cup (60 ml) unseasoned rice vinegar

½ cup (120 ml) cold water

½ tablespoon white (shiro) miso

1 teaspoon sugar

½ teaspoon fine sea salt

1½ cups (180 g) peeled carrots, sliced on the diagonal into ⅛-inch (3-mm) pieces

½ teaspoon togarashi (Japanese chile flakes)

1½ teaspoons sesame seeds, toasted (page 344)

1 clove garlic, smashed

In a small bowl, soak the wakame in the ½ cup (120 ml) of warm water for 5 to 10 minutes, then drain and squeeze out the excess water.

To make the brine, in a small saucepan, combine the seasoned and unseasoned rice vinegars, the ½ cup (120 ml) of cold water, miso, sugar, and salt. Bring to a bare simmer over low heat then remove from the heat.

In a heatproof container, combine the carrots, togarashi, sesame seeds, and garlic and pour the hot brine over the mixture. Let sit until it has come to room temperature, 1 or 2 hours. Add the wakame to the brine and carrot mixture. Stir to combine. Cover and refrigerate for at least 2 hours or up to 1 month. **MAKES ABOUT 2 CUPS (240 G)**

---

Cabbage salad tossed with shio kombu (salted kelp that has been simmered with soy sauce) is often served at izakayas (Japanese-style taverns) in Japan. The combination of shio kombu, toasted sesame oil, and toasted sesame seeds takes cabbage to a new level.

# CABBAGE SALAD TOSSED
## with shio kombu

½ small cabbage, cored

1½ tablespoons shio kombu

2 teaspoons toasted sesame oil

2 teaspoons sesame seeds, toasted (page 344)

Small lime wedges, for serving

Cut the cabbage into bite-size pieces. In a medium bowl, combine the cabbage, shio kombu, sesame oil, and sesame seeds. Mix well to coat the cabbage and distribute the other ingredients. Let sit for 10 minutes to develop the flavors. Serve with lime wedges for squeezing over. **SERVES 2 TO 4**

# BASIC RECIPES AND TECHNIQUES

## STOCKS

### SHELLFISH STOCK

**Makes about 2 quarts (2 l)**

6 cups shellfish shells from shrimp, lobster, and/or crab
Olive oil, for drizzling
½ cup (120 ml) dry white wine
1 large yellow onion, chopped
1 carrot, peeled and coarsely chopped
1 celery stalk, coarsely chopped
2 tablespoons tomato paste
½ teaspoon fennel seeds
Several sprigs parsley
1 bay leaf
1 teaspoon whole black peppercorns

Preheat the oven to 400°F (205°C). Break any thick shells of lobster or crab by putting them in a sealed, thick plastic bag and either rolling over them with a rolling pin or hitting them with a meat hammer or the bottom of a heavy pot to crush. Shrimp shells don't need breaking up.

Put the shells in a large roasting pan, drizzle with a little olive oil, and toss to coat. Roast for 8 minutes. Alternatively, sauté the shells in batches in a large sauté pan until lightly browned. This cooking/browning of the shells greatly enhances the flavor of the stock.

In a large stockpot, combine the roasted shells and cover with about 1 inch (2.5 cm) of water and heat to not quite a simmer. Don't let the water boil or stir the shells. Skim away the foam that will come to the surface. Boiling, stirring, and not skimming will cause the stock to be cloudy.

Once the stock has stopped releasing foam, add the wine, onion, carrot, celery, tomato paste, fennel seeds, parsley, bay leaf, and peppercorns. Bring to a simmer (don't boil) and cook for 30 minutes, skimming the foam if necessary.

Line a large, fine-mesh sieve with two layers of dampened cheesecloth and place the sieve over a large bowl. Strain the stock and discard the solids. Don't add salt to this stock at this time. You may want to reduce it for sauces or to concentrate its flavor. Add salt to taste then.

Let cool, cover, and refrigerate for up to 5 days or freeze up to 4 months (remember to leave some headroom at the top of your freezer container for the liquid to expand as it freezes).

### QUICK SHELLFISH STOCK

Always save shrimp shells (or lobster or crab shells) and store them in a plastic bag in your freezer. Then, when you need to make a good shellfish stock, all you have to do is to take one of your basic chicken stocks (or even canned low-salt, defatted chicken broth) and add as many shrimp shells as you have. You might also include a good splash or two of dry white wine. Bring the stock to a boil, reduce the heat, and simmer for 5 minutes. Strain and discard the shells, and now you have a delicious stock for your favorite fish soup or sauce.

### FISH STOCK

**Makes about 2 quarts (2 l)**

5 to 6 pounds (2.3 to 2.7 kg) mild white fish bones, trimmings, and/or heads
2 tablespoons olive oil
2 cups (220 g) chopped onion
1 cup (140 g) peeled, chopped carrots
2 cloves garlic, smashed
2 cups (480 ml) dry white wine
1 cup (50 g) coarsely chopped fresh flat-leaf parsley leaves and stems
½ teaspoon black peppercorns
½ teaspoon coriander seeds
About 5 quarts (4.7 l) water, or to cover

Rinse the fish parts well and remove and discard the gills if using fish heads. In a stockpot, heat the olive oil over medium heat and add the onion, carrot, and garlic. Cook until the vegetables are just beginning to color, about 10 minutes. Add the fish parts, wine, parsley, peppercorns, and coriander seeds. Add water to cover and bring to a boil over high heat.

Reduce the heat to a simmer, partially cover, and cook until flavorful, 30 to 45 minutes. Using a large spoon, carefully skim any scum or froth that rises to the surface. Remove from the heat and strain through a fine-mesh sieve set over a bowl. Let cool, cover, and refrigerate for 3 days. Using a spoon, remove any solidified fat from the surface of the stock. The stock may be frozen for up to 2 months (remember to leave some headroom at the top of your freezer container for the liquid to expand as it freezes).

# CHICKEN STOCK

**Makes about 1 gallon (3.8 l)**

6 to 8 pounds (2.7 kg to 3.6 kg) meaty chicken parts including legs, wings, backs, etc.
2 tablespoons olive oil
3 cups (330 g) chopped onion
1 cup (140 g) *each* chopped carrots and celery
6 large cloves garlic, crushed
1½ gallons (5.7 l) water
3 cups (720 ml) dry white wine

Rinse the chicken parts and set aside. In a deep stockpot, heat the olive oil and add the onion, carrots, celery, and garlic and sauté until just beginning to color. Add the chicken, water, and wine and bring just to a boil. Reduce the heat and simmer partially covered without boiling for 2 to 3 hours, skimming any foam from the surface (The reason we don't want to boil the stock at this stage is that it will become cloudy. It'll still taste good but usually we'd like to have it relatively clear, especially if we want it for a clear soup or sauce.) Remove from the heat and cool and strain through a fine-mesh sieve. Discard the solids. Refrigerate overnight or until fat has congealed on top. Remove and discard the fat. Store covered and refrigerated up to 5 days or frozen up to 6 months (remember to leave some headroom at the top of your freezer container for the liquid to expand as it freezes).

---

# GINGER CHICKEN STOCK

**Makes about 3 quarts (2.8 l)**

6 to 8 pounds (2.7 kg to 3.6 kg) meaty chicken parts
6 coins fresh ginger, smashed with the side of a cleaver or knife
6 green onions, smashed with the side of a cleaver or knife
1½ gallons (5.7 l) water

Rinse the chicken parts and place in a deep pot. Add the rest of the ingredients and bring to a boil and immediately reduce the heat. Gently simmer, partially covered, without boiling, for 2 to 3 hours, skimming any foam from the surface. Proceed as above. After straining and defatting, return stock to a clean pot and bring to a boil. Continue to boil uncovered until it is reduced by at least a third. Let cool, then refrigerate for up to 5 days or freeze up to 6 months. I like to freeze the reduced stock in standard ice cube trays. When frozen, I pop them out and put them in plastic freezer bags. Two cubes equals about ¼ cup (60 ml).

# HOW TO IMPROVE PURCHASED CHICKEN STOCK

Basically, to make store-bought stock better, what I do is to take the aromatic vegetables (onions, carrots, celery, garlic) and sauté them until they are lightly browned, then add them along with a bay leaf and one whole clove (the spice) to the canned or boxed stock. Figure on about 2 cups (480 ml) of raw vegetables to 6 cups (1.4 l) of stock, along with the bay and clove. Bring this to a boil, reduce the heat and simmer for 20 to 30 minutes, and you've added a lot of flavor to the stock.

---

# VEGETABLE STOCK

**Makes about 1 gallon (3.8 l)**

⅓ cup (75 ml) olive or other light vegetable oil
10 cups (1.1 kg) chopped onions and/or leeks
4 cups (560 g) chopped carrots
2 cups (200 g) chopped celery including tops
¼ cup (35 g) chopped garlic
4 cups (240) chopped fresh mushrooms, preferably cremini or portobello
1½ gallons (5.7 l) water
3 cups (720 ml) dry white wine
4 cups (720 g) chopped tomatoes, fresh or canned
2 teaspoons whole black peppercorns
3 whole bay leaves
2 cups (100 g) roughly chopped parsley leaves and stems

Heat the olive oil in a large pot and add the onions, carrots, celery, garlic, and mushrooms and very lightly brown over medium-high heat, stirring occasionally. Alternatively, you can toss the vegetables with the oil, spread out on a single layer and roast in a preheated 400°F (205°C) oven to lightly brown. Be sure to stir and turn occasionally.

Add the water, wine, tomatoes, peppercorns, bay leaves, and parsley, bring to a boil and immediately reduce the heat and simmer, partially covered, for 1½ hours. Carefully strain, cool, and refrigerate or freeze.

**NOTE** If you want your vegetable stock to have a little more body, add a cup or two (140 g or 280 g) of chopped white potatoes. The potato starch adds the body and mouthfeel but will make it a bit cloudy.

You could substitute 1 ounce (28 g) of dried porcini mushrooms soaked in warm water and chopped. Save the soaking water, strain it to catch any sand, and add it when you add the other liquids.

# DASHI

**Makes about 1 quart (960 ml)**

One 4-by-6-inch (10-by-15-cm) piece kombu seaweed
5 cups (1.2 l) water
1 ounce (1½ cups/28 g) dried bonito flakes (katsuobushi)

Wipe the kombu clean with a damp cloth. In a stockpot, combine the kombu and water and let sit for 1 hour. Bring just to a boil over high heat and add the bonito. Remove from the heat and let the bonito settle to the bottom (about 3 minutes). Let cool slightly, then carefully strain the broth through a fine-mesh sieve set over a large bowl. Discard the bonito. Reserve the kombu for another use, such as shredding for soup. Dashi can covered and refrigerated for up to 5 days or frozen for up to 1 month.

**NOTE** Dashi stock, flavored with seaweed and bonito flakes, is one of the cornerstones of Japanese cooking, the equivalent of our chicken, beef, or vegetable stocks. It is also eaten as a soup, with various additions and garnishes.

---

# KOMBU DASHI (VEGETARIAN)

Using kombu seaweed alone makes a delicate stock. In a bowl, combine 4 cups (960 ml) cold water and 1½ ounces (40 g) kombu, wiped clean and cut into small squares. Let stand overnight. Strain through a fine-mesh sieve set over a bowl; reserve the kombu for other uses. Alternatively, bring 4 cups (960 ml) water and 1¼ ounces (35 g) kombu to a boil, then turn off the heat and let sit for 30 minutes before straining.

---

# MUSHROOM DASHI

Follow the directions for kombu dashi, above, substituting dried shiitake mushrooms for the kombu.

---

# INSTANT DASHI POWDER

A quick alternative to making dashi from scratch is to use instant dashi powder, or granules. There are also vegetarian versions that use dried shiitake mushrooms in place of the bonito flakes. Many Japanese cooks will reluctantly tell you that they almost always use the powder since it is so simple. You'll find instant dashi in Japanese markets and also online. Some are packaged in "tea bags," which allow you to control the strength of the stock by removing the bag when it gets to the flavor intensity you like. Follow the package directions, as they vary by brand. The dry powder can also be used to flavor sauces and compound butters.

# COMPOUND BUTTERS

A flavored butter is one of the most delicious ways to finish nicely grilled, pan-roasted, or broiled fish or shellfish. The Hog Island Oyster Bars have an ever-changing group of these for their baked oysters. Simply place slices of the compound butter on top of the hot food to melt as you bring it to the table. Shape the butter by spooning the mixture onto a square of plastic wrap, folding the wrap over, and forming the butter into a sausage shape about 1½ inches (4 cm) in diameter. Twist the ends of the plastic wrap closed and refrigerate until firm. Store the butter in the refrigerator for up to 2 weeks and frozen up to 6 months (although once you know that they are there and start using them, they won't last that long!)

---

# MAITRE D'HOTEL BUTTER

**Makes ½ cup (115 g) compound butter**

½ cup (115 g) unsalted butter, at room temperature
1 teaspoon fresh lemon juice
2 tablespoons finely chopped fresh flat-leaf parsley
2 teaspoons minced shallot or green onion, white part only
Kosher salt and freshly ground pepper

In a medium bowl, beat the butter with a wooden spoon until smooth. Stir in the lemon juice, parsley, and shallot. Season with salt and pepper to taste. Wrap and refrigerate or freeze, following the instructions for compound butters (above).

---

# 'NDUJA BUTTER

**Makes ½ cup (115 g) compound butter**

½ cup (115 g) unsalted butter, at room temperature
4 ounces (115 g) 'nduja, at room temperature
1 tablespoon freshly grated Parmesan

In a medium bowl, beat the butter with a wooden spoon until smooth. Stir in the 'nduja and Parmesan. Wrap and refrigerate or freeze, following the instructions for compound butters (above).

**NOTE** 'Nduja is a spreadable type of spicy salami from Calabria, containing lots of spicy Calabrian chiles. Look for it online or in specialty markets.

# PORCINI BUTTER

**Makes ½ cup (115 g) compound butter**

⅓ cup (10 g) dried porcini
1 tablespoon olive oil
Kosher salt and freshly ground pepper
Soy sauce
½ cup (115 g) unsalted butter, at room temperature

In a heatproof bowl, soak the dried porcini in just enough warm water to cover until they are softened, about 20 minutes. Squeeze the excess water out of the soaked mushrooms.

In a skillet over medium-low heat, warm the olive oil. Add the reconstituted mushrooms and cook, stirring, until the moisture evaporates, about 5 minutes. Season with salt, pepper, and soy sauce to taste. Let cool completely.

Add the butter and mushrooms to the bowl of a food processor and process until smooth, scraping down the sides of the bowl as needed. Wrap and refrigerate or freeze, following the instructions for compound butters (facing page).

# MISO BUTTER

Beat ½ cup (115 g) room-temperature unsalted butter together with 2 tablespoons white (shiro) or yellow miso paste, 1 tablespoon minced fresh chives, 1 teaspoon minced garlic, and ½ teaspoon coarsely ground pepper. Wrap and refrigerate or freeze, following the instructions for compound butters (facing page).

# ANCHOVY BUTTER

Beat ½ cup (115 g) room-temperature unsalted butter together with 2 ounces (½ can/55 g) drained oil-packed anchovy fillets; 1 small clove garlic, finely grated or pounded to a paste; 1 tablespoon finely chopped fresh flat-leaf parsley; 1 pinch each of kosher or fine sea salt and freshly ground pepper; and a few drops of lemon juice to taste. Wrap and refrigerate or freeze, following the instructions for compound butters (facing page).

# MUSTARD-TARRAGON BUTTER

Beat ½ cup (115 g) of room temperature unsalted butter with 2 teaspoons grainy Dijon mustard, 1 teaspoon minced fresh tarragon, and kosher or fine sea salt and freshly ground pepper. Wrap and refrigerate or freeze, following the instructions for compound butters (facing page).

# ROASTED GARLIC BUTTER

Beat ½ cup (115 g) room temperature unsalted butter with 1 teaspoon fresh lemon juice, 2 tablespoons finely chopped fresh flat-leaf parsley (or a mixture of fresh herbs such as basil, chives, and parsley), 1 tablespoon roasted garlic puree (page 345), kosher or fine sea salt and freshly ground pepper. Wrap and refrigerate or freeze, following the instructions for compound butters (facing page).

# KIMCHI BUTTER

Beat ½ cup (115 g) room temperature unsalted butter with 3 tablespoons finely chopped kimchi. Wrap and refrigerate or freeze, following the instructions for compound butters (facing page).

# CHILE-LIME BUTTER

Beat ½ cup (115 g) room temperature unsalted butter with 1 tablespoon finely chopped shallot, 1 teaspoon grated fresh lime zest, 2 teaspoons fresh lime juice, ½ teaspoon minced fresh Thai or serrano chile (preferably red), and ½ teaspoon salt. Wrap and refrigerate or freeze, following the instructions for compound butters (facing page).

# HARISSA BUTTER

Beat ½ cup (115 g) room temperature unsalted butter with 2 tablespoons harissa paste, homemade (page 341) or store-bought. Wrap and refrigerate or freeze, following the instructions for compound butters (facing page).

# FLAVORED SALTS

Flavored salts, used for sprinkling on food just as it's being served, are a quick and easy way of finishing fish and shellfish dishes. Store all flavored salts in airtight containers in a cool dark place, especially in humid climates, for up to 6 months.

- **Sesame salt (gomashio)**, used in Japanese cooking, is a blend of 4 or more parts ground toasted sesame seeds to 1 part fine sea salt. It adds a nutty, earthy note when sprinkled on foods.

- **Fresh herb salt** can be made with any green, leafy herb, such as basil. Grind 1/4 cup (10 g) finely chopped basil with ¼ cup (70 g) coarse sea salt in a spice grinder until finely ground. Spread on a parchment-lined baking sheet and bake in a preheated 175°F (80°C) oven, or lowest possible setting, for 15 minutes, stirring occasionally. Turn off the oven and let the mixture dry for 30 minutes. If it's lumpy, pulse in a blender to smooth it out.

- **Nori salt** is simply nori ground with sea salt. Use whatever ratio of salt to nori that you like. Start with equal parts and adjust to your taste. I use seasoned nori (ajitsuke nori).

- **Chile salt** is great on seafood. Stir 2 teaspoons fine sea salt with 1 teaspoon pure chile powder, such as ancho or chipotle.

- **Pimentón salt** is especially good on grilled fish. Substitute 1 teaspoon pimentón for the chile powder in the above recipe.

- **Lavender salt** is excellent on grilled or roasted fish. In a coffee or spice grinder, combine 2 tablespoons food-grade lavender blossoms with ½ cup (120 g) fine sea salt; grind until fine.

- **Citrus salt** is good on almost anything, including grilled fish and shellfish, such as scallops. Stir 2 tablespoons grated citrus zest with ½ cup (120 g) fine sea salt and bake on a parchment-lined baking sheet for 1 hour in a preheated 225°F (110°C) oven. Use as is or pulse in a food processor for a finer texture.

- **Makrut lime salt** can be used on seafood of all kinds as well as tomatoes, corn, and other vegetables. In a mini processor, add 1 part finely chopped fresh makrut lime leaves to 4 parts coarse sea salt and pulse together until uniform. You'll get a salt with incredible aroma that will add a delicious lime flavor to anything.

# SAUCES

Many of the recipes include sauces, but I've included a few more that would be good to have in your cooking toolbox. A sauce can add delicious flavor and texture to any dish. Any of these will enhance a wide variety of fish or shellfish dishes.

## BASIL PESTO

**Makes about 1 cup (240 ml)**

3 large cloves garlic
2 bunches fresh basil leaves, firmly packed (3 cups/120 g)
1 to 2 tablespoons pine nuts
⅓ cup (75 ml) olive oil
¼ cup (25 g) freshly grated Parmesan or Asiago cheese
Fine sea salt and freshly ground pepper

In a small saucepan of boiling salted water, poach the garlic for 1 minute. Add the basil and blanch for 5 seconds. Immediately drain and plunge into a bowl of ice water to stop the cooking and set the bright green color. Drain and then squeeze out all the water that you can. Add to a blender along with the nuts, olive oil, and cheese; blend until smooth. Add salt and pepper to taste. Store in an airtight container in the refrigerator for up to 5 days or freeze for up to 3 months.

## KALE PESTO

**Makes 1 cup (240 ml)**

2 large cloves garlic, unpeeled
2 cups (130 g) chopped lacinato kale, tough center ribs removed and discarded
⅓ cup (30 g) shredded Parmesan cheese
2 tablespoons toasted pine nuts or walnuts (page 344)
½ cup (120 ml) extra-virgin olive oil
1 teaspoon finely grated lemon zest
Kosher salt and freshly ground pepper

Bring a large pot of salted water to a boil. Add the garlic and let simmer for 1 minute. Add kale then bring the water back to a boil, stirring until the kale softens, about 2 minutes.

Drain the kale and garlic and immediately plunge into cold water to stop the cooking and preserve the kale's green color. Drain again when cool. Remove the garlic, peel, and set aside. Squeeze the kale with your hands to remove as much of the water as possible.

Add the garlic, kale, and remainder of ingredients to a food processor. Process until the mixture is pureed to your liking. It should have a little texture. You may want to add more olive oil to reach desired consistency. Season to taste.

## SAUCE GRIBICHE

**Makes about 1⅓ cups (315 ml)**

3 large hard-boiled eggs (page 344), yolks and
    whites separated
1 tablespoon Dijon mustard
2 tablespoons chicken stock (page 333) or
    vegetable stock (page 333)
2 teaspoons fresh lemon juice
½ cup (120 ml) olive oil
1 tablespoon drained capers, chopped
1 tablespoon small cornichon pickles or black
    olives, finely diced

1 tablespoon chopped mixed fresh herbs, such as
    parsley, chives, tarragon, and chervil
Fine sea salt and freshly ground pepper

In a blender, combine the egg yolks, mustard, stock, and
lemon juice and puree until smooth. With the machine
running, gradually add the olive oil in a fine stream to form
a smooth sauce. Finely dice the egg whites and stir them
into the sauce along with the capers, pickles, and herbs.
Add salt and pepper to taste. Store covered in the refrigerator
for up to 2 days.

---

## CHIMICHURRI SAUCE

**Makes 1½ cups (360 ml)**

1 small bunch fresh flat-leaf parsley
1 small bunch fresh cilantro
¼ cup (7 g) fresh oregano leaves
1 tablespoon drained capers
⅔ cup (165 ml) olive oil
4 large cloves garlic, minced
1 small shallot, minced
2 tablespoons sherry or red wine vinegar
2 tablespoons fresh lemon juice
½ teaspoon crushed red pepper flakes
Kosher salt and freshly ground black pepper

Using a chef's knife with a rocking motion, mince the
leaves and tender stems of the parsley and cilantro. (Hand
chopping is preferable to using a food processor, which
tends to pulverize the herbs.) Add the oregano leaves and
capers to the pile and mince into the parsley and cilantro.
Transfer the mixture to a small bowl.

Stir in the olive oil, garlic, shallot, vinegar, lemon juice, and
crushed red pepper. Season with salt and pepper. Let sit at
room temperature for least 15 minutes. Taste and adjust the
seasoning. Store refrigerated in an airtight container for up
to 3 days.

## AIOLI

**Makes about 1¾ cups (420 ml)**

4 to 6 large cloves garlic, chopped
½ teaspoon fine sea salt
1 tablespoon fresh lemon juice
2 egg yolks
1¼ cups (300 ml) olive oil
1 to 2 teaspoons cold water if needed
Fine sea salt and freshly ground pepper

With a mortar and pestle or the side of a chef's knife,
vigorously mash the garlic with the salt to form a paste.
Add the paste to a blender or mini food processor along with
the lemon juice and egg yolks and pulse until mixture is well
combined. With the machine running, gradually add the olive
oil a few drops at a time, then in a very thin stream to form a
smooth, thick emulsion. Add the water if needed to thin the
sauce. The finished sauce should be thick enough to hold
its shape solidly on a spoon. Season to taste with salt and
pepper. Store covered in the refrigerator for up to 5 days.

---

## QUICK GARLIC AIOLI

Stir mashed garlic and lemon juice into good-quality store-
bought mayonnaise.

---

## SALSA VERDE

**Makes about 1 cup (240 ml)**

2 cups (100 g) coarsely chopped fresh flat-leaf parsley
½ cup (20 g) chopped fresh basil or mint
4 oil-packed anchovy fillets
2 tablespoons drained capers
2 tablespoons poached or roasted garlic (page 345)
1 tablespoon finely grated lemon zest
⅔ cup (165 ml) extra-virgin olive oil
Fine sea salt and freshly ground pepper

In a blender or food processor, combine the parsley, basil,
anchovies, capers, garlic, and zest to a food processor or
blender. With the machine running, gradually add the olive
oil until just blended. The sauce should still have a little
texture. Season to taste with salt and pepper. Store covered
in the refrigerator for up to 24 hours.

## AVOCADO AND TOMATILLO SALSA

**Makes 1 cup (240 ml)**

2 tomatillos, husked, rinsed, and coarsely chopped
1 teaspoon chopped garlic
1 teaspoon seeded and chopped serrano chile
2 tablespoons chopped green onion, including
    some green parts
2 tablespoons chopped fresh cilantro
Fresh lime juice, to taste
1 large ripe avocado, pitted, peeled, and coarsely chopped
Fine sea salt and freshly ground pepper

In a blender or food processor, combine the tomatillos, garlic, chile, green onion, cilantro, and lime juice to taste and pulse to finely chop. Add the avocado and pulse once or twice. The salsa should still have some texture. Season to taste with salt and pepper. Store in an airtight container in the refrigerator for up to 2 days.

---

## VIETNAMESE DIPPING SAUCE (NUOC CHAM)

**Makes about 1 cup (240 ml)**

⅓ cup (75 ml) fresh lime juice
3 tablespoons fish sauce
1 teaspoon minced red jalapeño or bird chile
½ teaspoon minced garlic
2 teaspoons rice vinegar
3 tablespoons sugar, or to taste
1 teaspoon fresh cilantro leaves, coarsely chopped

In a small nonreactive bowl, combine the lime juice, fish sauce, chile, garlic, vinegar, and sugar and stir until the sugar is dissolved. Let sit for at least 30 minutes before serving for the flavors to develop. Serve at once or cover and refrigerate for up to 3 days. Stir in the cilantro just before serving.

---

## ROMESCO SAUCE

**Makes about 2 cups (480 ml)**

1 large red bell pepper
6 ripe plum tomatoes
1 head garlic, halved, papery outer skin removed
1 red onion
½ cup (120 ml) plus 1 tablespoon Spanish extra-virgin olive oil,
    plus more for brushing
6 nora or cascabel chiles

¼ cup (35 g) blanched almonds
1 thick slice white bread, crusts removed
1 tablespoon sherry vinegar
1 teaspoon pimentón (smoked Spanish paprika)
Fine sea salt

Preheat the oven to 350°F (175°C). Put the bell pepper, tomatoes, garlic, and onion in a roasting pan and brush lightly with the olive oil. Roast until the vegetables are soft, about 25 minutes. Remove the pan from the oven and let cool.

Meanwhile, put the chiles in a heatproof bowl, cover with hot water, and let soak for 15 minutes. Drain, then remove the seeds and stems.

In a small sauté pan, heat the 1 tablespoon olive oil over low heat. Add the almonds and sauté to brown them lightly, about 1 minute. Pour the almonds into a bowl, reserving the pan, and let cool.

Raise the heat to medium and add the bread slice to the reserved pan. Toast until golden brown, about 30 seconds on each side. Transfer the bread to a plate, reserving the pan, and let cool.

Add the pureed chiles to the same pan and cook for 30 seconds. Remove from the heat.

Peel the cooled vegetables, then discard the stems and seed the bell pepper and tomatoes. In a food processor, combine the roasted vegetables, toasted almonds and bread, chile puree, vinegar, pimentón, and the remaining ½ cup olive oil. Process to form a thick sauce, the texture is up to you. Add salt to taste. Store covered and refrigerated for up to 7 days.

---

## COCONUT-PEANUT SAUCE

**Makes about 1 cup (240 ml)**

3 tablespoons natural peanut butter
1 teaspoon chili-garlic sauce
3 tablespoons chicken stock (page 333), vegetable
    stock (page 333), or water
⅓ cup (75 ml) stirred coconut milk
2 teaspoons brown sugar
2 tablespoons fresh lime juice
1 tablespoon soy sauce

In a blender, combine the peanut butter, chili-garlic sauce, stock, coconut milk, brown sugar, lime juice, and soy sauce, and blend until smooth. The sauce should have the texture of heavy cream. Store covered in refrigerator for up to 5 days. Return to room temperature before using.

## TARTAR SAUCE

**Makes about 2 cups (480 ml)**

1 cup (240 ml) good mayonnaise
1 large hard-boiled egg (page 344), chopped
1 tablespoon sweet pickle relish
2 teaspoons drained capers, chopped
1 tablespoon Dijon mustard
1 tablespoon finely chopped fresh chives
1 tablespoon finely chopped fresh flat-leaf parsley
Kosher salt and freshly ground pepper

In a small bowl, gently stir the mayonnaise, egg, relish, capers, mustard, chives, and parsley together. Season to taste with salt and pepper. Transfer to an airtight container and refrigerate for at least 1 hour before using. Store refrigerated for up to 3 weeks.

---

## PONZU SAUCE

**Makes about 1 cup (240 ml)**

½ cup (120 ml) fresh lime, lemon, or yuzu juice
2 tablespoons rice vinegar
⅓ cup (75 ml) soy sauce
2 tablespoons mirin
2 tablespoons light brown sugar
½ teaspoon fish sauce

In a small bowl, combine the lime juice, vinegar, soy sauce, mirin, brown sugar, and fish sauce and whisk to blend. Let sit for at least 1 hour before serving, or cover and refrigerate for up to 1 week.

**NOTE** Classic Japanese ponzu is made with the juice of a small, aromatic citrus called yuzu. It's difficult to find, so I've substituted lime or lemon juice.

---

## ARRABBIATA SAUCE

**Makes about 6 cups (1.4 l)**

¼ cup (60 ml) extra-virgin olive oil
1 yellow onion, chopped
1 tablespoon finely chopped garlic
½ teaspoon fine sea salt
1 or 2 teaspoons crushed red pepper flakes, or to taste
Two 28-ounce (800-g) cans whole San Marzano tomatoes
1 large bay leaf
Stock or water as needed
Freshly ground pepper
½ cup (20 g) coarsely chopped fresh basil leaves

In a large, heavy pan, heat the olive oil over medium heat, sauté the onions and garlic with the salt until translucent, about 5 minutes. Add the crushed red pepper and cook for just 30 seconds or until fragrant.

Put the tomatoes in a large bowl and crush them with your hands, leaving a few smaller chunks. Add to the pot with the onions and garlic and bring to a simmer. Add the bay leaf and reduce the heat to low, partially cover, and simmer gently, stirring occasionally and adding stock or water in ¼-cup (60-ml) increments to prevent sticking, until thickened, about 20 minutes. Season to taste with salt and pepper. Stir in the fresh basil leaves. Store covered and refrigerated for up to 7 days.

---

## DIJON-LEMON SAUCE

**Makes about ¾ cup (180 ml)**

½ cup (115 g) unsalted clarified butter (page 345)
3 large egg yolks
1 tablespoon fresh lemon juice
2 teaspoons Dijon mustard
Kosher salt and freshly ground white pepper

In a small saucepan, heat the butter until it just begins to bubble. In a blender, combine the egg yolks, lemon juice, and mustard and blend until the mixture is foamy. With the machine running, gradually add the clarified butter in a thin stream. Season to taste with salt and pepper.

---

## BLENDER HOLLANDAISE SAUCE

**Makes about 1 cup (240 ml)**

½ cup (115 g) unsalted butter
3 large egg yolks
2 teaspoons fresh lemon juice
1 teaspoon Dijon mustard
Kosher salt and freshly ground pepper

In a small saucepan over medium heat, melt the butter. Add the egg yolks, lemon juice, and mustard to a blender and pulse 2 or 3 times to combine. With the blender on low speed, slowly add the hot butter in a thin stream. Season with salt and pepper. Add more lemon juice if you'd like. Keep warm.

**NOTE** If the sauce curdles or "breaks" (separates), you can correct it by whisking in 1 or 2 teaspoons of boiling water, a drop at a time. If that doesn't work, add another egg yolk to a bowl and very slowly whisk in the broken sauce. Usually it will come back together with one of these methods.

## PAN-DEGLAZING SAUCE

**Makes about ⅔ cup (165 ml)**

3 tablespoons minced shallots or green onions
1 cup (240 ml) dry red or white wine
½ cup (120 ml) chicken stock (page 333), fish stock
  (page 332), or vegetable stock (page 333)
3 to 4 tablespoons unsalted butter, at room temperature
2 tablespoons finely minced fresh herbs, such as chives,
  parsley, basil, or a combination
Salt and freshly ground pepper

After sautéing food, pour off all but a couple of teaspoons of any fat from the sauté pan. Add the shallots and cook over medium heat until translucent, about 3 minutes. Add the wine and stock and stir with a wooden spoon to scrape up any browned bits from the bottom of the pan. Raise the heat to high and boil until the mixture is almost syrupy, about 5 minutes. Remove from the heat and whisk in the butter 1 tablespoon at a time; the sauce will thicken and become shiny. Whisk in the herbs and season with salt and pepper to taste. Pour over the sautéed food and serve immediately.

## WHITE WINE BUTTER SAUCE

**Makes about ¾ cup (180 ml)**

1 tablespoon olive oil
¼ cup (35 g) finely chopped shallots or green
  onions, white part only
¾ cup (180 ml) dry white wine
1 tablespoon grated lemon zest
1 cup (240 ml) chicken stock (page 333) or shellfish
  stock (page 332)
⅓ cup (75 ml) heavy cream
3 tablespoons unsalted butter, at room temperature
Fine sea salt and freshly ground pepper
Fresh lemon juice, to taste

In a heavy saucepan over medium heat, warm the olive oil Cook the shallots until translucent, about 2 minutes. Add the wine, zest, and stock. Raise the heat to high and cook to reduce the liquid by two-thirds. Add the cream and cook, stirring, until a light sauce consistency, about 5 minutes. Off heat, whisk in the butter 1 tablespoon at a time. The sauce will thicken and take on a shine. Season with salt, pepper, and lemon juice. Cover and keep warm over hot water for up to 30 minutes.

## BÉARNAISE SAUCE

**Makes about 1 cup (240 ml)**

⅓ cup (75 ml) dry white wine
⅓ cup (75 ml) white wine vinegar
2 tablespoons chopped shallots
3 tablespoons chopped fresh tarragon leaves and stems
8 black peppercorns
3 large egg yolks
1 cup (225 g) unsalted butter, melted
1 or 2 tablespoons warm water, if needed
Fine sea salt and freshly ground pepper

In a small saucepan, combine the wine, vinegar, shallots, 1 tablespoon tarragon, and the peppercorns. Bring to a boil over high heat and cook until reduced to about ¼ cup (60 ml), about 5 minutes. Remove from the heat. Strain through a fine-mesh sieve set over a bowl, pressing on the solids with the back of a spoon; discard the solids. Let cool slightly.

In a blender, combine the strained reduction and the egg yolks and pulse until smooth. With the machine running, gradually add the butter in a slow stream through the hole in the lid. Add the remaining 2 tablespoons tarragon and pulse once or twice. Thin the sauce if desired by whisking in a tablespoon or two of warm water. Season to taste with salt and pepper. If making ahead, cover and keep warm over hot tap water for up to 1 hour.

## POBLANO CHILE SAUCE

**Makes about 2 cups (480 ml)**

4 large poblano chiles
2 tablespoons canola or other neutral oil
1 small white onion, sliced
1 teaspoon thinly sliced garlic
½ teaspoon dried oregano, preferably Mexican
½ teaspoon ancho chile powder
½ cup (120 ml) crème fraîche or Mexican crema
⅓ cup (75 ml) chicken stock (page 333) or vegetable
  stock (page 333), or more as desired
Fine sea salt and freshly ground pepper

If using a gas stove, char the poblanos in the open flame of a stove-top burner, turning regularly until the skins are mostly charred, about 10 minutes. Alternatively, cut the chiles in half and char them skin side up under a hot broiler.

Put the chiles in a bowl and cover with plastic wrap for about 10 minutes to help loosen the charred skin.

Peel and discard the charred skin and remove and discard the stems and seeds. Cut the peppers into strips about ½ inch (2 mm) wide. Don't worry if you don't get all the charred bits off, and don't rinse the chiles, as this washes away much of the toasty flavor.

In a large skillet, heat the oil over medium heat and cook the onion until just beginning to color, about 5 minutes. Add the chile strips, garlic, oregano, and powdered chile and cook, stirring, for 2 minutes. Stir in the crème fraîche and stock and simmer until nicely thickened, about 2 minutes. Add more stock to thin, if desired. Season to taste with salt and pepper. Store, covered and refrigerated, for up to 3 days.

## VINEGAR-CREAM SAUCE

**Makes about 1¼ cups (300 ml)**

2 tablespoons unsalted butter
1 tablespoon olive oil
¼ cup (35 g) minced shallots or green onion
¼ cup (15 g) chopped fresh mushrooms
¼ cup (60 ml) pear vinegar
2 cups (480 ml) chicken stock (page 333)
1 cup (240 ml) heavy cream
½ cup (90 g) diced fresh pears
2 teaspoons finely chopped fresh herbs,
    such as chives, parsley, and tarragon
Fine sea salt and freshly ground pepper

In a sauté pan, melt the butter with the olive oil over medium-high heat. Add the shallots and mushrooms and cook until lightly colored. Add the vinegar and stock, raise the heat to high, and cook until slightly thickened, about 5 minutes. Strain through a fine-mesh sieve set over a bowl, pressing on the solids with the back of a spoon; discard the solids. Return the sauce to the pan, add the cream, and cook to reduce to a light sauce consistency. Stir in the fruit and herbs and season with salt and pepper. Cover and keep warm for up to 1 hour.

**NOTE** Depending on the strength or flavor of the vinegar, you can whisk 1 or 2 tablespoons more into the sauce for a more piquant finish. Use any fragrant fruit vinegar you like and match the fresh fruit to the vinegar. Serve with fish or shellfish.

## GUACAMOLE

**Makes about 2½ cups (575 g)**

4 medium ripe avocados, halved and pitted
⅓ cup (40 g) finely chopped white onion
2 tablespoons finely chopped fresh cilantro
1 teaspoon finely chopped jalapeño
3 tablespoons lime juice (about 1½ limes), or to taste
¼ teaspoon ground cumin
2 teaspoons kosher salt

Scoop the avocados into a bowl, discarding any browned areas. Using a fork, mash the avocado to your desired texture. Add the onion, cilantro, jalapeno, lime juice, cumin, and salt. Stir to combine. Season to taste with additional salt and lime juice if needed.

## SPICE MIXES AND PASTES

## ZA'ATAR SPICE MIX

**Makes ½ cup (100 g)**

2 tablespoons sesame seeds, toasted (page 344)
2 tablespoons ground sumac
2 tablespoons dried marjoram
2 tablespoons dried oregano
1 teaspoon kosher salt

Grind the sesame seeds in a spice grinder. In a small bowl, combine the ground sesame seeds, sumac, marjoram, oregano, and 1 teaspoon salt. Store in an airtight jar with a tight-fitting lid in a cool place for up to 3 months.

## CAJUN OR CREOLE SEASONING

**Makes a generous 3 tablespoons**

2 teaspoons sweet Hungarian paprika
1 teaspoon garlic powder
1 teaspoon onion powder
1 teaspoon *each* dried thyme, basil, and oregano
½ teaspoon cayenne pepper
1 teaspoon fine sea salt
½ teaspoon freshly ground black pepper

In a spice grinder, combine the paprika, garlic powder, onion powder, thyme, basil, oregano, cayenne, salt, and pepper. Pulse to grind to a fine powder. Store in an airtight jar with a tight-fitting lid in a cool place for up to 3 months.

## HARISSA PASTE

**Makes about 1½ cups (345 g)**

One 14-ounce (400-g) can fire-roasted piquillo
    peppers, drained
2 large drained oil-packed Calabrian chiles
1 tablespoon chopped garlic
¼ cup (13 g) chopped fresh flat-leaf parsley
1 tablespoon ground pasilla or ancho chile
1 teaspoon ground cumin
1 teaspoon ground coriander
Juice of ½ lemon
⅓ cup (75 ml) olive oil
2 teaspoons salt

In a blender or food processor, combine all the ingredients and process to a smooth paste. Store covered and refrigerated for up to 3 months.

# LAKSA PASTE

**Makes 1 cup (230 g)**

2 tablespoons chili-garlic sauce, or to taste
⅓ cup (45 g) chopped shallots
⅓ cup (45 g) chopped macadamia nuts or blanched almonds,
   toasted (page 344)
¼ cup (25 g) peeled and finely chopped ginger
2 tablespoons coriander seeds, crushed
1 teaspoon shrimp paste, or 2 tablespoons fish sauce
Juice and grated zest of 2 limes
2 teaspoons sugar
2 tablespoons canola oil or other neutral oil
1 teaspoon toasted sesame oil
½ cup (120 ml) or so coconut milk

In a blender, combine the chili-garlic sauce, shallots, macadamias, ginger, coriander, shrimp paste, lime juice and zest, sugar, canola oil, and sesame oil and process for a minute or two or until very smooth. Pour into a small saucepan and cook over medium heat, stirring constantly until fragrant, 4 to 5 minutes. Stir in the coconut milk and cook 2 to 3 minutes more. Let cool. To store, cover and refrigerate for up to 1 week or freeze for up to 3 months.

## OTHER PANTRY ESSENTIALS

# TOASTED RICE POWDER

Thai toasted-rice powder (*khao khua*) is made by very slowly toasting sticky rice grains to a golden brown and then grinding them to a coarse powder. It adds texture and a nutty flavor to dishes. Sticky rice is also sold as "sweet" and "glutinous" rice.

**Makes ½ cup (100 g)**

¾ cup (150 g) Thai sticky rice

Put the rice in a large stainless-steel skillet and cook over medium heat, stirring regularly and shaking the pan to keep the rice in an even layer, until it is golden brown, 10 to 12 minutes. If the rice begins to burn, lower the heat.

Spread the rice on a baking sheet and let cool to room temperature. Using a spice grinder, grind to a coarse powder like coarse ground coffee. Store in an airtight container for up to 3 months.

# SUSHI RICE

**Makes 3 cups (615 g)**

1½ cups (300 g) sushi rice
One 2-inch (5-cm) piece kombu seaweed
1 tablespoon sugar
½ teaspoon kosher salt
3 tablespoons rice vinegar

In a fine-mesh strainer, rinse the rice repeatedly with cold running water, until the water runs clear. Transfer the rice to a saucepan with 1½ cups (360 ml) water; let sit for 30 minutes.

Gently wipe the kelp with a clean, dry cloth, leaving as much of the white powder as you can on the surface. Place on top of the rice.

Bring the rice to a boil over medium heat, then reduce the heat to low and cover. Simmer for 12 minutes, then remove the saucepan from the heat, and let sit, covered, for another 12 to 15 minutes.

In a small saucepan over low heat, combine the sugar, salt, and vinegar, stirring to dissolve the sugar. Discard the kombu, then transfer the rice to a large, shallow container, preferably wooden. Sprinkle the rice with the vinegar mixture. Let the rice cool to just above room temperature. Fluff the rice with a damp wooden paddle, then cover the container with a damp kitchen towel until ready to use.

# STICKY RICE

Sticky rice is a type of rice commonly sold as "glutinous rice" (though it has no gluten) or "sticky rice". As its name implies, after cooking, it really is very sticky. It is rarely served plain. To cook, rinse in several changes of water, then soak for 2 hours in water to cover. Typically, it's steamed, but you can also make it in a rice cooker or on top of the stove. Follow the package directions.

# GARLIC-LEMON BREAD CRUMBS

**Makes about 2 cups (200 g)**

1 small (12-ounce/340-g) coarse-grained bread, such
   as ciabatta
2 tablespoons extra-virgin olive oil
2 teaspoons finely chopped garlic
2 teaspoons finely grated lemon zest
1 tablespoon finely chopped fresh flat-leaf parsley
Fine sea salt and freshly ground pepper

Preheat the oven to 350°F (175°C). Cut the bread into ¼-inch- (6-mm-) thick slices, place on a baking sheet, and bake until dry and crunchy, about 12 minutes. Break up the slices with your hands, add to a food processor, and pulse into coarse crumbs. Be careful not to overprocess.

In a medium skillet, heat the olive oil over medium heat. Add the garlic and stir until it just begins to color, about 2 minutes. Add the bread crumbs, lemon zest, and parsley and stir until the crumbs are lightly coated. Season with salt and pepper to taste and remove from the heat. Let cool. Set aside to use now or cover and refrigerate for up to 5 days.

------------

## ANCHOVY-PARMESAN BREAD CRUMBS

### Makes 1 generous cup (80 g)

¼ cup (60 ml) extra-virgin olive oil
4 oil-packed anchovies, drained
1 cup (80 g) panko (Japanese bread crumbs) or other coarse
    bread crumbs
1 tablespoon freshly grated Parmesan
2 teaspoons finely chopped fresh chives
1 teaspoon grated lemon zest
Fine sea salt and freshly ground pepper

In a large skillet, heat the olive oil over medium heat. Add the anchovies and stir constantly to melt them into the olive oil, about 3 minutes. Add the panko and cook, stirring, until nicely browned, about 2 minutes. Off heat, stir in the Parmesan, chives, and zest. Add salt and pepper to taste. Let cool. Store in an airtight container at room temperature for up to 3 days.

**NOTE** Seasoned bread crumbs have a multitude of uses, including as a garnish for fish of any kind.

------------

## GARLIC CROUTONS

### Makes 3 cups (130 g)

⅓ cup (75 ml) olive oil
2 large cloves garlic, bruised with the side of a knife
3 cups (170 g) 1-inch (2.5-cm) cubes cut from day-old rustic
    bread with crusts removed
2 tablespoons minced fresh flat-leaf parsley
1 teaspoon grated lemon zest
Fine sea salt and freshly ground pepper

Preheat the oven to 375°F (190°C).

In a large sauté pan, heat the olive oil over medium heat and sauté the garlic until it just begins to color. Don't let the garlic burn, or it will become bitter. Using a slotted spoon, remove the garlic from the olive oil.

In a medium bowl, toss the bread cubes with the oil until well coated and spread on a wire rack set in a baking sheet. Toast in the oven until the cubes are nicely golden on all sides, 10 to 12 minutes. The croutons should be crisp but still somewhat soft in the center.

Pour the croutons into a medium bowl and toss with parsley, lemon zest, and salt and pepper while still warm. Use now, or let cool, pour into an airtight container, and store for up to 2 weeks.

------------

## CROSTINI

*Crostini* is an Italian term that basically translates to "little toasts." They are easily made by thinly slicing a baguette, usually at an angle. Brush the baguette slices with olive oil, then arrange on a baking sheet at toast until lightly browned on both sides under a hot broiler or in a hot oven. They can also be toasted on a grill. Bruschetta are similar, but usually are cut a little thicker.

------------

## PETER'S NEW YORK PIZZA DOUGH

### Makes 36 ounces (1 kg) or three 14-inch (35.5-cm) pizzas

4⅔ cups (630 g) unbleached bread flour
1½ teaspoons kosher salt
1 teaspoon instant yeast
2 tablespoons granulated sugar, brown sugar, or honey
1½ cups (360 ml) plus 2 tablespoons room-temperature water
3 tablespoons olive oil

In the bowl of a stand mixer fitted with the paddle attachment, combine the flour, salt, yeast, and sugar. Add the water and stir on slow speed for 3 minutes to form a coarse, shaggy dough.

Switch from the paddle to the dough hook. Add the olive oil, increase the speed to medium, and mix for an additional 2 to 3 minutes to make a coarse, tacky dough. If there is any dry flour in the bowl add more water 1 teaspoon at a time while mixing. Let the dough rest for 5 minutes to fully hydrate.

On medium high speed, mix for another 2 to 3 minutes to make a smooth dough, adding more flour or water as needed. The dough should be soft, supple, and satiny to the touch, and spring back when pressed with a wet finger.

Lightly oil a bowl or heavy-duty zip-top bag and place the dough in it. If using a bowl, cover it with plastic wrap. Refrigerate for anywhere from 12 to 72 hours. The dough can be wrapped tightly in plastic wrap and frozen for up to 1 month; thaw before using.

## TECHNIQUES

### POACHED EGGS

Bring a saucepan half-filled with water to a bare simmer. Add 1 or 2 teaspoons white vinegar (to help set the whites more quickly), then gently add 1 to 3 large eggs to the water. Cook until the white is set and the yolks is still runny, about 4 minutes. You can also use stock, milk, or court bouillon to add a bit of flavor.

---

### HARD-BOILED EGGS

Bring a deep saucepan of water to a boil and carefully add the eggs. Adjust the heat to a gentle boil and cook, uncovered, for 7 minutes. Set the pan aside and allow the eggs and water to cool a bit, about 5 minutes. Drain the eggs and place them in a bowl of cold water. Crack each egg completely, starting on the rounded end and peel under cold running water.

---

### FRIED HERBS

Leafy herbs such as basil, parsley, and sage are delicious fried crisply. Add about an inch (2.5 cm) of oil to a small, deep saucepan and heat to 350°F (175°C) on a deep-frying thermometer. Add the herbs in small batches, leaving them in the oil for 10 to 20 seconds or so or until they are crisp and crystalline looking. Remove from the oil with a spider or slotted spoon and drain on paper towels. Set aside. Save the oil for another use, such as frying eggs or drizzling on soup. The oil will now have a distinctive herb flavor.

### FRIED CAPERS

When capers are fried, they take on a distinct flavor and texture, which I really like. All you need to do is to drain them well, pat dry with paper towels, and then fry in small batches in ½ inch (12 mm) or so of hot (350°F/175°C on a deep-frying thermometer) olive oil until the buds begin to open and are lightly browned and crisp, about 2 minutes. Drain on paper towels. This can be done a few hours in advance.

---

### FRIED SHALLOTS

We often associate shallots with French and European cooking, but when fried, they are widely used in Southeast Asian cooking for garnish. They are very simple to make. Thinly slice the shallots and add ½ inch (12 mm) of hot (350°F/175°C on a deep-frying thermometer) vegetable oil. Fry until golden brown, about 3 minutes. Drain on paper towels and store tightly covered for up to 2 weeks. Fried shallots are widely available in well-stocked markets if you don't want to make your own.

---

### TOASTING NUTS AND SEEDS

Lightly toasting nuts and seeds before using in a recipe is always recommended; it brings out the flavor of both. Add nuts or seeds to a small dry skillet over medium heat and cook, stirring regularly, until they are lightly golden. A good timing guide is that when you smell their fragrance, they are done. Immediately transfer to a plate to cool. Store tightly covered for up to 2 weeks.

---

### TOASTING SPICES

Lightly toasting spices brings out their flavor. Add whole or ground spices to a small dry skillet over low heat and cook, stirring continuously, just until fragrant. Immediately transfer to a plate to cool. Use a mortar and pestle or a spice grinder to grind the spices if required by the recipe. The toasted spices are best used the same day.

## TOASTING BREAD CRUMBS

Breadcrumbs can be of many sizes depending on what you desire. I like using a rotary hand grater, but you could also place dried bread in a zip-top plastic bag and crush it with a rolling pin. To toast them, spread the bread crumbs on a baking sheet and bake in a 350° (175°C ) oven for 8 to 10 minutes, or until they are lightly browned. Stir once or twice. Store in an airtight container in a cool, dry spot.

## SEGMENTING CITRUS FRUIT

Cut the ends off the citrus fruit. Stand the fruit on one end and, with a small sharp knife, remove all the peel and white pith by slicing from top to bottom all the way around the fruit, following the contour of the fruit. Cut between the segments on each side of the membrane to release the segments. Squeeze the membranes over a small bowl to reserve the juice.

## CLARIFIED BUTTER

Clarified butter (also known as drawn butter), the golden liquid left behind when the milk solids and water have been removed, is the perfect fat to sauté or fry with. It has a very high smoke point and a pure, buttery taste.

To make clarified butter, simply melt unsalted butter in a small, heavy saucepan over low heat. It will separate as it melts, with foam rising to the top and the milk solids falling to the bottom. Skim off the foam and reserve the foam. Take the butter off the heat and let cool for 5 minutes or so. Do a final skim of the foam, then pour the clear golden liquid carefully into a glass container, leaving the cloudy milk solids behind. Store tightly closed in the refrigerator for 6 to 8 months.

## ROASTING, POACHING, AND TOASTING GARLIC

A simple way of taming garlic's strong taste is to roast, poach, or toast it first. Roasted, poached, or toasted garlic can be stored in a tightly covered container in the refrigerator for up to 1 week.

**To roast garlic:** Cut off the top quarter of each garlic head to expose the cloves. Drizzle with a little olive oil and season with salt and pepper. Loosely but completely wrap each head in a piece of aluminum foil and roast in a preheated 400°F (205°C) oven until the garlic is very soft and lightly browned, about 45 minutes. To use, simply squeeze the buttery soft garlic out of the garlic head.

**To poach garlic:** Separate but don't peel the cloves. Put in a small saucepan and add water to cover by at least ½ inch (12 mm). Place over high heat and bring to a boil. Immediately drain and repeat the process again. Rinse in cool water to cool off the cloves. Remove and discard the skins.

**To toast garlic:** Separate the unpeeled cloves and place them in a dry sauté pan over medium heat. Shake and turn them occasionally until the cloves develop toasty brown spots on the skin. Remove, let cool, and slip off the skins.

# INDEX

## A

abalone, 34–35
  Pan-Fried Abalone, 85
  Rice Porridge with Abalone, 83
Achiote Paste, 214
Aioli, 337
  Mango Aioli, 172
  Orange-Caper Aioli, 156
  Quick Garlic Aioli, 337
  Smoked Paprika Aioli, 60
  Tarragon Aioli, 145
anchovies, 272, 286. *See also* boquerones
  Anchoïade, 292
  Anchovy Butter, 335
  Anchovy-Parmesan Bread Crumbs, 343
  Bagna Cauda, 292
  John's Caesar Salad, 291
  Pan Bagnat, 297
  Spaghetti alla Rustica, 294
Arrabbiata Sauce, 339
avocados
  Ahi Tuna Ceviche with Mango and
    Avocado, 255
  Avocado and Tomatillo Salsa, 338
  Bay Scallops and Avocado with Miso
    Dressing, 74
  Crab, Avocado, and Golden Beet Salad
    with Lime Vinaigrette, 143
  DLTA: Dulse, Lettuce, Tomato, and
    Avocado Sandwiches, 324
  Guacamole, 341
  Halibut Crudo with Fennel, Green Apple,
    and Avocado, 226
  Sesame-Crusted Seared Tuna with
    Avocado Salad and Sesame-Miso
    Vinaigrette, 262

## B

bacon
  Crab and Corn Chowder with Bacon and
    Wild Mushrooms, 140
  Grilled Trout with Herbs and Bacon, 182
  Hangtown Fry, 46
  Pan-Seared Sturgeon with Pancetta,
    Capers, and Lemon, 268
  Shad Roe with Bacon and Lemon, 220
  Steamed Bacon-Stuffed Sole, 243
Bagna Cauda, 292

Basil Pesto, 336
Béarnaise Sauce, 340
black cod. *See* sablefish
Blini with Smoked Salmon and Caviar, 309
boquerones, 286
  Homemade White Anchovies in Vinegar
    (Boquerones), 275
  Lime-Pickled Anchovies, aka "California
    Boquerones," 276
  Tomato Toasts with Serrano Ham and
    Boquerones, 288
  Tuna-Stuffed Eggs with Boquerones, 288
bottarga, 302
  Spaghetti with Bottarga, 313
Bouillabaisse, California, with Rouille, 87
Brandade (Salt Cod Gratin), 319
branzino, 191
  Branzino Baked in a Salt Crust, 219
  Roasted Whole Branzino, 219
bread crumbs
  Anchovy-Parmesan Bread Crumbs, 343
  Garlic-Lemon Bread Crumbs, 342–43
  toasting, 345
Bruschetta with Grilled Calamari, Tomatoes,
  and Goat Cheese, 98
butter
  Anchovy Butter, 335
  Calabrian Chile Butter, 50
  Chile-Lime Butter, 335
  Chipotle-Bourbon Butter, 41
  clarified, 345
  flavored, 334
  Harissa Butter, 41, 335
  Kimchi Butter, 335
  Maitre d'Hotel Butter, 334
  Mendocino Miso Butter, 42
  Miso Butter, 335
  Mustard-Tarragon Butter, 335
  'Nduja Butter, 334
  Porcini Butter, 335
  Roasted Garlic Butter, 335

## C

cabbage
  Cabbage Salad Tossed with Shio
    Kombu, 328
  Cabbage Slaw, 201

  Grilled Squid Noodle Salad with Mango,
    Cabbage, and Cucumber, 105
  Napa Cabbage–Apple Slaw, 211
Caesar Salad, John's, 291
Cajun or Creole Seasoning, 341
capers, fried, 344
Caponata, 241
Carrots, Pickled, with Wakame
  and Miso, 328
catfish, 188
  Southern Fried Catfish, 199
caviar, 302
  Blini with Smoked Salmon and Caviar, 309
  Caviar Toasts, 309
Celery Root Salad, Scallops with, 78
cheese
  Anchovy-Parmesan Bread Crumbs, 343
  Bruschetta with Grilled Calamari,
    Tomatoes, and Goat Cheese, 98
  Cheese Grits, 205
  Greek Shrimp Saganaki with Tomatoes,
    Olives, and Feta, 131
  Parmesan Custards with
    Salmon Roe, 310
  Rock Shrimp Quesadillas with Oaxacan
    Cheese and Tomatoes, 126
chicken
  Chicken Stock, 333
  Ginger Chicken Stock, 333
  Japanese Egg Custards with Shrimp, 127
  Thai Shrimp and Chicken Meatball
    Soup, 130
Chilean sea bass, 190
  Achiote-Grilled Sea Bass and Citrus Salad,
    214
  Pan-Seared Sea Bass with Ham Hocks and
    Savory Red Wine Sauce, 216
chiles
  Calabrian Chile Butter, 50
  Chile-Lime Butter, 335
  Chipotle-Bourbon Butter, 41
  Chipotle Mayonnaise, 149
  Cilantro-Poblano Sauce, 61
  Fresno Chile Mignonette, 39
  Mango-Jalapeño Salsa, 36
  Poblano Chile Sauce, 340–41
  Thai Crab Curry with Chiles, Ginger,
    and Lime Leaves, 150

Chimichurri Sauce, 337

Chirashi Sushi, 323

chowders
Crab and Corn Chowder with Bacon and
Wild Mushrooms, 140
Hog Island Clam Chowder, 52
Smoky Salmon and Potato Chowder, 173

cilantro
Cilantro Crema, 201
Cilantro-Poblano Sauce, 61

Cioppino, 88

citrus. See also individual fruits
Achiote-Grilled Sea Bass and
Citrus Salad, 214
Candied Citrus Mignonette, 39
Citrus Salsa, 201
segmenting, 345
Smoked Salmon, Citrus, and Fava Bean
Salad, 167

clams, 30–32. See also geoducks
Clam Fritters with Smoked-Paprika
Aioli, 60
Clams Casino, 51
Clams Casino Pizza, 62
Clam Shack Fried Clams, 54
Clam Steamers with Chorizo, Greens, and
Calabrian Chile Butter, 50
Clams with Cherry Tomatoes, Herbs, and
Crème Fraîche, 57
Clams with Cilantro-Poblano Sauce, 61
Hog Island Clam Chowder, 52
Linguine with Clams, 58
Paella with Clams, Shrimp,
and Chorizo, 91
Rigatoni with Grilled Squid, Clams,
and Heirloom Tomatoes, 106
Saigon Clams, 58
Sake-Steamed Clams with Shimeji
Mushrooms, 61
Stuffed Clams, 55

Coconut-Peanut Sauce, 338

cod, 189. See also salt cod
Baked Cod with Ras el Hanout Onion
Jam, 212
Beer-Battered Fish and Chips, 206
Panko-Fried Fish, 208
Seafood Sausages, 213

Coquilles Saint-Jacques, 75

corn. See also grits
Corn Bread–Oyster Stuffing with
Thyme and Fennel, 44
Crab and Corn Chowder with Bacon and
Wild Mushrooms, 140
Creamy Corn Sauce, 82
Creamy Polenta, 177
Seared Corn Sauce, 174

crab, 116–18
Crab and Corn Chowder with Bacon and
Wild Mushrooms, 140
Crab, Avocado, and Golden Beet Salad
with Lime Vinaigrette, 143
Crab Cakes with Tarragon Aioli, 145
Crab Deviled Eggs, 144
Crab Hush Puppies, 138
Crab in Wine and Vermouth, 144
Crab Louis Salad, 146
Green Pea Soup with Crab, 139
Soft-Shell Crab Sandwiches with Chipotle
Mayonnaise, 149
Thai Crab Curry with Chiles, Ginger, and
Lime Leaves, 150

crayfish, 121
Crayfish Étouffée, 157
Peel 'n' Eat Crayfish, 158

Crostini, 343

Croutons, Garlic, 343

D

Dashi, 334
Kombu Dashi (Vegetarian), 334
Mushroom Dashi, 334
powder, instant, 334

deep-frying tips, 208

DLTA: Dulse, Lettuce, Tomato, and Avocado
Sandwiches, 324

dogfish shark, 225

dressings. See also vinaigrettes
Green Goddess Dressing, 169
Herb Dressing, 97
Kalamata Dressing, 110
Lime Citronette, 265
Louis Dressing, 146
Miso Dressing, 74
Spicy Lime Dressing, 76
Tofu Caesar Dressing, 291

E

eggs
Crab Deviled Eggs, 144
Hangtown Fry, 46
hard-boiled, 344
Japanese Egg Custards with Shrimp, 127
poached, 344
Salt Cod Cakes with Poached Eggs and
Romesco Sauce, 317
Tuna-Stuffed Eggs with Boquerones, 288

F

Fennel, Pickled, 299

fish. See also individual fish
Beer-Battered Fish and Chips, 206
buying, 20
California Bouillabaisse with Rouille, 87
canned, tinned, and jarred, 284, 286
Cioppino, 88
collars, 253
cooking frozen, 21
filleting, 164, 225, 272
Fish Stock, 332
fresh vs. frozen, 21
Panko-Fried Fish, 208
plank-grilling, 178
raw, 23
removing pin bones from, 164
safety, 23
scaling, 164
Seafood Larb, 231
skinning, 164
storing, 23

flounder, 224

Flounder Amandine, 242
Peruvian Ceviche with Leche de Tigre, 228

fluke, 225
Peruvian Ceviche with Leche de Tigre, 228

Furikake, 326

G

garlic
Aioli, 337
Garlic Cream, 314
Garlic Croutons, 343
Garlic-Lemon Bread Crumbs, 342–43
Green Garlic Mussels, 72
poaching, 345
Quick Garlic Aioli, 337
Roasted Garlic Butter, 335
Roasted-Garlic Sabayon, 79
roasting, 345
toasting, 345

Gazpacho, Wine Country, with Shrimp, 124

geoducks, 31, 32
Geoduck Ceviche with Calabrian Chile
Sauce, 65
Geoduck Fritters, 65

ginger
Ginger Chicken Stock, 333
Ginger-Soy Dipping Sauce, 129
Ginger-Soy Salmon with Soba Noodle
Salad, 170

Gravlax, Quick Salmon, 168

Green Goddess Dressing, 169

green onions
    Broiled Mackerel with Butter and Green
        Onions, 282
    Korean Green Onion Pancakes
        with Squid, 103
grits
    Cheese Grits, 205
    Shrimp and Grits, 134
grouper, 190
    Braised Grouper Cheeks with Green
        Tomato Salsa Verde, 217
Guacamole, 341

## H

haddock, 189
    Beer-Battered Fish and Chips, 206
    Panko-Fried Fish, 208
hake, 189
halibut, 224
    Fish Bone Marrow with Grilled Bread, 253
    Halibut Crudo with Fennel, Green Apple,
        and Avocado, 226
    Oven-Fried Cornmeal-Crusted
        Fish Sticks, 236
    Panko-Fried Fish, 208
    Pan-Seared Halibut with Mediterranean
        Marinade, 234
    Peruvian Ceviche with Leche
        de Tigre, 228
    Poached Halibut in Court Bouillon, 232
    Steamed Halibut with Thai Curry Cream
        Sauce and Chard, 233
ham. See also prosciutto
    Pan-Seared Sea Bass with Ham Hocks and
        Savory Red Wine Sauce, 216
    Tomato Toasts with Serrano Ham and
        Boquerones, 288
Hangtown Fry, 46
harissa
    Harissa Butter, 41, 335
    Harissa Paste, 341
herbs, fried, 344
herring, 272
    Pickled Herring Rollmops with Crème
        Fraîche and Pumpernickel, 278
Hog Island Oyster Company
    about, 12
    sustainable seafood and, 19
Hogwash, 39
Hollandaise Sauce, Blender, 339
Honey-Lemon Vinaigrette, 167
Hush Puppies, Crab, 138

## K

Kale Pesto, 336
Kimchi Butter, 335

## L

laksa
    Laksa Paste, 342
    Shrimp Laksa Soup with Noodles, 133
Larb, Seafood, 231
lemons
    Dijon-Lemon Sauce, 339
    Garlic-Lemon Bread Crumbs, 342–43
    Honey-Lemon Vinaigrette, 167
    Lemon-Caper Vinaigrette, 239
limes
    Chile-Lime Butter, 335
    Lime Citronette, 265
    Lime-Pickled Anchovies, aka "California
        Boquerones," 276
    Lime Vinaigrette, 143
    Spicy Lime Dressing, 76
lingcod, 189
    Lingcod Sliders with Napa Cabbage–
        Apple Slaw, 211
lobster, 119–20
    Grilled Lobster with Roasted Garlic Butter,
        152
    Lobster Bisque, 155
    Lobster Potpies, 155
    Lobster Rolls, 152
    Lobster Watercress Salad with
        Orange-Caper Aioli, 156
    Stir-Fried Lobster in Black Bean
        Sauce, 151
Louis Dressing, 146

## M

mackerel, 273
    Baked Mackerel with Daikon, Soy, and
        Lemon, 283
    Broiled Mackerel with Butter and Green
        Onions, 282
    Fried Whitebait, 279
    Mackerel "En Saor," 281
mahi mahi, 249
    Grilled Mahi Mahi Brochettes, 267
    Grilled Mahi Mahi with Chimichurri, 267
Maitre d'Hotel Butter, 334
mangoes
    Ahi Tuna Ceviche with Mango and
        Avocado, 255
    Grilled Squid Noodle Salad with Mango,
        Cabbage, and Cucumber, 105

Mango Aioli, 172
Mango-Jalapeño Salsa, 36
Maple Vinaigrette, 181
marinades
    Mediterranean Marinade, 234
    Tiger's Milk Marinade, 228
mayonnaise
    Chipotle Mayonnaise, 149
    Pesto Mayonnaise, 102
    Spicy Mayonnaise, 109
    Sriracha Mayonnaise, 261
miso
    Mendocino Miso Butter, 42
    Miso Butter, 335
    Miso Dressing, 74
    Miso Soup with Tofu and Wakame, 324
    Pickled Carrots with Wakame and
        Miso, 328
    Sesame-Miso Vinaigrette, 262
monkfish, 225
    Monkfish Carpaccio, 244
    Monkfish with Dijon-Lemon Sauce, 244
mushrooms
    Beth's Oyster Gratin with Oyster
        Mushrooms, 47
    Cod-Stuffed Piquillo Peppers with Garlic
        Cream and Chanterelles, 314
    Crab and Corn Chowder with Bacon and
        Wild Mushrooms, 140
    Mushroom Dashi, 334
    Porcini Butter, 335
    Sablefish with Chanterelles and Parsley
        Sauce, 195
    Sake-Steamed Clams with Shimeji
        Mushrooms, 61
mussels, 33
    Baked Mussels with Herb, Ginger, and
        Peanut Pesto, 71
    Billi Bi Mussel Soup, 69
    Classic Steamed Mussels, 66
    Green Garlic Mussels, 72
    Mussel Escabeche, 68
    Mussels Cooked with Pine Needles, 66
    Spicy Thai Red Curry Mussels, 72
mustard
    Dijon-Lemon Sauce, 339
    Mustard-Tarragon Butter, 335

## N

'Nduja Butter, 334
Niçoise Salad with Olive Oil–Poached
    Tuna, 265
Nuoc Cham (Vietnamese Dipping
    Sauce), 338
nuts, toasting, 344

# O

octopus, 95
  Baby Octopus with Green Olive
    Relish, 108
  Seared Octopus with Roasted Potatoes, 110
  Takoyaki (Japanese Octopus Balls), 109
  Tartines with Octopus and
    Pickled Fennel, 299

olives
  Greek Shrimp Saganaki with Tomatoes,
    Olives, and Feta, 131
  Green Olive Relish, 108, 250
  Kalamata Dressing, 110
  Sablefish with Tomatoes, Pine Nuts,
    and Olives, 198
  Salt Cod, Orange, and Black Olive
    Salad, 316

onions, 24. See also green onions
  Ras el Hanout Onion Jam, 212

Orange-Caper Aioli, 156

orange roughy, 191

oysters, 28–29
  Beth's Oyster Gratin with Oyster
    Mushrooms, 47
  Butter-Poached Oysters, 43
  Corn Bread–Oyster Stuffing with Thyme
    and Fennel, 44
  Curried Oyster Soup, 47
  Grilled Oysters, 41
  Hangtown Fry, 46
  Oyster Po' Boys, 49
  Oyster Sangrita Shooters, 43
  Oysters on the Half Shell, 36
  Oysters Rockefeller, 42

# P

Paella with Clams, Shrimp, and Chorizo, 91

Pan Bagnat, 297

pancakes
  Blini with Smoked Salmon and Caviar, 309
  Korean Green Onion Pancakes with
    Squid, 103

Paprika Aioli, Smoked, 60

Parsley Sauce, 195

pasta and noodles
  Bucatini with Sardines and Bread
    Crumbs, 298
  Ginger-Soy Salmon with Soba Noodle
    Salad, 170
  Grilled Squid Noodle Salad with Mango,
    Cabbage, and Cucumber, 105
  Linguine with Clams, 58
  Pasta with Salmon Caviar and Smoked
    Salmon, 310

Rigatoni with Grilled Squid, Clams, and
    Heirloom Tomatoes, 106
  Sablefish Coconut Curry with
    Vermicelli, 196
  Seafood Spaghetti Carbonara, 86
  Shrimp Laksa Soup with Noodles, 133
  Spaghetti alla Rustica, 294
  Spaghetti with Bottarga, 313
  Spaghetti with Uni and Ikura, 322
  Tuna Spaghetti, 294
  Tuna "Tonnato" Penne, 293

Pea Soup, Green, with Crab, 139

pepper, black, 24

peppers. See also chiles
  Cod-Stuffed Piquillo Peppers with Garlic
    Cream and Chanterelles, 314

pesto
  Basil Pesto, 336
  Herb, Ginger, and Peanut Pesto, 71
  Kale Pesto, 336
  Pesto Mayonnaise, 102

pizza
  Clams Casino Pizza, 62
  Peter's New York Pizza Dough, 343

plank-grilling, 178

Po' Boys, Oyster, 49

poke, 226
  Ahi Tuna Poke, 257

Polenta, Creamy, 177

pollock, 189

Ponzu Sauce, 339

potatoes
  Beer-Battered Fish and Chips, 206
  Seared Octopus with Roasted
    Potatoes, 110
  Smoky Salmon and Potato Chowder, 173

Potpies, Lobster, 155

prawns, 114–15. See also shrimp

prosciutto
  Prosciutto-Wrapped Swordfish with Kale
    Pesto, 254
  Tamari-Zuchi Rice Balls, 258

# Q

Quesadillas, Rock Shrimp, with Oaxacan
    Cheese and Tomatoes, 126

# R

Rémoulade Sauce, 158

rice
  Chirashi Sushi, 323
  Paella with Clams, Shrimp,
    and Chorizo, 91

Rice Porridge with Abalone, 83
  Sticky Rice, 342
  Sushi Rice, 342
  Tamari-Zuchi Rice Balls, 258
  Toasted Rice Powder, 342
  Uni Mini Hand Rolls, 322

rockfish, 188
  "Red Snapper" Veracruz Style, 204
  Rockfish Tacos with Citrus Salsa and
    Cabbage Slaw, 201
  Spicy Rockfish Ceviche with
    Cucumber, 202
  Steamed Rockfish with Ginger, 202

roe, 302. See also bottarga; caviar
  Chirashi Sushi, 323
  Parmesan Custards with Salmon
    Roe, 310
  Pasta with Salmon Caviar and Smoked
    Salmon, 310
  Shad Roe with Bacon and Lemon, 220
  Spaghetti with Uni and Ikura, 322
  Taramosaláta with Warm Pita Breads, 311

Romesco Sauce, 338

# S

sablefish (black cod), 188
  Baked Sablefish with Tomatoes and
    Capers, 194
  Sablefish Coconut Curry with
    Vermicelli, 196
  Sablefish with Chanterelles and Parsley
    Sauce, 195
  Sablefish with Tomatoes, Pine Nuts, and
    Olives, 198
  Smoked Sablefish, 193

Saganaki, Greek Shrimp, with Tomatoes,
    Olives, and Feta, 131

salmon, 162–64
  Blini with Smoked Salmon and
    Caviar, 309
  Ginger-Soy Salmon with Soba Noodle
    Salad, 170
  Grilled Salmon Salad with Green Goddess
    Dressing, 169
  Pan-Roasted Salmon with Seared Corn
    Sauce, 174
  Pasta with Salmon Caviar and Smoked
    Salmon, 310
  Plank-Roasted Cured Salmon, 178
  Quick Salmon Gravlax, 168
  Salmon Cakes with Mango Aioli, 172
  Salmon Tartare with Cucumber, 168
  Slow-Cooked Salmon with Red Wine
    Sauce and Butter-Braised Chard, 179
  Smoked Salmon, Citrus, and Fava Bean
    Salad, 167
  Smoky Salmon and Potato Chowder, 173

Sous Vide Salmon with Creamy
    Polenta, 177
Stove-Top Smoked Salmon, 165
Tamari-Zuchi Rice Balls, 258
Tea-Smoked Salmon with Cucumber
    Salad, 176
salt, 24
    Branzino Baked in a Salt Crust, 219
    flavored, 336
salt cod, 302–3
    Cod-Stuffed Piquillo Peppers with Garlic
        Cream and Chanterelles, 314
    Salt Cod Cakes with Poached Eggs and
        Romesco Sauce, 317
    Salt Cod Gratin (Brandade), 319
    Salt Cod, Orange, and Black Olive
        Salad, 316
sand dabs, 224
    Sand Dabs with Lemon-Caper
        Vinaigrette, 239
sandwiches
    DLTA: Dulse, Lettuce, Tomato, and
        Avocado Sandwiches, 324
    Lingcod Sliders with Napa Cabbage–
        Apple Slaw, 211
    Lobster Rolls, 152
    Oyster Po' Boys, 49
    Pan Bagnat, 297
    Soft-Shell Crab Sandwiches with Chipotle
        Mayonnaise, 149
    Tartines with Octopus and
        Pickled Fennel, 299
    Tuna Burgers with Sriracha
        Mayonnaise, 261
sardines, 272, 286
    Bucatini with Sardines and
        Bread Crumbs, 298
    Fried Sardines with Tomato-Caper
        Topping, 274
    Fried Whitebait, 279
    Grilled Sardines in Grape Leaves, 274
sauces and salsas. See also Aioli; pesto
    Arrabbiata Sauce, 339
    Avocado and Tomatillo Salsa, 338
    Bagna Cauda, 292
    Balsamic Butter Sauce, 183
    Blender Hollandaise Sauce, 339
    Candied Citrus Mignonette, 39
    Chimichurri Sauce, 337
    Cilantro-Poblano Sauce, 61
    Citrus Salsa, 201
    Classic BBQ Sauce, 42
    Coconut-Peanut Sauce, 338
    Creamy Corn Sauce, 82
    Creamy Shrimp Sauce, 237
    Dijon-Lemon Sauce, 339
    French Mignonette, 36
    Fresno Chile Mignonette, 39

Ginger-Soy Dipping Sauce, 129
Green Peppercorn Sauce, 239
Green Tomato Salsa Verde, 217
Hogwash, 39
Mango-Jalapeño Salsa, 36
Pan-Deglazing Sauce, 340
Parsley Sauce, 195
Poblano Chile Sauce, 340–41
Ponzu Sauce, 339
Red Wine Sauce, 179
Rémoulade Sauce, 158
Roasted-Garlic Sabayon, 79
Romesco Sauce, 338
Salsa Verde, 337
Sauce Gribiche, 337
Savory Red Wine Sauce, 216
Savory Vanilla Butter Sauce, 81
Seared Corn Sauce, 174
Takoyaki Sauce, 109
Tartar Sauce, 339
Vietnamese Dipping Sauce
    (Nuoc Cham), 338
Vinegar-Cream Sauce, 341
White Wine Butter Sauce, 340
sausage
    Clam Steamers with Chorizo, Greens, and
        Calabrian Chile Butter, 50
    Paella with Clams, Shrimp, and Chorizo, 91
    Seafood Sausages, 213
scallops, 33–34
    Bay Scallops and Avocado with Miso
        Dressing, 74
    Coquilles Saint-Jacques, 75
    Grilled Scallop and Asparagus Salad with
        Spicy Lime Dressing, 76
    Scallop Ceviche, 74
    Scallops with Celery Root Salad, 78
    Seared Scallops with Coppa and Creamy
        Corn Sauce, 82
    Seared Scallops with Roasted-Garlic
        Sabayon, 79
    Seared Scallops with Savory Vanilla Butter
        Sauce, 81
seafood. See also individual seafoods
    buying, 20
    California Bouillabaisse with Rouille, 87
    Cioppino, 88
    safety, 23
    Seafood Larb, 231
    Seafood Sausages, 213
    Seafood Spaghetti Carbonara, 86
    storing, 23
    sustainable, 17–19
sea urchins. See uni
seaweed and sea vegetables, 306–7
    Cabbage Salad Tossed with
        Shio Kombu, 328
    Chirashi Sushi, 323

Dashi, 334
DLTA: Dulse, Lettuce, Tomato, and
    Avocado Sandwiches, 324
Furikake, 326
Heirloom Tomato, Uni, and Wakame
    Salad, 321
Kombu Dashi (Vegetarian), 334
Miso Soup with Tofu and Wakame, 324
Pickled Carrots with Wakame and
    Miso, 328
Pickled Cucumber, Wakame, and Sesame
    Salad, 327
Seaweed Chips, 326
seeds, toasting, 344
shad, 191
    Broiled Shad with Butter and
        Lemon, 220
shallots, fried, 344
shellfish. See also individual shellfish
    Quick Shellfish Stock, 332
    Shellfish Stock, 332
shrimp, 114–16
    Chirashi Sushi, 323
    Creamy Shrimp Sauce, 237
    Greek Shrimp Saganaki with Tomatoes,
        Olives, and Feta, 131
    Grilled Shrimp with Salsa Verde, 127
    Japanese Egg Custards with Shrimp, 127
    Paella with Clams, Shrimp, and
        Chorizo, 91
    Rock Shrimp Cakes with Avocado and
        Tomatillo Salsa, 135
    Rock Shrimp Quesadillas with Oaxacan
        Cheese and Tomatoes, 126
    Seafood Sausages, 213
    Shrimp and Grits, 134
    Shrimp Laksa Soup with Noodles, 133
    Shrimp Rice Paper Rolls, 122
    Shrimp Tempura with Ginger-Soy Dipping
        Sauce, 129
    Southwestern Shrimp Cocktail, 125
    Thai Shrimp and Chicken Meatball
        Soup, 130
    Wine Country Gazpacho with
        Shrimp, 124
smelt. See whitebait
snappers, 188
    Blackened Red Snapper with Cheese
        Grits, 205
    "Red Snapper" Veracruz Style, 204
sole, 224
    Petrale Sole Caponata, 241
    Petrale Sole with Green Peppercorn
        Sauce, 239
    Sole Quenelles with Creamy Shrimp
        Sauce, 237
    Steamed Bacon-Stuffed Sole, 243

soups. *See also* chowders
    Billi Bi Mussel Soup, 69
    Curried Oyster Soup, 47
    Green Pea Soup with Crab, 139
    Lobster Bisque, 155
    Miso Soup with Tofu and Wakame, 324
    Shrimp Laksa Soup with Noodles, 133
    Thai Shrimp and Chicken Meatball Soup, 130
    Wine Country Gazpacho with Shrimp, 124
spices, 24
    Cajun or Creole Seasoning, 341
    toasting, 344
    Za'atar Spice Mix, 341
squid, 94
    Braised Squid with Tomato, Harissa, and Fregola, 100
    Bruschetta with Grilled Calamari, Tomatoes, and Goat Cheese, 98
    Crispy Calamari with Pesto Mayonnaise, 102
    Fried Salt and Pepper Squid, 99
    Grilled Squid Noodle Salad with Mango, Cabbage, and Cucumber, 105
    Herbed Cast-Iron Squid, 97
    Korean Green Onion Pancakes with Squid, 103
    Rigatoni with Grilled Squid, Clams, and Heirloom Tomatoes, 106
Sriracha Mayonnaise, 261
stocks. *See also* Dashi
    Chicken Stock, 333
    Fish Stock, 332
    Ginger Chicken Stock, 333
    improving store-bought, 333
    Quick Shellfish Stock, 332
    Shellfish Stock, 332
    Vegetable Stock, 333
striped bass, 191
Stuffing, Corn Bread–Oyster, with Thyme and Fennel, 44
sturgeon, 249
    Pan-Seared Sturgeon with Pancetta, Capers, and Lemon, 268
sushi
    Chirashi Sushi, 323
    Sushi Rice, 342
    Uni Mini Hand Rolls, 322
Swiss chard
    Butter-Braised Chard, 179
    Steamed Halibut with Thai Curry Cream Sauce and Chard, 233
swordfish, 248
    Fish Bone Marrow with Grilled Bread, 253

Grilled Swordfish with Green Olives and Oranges, 250
Prosciutto-Wrapped Swordfish with Kale Pesto, 254

T

Tacos, Rockfish, with Citrus Salsa and Cabbage Slaw, 201
Takoyaki (Japanese Octopus Balls), 109
Tamari-Zuchi Rice Balls, 258
Taramosaláta with Warm Pita Breads, 311
tarragon
    Mustard-Tarragon Butter, 335
    Tarragon Aioli, 145
Tartar Sauce, 339
Tiger's Milk Marinade, 228
tilapia, 190
    Grilled Tilapia with Herb Sabayon, 209
tofu
    Miso Soup with Tofu and Wakame, 324
    Tofu Caesar Dressing, 291
Tomatillo Salsa, Avocado and, 338
tomatoes
    Arrabbiata Sauce, 339
    Baked Sablefish with Tomatoes and Capers, 194
    Braised Squid with Tomato, Harissa, and Fregola, 100
    Bruschetta with Grilled Calamari, Tomatoes, and Goat Cheese, 98
    Clams with Cherry Tomatoes, Herbs, and Crème Fraîche, 57
    DLTA: Dulse, Lettuce, Tomato, and Avocado Sandwiches, 324
    Fried Sardines with Tomato-Caper Topping, 274
    Greek Shrimp Saganaki with Tomatoes, Olives, and Feta, 131
    Green Tomato Salsa Verde, 217
    Heirloom Tomato, Uni, and Wakame Salad, 321
    Rigatoni with Grilled Squid, Clams, and Heirloom Tomatoes, 106
    Rock Shrimp Quesadillas with Oaxacan Cheese and Tomatoes, 126
    Sablefish with Tomatoes, Pine Nuts, and Olives, 198
    Tomato Granita, 39
    Tomato Toasts with Serrano Ham and Boquerones, 288
    Wine Country Gazpacho with Shrimp, 124
trout, 163
    Fried Trout Agrodolce, 185
    Grilled Trout with Herbs and Bacon, 182

Pan-Fried Trout with Balsamic Butter Sauce, 183
    Smoked Trout Salad with Maple Vinaigrette, 181
tuna, 248–49, 286
    Ahi Tuna Ceviche with Mango and Avocado, 255
    Ahi Tuna Poke, 257
    Albacore Tuna Preparation, 259
    Chirashi Sushi, 323
    Fish Bone Marrow with Grilled Bread, 253
    Niçoise Salad with Olive Oil–Poached Tuna, 265
    Olive Oil–Poached Tuna, 264
    Sesame-Crusted Seared Tuna with Avocado Salad and Sesame-Miso Vinaigrette, 262
    Tamari-Zuchi Rice Balls, 258
    Tuna Burgers with Sriracha Mayonnaise, 261
    Tuna Spaghetti, 294
    Tuna-Stuffed Eggs with Boquerones, 288
    Tuna "Tonnato" Penne, 293
    Za'atar-Seared Albacore Tuna, 264
turbot, 225

U

uni (sea urchins), 303–4
    Heirloom Tomato, Uni, and Wakame Salad, 321
    Spaghetti with Uni and Ikura, 322
    Uni Mini Hand Rolls, 322
    Uni with Horseradish Cream, 321

V

Vanilla Butter Sauce, Savory, 81
Vegetable Stock, 333
vinaigrettes
    Honey-Lemon Vinaigrette, 167
    Lemon-Caper Vinaigrette, 239
    Lime Vinaigrette, 143
    Maple Vinaigrette, 181
    Sesame-Miso Vinaigrette, 262
Vinegar-Cream Sauce, 341

W

whitebait, 272
    Fried Whitebait, 279
whiting, 189

Z

Za'atar Spice Mix, 341

# ACKNOWLEDGMENTS

There are many to thank for their help and participation in this book. The founders: John Finger, Michael Watchorn, and Terry Sawyer first for their vision in creating Hog Island Oyster Company. Certainly, the chefs and crews at Hog Island Oyster Bars are to be applauded for their hard work and creative contributions to the book. They are a young, tough, energetic group that I admire greatly. Remy Anthes, creative marketing manager at Hog Island, who helped shepherd most of the moving parts in the creation of the book. Gary Fleener, the PhD in charge of science, sustainability, and farm education at Hog Island, brought his skills as an educator and science expert to all parts of the book, helping to keep it focused and accurate.

The extraordinary group of restaurant friends who also contributed to the book, including Stuart Brioza, Jeremy Sewall, Peter Reinhart, Renee Erickson, Bryan Rackley, Barton Seaver, Josh Silvers, Gustavo Arana Dagnino, Sallie Miller, Gwen Gunheim, and Beth Snow.

Thanks also to Sheila Bowman of the Monterey Bay Aquarium for her help with the sustainable seafood information.

The crew at Cameron Books, without whom this wouldn't have happened. Kim Laidlaw, who was our tireless editor, and helped shape the book and bring focus. Pippa White, editorial director, and many others. How do they make something as complicated as this happen?

Ashley Lima, who provided beautiful and delicious photography. Laurie Mayhan Sawyer for her helpful illustrations.

Our gang of recipe testers who helped us make sure the recipes worked.

Leslie Stoker, literary agent extraordinaire, who brought calm insight into all phases of the book, and Beth Snow, who helped me keep all parts of the book on track and organized. I couldn't have done it without her. She is a gem.

Creating a book is an extraordinary example of the importance of teamwork, as is growing and selling oysters and other seafood. We all hope you enjoy our efforts.

---

**CAMERON + COMPANY**
149 Kentucky Street, Suite 7
Petaluma, CA 94952
cameronbooks.com

Publisher *Chris Gruener*
Creative Director *Iain R. Morris*
Editorial Director *Pippa White*
Senior Art Director *Suzi Hutsell*
Managing Editor *Jan Hughes*
Editorial Assistant *Krista Keplinger*

Executive Editor *Kim Laidlaw*
Photographer *Ashley Lima*
Illustrator *Laurie Mahan Sawyer*
Art Director/Stylist *Margaux Keres*
Food Stylist *Emily Caneer*
Food Stylist Assistant *Carrie Beyer*
Copy Editor *Carolyn Miller*
Proofreader *Amy Treadwell*
Props *Rule&Level Prop House*
Indexer *Ken DellaPenta*

CAMERON + COMPANY would like to thank John Finger, Gary Fleener, and Remy Anthes at Hog Island Oyster Co. for all their tireless help and encouragement.

Text and photographs copyright © 2023 John Ash
Illustrations copyright © 2023 Laurie Mahan Sawyer

Recipes on the following pages have been reprinted with permission: 31 (top), 43 (bottom), 49, 57, 62, 106, 172, 173, 174, 179, 181, 217, 228, 262, 276, 281, 297, 299

Library of Congress Cataloging-in-Publication Data available.

ISBN: 978-1-951836-87-0

10 9 8 7 6 5 4 3 2 1

Printed in China